LONGMAN STUDY GUIDES

GCSE

English
Literature

Trevor Gamson
Julie Grover

LONGMAN

LONGMAN STUDY GUIDES

SERIES EDITORS: Geoff Black and Stuart Wall

Titles available

Biology
Business Studies
Chemistry
Design and Technology
Economics
English
English Literature
French
Geography
German
Information Technology

Mathematics
Mathematics: Higher Level
Music
Physics
Psychology
Religious Studies
Science
Sociology
Spanish
World History

Addison Wesley Longman Ltd,
Edinburgh Gate, Harlow,
Essex CM20 2JE, England
and Associated Companies throughout the world.

© Addison Wesley Longman 1997

First Published 1997

ISBN 0582-30483-0

British Library Cataloguing-in-Publication Data
A catalogue record for this book is available from the British Library.

Set by 16 in 9.75/12pt Sabon

Produced by Longman Singapore Publishers Pte
Printed in Singapore

▶ CONTENTS

► EDITORS' PREFACE

Longman Study Guides have been written by the people who set and mark the exams – the examiners. Examiners are aware that, due to lack of practice and poor preparation, some students achieve only the lowest grades: they are not able to effectively show the examiner what they know. These books give excellent advice about exam practice and preparation, and organising a structured revision programme, all of which are essential for examination success. Remember: the examiners are looking for opportunities to *give* you marks, not take them away!

Longman Study Guides are designed to be used throughout the course. The self-contained chapters can be read in any order appropriate to the stage you have reached in your course. The examiner guides you through the essential parts of each topic, making helpful comments throughout.

We believe that this book, and the series as a whole, will help you establish and build your basic knowledge and examination technique skills. For additional help with exam practice and revision techniques, we have published a series called **Longman Exam Kits**, which are available from all good bookshops, or direct from Addison Wesley Longman.

GEOFF BLACK AND STUART WALL

► AUTHORS' PREFACE

We hope this book will help you throughout your GCSE course and enable you to be successful in both your coursework and your examination. There are no correct answers in English Literature but there are questions that can be usefully asked. The first aim of this book is to show you the right kinds of questions to ask about poetry, plays and novels. This will enable you to develop your own ideas and your own response. The second aim is to help you write interestingly and appropriately about the literature you have studied. Each chapter contains passages quoted from a great variety of works, many from set books. We hope that these will give you a taste of a range of literature and stimulate your interest and appetite.

We have received a great deal of help and support whilst we have been writing this book. We are particularly grateful to Stuart Wall for his encouragement, to Stuart Sillars for his careful scrutiny of the text and the many suggestions he made to improve its clarity, and to Philip Grover for countless discussions about literature.

JULIE GROVER AND TREVOR GAMSON

⊳ **INFORMATION ABOUT THIS BOOK**

This book has been written as a course companion for use throughout your GCSE course in English Literature. The first chapter focuses on examination requirements, including information about the aims of a GCSE in English Literature, assessment, types of examination and questions set, and the particular requirements of the main examination boards. The second chapter gives advice about the skills required for English Literature, including information about how to approach coursework, on the different types of question set and on preparing for and sitting the examination. You should read these first two chapters carefully as they give invaluable advice which will be useful throughout your English Literature course.

Each of the remaining chapters, 3 to 18, deals with an important aspect of poetry, drama or prose. Each chapter starts with a **Getting Started** section which is an introduction to the chapter. This includes a **Topic Chart**, a table which, at a glance, shows which parts of the chapter are relevant to a particular examination board's requirements. You should use this to identify whether topics in a specific chapter are covered by your examination board. The chart can also be used to check your study and revision progress over the two years. A Topic Chart looks like this:

MEG	NEAB	NICCEA	SEG	LONDON	WJEC	IGCSE	TOPIC	STUDY	REVISION 1	REVISION 2
✓	✓	✓	✓	✓	✓	✓	Imagery			
✓	✓	✓	✓	✓	✓	✓	Language			

Key to the initials	
MEG	Midland Examination Group
NEAB	Northern Examinations and Assessment Board
NICCEA	Northern Ireland Council for the Curriculum, Examinations and Assessment
SEG	Southern Examining Group
LONDON	EDEXCEL Foundation
WJEC	Welsh Joint Education Committee
IGCSE	International General Certificate of Secondary Education

Each topic listed is then explained in the **What you need to know** section – the core of the chapter. This section contains passages from texts which can be used as exercises to test your understanding, and is followed by **Additional examples** of questions and answers.

Coursework is an important part of a GCSE in English Literature. In each chapter, therefore, suggestions for coursework are given together with an example task and suggested coursework answer.

To help you practise what you have just learnt, there are then a series of examination questions with suggested answers in one of the following two formats:

⊳   a tutor's answer with some useful notes.
⊳   a student's answer with examiner's comments.

Do not look at the answers until you have attempted to answer the questions yourself. Although there are no correct answers in English Literature, the suggested answers may show you a more appropriate way of answering the question. The students' answers, some of which are excellent A-grade answers and some of which may have faults or weaknesses, will help you to see what problems are identified by examiners and where you could improve your examination answers.

The table at the end of the examination answers can be used to identify the assessment objectives covered in the questions. The first column in the table indicates the question number, the second shows the assessment objectives as listed by the examination boards in their syllabuses. They appear in the table by their number as follows.

Question	Assessment Objective(s)	Pre-20th century	20th century
Coursework task	1	✓	
1	2, 4	✓	
2	3		✓

A syllabus requires candidates to demonstrate the ability to:

1. respond to texts critically, sensitively and in detail, selecting appropriate ways to convey their response, using textual evidence as appropriate;
2. explore how language, structure and forms contribute to the meaning of texts, considering different approaches to texts and alternative interpretations;
3. explore relations between texts, selecting and evaluating relevant material;
4. understand literary tradition and appreciate social and historical influences and cultural contexts.

Columns three and four indicate whether the text was written before or after 1900. At the end of each chapter there is a summary box which briefly identifies the key points about topics covered in the chapter. You should check that you know, and understand more fully, each of the key points listed.

ACKNOWLEDGEMENTS

We are grateful to the following for permission to reproduce copyright material:

Anvil Press Poetry Ltd for the poems 'Mrs Skinner, North Street' from *The Other Country* by Carol Ann Duffy (1990) and 'Human Interest' from *Standing Female Nude* by Carol Anne Duffy (1985); Broadside Press for an extract from the poem 'The Black Narrator' by Ahmed Alhamisi; the author, Alan Brownjohn, for an extract from his poem 'Skipping Rhyme'; Jonathan Cape Ltd on behalf of the Estate of Robert Frost for an extract from the poem 'Out, Out-' from *The Poetry of Robert Frost* edited by Edward Connery Latham; Carcanet Press Ltd for an extract from the poem 'Blue Girls' from *Selected Poems* by John Crowe Ransom; Faber & Faber Ltd for an extract from *The Lord of the Flies* by William Golding; Editions Gallimard for the Literary Estate of Jacques Prevert/the Literary Executor of the translator Paul Dehn, for the poem 'Exercise Book' by Jacques Prevert from *Paroles (Le Point de Jour NRF)* copyright Librairie Gallimard, Paris. The translation originally appeared in *Romantic Landscape* by Paul Dehn (Hamish Hamilton, 1952); GRM Associates, Inc, agents for the Estate of Ida M Cullen, for the poem 'Yet Do I Marvel' from *Color* by Countee Cullen, copyright 1925 by Harper & Brothers, copyright renewed 1953 by Ida M Cullen; the author's agent for extracts from *Brighton Rock* by Graham Greene (William Heinemann Ltd) and *The Power and the Glory* by Graham Greene (The Bodley Head); William Heinemann Ltd for extracts from *To Kill a Mockingbird* by Harper Lee and *Of Mice and Men* by John Steinbeck; The Estate of James Joyce for an extract from *A Portrait of the Artist as a Young Man* (Jonathan Cape 1956); Laurence Pollinger Ltd and the Estate of Frieda Lawrence Ravagli for an extract from *The Rainbow* by D H Lawrence; the author's agent for the poem 'Prayer Before Birth' by Louis MacNeice from *Collected Poems* (Faber & Faber); Greene & Heaton Ltd for extracts from *The Crucible* by Arthur Miller (Penguin Books Ltd), copyright © Arthur Miller, 1952, 1953, *Death of a Salesman* by Arthur Miller, copyright © 1948, 1949, 1951, 1952 by Arthur Miller, renewed 1975, 1976, 1979, 1980, and *A View from the Bridge* by Arthur Miller (Penguin Books Ltd) copyright © Arthur Miller, 1955, 1957; John Murray (Publishers) Ltd for the poem 'Slough' from *Collected Poems* by John Betjeman; New Directions Publishing Corporation for the poem 'Fragrance of Life, Odor of Death' from *The Freeing of the Dust* by Denise Levertov, copyright © 1973 by Denise Levertov; The Orion Publishing Group Ltd for the poem 'Cynddylan on a Tractor' from *Collected Poems by R S Thomas* (J M Dent); Oxford University Press for the first 12 lines from the poem 'Your Attention Please' from Peter Porter's *Collected Poems* (1983) and the poem 'From the Motorway' from *The Collected Poems of Anne Stevenson 1955-1995*; the author's agent on behalf of George Orwell for an extract from *Animal Farm* Copyright © Mark Hamilton as literary executor of the Estate of the late Sonia Brownell Orwell and Martin Secker and Warburg Ltd; Penguin Books Ltd for the poem 'A thousand years, you said' by Lady Heguri from *The Penguin Book of Japanese Verse* translated by Geoffrey Bownas and Anthony Thwaite (1964), copyright © Geoffrey Bownas and Anthony Thwaite, 1964; Random House UK Ltd for an extract from the poem 'The Future' from *Fifteen to Infinity* by Ruth Fainlight (Hutchinson); James MacGibbon, the executor of the Estate of Stevie Smith, for the poem 'Not Waving but Drowning' by Stevie Smith from *The Collected Poems of Stevie Smith* (Penguin 20th Century Classics); the Society of Authors on behalf of the Literary Trustees of Walter de la Mare for an extract from the poem 'The Dove said, "Coo"' by Walter de la Mare; the author's agent for extracts from poems 'The Force that through the Green Fuse Drives the Flower' and 'Do not go Gentle into that Goodnight' from *The Poems by Dylan Thomas* (J M Dent); the Revd. P J Hanson for the Trustees of Katherine Tynan Estate for the poem 'Joining the Colours'; A P Watt Ltd on behalf of Michael Yeats for the poem 'The Lake of Innisfree' from *The Collected Poems of W B Yeats* and an extract from the poem 'At the grey round of the hill' by W B Yeats.

We are also grateful to the following Examination Groups for permission to reproduce questions from past papers: EdExcel Foundation (London), Midland Examining Group (MEG), Southern Examining Group (SEG), Welsh Joint Education Committee (WJEC). Whilst permission has been granted to reproduce their questions, the answers, or hints on answers are solely the responsibility of the authors and have not been provided or approved by the Group.

SOME USEFUL TERMS

Here are some definitions of some useful terms. They appear in the book but are brought together here for easy reference.

Alliteration	The repetition of the same consonant sound, as in 'Billy the Bully'.
Ambiguity	Word or phrase which has a double meaning.
Aside	When a character in a play turns away from the action on stage and speaks directly to the audience as though the other characters cannot hear.
Assonance	The repetition of vowel sounds, as in 'green trees'.
Ballad	A poem that tells a story in a simple and straightforward way, usually in four-line stanzas.
Chorus	A character, or a group, in a play who comments on the action.
Comedy	Nowadays a work that makes you laugh, but it used to mean a work with a happy ending.
Couplet	Two lines of verse which rhyme.
Dialogue	Two or more characters speaking to each other. We also speak about the 'dialogue of a play', meaning all the words that are spoken.
Diction	The words a poet chooses to use.
Dramatic irony	Occurs when a character says something that has a different meaning for the audience from the one it has for the character. This happens when the audience knows more about a situation than the character who is speaking.
Fiction	Anything that is not fact.
First person	Using 'I' in speech or writing, as in: 'I shall tell you the story of what happened to me when I was six.'
Free verse	Verse that has neither rhyme nor rhythm.
Genre	A kind of writing. Poetry is one genre of literature, plays are another and prose is a third genre.
Iambic pentameter	A line of poetry made up of ten syllables, with alternating light and heavy beats, as in: 'Is this the face that launched a thousand ships?' A great deal of English poetry has been written in iambic pentameter.
Imagery	Writing that creates a picture in your mind, usually through the use of comparisons.
Irony	Saying one thing but meaning the opposite, as in Jane Austen's famous opening sentence of Pride and Prejudice: 'It is a truth universally acknowledged that a single man in possession of a good fortune, must be in want of a wife.'
Juxtaposition	Putting two things side by side in order to show a relationship between them.
Metaphor	A comparison that says one thing is another thing, rather than saying one thing is like another, as in: 'She was a rose of fairest hue.'
Metre	A regular rhythm in verse.
Narrative	A story. It can be a novel, a short story, poem or simply spoken.
Narrator	Someone who tells a story.
Novel	A long fiction story in prose.
Onomatopoeia	A word which shows its meaning through its sound, as in 'plop'. We sometimes say that the sound echoes the sense.
Personification	Writing of things or ideas as if they were persons, for example Old Father Time.
Prose	Any piece of continuous writing that is not verse or dialogue.
Quatrain	Four lines of verse.
Rhyme	Words which have the same sounds except for the first consonant, as in 'hot' and 'pot', placed at the end of the lines in poetry, or sometimes at fixed points in the middle.
Rhythm	The movement of language in speech, verse or prose. It does not have to have a regular beat.
Simile	A comparison which uses like or as, as in: 'My love is like a red, red rose.'
Soliloquy	A speech in a play which represents the character thinking. It is usually spoken when the character is alone on stage.
Sonnet	A poem of fourteen lines, rhyming in a particular way, see Chapter 6.

Stanza The correct term for the groups of lines a poem is divided into, often mistakenly called a verse.

Symbol A thing which stands for something else. A flag stands for a country and is a symbol that everyone recognizes. Writers invent their own symbols.

Theme The central idea of a piece of writing.

Tragedy A play, or sometimes a novel or a poem, with an unhappy ending. It must be serious and it usually shows the suffering of a good or great character whose life is spoiled by a weakness or by the workings of fate.

Verse The proper word for poetry.

Examination requirements

▷ **GETTING STARTED**

This book sets out to help you develop the skills you need as a candidate for GCSE Key Stage 4 English Literature. It will explain the concepts you need to understand and help you to study effectively the three areas of literature – poetry, drama and prose. It will also suggest how to write assessed coursework and answer exam questions. No matter which board's examination you are taking you will find every chapter relevant. You can turn to a particular chapter to help you with a specific problem; but, if you work your way through the whole book, it will help you to answer all the required questions and to write the required coursework units. At the end of each topic-based chapter you will find a summary box for you to check what you have learnt.

▶ **WHAT YOU NEED TO KNOW**

▶ **General aims**

The kind of **skills** which an English course should aim to develop have been set out nationally. They are to enable the candidate to:

1   develop their ability to read, understand, enjoy and respond to all types of literary texts; recognize and appreciate themes and attitudes and the ways in which authors achieve their effects; develop information retrieval strategies for the purposes of literary study;

2   develop their awareness of personal, social and cultural significance in the study of literature;

3   develop their ability to construct and convey meaning in written and spoken language, using correct grammar and Standard English (except in contexts where non-standard forms are needed for literary purposes), matching style to audience and purpose.

These are the general aims. In your English Literature course you will pursue these aims by studying the three areas of literature – poetry, drama and prose. Prose is any piece of continuous writing, like a novel or a short story. These different types of writing are called 'genres', and the books are called 'texts'.

▶ **Specific aims**

You will be expected to know the context of each text and show you have understood what you have read. You will also be expected to show an appreciation of the texts. This means being able to write about what is interesting in each text. In practice this means writing about the characters, the writer's ideas and the way the book is written. Finally you will be expected to have your own views and feelings about the text.

Examination boards set out their specific aims in the marking guidelines which they publish with their specimen questions. Obtain a copy from the board of your choice and look carefully at the descriptors which are published to show what is required to achieve each grade boundary. Boards now publish detailed marking schemes. These will give you clear indicators of the type of response which is required for each question.

Areas of study

During your course you will be expected to study a substantial volume of literature. Not only will you study works from the three genres of drama, poetry and prose, but you will also, from time to time, be required to write comparative studies of texts. You may be asked to make a study of a particular genre. One key development is the emphasis now placed on the importance of the following:

▶   literary tradition
▶   historical influences
▶   social influences
▶   cultural contexts.

So, as you read your book, be aware of the wider implications. Do not regard a book as an entity in itself. Be on the look-out for its place in the development of literature and the social and cultural implications of what the writer is trying to put across.

▶ **Assessment**

The examination takes the form of a written paper taken at the end of the course and a number of coursework units. The coursework is mostly written but may also include some oral assessment.

The percentage of marks awarded is:

Terminal Examination: 70%
Coursework: 30%.

The requirements of individual boards are set out below.

▶ **Levels of written examination**

Examination boards offer qualifications at *two* levels. These levels are called **tiers**.

Tiers

Examination boards divide their examination entry into two tiers, the Foundation Tier and the Higher Tier.

The Foundation Tier enables GCSE candidates to obtain Grades from G to C. The Higher Tier offers Grades from D to A*.

When you choose the tier to enter for, think very carefully. You will have noticed that if you enter for the Higher Tier and fall below Grade D in your final assessment, then you will receive a U Grade (unclassified)! The Foundation Tier is a safer bet if what you wish to obtain is a Grade C. If, however, you require a higher qualification, to proceed to higher education, say, then you must enter yourself for the Higher Tier. One board (the Northern Ireland Council for the Curriculum, Examinations and Assessment) will, in exceptional circumstances, award a Grade E on the Higher Tier.

Some boards set identical questions for both the Foundation and the Higher Tiers. Others vary the questions between tiers.

Course weighting

You will be required to take one examination paper and submit one folder of coursework. The weighting is:

Coursework	30%
Terminal Examination	70%
Total	100%.

Sometimes you can use the same set texts for both examination and coursework. There are exceptions, though. Check the syllabus very carefully.

▷ **Specific requirements**

Twentieth-century and pre-twentieth-century texts

There are strict regulations governing the combination of books you are required to study. Each examination board will require you to study books written before the twentieth century as well as books written during the present century. So obtain a copy of the board's syllabus before you begin your course of study. Note the various combinations of set texts. This will save you hours of wasted effort.

Combined courses

It is possible to take a combined English and English Literature course. This book is a preparation for the English Literature course, but the advice given would enable you to use your knowledge and expertise in a combined course.

▷ **Types of questions**

Set books

The questions are based on a variety of stimuli. These are set texts, anthologies of pre-released material and books taken from wider reading.

The questions are what you might expect from studies of poetry, prose and drama. But be aware of the emphasis now placed on the sub-text of a work of literature. Not only will you be asked the traditional questions about character, plot or author's technique, for example; you may also be required to discuss a particular book in relation to its historical or social background. A novel by Dickens or Hardy would fall into these categories. In addition you should be aware of a text's cultural implications, as in, say, *Roll of Thunder Hear My Cry* or the poetry of Grace Nichols.

Open book

One board (the Southern Examining Group) offers a syllabus which permits the candidates to take copies of the set texts into the examination. This is not the soft option it appears to be. It may seem an easier option, because it cuts out all that dreadful learning of quotations. But it has a serious purpose. It enables candidates to really engage the text. Unhampered by the need to remember massses of information, they are freed to explore the way a book has been written. It is not designed for the lazy who idle their way through two years of 'study' in the vain hope they can make up lost ground in the exam itself.

Anthology

Each board publishes a collection of writing for study. Some term these collections anthologies; others refer to them as pre-released material. When you send off for a copy of the syllabus, make sure you order an anthology. This is an essential part of the course.

▷ **Coursework**   A coursework unit takes various forms. It could take the form of a traditional essay. It might be a piece of empathetic writing based on one of your texts for study. Chapters 3 to 18 contain suggestions for coursework. The more imaginative your response, the more you will impress the moderator who assesses your portfolio.

Whatever the form coursework takes, you should be aware of the restrictions. Most boards insist on a balance between pre-twentieth- and twentieth-century texts.

Because the work is carried out over a period of time, you should take great care over the final presentation. It must not only look neat and tidy, but the spelling, punctuation and expression should be accurate, as it should be in the written exam.

REQUIREMENTS OF THE BOARDS

▷ **EDEXCEL Foundation (London Examinations)**

There are *two* options.

Option 1

Written examination paper of 2 hours 30 minutes (70%)

Three questions on each of the following:

> pre-twentieth-century poetry
> twentieth-century prose
> twentieth-century drama.

Coursework portfolio

Three units:

> pre-twentieth-century drama unit
> pre-twentieth-century prose unit
> twentieth-century poetry unit.

Option 2

Written examination paper of 2 hours 30 minutes (70%)

Three questions on each of the following:

> pre-twentieth-century poetry
> pre-twentieth-century prose
> twentieth-century drama

Coursework portfolio

Three units:

> pre-twentieth-century drama unit
> twentieth-century prose unit
> twentieth-century poetry unit

▷ **Midland Examining Group (MEG)**

(a) Written exam   Set book examination paper of 2 hours 30 minutes (70%)

(Foundation Tier: Component 11 or 12; Higher Tier: Component 21 or 22)

> Section A: Post-1900 drama: Set book

Section B: Pre-1900 prose: Set book
Section C: Post-1900 poetry: Set book or MEG pre-released selection.

Task – 3 questions, one from each section.

(b) Coursework unit (30%)

Genres must include:

prose written since 1900
poetry written before 1900
drama written before 1900.

There must be work that explores:

comparisons between texts
historical and social influences
cultural contexts.

At least one response must be in own handwriting.

▷ **Northern Examinations and Assessment Board (NEAB)**

NEAB offers *two* alternative schemes of assessment:

Alternative A: Anthology

Written examination paper of 2 hours 30 minutes (70%)

Section A (35%) Prose   Candidates answer one question based on prose contained in an NEAB anthology.

Section B (35%) Poetry   Candidates answer one question based on pre-twentieth-century/twentieth-century poetry contained in an NEAB anthology.

Coursework (30%)

Shakespeare*
wide reading*
twentieth-century drama.
*Optional cross-over for English coursework.

Alternative B: Set texts

Written examination paper of 2 hours 30 minutes (70%)

Section A (35%) Twentieth-century prose   Candidates answer one question from a list of prescribed twentieth-century prose texts.

Section B (35%) Twentieth-century drama   Candidates answer one question from a list of prescribed twentieth-century texts.

Coursework (30%)

Shakespeare*
wide reading*
pre-twentieth-century/twentieth-century poetry
* Optional cross-over for English coursework.

▷ **Northern Ireland Council for the Curriculum, Examinations and Assessment (NICCEA)**

(a) Written examination paper of 2 hours 30 minutes (70%)

Candidates will answer *one* question from each section.

Section A: Shakespeare
Section B: drama written after 1900
Section C: prose written after 1900.

(b) Coursework (30%)

The *three* best assignments which address the following:

prose written before 1900
poetry written before and after 1900.

▷ **Southern
Examining Group
(SEG)**

SEG offers three versions of assessment.

Version 1

(a)   Coursework folder
(b)   One written examination paper which does not permit candidates to have access in the examination to copies of the set texts.

Version 2

(a)   Coursework folder
(b)   One written examination paper which permits candidates to have access in the examination to copies of set texts.

Version 2 External

This is available to external candidates. For this version, coursework folders will be externally marked by SEG.

Assessment pattern

Written examination paper of 2 hours (70%). In addition 15 minutes reading time will be allowed, in which to study the paper and plan answers.

Three prescribed texts:

one drama
one poetry
one prose.

Work on relationships and comparisons between texts.

Coursework (30%)

Minimum of *three* texts chosen by the centre:

one drama
one poetry
one prose.

Work on relationships and comparisons between texts.
NB   Set texts offered in the written examination may not be used in the coursework. By the end of the assessment candidates will have offered answers on drama, poetry and prose published both before *and* after 1900.

▷ **Welsh Joint
Education
Committee (WJEC)**

The Board offers *two* syllabuses.

Syllabus A

(a) Written examination paper 2 hours 30 minutes (70%)

Section A: prose (30%)
Close reading of extract from set text.
Extended writing on set text.

Section B: drama (30%)
Close reading of extract from set text
Extended writing on set text.

Section C: poetry (10%)
Guided response to unseen poem.

(b) Coursework (30%)

Poetry ⎱
Poetry ⎰ including pre- and post-1900 works.
Prose ⎱ texts to be chosen so that pre- and post-1900
Drama ⎰ works in each genre are covered across coursework and written paper.

Syllabus B

(a) Written examination paper 2 hours 30 minutes (70%)

Section A: prose anthology (26%)
Close reading of extract.
Extended writing on anthology.

Section B: poetry anthology (26%)
Close reading of extract.
Extended writing on anthology.

Section C: drama (18%)
Extended writing on set texts.

(b) Coursework (30%)

Poetry pre-1900
Prose pre-1900
Drama (pre- and post-1900 to be covered across coursework and written examination paper).
Wider reading (any genre, pre- or post-1900).

▷ **International General Certificate of Education (IGCSE)**

The Board offers *three* schemes of assessment.

Literature with coursework (syllabuses 0486–0489)

Paper 1: Open books. Written examination paper 2 hours 15 minutes (70%)

One text-based and two essay questions on each prescribed text.

Paper 2: Coursework – school-based assessment (30%)

Literature without coursework (syllabuses 0486–0489)

Paper 1: Open books. Written examination paper 2 hours 15 minutes (70%)

One text-based and two essay questions on each set text.

Paper 3: Unseen (1 hour)

Literature without coursework (syllabus 0486 only)

Paper 4: Closed books. Written examination of 2 hours 30 minutes (100%)

One passage-based and two essay questions on each prescribed text. Candidates will enter for Paper 4 only.

▷ **Names and addresses of the examination boards**

London
EDEXCEL Foundation
Stewart House, 32 Russell Square, London, WC1B 5DN
Tel: 0171 331 4000
Fax: 0171 753 4592
Advice line: 0171 753 4556

MEG
Midland Examining Group
Head Office: Syndicate Buildings, 1 Hills Road, Cambridge, CB1 2EU
Tel: 01223 553311
Fax: 01223 460278

NEAB
Northern Examinations and Assessment Board
Devas Street, Manchester, M15 6EX
Tel: 0161 953 1180
Fax: 0161 273 7572

NICCEA
Northern Ireland Council for the Curriculum, Examinations and Assessment
29 Clarendon Road, Belfast, BT1 3BG
Tel: 01232 261200
Fax: 01232 261234

SEG
Southern Examining Group
Stag Hill House, Guildford, Surrey, GU2 5XJ
Tel: 01483 506506
Fax: 01483 300152

WJEC
Welsh Joint Education Committee
245 Western Avenue, Cardiff, CF5 2YX
Tel: 01222 265000
Fax: 01222 575994

IGCSE
International General Certificate of Education
University of Cambridge Local Examinations Syndicate,
1 Hills Road, Cambridge, CB1 2EU
Tel: 01223 553311
Fax: 01223 553311

When contacting examination boards, ask for the Publications Department. Always indicate which syllabus you require. A charge is normally made.

Coursework and examination techniques

GETTING STARTED

English Literature is not a subject that depends entirely on learning facts. GCSE syllabuses recognize this, particularly in open-book exams. But whatever the type of exam, the emphasis is on *demonstrating various skills*. You are asked to show you have *understood* and *appreciated* the literature *you* have read. This does mean *you* and not the teacher.

To do this you need to read attentively and write effectively about what you have read.

In this chapter we look at a number of approaches which will help you prepare for both coursework and exam assessments. We also look at the different types of questions.

WHAT YOU NEED TO KNOW

▷ **Reading well**

We read all the time. We learn how to do this when young. Nothing to it! However, reading literature is vastly different from the sort of reading for information we do every day. Literature uses words at full stretch, and every single one has to be attended to. So turn off the hi-fi, and the television, and really concentrate. The Walkman can have a useful function – there are arguments for and against – but it does enable you to listen to a text while you are jotting down notes and making observations.

It is no good 'skipping' to get the gist, or general drift, of a book. Read the book carefully to the end.

Develop good reading habits. Read with a pen and notebook – always have a notebook with you, for those inspired thoughts! Keep a dictionary handy. You will need to look up new or unusual words. Jot down the words as you go along and revise them with a dictionary at the end of a chapter, scene or poem.

Be careful not to read too fast. Know your own rate and stick to it. Eating up pages too quickly only produces indigestion. Skim reading has its place, but you will always have to go back over the text.

Pause at the end of a chapter or scene to let its meaning sink in. Note how you felt towards it. Think about its possible meanings. If it raises questions, jot them down and put them to your teacher and discuss them with your friends. You can learn from someone else's opinions.

When your mind begins to wander, stop work. Read for twenty minutes with close attention, then stop. Do something different – go for a walk and let the ideas sink in. Return to your reading and do another concentrated stint. Gradually your periods of study will get longer.

When you have read to the end, re-read. Do not do this immediately. Leave a reasonable gap between one book and the next. Literature matures like good wine in a cellar. You will enjoy the second tasting so much more.

Poetry, in particular, needs careful reading and many re-readings. Do not expect to understand everything immediately. Many modern poems start deliberately with a puzzle for the reader to solve. Some apparently 'easy' poems may contain depths of meaning which surface only after much study. Most poetry is concentrated stuff.

A good literature guide such as *York Notes* and *York Handbooks*, which are also published by Longman, will help you to understand your chosen text. They provide you with ideas, and explain any difficulties.

▷ **Personal response**

Examiners are looking for your personal response to literature. This is why your own careful reading and questioning are so important. You can learn all about your own appreciation of a writer's work.

A word of warning. A personal response does not mean writing, 'I love this poem because it reminds me of when I had a wonderful holiday in Cornwall' or 'The poet uses language in such a fascinating way I can see the things actually happening.'

Your understanding must be disciplined. Your response must be seen through a rational discussion of the text. Through your discusssion of, say, theme, character or language, your response will be made clear.

There is no right or wrong answer to questions set on literature. This does not mean that you can write anything and it will be accepted. What the examiner requires is an argument which is supported by evidence drawn from the text. Provided you can make out a reasonable case and prove it then you are home and dry. So you cannot, for example, claim you feel a character is a liar or a cheat if there is nothing in the text to suggest it.

▷ **Making notes**

This is a skill vital to any study of books. Your notes must be brief but sufficient for your purpose. Some students' notes are as long as the book itself! Notes are an aid to study, not a chore. Notes help you to:

▶ remember what you have read
▶ organize what you have read into different areas of study
▶ prepare your essays.

Important ways in which to use notes are to:

▶ make a brief summary at the end of each chapter of a novel;
▶ identify the diction, imagery, figurative language, rhyme, rhythm, sounds and overall effect of a poem;
▶ remember character, plot, theme, language, staging, conventions of a play;
▶ understand the narrative, plot, character, setting, theme and language of a novel or short story.

Here is one way to approach note-taking on a play. First, read the play. As you complete each scene, (a) note the characters in the scene and (b) make brief notes on what happens *and* the significance of these events. If possible do this on one side of A4, at most two sides.

Then you could colour code the characters/events with marker pen. This will save hours of time when you come to prepare essays and coursework assignments. A brief glance will focus your attention on the significant scenes. For the purposes of a particular question, you can then ignore the rest of the play.

When you are revising the play, it is a good idea to combine these concise notes with your re-reading of the text, an ideal combination of specific points and an overall view of the play. You will not always find every aspect listed here in every text you read, but by looking for them you will be establishing good practice. Well-prepared notes will enable you to write your coursework assignments and revise for the exams. The following chapters will tell you the types of likely questions and give some worked answers for guidance.

▷ Essay techniques

First of all, make sure you understand what the question means. You will receive marks only for showing an understanding of the question. Too many students see the title of a book and proceed to write about it, ignoring the question altogether. If in doubt, ask your teacher.

Find the *key* word or words. Look at this question:

'MEG, Higher Tier'

Many of the poems in this selection of war poems create a powerful atmosphere and sense of place.
Which two poems do you think do this most successfully?
You will need to refer closely to the language of the poems in your answer.

You are asked first to consider two things: the powerful atmosphere and sense of place.

More importantly, you are asked to do this by showing the effective way in which the poets use language to create atmosphere and sense of place. This does *not* mean a description of some places in the poems, or the sort of answer referred to earlier: 'The poet creates an atmosphere so skilfully that you can almost feel that you are there.' A discussion of various uses of language is what the question requires. And that is what you have to provide. Limit your answer to a discusion of *two* poems, neither more nor less.

Planning the essay

Planning is the key to every successful essay. Follow these seven stages:

1. Study the question carefully, particularly the key words.
2. Look at your notes on the relevant sections of the book. This is why colour coding of notes is so important.
3. Make a list of points/arguments/statements you wish to make.
4. Find a quotation or two to illustrate each stage of your argument.
5. Put the arguments and quotations into a sensible order.
   A useful tip is to use separate pieces of paper so that, when you have prepared all the points and quotations, you can shuffle them into a sensible order. If you have a PC your task is simplified. What you must not do is start with a blank piece of A4 in front of you and write an essay from cold. You will dry up after half a side. Without careful planning you will be putting down arguments in the wrong order. The conclusion may appear on the first page! A common cause of frustration.
6. When everything is in place, you may then write your introduction. Keep this short and simple. Do not try to impress with examples of your deathless prose.
   Faced with the question about war poets mentioned above, start this way: 'The poets create a powerful atmosphere and a sense of place in interesting ways. One is . . .' This generalized opening sentence may look rather vague, but it gets you into the essay

quickly. Now you can start rolling out your prepared arguments. A simple opening saves precious time in the exam room and prevents you wasting coursework time.

7. Write the conclusion, which is not a lengthy summary of what has gone before. Weak conclusions are simply the first halves of essays dressed up in different language.

When you have presented all your arguments you may find a neat twist, or some further possibilities not mentioned previously.

Basic structure of the paragraph

Good critical writing is based on *three* stages.

1. Make a point or argument.
2. Illustrate with an apt quotation.
3. Show how the quotation explains the point. This serves to modify your original point and add subtle arguments along the way, leading easily to . . .
4. The next paragraph, and so on.

This approach will prevent repetition. Too many students make a point, then repeat it in different words, then repeat it . . . An apt quotation immediately focuses the reader's attention. It gives you something to discuss, and it leads on naturally to other points.

With this method you will save time and achieve success.

▷ Coursework

One of the advantages of coursework is that you can produce different types of writing from the traditional essay. Planning coursework gives you an opportunity to get involved in the decision-making process. You may be able to bend the ear of a sympathetic teacher to angle your coursework task to suit your interests.

There are many coursework possibilities. You could:

▷ **Write a review of a novel.** You could comment on the way the story is told, the background, the characters and your response to the author's ideas.

▷ A different approach is to **take a work written in one form and change it into another.** For instance, you could turn a chapter of a novel into a scene from a play, or change a scene into a short story.

Turning a chapter into a scene involves identifying the dialogue and presenting it in play format. You may need to invent extra dialogue. This is a sensitive operation. You need to understand the characters, so that you make them speak in character. The description becomes stage directions – not too many – a play isn't all stage directions. If you are really clever, you will be able to re-present some of the action as dialogue. This task demands a high degree of imagination. You must be able to visualize the story in terms of real people acting out the story on stage.

▷ **Write an extra scene or episode** for a play or a novel. This again requires imagination, and an understanding of the author's style. It's an interesting task, but be aware of the problems before you start.

▷ **Try empathetic writing.** This allows you to write imaginatively. For example, the task may be: 'Imagine you are Wilfred Owen. Write a letter home from the front.' To do this you need to understand First World War poetry, the conditions at the front and the ways the writers/soldiers were reacting to their experiences in Flanders.

▷ **Write as a journalist.** As a reporter give a graphic account of the trial scene in *The Merchant of Venice* or as a political correspondent write an article about the problems of the succession to the Scottish throne, based on your study of Macbeth.

▷ **Keep a diary.** As a character in fiction write a diary to cover a period of time. For example, as Jane Eyre you might write about the period when you were getting to know Mr Rochester.

Suggestions for coursework are given in each chapter.

▷ Preparing for the exam

You have read and re-read your books. You have made notes. So what is left to do? In the exam room the emphasis will be on *speed*. You will have little time to think. Therefore you should do as much organizing of your thoughts as you can before you get there.

Go over your notes carefully. *Make a list of all possible questions* on each set book. There are exam questions in every chapter to help you. Your teacher can give you others. If you are studying alone you can look in the local library for specimen papers, or you can write direct to the examination board. Do not just look at questions on your own set books. Questions on other books will show you other things that are likely to be asked. Adapt questions on other books to your own set books. Simply doing this makes you think about the works you have studied.

Work out the answers to a number of these questions. Take some as far as the planning stage. Write out others in full. Try to do a variety of different kinds of questions. As you do this work it will become clear that some passages in your texts are particularly important because they keep cropping up in your answers. Go back to the texts and read these passages carefully.

You will be expected to be able to *quote from plays*. Compile a list of useful quotations to illustrate character, theme or language. Quotations should be one or two lines long.

To revise poems you should read through each one, in full, alongside your notes. You need to be able to *quote from poems* too. Choose quotations which show a particular point about the subject or the language of the poem.

Finally you need to practise answering questions *in the time allowed*. Find out from past papers how much time you are allowed to answer each question. When you have done all your revision on a text, choose a question. Make sure you will not be interrupted. Set the alarm clock and write your answer. If you do this several times for different texts you will develop a feeling for the length of time a question takes and you will have far less trouble in the exam room. All this is hard work and, above all, takes time. Never think you can skimp on the time and get a good grade. Do not be fooled by people who say they are not doing any revision. They probably are in secret. Most of us have to work hard to get through our exams.

▷ Types of questions

On the exam paper you should expect *three* types of question on the set books or the anthology:

   i)   the traditional essay;
   ii)   an extract, followed by one question, often accompanied by bullet points;
   iii) a structured question, often on an extract.

The traditional essay

For this you are given a title, which you then have to plan and write as you did for coursework. This may be a general title which you are asked to apply to one of your set texts. For example, 'Relationships between people are difficult.' Write about the difficult relationships in, and show how they develop in, your set book. You are often offered alternative titles on each of your set books. Making a brief plan in the exam is vital as it prevents you omitting key points. Read the question carefully and find the key word or words. Make sure you know precisely what the question is asking for. It is easy under stress to assume the question means one thing when, in fact, the examiners want something slightly different. So take your time. Read the question, carefully. Think. Plan. Then write.

Questions on an extract

The extract passage takes one of two forms. It could be an extract from one of the texts you are studying, or it could be taken from the board's anthology.

Usually one or two general questions are set. On drama a question might require you to comment on the character of one of the speakers or discuss the audience reaction to a scene. A poem or prose extract might be accompanied by a question on the author's methods of writing.

The only real way to prepare for this type of question is to revise your texts thoroughly. Pay particular attention to an author's techniques. Once you have understood a writer's methods, make a checklist and learn them. Note also the sections of the text where typical examples of his or her style are to be found.

Structured questions

These questions suggest some areas to be covered in your essay. For example:

In *Animal Farm* Boxer is obviously very popular with the animals. How do you think he will be remembered by the animals? In your answer, you may wish to consider the following:

▶ Boxer's character
▶ his actions
▶ his attitude to the revolution
▶ his relationships with the other animals.

This is a very useful type of question. It serves to jog your memory and stimulates thought on the book. It provides a plan so all you have to do is put some flesh on the question's skeleton.

Each section of the book has a section on examination questions, which will show you the possible variety.

▷ Open-book exams

The difference between an open-book exam and a traditional exam is that you take copies of texts in with you. They may be lightly annotated and are there for you to refer to so that you can refresh your memory of a passage you want to use as illustration. For an extract question, instead of the passage being printed on the exam paper, you will be asked to look it up in your own text. Having the text there with you is comforting but not as useful as you might at first think. You can spend an awful lot of time looking through a text for a particular passage if you do not know precisely where to look. So you have to know your text as thoroughly as for a traditional exam. One advantage is that you can look up quotations and so quote accurately.

▷ In the exam

If you stay up late the night before the exam, or get up at the crack of dawn to do some last-minute revision, you will not be at your best in the exam itself. Try to arrive feeling relaxed and refreshed. Make sure you have everything you need with you: pens, and texts if it is an open-book exam. Wear comfortable clothes.

When you are shown to your place, try to settle down and shut everything else out of your mind before you are told to start.

Look through the paper and find the questions on your set books. Read all these questions carefully and decide which ones you are going to answer.

Most importantly, do the right number of questions. Read the directions carefully. In preparation get to know what your exam paper will look like by working through specimen papers or past papers. Every year candidates do badly because they do not finish the paper. Do not spend too long on one question and have no time to do the required number of questions. Good luck!

Reading to understand poetry

> **GETTING STARTED**

Poetry is often considered to be the most difficult part of an English Literature course. It is felt by many people to be strange and alien. This is hardly surprising. Poetry is not part of our everyday experience nowadays, though it used to be. Ballads were once popular entertainment and right up to the present century poets were valued as story-tellers. What is more, it is not always immediately clear what a poem is about; even when we understand all the words separately we may not understand the way the poet has put them together. Examiners require that you should be able to give an adequate account of the surface meaning of a poem. If even this is difficult, how can you hope to go beyond to the deeper meaning and develop the personal response that the examiners are looking for?

The first thing to accept is that if you can't grasp the meaning of a poem on first reading you should not give up in despair or dismiss it as rubbish. Poetry is the most intense and concentrated language there is. It yields up its meanings, its many meanings, slowly. We have to read and re-read. Start by reading aloud and after that try to hear the poem in your head as you read.

Secondly, reading poetry is, in a sense, a different skill from ordinary reading and so we have to learn to do it. You may have to learn it for the purposes of the exam but you will discover that, like any other skill, it will stay with you. The impressions made on us as we read are created by the kinds of words the poet uses. This chapter will help you to begin to read poetry with understanding by showing you some of the things you should be looking for.

The topics in this chapter are applicable to all exam boards.

MEG	NEAB	NICCEA	SEG	LONDON	WJEC	IGCSE	**TOPIC**	STUDY	REVISION 1	REVISION 2
✓	✓	✓	✓	✓	✓	✓	Diction			
✓	✓	✓	✓	✓	✓	✓	Tone			
✓	✓	✓	✓	✓	✓	✓	Associations			
✓	✓	✓	✓	✓	✓	✓	Ambiguity			
✓	✓	✓	✓	✓	✓	✓	Imagery			
✓	✓	✓	✓	✓	✓	✓	Response			

WHAT YOU NEED TO KNOW

▷ Diction

The words which poets use, the vocabulary, is frequently called the **diction**. The choice of diction gives a poem its character – elevated and lofty or colloquial and down to earth, serious or lighthearted.

A great deal of the mood of a poem comes from the impression we receive from the diction.

Poets writing in English have half a million words to call on. They may resurrect a long dead word if it suits them or on other occasions invent words and leave the reader to work out the meaning. Shakespeare was the greatest such inventor and many of his words have since passed into the English language. Do not assume a word is invented, though, until you have scoured the dictionary. Newly coined words, or the archaic ones dug up from past centuries, stand out because they are unusual. They surprise us, which is presumably why the poet went to the trouble of using them.

Here are two contrasting styles. One has very elevated formal diction, the other is colloquial and conversational:

> i)   Avenge, O Lord, thy slaughtered saints, whose bones
>   Lie scattered on the alpine mountains cold.
>
>   (John Milton)

> ii) Lawd, Son, whut um go do with you?
>   You makes me so mad
>   I don't know whut to do!
>
>   (Betty Gates)

The first poet has a different purpose from the second. Milton is addressing an all-powerful God. A poet could address God in the way Betty Gates talks to her son in the second extract but we would then get a very different impression of the relationship between the poet and God.

One of the first things to note about a poem is the general effect of the diction. You should note all unusual words and ask yourself what their effect is.

'Do you have a good dictionary? Always have one near when you are reading or writing.'

▷ Tone

Growing out of the poet's choice of diction is the **tone** of a poem. You may find it helpful to think of it as tone of voice or to imagine the poet speaking. The question to ask is 'What is the poet's attitude to the subject?' This may change as the poem progresses, as the tone is not necessarily the same all the way through. Tone often changes from stanza to stanza and sometimes single lines have a marked tone of their own. Finding words for the tone demands careful distinctions. Can you briefly describe the tone of these lines?

> I have had playmates, I have had companions
> In my childhood days, in my joyful schooldays
> All, all are gone, the old familiar faces.
>
>   (Charles Lamb)

'Regret for the past' would sum it up adequately. The tone of the next poem is also regretful but it is different:

> A thousand years you said
> As our hearts melted.
> I look at the hand you held
> And the ache is hard to bear.
>
>   (Lady Heguri)

Here the regret is more painful and there is also a suggestion of resentment at betrayal. These distinctions are important.

When you study a poem hear it in your head. Try to decide what the poet's tone is, and if it changes during the course of the poem.

'Ask your teacher or local library if there are recordings available of the poems you are studying.'

▷ Associations

Poets choose their words with extreme care so we must look at them with equal care. Ordinarily we use words to convey information in a fairly straightforward way. But words are loaded. They communicate shades of meaning and feelings. Would you rather be described as 'skinny' or 'slim'? Words with more or less the same literal meanings carry senses which make us react differently. Some words seem naturally attractive because of their **associations**, some equally naturally unattractive. 'Golden' would be an example of the first, 'murky' an example of the second. Poets make use of this ability of words to prompt particular **reactions**: they choose words very deliberately for their associations and connotations. When the sun is described as blood-red we feel there is something dangerous or sinister about it because of the associations of blood. A sun that is as red as a poppy has more comfortable associations.

Here is a description of a dead lamb:

> I saw on the slant hill a putrid lamb,
> Propped with daisies.
>
> (Richard Eberhart)

The poet chooses 'putrid' because he wants to show the dead animal as unpleasant. He could have achieved a quite different effect by describing the lamb as though it were asleep. Why, though, does he include 'daisies'? They are pretty, charming little flowers, often associated with children. The poet seems to be deliberately bringing together the prettiness and nursery rhyme associations of the daisies (and lambs) with the horrid associations of 'putrid'. It is the associations which make the lines more than just a statement about a lamb lying dead on a hillside because they affect your reactions to the words.

'Look for associations.'

Try to be aware of the associations of words as you read and the reactions they provoke in you.

▷ Ambiguity

Double meanings, or **ambiguities**, abound in poetry because the poet tries to concentrate a great deal into a few words. It is one of the ways that poetry is made so rich and complex. When Robert Frost writes:

> And miles to go before I sleep.

he means both that he has a long way to ride and that he has many more things to do before the end of his life.

You must always be on the look out for words which mean more than at first appears. On the other hand you do not need to look on the whole of poetry as a trap, with double meanings lurking everywhere.

▷ Imagery

This is one of the most frequently used terms in talking about poetry. Put simply it means using language to convey sense impressions. An **image** will do more than just state that we can see, hear, feel, smell or taste something. The poet will try to create the experience in our imagination. Wordsworth describes how, while he is rowing across a lake at night, he suddenly becomes aware of a huge cliff:

> the huge cliff
> Rose up between me and the stars, and still,
> With measured motion, like a living thing,
> Strode after me.

This immediately conjures up a picture of the rock towering over him and seeming to move with him. **Visual** imagery of this kind is very frequent in poetry.

But poets are concerned with all five senses so imagery can also be **aural**, to do with sound:

> Listen! you hear the grating roar
> Of pebbles which the waves draw back, and fling,
> At their return, up the high strand,
>
> (Matthew Arnold)

Here we are invited to imagine the sound of the pebbles which the poet creates with the words 'grating roar' before we are given a picture of the waves flinging them up the beach.

Imagery can be **tactile**, to do with touch:

Against the rubber tongues of cows and the hoeing hands of men
Thistles spike the summer air

(Ted Hughes)

Calling the cows' tongues 'rubber' gives us a very strong impression of what the touch of the thistles against them would be like. The language is both visual and tactile because we can both see and feel the spike of the thistles.

Imagery can be to do with **smell**, as in this description of a fight between a knight and a mythical beast:

Therewith she spew'd out of her filthy maw
A floud of poison horrible and black,
Full of great lumps of flesh and gobbets raw,
Which stunke so vildly, that it forst him slacke
His grasping hold, and from her turne him backe.

(Edmund Spenser)

The poet says that the beast's vomit 'stunke so vildly'. But it is the associations of words like 'spew'd', 'filthy' and 'poison', together with the visual images of 'great lumps of flesh and gobbets raw', which turn our stomach in disgust.

Taste is notoriously difficult to describe and is probably the sense referred to least in poetry. Here is one example:

O, for a draught of vintage! that hath been
Cool'd a long age in the deep delved earth,
Tasting of Flora and the country green,

(Keats)

Perhaps only drinkers of Elderflower or Cowslip wine can really appreciate the flavour of Keats' vintage. More likely, he was not really expecting to create the sensation of taste but relying on the power of association with flowers and the countryside to produce an effect.

On many occasions poets will use imagery referring to *several senses* to express their meaning. Notice how in the following stanza the poet uses four of the five senses to evoke the purity and beauty of his lady:

Have you seen but a bright lily grow
    Before rude hands have touched it?
Have you marked but the fall of snow
    Before the soil hath smutched it?
Have you felt the wool of the beaver,
    Or swan's down ever?
Or have smelt o' the bud o' the brier,
    Or the nard i' the fire?
Or have tasted o' the bag of the bee?
Oh so white, oh so soft, oh so sweet is she!

(Ben Jonson)

Sometimes poets will deliberately *jumble the senses*. They may talk about sights in terms of sound, or touch in terms of taste. To speak of 'bitter sorrow' is to transfer taste sensations to an emotion. In these lines Elizabeth Barrett Browning uses a colour to describe a voice which she hears answering her:

'Guess now who holds thee?' – 'Death,' I said. But there,
The silver answer rang, – 'Not Death, but Love.'

Colour is quite frequently used like this. We often talk about feeling blue when we mean sad. It is not a great step from that to imagine the colour of the sound of trumpets – many of us might say red. This technique (called **synaesthesia**) is yet another way of intensifying expression and making it fresh and new.

Look at the kinds of images used in a poem. Which of the senses is the poet appealing to? When you have looked at individual images in a poem you should notice if any of them can be grouped together. Many poems have clusters of images of the same kind. There may be a contrast between two images or sets of images.

▷ **Response**

The examiners are looking for a **personal response** to poetry. This does not just mean asserting opinions – 'I think this is a good poem' is not going to get you very far. If you can say 'This is an interesting poem because . . .' and then give some reasons for your reactions, that is far better. In theory it is just as valid to say 'I don't like this poem because . . .', but in practice it is rather difficult to write well about negative responses.

The techniques mentioned in this chapter should begin to give you an idea of what to look for and what to base your opinions on. While you are reading a poem try to keep in mind the various attributes of poetry mentioned in this chapter. At the same time notice if the poem stirs in you any particular feelings or responses. If it does, try to decide which of the poet's words, phrases or ideas are responsible for the effect. If it does not, do not worry. We cannot feel things to order and it may be that studying the poem will awaken a response. At the very least, study will give you an appreciation of the poet's skill and provide you with material for your writing.

▷ **Additional examples**

Use the following examples as exercises to see if you have understood everything so far. Work through them and then read the key at the end.

1 What can you say about the diction and tone of this stanza?
　　Fear no more the heat o' the sun,
　　　　Nor the furious winter's rages;
　　Thou thy worldly task hast done,
　　　　Home art gone, and ta'en thy wages;
　　Golden lads and girls all must
　　As chimney-sweepers, come to dust.

2 Explain the ambiguity of this line:
　　He that is down needs fear no fall,

'What senses is the poet appealing to? What are the contrasts?'

3 What kinds of imagery are used here?
　　　　　　Fragrance of Life, Odor of Death
　　All the while among
　　the rubble even, and in
　　the hospitals, among the wounded,
　　　　　　not only beneath
　　　　　　lofty clouds

　　　　　　　in temples
　　　　　　by the shores of lotus-dreaming
　　　　　　lakes
　　a fragrance:
　　flowers, incense, the earth-mist rising
　　of mild daybreak in the delta – good smell
　　of life.

　　It's in America
　　where no bombs ever
　　have screamed down smashing
　　the buildings, shredding people's bodies,
　　tossing the fields of Kansas or Vermont or Maryland into the air
　　to land wrong way up, a gash of earth guts . . .
　　it's in America, everywhere, a faint seepage,
　　I smell death.

Key to the examples

1 William Shakespeare. The diction is fairly simple, easy to understand and down to earth, but quite formal. Several words (o', thou, art) show that it was not written in this century. The tone is grave and calmly philosophical: he speaks of death as taking wages and going home, the end of life as completing a task. The phrase 'Golden lads and girls' is warm and affectionate.

(continued)

(continued)

2 John Bunyan. 'He that is down' could mean both physically down – on his knees, or in the gutter – or it could mean mentally or spirtually down, perhaps depressed or humble. Such a person need have no fear of falling down physically or from a mental height, whether of excitement or of pride. In the case of a word like 'down', which can have so many applications, we need the rest of the poem to show us which particular meaning, or meanings, the poet is thinking of. The next line of Bunyan's poem is 'He that is low, no pride', which shows us how to take the first line. Because the poem opens with the general word 'down' we think of all sorts of interpretations before the second line points us towards a specific one. This ambiguity gives a depth and richness to the lines.

3 Denise Levertov. A great many of the images in this poem are of war-smashed buildings and shredded bodies; the land devastated and in chaos. Most of these are visual images, though there is one sound image of bombs screaming. However, the poem is organized around two contrasting smells, which the poet equates with life and death, as the title tells us. The poet evokes the first, the fragrance of life, with strong images of the scent of flowers, particularly the lotus, incense and the smell of the damp earth rising in the morning mist. The second odour she evokes indirectly in 'a gash of earth guts'. This, too, is a visual image but the associations of the dreadful pungent smell of guts are strong, especially when she states, 'I smell death.' This is the smell that seems to be buried in America and is seeping out everywhere.

▶ SUGGESTIONS FOR COURSEWORK

1 Choose three poems by a set author or from an anthology. Analyse the type of diction and imagery used.
2 Choose a theme common to poems from different centuries. Make a comparative study of the different language found in each poem.
3 Choose one of your poets for study. Imagine that you are to interview the poet for radio, asking him or her about the way in which the poems have been written.

▷ **Coursework task** Read the following poem by Robert Frost. As you read try to imagine the scene in your mind. Re-write the poem as if it were a scene from a play. Expand the dialogue, actions and details of the poem to create characters and their situation. Try to re-create the feelings of the poem in your writing.

'Out, Out –'
The buzz saw snarled and rattled in the yard
And made dust and dropped stove-length sticks of wood,
Sweet-scented stuff when the breeze drew across it.
And from there those that lifted eyes could count
Five mountain ranges one behind the other
Under the sunset far into Vermont.
And the saw snarled and rattled, snarled and rattled,
As it ran light, or had to bear a load.
And nothing happened: day was all but done.
Call it a day, I wish they might have said
To please the boy by giving him the half hour
That a boy counts so much when saved from work.
His sister stood beside them in her apron
To tell them 'Supper'. At the word, the saw,
As if to prove saws knew what supper meant,
Leaped out at the boy's hand, or seemed to leap –
He must have given the hand. However it was,
Neither refused the meeting. But the hand!
The boy's first outcry was a rueful laugh,
As he swung towards them holding up the hand
Half in appeal, but half as if to keep
The life from spilling. Then the boy saw all –

Since he was old enough to know, big boy
Doing a man's work, though a child at heart –
He saw all spoiled. 'Don't let them cut my hand off –
The doctor, when he comes. Don't let him, sister!'
So. But the hand was gone already.
The doctor put him in the dark of ether.
He lay and puffed his lips out with his breath.
And then the watcher at his pulse took fright.
No-one believed. They listened at his heart.
Little – less – nothing! – and that ended it.
No more to build on there. And they, since they
Were not the one dead, turned to their affairs.

▷ **Suggested answer**

[*At the back of the stage is a white-painted porch of a farmhouse. The back drop shows trees and mountains rising into the distance. Gold light to show that day is waning to evening and the sun is setting. Downstage a man and a boy, tall but young, are cutting logs into short lengths with a buzz saw. The ground is littered with sawdust. The sound of the saw is continuous but its note changes as it bites into the wood. The man works with methodical concentration but the boy gazes around as he waits for the next log to be cut and occasionally glances towards the house expectantly. There is no resentment in the way he works, just youthful impatience for the task to be ended. A young woman in an apron comes out on to the porch.*]

SIS   [*calling to be heard above the saw*] Supper! [*Seeing she is not heard she crosses to where the man and the boy are working.*] Supper.

[*The boy looks up with a smile and starts to speak but in his moment of inattention the saw catches his wrist.*]

PA   [*not seeing*] Good, I'm hungry.

BOY   [*with a gasp, half-laughing*] No! Stupid. Look. What shall I do? [*The pain reaches him and he falls to his knees.*]

PA   What? Oh my God! [*He lunges to switch off the saw.*]

SIS   Oh lord!

PA   Quick, call your mother, get bandages. Go on!

SIS   [*running, shouting*] Mother, Ma, Ma.

PA   I'll get the doctor. He'll stitch you up. Can you walk? Here, I can carry you – just.

[*The girl and the mother return.*]

MA   O my boy, what have you done? Come, let me help you. [*to the girl*] Go and get a bowl of warm water. Just get him as far as the porch. Good. There now. [*They sit him in a chair.*] I can manage him now.

PA   I'll go and get Dr Lester. Be as quick as I can. [*Exit*]

MA   Yes, you go. Be quick. I'll try and stop the bleeding.

[*Sis returns with a bowl which she sets on the floor. Ma is tying a bandage tightly round the boy's arm to stem the flow of blood.*]

SIS   What can I do?

MA   Just bathe his wrist and hold it together until the doctor comes.

SIS   I can't do that.

MA   Then go and get him a tot of rum while I do it.

BOY   I can hold it myself.

MA   [*cleaning and bandaging*] No, leave it be. You just be still. However did you do it?

BOY   I don't know. It just seemed to grab me.

SIS   [*coming back with the rum*] Here you are.

BOY   I don't like it.

MA   Never mind, just drink it. I always said you were too young to work that saw. There, I've done what I can. Sit still now. And you sit with him. Make sure he doesn't move. Doctor won't be long and your brother will be back soon. [*She tidies the things used to dress the wound and carries them out.*]

SIS   Does it hurt badly?

BOY   Yes, of course it does.

SIS   It's still bleeding.

BOY   Don't let him cut my hand off – the doctor, when he comes. Don't let him, Sis. What use will I be on the farm without a hand!

SIS   Don't worry, the doctor'll fix it. How do you feel now?

BOY   Don't know. My arm feels tight, and I feel woozy.

SIS   That's the rum. You just rest.

[Pause and silence. The boy's head lolls to one side as he half-sleeps. His sister watches anxiously. The father returns with the doctor, who hurries to his patient. At the sound of their footsteps the mother returns from inside the house. The family watch silently as the doctor kneels to examine the boy.]

DR LESTER   Whoever put on this tourniquet knew what they were doing. Now let's have a look at him. Hm, yes, the bleeding's almost stopped. Good, good. *[He turns away, apparently to look for something in his bag, but really he is thinking.]* You have another son, don't you, an elder?

PA   Yes, he's gone over to Long Meadow to mend a wall but he'll be back after sundown.

DR LESTER   Right, well, I'm going to have to do a little mending here myself, but it won't hurt. Do you know what ether is? I shall give you some of this and you won't feel a thing.

BOY   You're going to cut it off aren't you?

DR LESTER   I'm afraid I have to. The arm has been too severely severed to heal. Fortunately the cut is clean so we shouldn't have any worries once we've cleaned it up.

BOY   But my hand will have gone. I shan't have a hand. How can I help Pa, how can I run a farm of my own with only one hand? I shall be a cripple.

MA   Don't talk that way, you won't be a cripple.

PA   That's enough son. Doctor'll do what he can for you. What's done can't be undone.

[A bed is pushed to the middle of the stage and the lights shrink to a pool around the bed where the boy lies unconscious. His hand has been operated on and his arm, cleanly bandaged, lies straight at his side on top of the counterpane. His mother sits beside the bed watching him. There is a regular little 'pfft' sound from the boy's lips as he breathes out. His sister appears at the edge of the lighted area, as if entering a bedroom. She whispers.]

SIS   Ma!

MA   No need to whisper, he's sound asleep.

SIS   William's home. Do you want me to sit here for you?

MA   Yes, there's nothing to worry about. He's sleeping quietly. Just call me if there's any change.

[Ma goes and Sis takes her place. Silence settles over the scene. For a long time Sis gazes at her brother's face then, becoming bored, wanders to the edge of the light and appears to be looking out of the window. After a while she resumes her seat and settles again. Then she sits up. The 'pfft' sound has stopped. She bends forward and quickly puts a hand on the boy's chest. With a little gasp she gets up and calls.]

SIS   Ma! Ma, Pa! *[She returns to the side of the bed. Her father is the first to enter.]*

PA   What is it?

SIS   He's stopped breathing.

PA   Let's see. *[He goes round to the other side of the bed and picks up his son's good hand, feeling the pulse.]*

MA   *[coming in quickly]* What's to do?

SIS   He's stopped breathing, Ma.

MA   But he was all right when I left. I've only been gone a few minutes. What happened?

SIS   Nothing. He was going on quite quiet and I was watching him and then he just stopped. Nothing else.

PA   His pulse is still beating. Here, you feel.

MA   *[carefully pulling back the bedclothes and kneeling to listen to his heart]* Yes I can feel it, but it's so faint.

PA   I'll send William for the doctor again. *[He goes towards the door.]*

MA   I can't believe it.

PA   What?

MA   I can't believe it. It didn't seem bad enough for that.

PA   *[coming back and feeling the pulse again]* Nothing.

[Pause.]

SIS   What shall we do?

MA   Better get the doctor anyway.

EXAMINATION QUESTIONS

▷ **Question 1**   You will find that the examination boards have produced anthologies of literature for study. The WJEC has included in theirs this poem by Carol Ann Duffy. Read it carefully and then answer the question that follows.

Mrs Skinner, North Street

Milk bottles. Light through net. No post. Cat,
come here by the window, settle down. Morning
in this street awakes unwashed; a stale wind
breathing litter, last night's godlessness. This place
is hellbound in a handcart. Cat, you mark
her words. Strumpet. Slut. A different man
for every child; a byword for disgrace.

Her dentures grin at her, gargling water
on the mantelpiece. The days are gone
for smiling, wearing them to chatter down the road.
Good morning. Morning. Lovely day. Over the years
she's suffered loss, bereavement, loneliness.
A terrace of strangers. An old ghost
mouthing curses behind a cloudy, nylon veil.

Scrounger. Workshy. Cat, where is the world
she married, was carried into up a scrubbed stone step?
The young louts roam the neighbourhood.
Breaking of glass. Chants. Sour abuse of aerosols.
That social worker called her *xenophobic*. When he left
she looked the word up. Fear, morbid dislike, of strangers.
Outside, the rain pours down relentlessly.

People scurry for shelter. How many hours
has she sat here, Cat, filled with bitterness
and knowing they'll none of them come?
Not till the day the smell is noticed.
Not till the day you're starving, Cat, and begin
to lick at the corpse. She twitches the curtain
as the Asian man next door runs through the rain.

Write about this poem by Carol Ann Duffy. You may wish to think about:

▶   what the poem is about;
▶   who the speaker is in the poem;
▶   the way the poem is written;
▶   why the poem makes an impact on you;
▶   anything else you think is important.

▷ **Question 2**   Read this poem very carefully and then answer the question which follows.

'SEG Foundation Tier.'

Cynddylan on a Tractor

Ah, you should see Cynddylan on a tractor.
Gone the old look that yoked him to the soil;
He's a new man now, part of the machine.
His nerves of metal and his blood oil.
The clutch curses, but the gears obey
His least bidding, and lo, he's away
Out of the farmyard, scattering hens.
Riding to work now as a great man should,
He is the knight at arms breaking the fields'

Mirror of silence, emptying the wood
Of foxes and squirrels and bright jays.
The sun comes over the tall trees
Kindling all the hedges, but not for him
Who runs his engine on a different fuel.
And all the birds are singing, bills wide in vain,
As Cynddylan passes proudly up the lane.

(R. S. Thomas)

How does the poet show the readers what he thinks about Cynddylan's change from the old horse-drawn plough to the tractor? You should look closely at the poets' words and phrases.

▷ **Question 3**

'London Higher and Foundation Tiers.'

Read the following poems very carefully several times and then show connections and comparisons between them. Remember to use words and phrases from the poems to support what you have to say.

From the Lucy Poems

She dwelt among the untrodden ways
    Beside the springs of Dove
A Maid whom there were none to praise
    And very few to love:

A violet by a mossy stone
    Half hidden from the eye!
Fair as a star, when only one
    Is shining in the sky.

She lived unknown, and few could know
    When Lucy ceased to be;
But she is in her grave, and oh,
    The difference to me!
A slumber did my spirit seal;
    I had no human fears:
She seemed a thing that could not feel
    The touch of earthly years.

No motion has she now, no force;
    She neither hears nor sees;
Rolled round in earth's diurnal course,
    With rocks and stones and trees.

(William Wordsworth)

Remember

Remember me when I am gone away,
Gone far away into the silent land;
When you can no more hold me by the hand,
Nor I half turn to go, yet turning stay.
Remember me when no more day by day
You tell me of our future that you plann'd
Only remember me; you understand
It will be late to counsel then or pray.
Yet if you should forget me for a while
And afterwards remember, do not grieve:
For if the darkness and corruption leave
A vestige of the thoughts that once I had,
Better by far you should forget and smile
Than that you should remember and be sad.

(Christina Rossetti)

Show connections and comparisons between these two poems. You might find it helpful to consider the following:

▷ both poems are about death and the loss of a loved one;
▷ similarities in the tone in which they are both written;
▷ your personal response to both poems.

 EXAMINATION ANSWERS

▷ **Question 1** *Notes and tutor's answer*

Notes
Read these notes through and try writing your own answer. Do this before reading the one given below.

This question is set out very well because it directs you to the things the examiners are expecting, and it gives you a ready-made outline for your answer.

They want you to say what the poem is about and examine how it is written. They have given you useful headings to start you thinking and trigger your own personal reaction to the poem. Use what you learnt in the chapter to answer the separate sections of the question.

In order to write successfully about poetry always carry out the following procedure:

1 Read through the poem slowly at least twice. If you are not in a position to read aloud, try to hear the poem in your head.
2 Read through the questions.
3 Go back over the poem and underline words and phrases relevant to each question. You may care to colour code material to be included under each heading. Jot down useful notes in the margin.
4 Write your answer in *five* paragraphs, one for each heading. Now write your answer before reading the suggested answer which follows.

Suggested answer
The poem is about an old woman who lives in a slum area. She lives a lonely life with a cat as her only companion. The poem traces her life from the day she got married and was carried over 'her scrubbed stone step' until the present day. Over the years she lost her friends and relatives until she now lives among strangers. She peeps from behind her curtains at her new neighbours. She sits with her cat waiting for her life to end. The area is described as run down, inhabited by social outcasts, terrorized by hooligans and scarred by graffiti.

'Explains the surface meaning.'

The speaker is a nosy neighbour who obviously dislikes Mrs Skinner by criticizing her gossiping ways. She seems to be like Mrs Skinner herself. When the neighbour wonders how many hours Mrs Skinner has been sitting there, the reader might wonder how long the neighbour has been sitting watching too. As Mrs Skinner watches the Asian from behind her curtain, the speaker of the poem is also keeping her eye on Mrs Skinner.

'Identifies the speaker and makes an important comment.'

The poem is written in a conversational style. The expression is disjointed. The short phrases ('Milk bottles. Light through net.') seem to represent the observations of the speaker of the poem, almost as though the speaker is telling the reader what she sees as she is looking at something. The terse language indicates the speaker's bitterness ('Strumpet. Slut'.). The poet uses depressing imagery ('breaking of glass' 'sour abuse of aerosols') to underline the sadness of Mrs Skinner's life. There is a bitter tone in the descriptions of the weather. The poet uses images of dirt and decay ('street awakes unwashed', 'a stale wind') to emphasize the overall feeling of misery.

'Explores the poet's use of language and imagery.'

The way the poet shocks the reader impressed me. The vivid picture at the end of the cat licking at the corpse of Mrs Skinner I found particularly effective. This seemed to sum up the feelings of emptiness and horror in the poem. The way that Mrs Skinner twitches the curtain seems to suggest how Mrs Skinner herself will twitch as she dies.

'Identifies impact.'

One puzzling feature in the poem is the cat. At first it seemed as though the cat belonged to the speaker of the poem because it looks as though her cat is being told to 'come here by the window'. As the poem proceeds, however, it becomes clear that the cat belongs to Mrs Skinner, because in the final stanza the Cat will lick at Mrs Skinner's corpse. So what begins as a puzzle becomes quite an effective device. The cat is a means of drawing the speaker of the

'Interesting observation.'

poem and Mrs Skinner closer together. It also serves to draw the reader into the poem, as I became involved more closely in the poem.

▷ **Question 2**   *Student's answer – examiner's comments*

'Identifies key idea.'

The poet shows what he thinks about the change by the ways in which he describes the farmer. He does this in two main ways. First, he describes the way his life has changed. He describes Cynddylan as a farmer who used to be close to the soil ('yoked . . . to the soil'). But now he has changed to become someone who does his work by using machinery.

Secondly, not only has his way of life changed. His attitudes have changed as well. He has forgotten about the old country ways. He rides his tractor as though he has lost sympathy with the farm animals ('scattering hens'). He has lost his love of the countryside and its creatures:

'Identifies another key idea.'

> *emptying the wood*
> *Of foxes and squirrels and bright jays.*

The poet conveys his thought through the imagery he chooses. Cynddylan is now a farmer who is so used to using machinery that he seems to have become a machine himself:

> *His nerves of metal and his blood oil*

The tone of the poem is mechanical too:

> *but the gears obey*
> *His least bidding*

The farmer is so obsessed with his new way of farming that he does not notice what is going on around him:

'Shows how the poet uses imagery.'

> *And all the birds are singing, bills wide in vain,*

'Draws the points together.'

The poet imagines Cynddylan as a modern type of knight. This is a neat way of relating a medieval man dressed in metal to a modern farmer who seems to be made of metal. The only difference is that today's farmer, instead of going about the country doing good, ruins the countryside.

▷ **Question 3**   *Student's answer – examiner's comments*

'Identifies a connection.'

In both poems the feelings of separation through death are being considered. In the 'Lucy' poem Wordsworth is grieving for the loss of a departed lover. Christina Rossetti is beseeching her loved one to remember her when she herself is dead.

Wordsworth reflects upon the time when he knew Lucy and sees her living a secluded life close to nature. He puts her in a physical setting ('Beside the springs of Dove'). He compares her to things of beauty in nature:

> *A violet by a mossy stone*
> *. . . Fair as a star, when only one*
> *Is shining in the sky.*

(continued)

(continued)

Now she is dead he imagines her bound up with nature, as though she has become part of the earth rolling through space:

> *Rolled round in earth's diurnal course,*
> *With rocks and stones and trees.*

On the other hand, Rossetti writes about her lover by focusing on moments in their relationship. She describes the moment when lovers half-turn from each other. She writes about lovers forgetting each other. She concludes her thoughts by writing that it would be better to forget and be happy than become depressed through remembrance:

> *Better by far you should forget and smile*
> *Than that you should remember and be sad*

'Identifies comparisons.'

Although both poets have different perspectives, one looking forward and the other back, there are some similarities in the tone. Both have a sense of isolation. Wordsworth describes Lucy as dwelling 'among the untrodden ways' and 'She lived unknown'. Rossetti concentrates on the two lovers to the exclusion of the world. Thus the subjects of both poems represent romantic ideals of living out their love in isolation.

'Identifies similar tone.'

There is a sombre tone in both poems, produced by diction and imagery related to death and separation. Wordsworth writes:

> *she is in her grave*
> *. . . She neither hears nor sees;*

Rossetti talks of the 'darkness and corruption' of the grave.

There is an atmosphere of silence. Rossetti pictures herself going into 'the silent land'. Wordsworth imagines his thoughts of Lucy being sealed by a slumber. The feeling of quiet is emphasized by the lack of movement. Wordsworth states that Lucy has 'No motion'. Rossetti captures the stillness of the moment when lovers half-turn to leave. Some things are not quite in focus. Wordsworth's violet is 'Half hidden from the eye!', while Rossetti

'Different types of tone.'

writes about the vestige of a thought.

I am not really attracted to either of the poems. Wordsworth seems to have a very individual view of death with the dead Lucy being rolled around like the earth. The poet tries to link Lucy to nature even in death, which is an argument based on a personal point of view. Rossetti, on the other hand, is too sentimental for my taste. It seems rather weak to conclude a poem about remembering the sadness of things by writing it would be

'Clear personal response.'

better for the loved one to 'forget and smile' if the memory proves to be too painful.

'This essay answers the question. The only problematic paragraph is the one which gives a personal response. The candidate gives valid reasons for not being attracted to either poem. It is a courageous but dangerous line to take. Remember that the candidate has challenged the writing of established writers. Fortunately sensible reasons are put forward to support the opinions. Had reasons not been given, a conclusion based on personal feeling alone would have detracted from the quality of the essay as a whole.'

Question	Assessment Objective(s)	Pre-20th century	20th century
Coursework task – Robert Frost	1, 4		✓
1 'Mrs Skinner, North Street'	1, 2		✓
2 'Cynddylan on a Tractor'	1, 2, 4		✓
3 'From the Lucy Poems', 'Remember'	1, 2, 3	✓	

SUMMARY

The key points to remember in the study of poetry are:

▷ **Diction** – the type of words a poet uses gives the poem its character and tone.

▷ **Tone** – the 'voice' of a poet; the tone can change throughout a poem.

▷ **Associations** – note the associations of particular words, the further meaning or meanings words can conjure up.

▷ **Double meanings** or **ambiguities** give poetry richness and complexity.

▷ **Imagery** – the most frequently used term when discussing poetry – look for the way imagery appeals to our different senses.

▷ **Response** – examiners are looking for a personal response, which must be based on reason and not simply be a matter of prejudice.

Figurative language

 GETTING STARTED

Most questions on poetry ask you to make some comment on the poet's use of language. It is often the case that the way in which ideas are expressed in a poem is more important than the ideas themselves. This chapter and the next three deal with different aspects of the language of poetry. If you work your way through all four chapters you should be equipped to deal with any question which asks for a comment on the poet's use of language. We begin with figurative language, or figures of speech, because without an understanding of this kind of language a great deal of poetry is a closed book to the reader. We have seen how poetry works through association and suggestion. Its purpose is not primarily to convey information but to suggest mood and atmosphere, pictures and impressions, attitude and emotion. Above all, perhaps, pleasure in itself. Because it has so much to do at once, much poetic language is highly concentrated and so sometimes puzzling at first. Many of the puzzles can be solved by understanding figurative language, or imagery as it is sometimes called, and why a poet uses it.

The topics covered in this chapter are applicable to all exam boards.

MEG	NEAB	NICCEA	SEG	LONDON	WJEC	IGCSE	TOPIC	STUDY	REVISION 1	REVISION 2
✓	✓	✓	✓	✓	✓	✓	Simile			
✓	✓	✓	✓	✓	✓	✓	Metaphor			
✓	✓	✓	✓	✓	✓	✓	Personification			

WHAT YOU NEED TO KNOW

▷ **Simile**   A **simile** is a comparison. We all know and use hundreds:

▶ She looked as white as a sheet.
▶ My feet are like blocks of ice.
▶ She was as cool as a cucumber.
▶ He's like a bear with a sore head.

The essential elements in a simile are the two things that are being compared, and a word or phrase which links them. In the above examples the link is 'as' or 'like'. It could also be 'seemed' or 'resembled' or a phrase like 'similar to'.

When we are telling others about something we have done we are often asked, 'What was it like?' In reply we may struggle to find a comparison that will convey the experience we want to describe. Sometimes a ready-made simile is usefully to hand. 'It was like an oven in there', we may say, to convey the heat of a room. When there is no off-the-peg comparison available we often resort to a general description like, 'It was awful', or 'Great!' No poet can duck out like that. Faced with the same need to convey experience the poet has to try to avoid old similes and invent something fresh and new that really brings the comparison and the experience alive. When Robert Burns wrote:

> My love is like a red red rose,

'Don't confuse every use of the word "as" with a simile; look for two things which are being compared.'

it probably did not seem the stale cliché that years of Valentine verses have made it. Even so, Robert Browning's comparison of a woman to a flower is more original and precise:

> On her neck the small face buoyant, like a bell-flower on its bed.

This is not to say the Browning is better than the Burns. They have different effects. Burns is simple and direct. Browning's picture of the little head carried on the slender neck like a flower on a stem in a garden bed is more complicated. Nevertheless he is still comparing a woman to a flower. Some similes present us with comparisons that only the poet could have thought of and we have to pause and consider the validity of:

> There's a certain Slant of light,
> Winter Afternoons –
> That oppresses, like the Heft
> Of Cathedral tunes.

Here Emily Dickinson is comparing two things which oppress her: the light on a winter afternoon and a tune like those played in church. The church tune has a heaviness ('Heft'); the winter light also strikes her as heavy. Both things weigh on her feelings in a way that is purely personal. The sense of heaviness that comes from the cathedral tune is probably more general and easily understood. She tries to communicate the despair that the slant of light on a winter afternoon brings to her soul by comparing the feeling that they both produce. This is a simile that we have to work at a little, but if we do so we add something of Emily Dickinson's experience to our own.

Look at the similes in the poems you are studying. Are they good and original? Do they make you see things in a new way?

▷ **Metaphor**   A **metaphor** is also a comparison, but in this case the linking word is omitted so that the two things being compared become even more closely identified. Instead of saying 'the girl is like a flower', we say 'the girl *is* a flower'. This is much more forceful.

We find ourselves using metaphors in everyday situations when we want to express extremes. We might exclaim, 'I'm starving' or 'I'm dying for a drink'. We are really comparing the intensity of our hunger or thirst with that of a dying person. How many times have you heard the expression, 'at the end of the day'? This is a metaphor, and a very overworked one, which compares reaching a conclusion, or coming to the end of something, with the day ending.

Poets tend to use metaphors more than similes because they are more forceful and more concise. We understand them in the same way as similes. Look at the two parts of the comparison presented and ask what similarity the poet has seen there. Marianne Moore says:

> the sea is a collector, quick to return that rapacious look

She does not explain why. We have to work out how the sea can be greedy and a collector. Perhaps because it takes lives. The poem is called 'A Grave' which would point to the same meaning. Titles often give clues to meaning.

Here is an effective use of quite common metaphors:

> Old age should burn and rave at close of day

There are two metaphors here. The first compares the anger of the old with a fire, by using the word 'burn'. The second compares the end of life with the end of a day. The poet, Dylan Thomas, increases their effectiveness by coupling the two metaphors together and by using the word 'burn' alone. He doesn't add 'with anger' but leaves the reader to work out what old age should burn with. This leaves the meaning open. The burning might be with pride or hatred as well as anger. Or it might simply mean that the old should carry on living as strongly and intensely as ever, refusing to give in.

Metaphors are often contained in single words, as in Andrew Marvell's:

> My vegetable love should grow

This is startling. In what way can his love for a woman be like a vegetable? Does he mean that love is like a seed: once planted it takes root and grows? Why not a weed then? A vegetable has to be cultivated. Perhaps his love is more like a cultivated plant than a weed; earthy but cultivated. This is the way we have to work towards the poet's meaning – by looking at all the possibilities that the comparison throws up and selecting those that are helpful in the context of the poem.

In the following poem Stevie Smith appears at first to be writing about a man who is literally drowning:

> Nobody heard him, the dead man,
> But still he lay moaning:
> I was much further out than you thought
> And not waving but drowning.
>
> Poor chap, he always loved larking
> And now he's dead
> It must have been too cold for him his heart gave way
> They said.
>
> Oh, no no no, it was too cold always
> (Still the dead one lay moaning)
> I was much too far out all my life
> And not waving but drowning.

But by the time we reach the end we realize that the whole poem has to be read metaphorically. When the poet writes 'I was much further out than you thought' she seems to be describing a man in the sea. When we come to 'I was much too far out all my life' it is clear that the sea has become a metaphorical one – the sea of life, if you like. In the light of this we look back and find other metaphors which we took for literal statements: not the sea but the whole of life was 'too cold'; 'his heart gave way' not from coronary thrombosis but a spiritual heart failure – he lost the heart, the will, to go on. This makes the poem much more poignant.

I admire the skill with which Stevie Smith utilizes metaphor here, so that the poem has to be read on two different levels.

Once you become accustomed to reading in this unliteral way, much difficult poetry becomes easier. Even so do not expect everything to be made suddenly easy. Understanding metaphors may be a key, but the locks still have to be worked at.

Do the poets you are reading use metaphors a lot or a little? What kinds of comparisons do they make?

▷ Personification

Personification is a particular kind of metaphor in which inanimate objects or abstract ideas are spoken of as if they are people. Death is often personified, and so is time. Often, but not always, they begin with a capital letter when they are personified. Ruth Fainlight personifies the future and speaks of it as a timid woman:

> The future is timid and wayward
> and wants to be courted, will not
> respond to threats or coaxing,
> and hears excuses only
> when she feels secure.

The poem goes on to picture this shy person, the future, frightened by aggression, lurking in a corner like a nun.

Keats uses personification in 'Ode to Melancholy' to bring to life a number of abstractions. He speaks of Melancholy as 'she':

> She dwells with Beauty – Beauty that must die,
> And Joy, whose hand is ever at his lips
> Bidding adieu; and aching Pleasure nigh,
> Turning to poison while the bee mouth sips:
> Ay, in the very temple of Delight,
> Veiled Melancholy has her sovran shrine,

This method of personification allows Keats to create a series of images. By calling Melancholy 'she', and by saying she lives with Beauty, he creates a nebulous sense of two goddess-like beings. The next line has a more specific image: Joy is seen as a man who seems to be forever caught in the act of kissing his fingers in a gesture of farewell. A little later Melancholy is pictured shrouded in a veil.

In Keats' famous 'Ode to Autumn' the season is personified in a number of ways. The seasons are favourite subjects for personification, so are the months – May is often seen as a young girl, December as an old man. Wind, rain and the sun are frequently personified. Personification enables a poet to develop a character and a personality for any idea or object.

▷ **Additional examples**

Identify the similes, metaphors and personifications in the following lines by writing down the two things that are being compared. Notice how the poet chooses unusual or out of the ordinary objects and try to explain why.

1 Anger lay by me all night long,
   His breath was hot upon my brow,
   He told me of my burning wrong,
   All night he talked and would not go.

2 Ears like bombs and teeth like splinters,
   A blitz of a boy was Timothy Winters.

3 White poems
   are daggers, guns. cops.
   piercing hearts in weird designs
   Black poems are beautiful
   egyptian princesses.

4 Day after day, day after day,
   We stuck, nor breath nor motion,
   As idle as a painted ship
   Upon a painted ocean.

5 Nothing is so beautiful as Spring –
   When weeds in wheels shoot long and lovely and lush;
   Thrush's eggs look little low heavens, and thrush,
   Through the echoing timber does so rinse and wring
   The ear, it strikes like lightnings to hear him sing

6 *Poppies in October*

   Even the sun clouds this morning cannot manage such skirts
   Nor the woman in the ambulance
   Whose red heart blooms through her coat so astoundingly –

Key to the examples

1   Elizabeth Daryush personifies anger as a man who lies beside her all night talking to her of his grievances. By doing this she makes anger into something outside herself, a persistent presence over whom she has no control.

2   Charles Causeley's similes comparing Timothy Winters' ears to bombs and teeth to splinters are not visual images. It is not helpful to picture large black objects on the side of Timothy's head. Rather they give a general impression of the boy's untidiness and neglect. This is summed up in the metaphor 'A blitz of a boy'. This suggests two things. First, Timothy himself looks as though a bomb has hit him. Secondly, his behaviour is so unrestrained that other people feel he is like a bomb about to go off. The whole stanza portrays someone in need of loving care.

3   Ahmed Alhamisi's first metaphor compares poems written by white people to three threatening things: daggers, guns and cops, to show how he feels threatened and oppressed by white culture. He picks up the idea of daggers again when he speaks of 'piercing hearts'. That is, he extends the original metaphor and shows how the poems, like daggers, can hurt.

   His second metaphor compares black poems to Egyptian princesses. By doing this he makes black poems seem exotic and rich and rare. Princesses have a high status so the comparison confers that same status on the poems. He makes the princesses Egyptian because he wants a connection with the African continent and Egypt is a part of Africa with a long and distinguished culture.

4   Coleridge's simile compares a becalmed ship to a painting. He suggests the absolute stillness of the ship and the sea. It seems that, as with a painting, there is no possibility of movement.

5   Gerard Manley Hopkins' first simile compares weeds, perhaps grasses, to wheels. They grow from a centre point and spread in a circle on the ground. Secondly he compares the blue of a thrush's eggs to the blue of the sky. Both these are visual images which encourage us to picture the Spring but the next metaphor is an aural or sound image which suggests the sound of Spring. He compares the thrush's song to something which rinses out and wrings the ear. This makes the song very pure and clear. The simile comparing the effect on the ear to lightning adds force and directness to the purity.

6   Sylvia Plath's title is important because without it we would not know she was talking about poppies. The first line is complicated by a double metaphor. She sees the red petals of the poppy as skirts. The red swirling clouds of the sunrise also remind her of skirts. But the red of the sunrise is not as vivid as the poppies. The next lines are very unexpected. What is the connection between poppies and the woman in the ambulance? And why does it seem that we can see her heart through her coat? The connection is in the phrase 'red heart blooms'. We take 'red' to be the colour of blood and therefore of life. Despite being in the ambulance the woman is full of life, she is blooming. So much so that we can imagine her heart beating. Even so, she is not so vibrantly alive as the poppies. 'Blooms' is the metaphorical word. If the poet had used 'beats' the connection with the poppies would have been lost.

SUGGESTIONS FOR COURSEWORK

1   Choose a poem from your set texts. Re-write it using imagery different from the poet's own. Write a comparative study of the two versions to indicate which imagery you prefer and why.

2   Choose a poem written about/based on an individual. Imagine that you have been asked to interview that person. Ask him or her to give their opinions of the imagery which has been used to describe them.

3   Write a poem in the style of your favourite poet. Then write a brief essay about elements in the poet's technique you find interesting.

▷ **Coursework task**   Write a poem in the style of your favourite poet. Then write a brief essay about elements in the poet's technique you find interesting.

My poem is based on Adrian Henri's 'Talking After Christmas Blues'.

My Grumbling Birthday Blues

Well I woke up this mornin' it was my birthday
And the sun was shining the day away
I saw the presents lying on the floor
Looked at the pile of gifts against the door
there was
    a red parcel
     a blue parcel
      a green parcel
       bright string
– but no you

So I went to the bathroom to have a shave
My eyes in the mirror looked like I'd been on a rave
I gazed at the aftershave and the toothbrush
I pulled a face; my tears began to gush
there was
    toilet soap
     toothpaste
      talcum
       aspirin
– but no you

Now I'm a year older and it's birthday time
I'm lookin' in the mirror an' feeling fine.
Happy Birthday! My friends have forgot
I know a girl I once loved a lot
there was
    more toilet soap
     more toothpaste
      more talcum
       more aspirin
– but no you

So I turn off the light
And stare at the night
I reach into my coat
And pull out my trusty cut-throat
there'll be
    Ninety Seven
     Ninety Eight
      Ninety Nine
       And a whole new century
– all of them without you.

What I like about Henri's style is that he bases his writing on blues and pop music. He breaks away from the traditional way of writing. His poem about Christmas starts like a real blues: 'Well I woke up this mornin' it was Christmas Day'. He even drops the final 'g' in 'morning' as you might expect of a blues singer.

The language is easy to understand. He writes about everyday things using everyday language. Instead of the poetic descriptions you might expect, you find 'mashed potato' and 'dry Martini'. He writes in a way that speaks to people of today. He clearly believes that the language of poetry is really no different from the language ordinary people use.

His chorus section is effective. He uses ordinary things or seasons to build up to the climax 'but no you'. The sadness of missing his girl is stressed by repeating the final chorus line.

I like the way in which he switches in each stanza from happiness to sadness. In the first stanza 'the birds were singing' but soon he realizes that his girl was not there. Later on he was 'feeling fine' but two lines further on he writes: 'it hurts a lot'. This movement from optimism to pessimism emphasizes the sadness the poet is feeling.

EXAMINATION QUESTIONS

Whether you are answering a question on a set text or a poem taken from an anthology, you will frequently have to comment on figurative language; examiners often comment on how badly candidates answer this part of a question. Because it is so difficult a successful answer attracts the examiner's attention.

Questions on figurative language may appear in both the Foundation and the Higher Tiers. They will often appear in the bullet points which are included to direct your thinking.

They take various forms. Here are some examples.

▶ Comment on the language the poet uses.
▶ Select and comment on some interesting phrases.
▶ Comment on the ways in which the poet presents the argument.
▶ Comment on the way in which the poem is written.

Such prompts require you to do several things – comment on tone, diction, rhythm and so on. But they also require you to write about the poet's use of figurative language.

▷ **Question 1**

'London Anthology.'

Comment on the effectiveness of the language used in 'Joining the Colours'.

Joining the Colours (West Kents, Dublin, August 1914)

There they go marching all in step so gay!
    Smooth-cheeked and golden, food for shells and guns
Blithely they go as to a wedding day,
    The mothers' sons.

The drab street stares to see them row on row
    On the high tram-tops, singing like the lark.
Too careless-gay for courage, singing they go
    Into the dark.

With tin whistles, mouth-organs, any noise,
    They pipe the way to glory and the grave;
Foolish and young, the gay and golden boys
    Love cannot save.

High heart! high courage! the poor girls they kissed
    Run with them: they shall kiss no more, alas!
Out of the mist they stepped – into the mist
    Singing they pass.

Katherine Tynan

▷ **Question 2**

'MEG set text. Foundation or Higher Tier.'

Comment on the language used in the poem 'From the Motorway' by Anne Stevenson.

From the Motorway

Everywhere up and down the island
Britain is mending her desert;
marvellous we exclaim as we fly on it,
tying the country in a parcel,
London to Edinburgh, Birmingham to Cardiff,
No time to examine the contents

thank you, but consider the bliss of
sitting absolutely numbed to your
nulled mind, music when you want it,
while identical miles thunder under you,
the same spot coming and going
seventy, eighty times a minute,

till you're there, wherever there
is, ready to be someone in
Liverpool, Leeds, Manchester,
they're all the same to the road,
which loves itself, which nonetheless
here and there hands you trailing

necklaces of fumes in which to be
one squeezed breather among
rich and ragged, sprinter and staggerer,
a status parade for Major roadworks
toiling in his red-rimmed triangle,
then a regiment of wounded triangle orange witches

defending a shameless naked
(rarely a stitch of work on her)
captive free lane,
while the inchlings inch on
without bite or sup, at most
a hard shoulder to creep on,

while there on all sides,
lie your unwrapped destinations,
lanes trickling off into childhood
or anonimity, apple-scented villages
asleep in their promise of being
nowhere anyone would like to get to

EXAMINATION ANSWERS

▷ **Question 1**   *Notes and tutor's answer*

Notes
Read notes 1–5 and then attempt your answer to the question.

1   Underline words and phrases that you think worthy of comment.
2   Identify similes, metaphors and personification by means of a note in the margin (S, M or P will serve).
3   Think back to what you learnt in Chapter 3 and underline anything else you think worthy of comment.
4   Try to write something about everything you have underlined but do not simply put 'This is a simile', 'This is a metaphor'. Instead use your knowledge of figures of speech to pick out interesting phrases to comment on. You will score marks for a sensible selection and what you have to say about the effect of the poet's comparisons.
5   Do not worry if it does not come easily at first. Go back and re-read the chapter, several times if necessary.

Suggested answer
You may have underlined some or all of the following:

▶   **Similes**   as to a wedding day, singing like the lark
▶   **Metaphors**   golden, food for shells and guns, they go Into the dark, out of the mist they stepped – into the mist . . . they pass
▶   **Personification**   drab street stares, Love cannot save
▶   **Other Evocative language**   careless-gay, They pipe the way to glory and the grave.

In 'Joining the Colours' Katherine Tynan sees happy troops ('in step so gay!') joyfully leaving for the front. The bands are playing and the men's girl friends are waving them goodbye – for the last time. The poet sees the underlying truth of the scene. She sees the troops as cannon-fodder, the guns waiting to eat them up. The soldiers are referred to as being 'golden' like things of great value, or people who belonged to a Golden Age when everything was perfect. The soldiers are as happy as if they were going to church to be married ('as to a wedding day') instead of their own funeral ('they go into the dark').

'Relates imagery to the poem's meaning.'

'The significance of the personification.'

The drab street is seen as a spectator of the scene. But the street 'stares' as though it cannot believe what is happening. The troops are singing happily ('like the lark') as though it is all a game. But they are condemned to their fate. Even love 'cannot save them'.

The poet states that the soldiers are not famous. No one knows where they came from ('Out of the mist they stepped') and their future is obscure ('into the mist . . . they pass').

A line which seems to sum up the atmosphere of the march past and underline its meaning is: 'They pipe the way to glory and the grave'. The music signifies two things. It is played to accompany soldiers marching in triumph, but it can soon change its tune to a funeral march.

Compare your version with this. Were you able to explain the comparisons in the figures of speech? If you were able to identify the figurative language, but struggled to explain it, go back over this answer and study it carefully. Practise this type of exercise by selecting a poem from your anthology, and attempting it yourself.

▷ **Question 2**   *Student's answer – examiner's comments*

The poet has an interesting choice of language to express her attitudes towards motor-ways. She begins in the first stanza by summing up what she considers the present-day situation to be. Motorways are as lifeless as deserts, and we seem to be constantly repairing them. She continues by comparing the motorway system to a parcel with the north/south and east/west roads like string securing the wrapping. This is an effective image which enables the reader to visualize the system.

'Identifies a key point.'

The contents of the parcel are, however, unknown, because the motorist is driving fast with no time to look at the contents. The poet returns to this idea throughout the poem. The scenery is repetitive and meaningless:

identical miles thunder under you

'Imagery seen as thematic.'

The cities the motorways pass through 'are all the same'.

Worse, as far as the poet is concerned, the motorist is surrounded by 'necklaces' of fumes. These are not, however, bright and attractive; they tighten round the driver's throat. The poet may be referring to the practice of necklacing as a punishment. The theme of pollution and its effect on the drivers is continued in the 'red-rimmed triangle'. Here the poet neatly transfers the sore eyes of the motorist to his hazard triangle.

'Sees the sinister significance of the imagery.'

The humans behind the wheels are reduced to lesser beings. The poet calls them 'inchlings' who have no 'shoulder to creep on' or should it be 'shoulder to cry on'? The poet's complexity of language is very effective here.

'Spots the pun.'

She returns to the theme of parcels in the final stanza with the 'unwrapped destinations'. Finally, she introduces some tempting slip-roads, taking the motorist off into nostalgia for childhood, or into ideal villages ('apple-scented'). These are 'asleep' safe in the knowledge that no one would like to go to them.

'Key change of image.'

The poet uses the poem as an opportunity to satirize the present-day motorist with his urge to show off his wealth and position in 'a status parade'. But the show-off is reduced to a crawl. He becomes a 'staggerer'. He crawls past useless traffic works, which the writer laughingly compares to a streaker 'shamelessly naked (rarely a stitch of work on her)'. The streaker is, of course, stationary – like the traffic.

'Writes imaginatively about comic images.'

The poet by her use of figurative language has effectively captured the experience of many motorway travellers.

'Simple conclusion.'

'This is effective. It identifies key themes by identifying and explaining the figurative language. It is quite wide ranging, recognizing the comic as well as the more serious images.'

Question	Assessment Objective(s)	Pre-20th century	20th century
Coursework task – Adrian Henri	1, 2, 3, 4		✓
1 'Joining the Colours'	1, 2		✓
2 'From the Motorway'	1, 2		✓

SUMMARY

▷   A **simile** is a comparison using the words 'as' or 'like'.

▷   A **metaphor** is a comparison which does not use these words.

▷   **Personification** compares things to people.

▷   Poets use these comparisons to show the nature of their subject, often in ways we have not thought of before.

Rhyme

▶ **GETTING STARTED**

This chapter, like the following one, sets out to help you appreciate an important technical aspect of poetry. Understanding rhyme will enable you to answer those questions in the exam which ask you to comment on the language and form of a poem. It will also provide you with interesting ways of looking at poetry which will be useful for your coursework.

Do not confuse rhyme with rhythm. Some people tend to mix them up, perhaps because of the spelling. Rhyme is two words which sound the same apart from the first consonant, like 'meet' and 'feet'. Rhythm will be dealt with in the next chapter.

For several centuries far more poetry was written in rhyme than was not, so that poetry and rhyme were thought of as almost synonymous (meaning the same thing). But poetry does not have to rhyme and in this century many poets have chosen to write in unrhymed verse. In fact, if your reading has been mainly of twentieth-century poetry you may need to accustom yourself to rhymed verse so that you can appreciate it properly.

We learn to use rhymes very early in life and most children take a delight in rhyming, so that later on we may come to think of rhyme as 'childish'. Of course, it is not. We also hear rhyme used in other places, by advertisers, for instance, and in games and jingles. If your experience of rhyme is limited to such things then you might find it difficult to accept its use for more serious purposes. The remedy is to widen your experience. The following poem by William Blake has a lot in common with a jingle but it is clearly profoundly serious.

> My mother groan'd! My father wept
> Into the dangerous world I leapt:
> Helpless, naked, piping loud:
> Like a fiend hid in a cloud.
>
> Struggling in my father's hands,
> Striving 'gainst my swaddling bands,
> Bound and weary I thought best
> To sulk against my mother's breast.

If at the end of the first stanza you are reminded of 'Twinkle Twinkle Little Star' that is because Blake's poem rhymes in the same way and has the same rhythm as the nursery rhyme. The poem is also about a baby. But nothing else about it is pretty and nurserylike. Read it through several times and pay attention to the harsh words the poet uses. They may make you feel quite uncomfortable about this particular baby. Look at a collection of Blake's poetry and you will find more poems written in a simple style which nevertheless are very serious.

The topics covered in this chapter are applicable to all exam boards.

MEG	NEAB	NICCEA	SEG	LONDON	WJEC	IGCSE	**TOPIC**	STUDY	REVISION I	REVISION 2
✓	✓	✓	✓	✓	✓	✓	The purpose of rhyme			
✓	✓	✓	✓	✓	✓	✓	Types of rhyme			
✓	✓	✓	✓	✓	✓	✓	Patterns of rhyme			

WHAT YOU NEED TO KNOW

 The purpose of rhyme

'Note the spelling of rhyme. Many students spell this wrongly.'

If you have ever tried to write a rhyme scheme, particularly a complicated one, you will know how difficult it can become. Finding the word that fits the rhyme and the meaning often proves to be such a struggle that inexperienced or less skilful poets fail in the attempt. They cannot find a perfect rhyme, the meaning becomes twisted or lines have to be padded out with vague phrases. Even very good poets sometimes seem to have chosen a word because it fits the rhyme scheme and not because it really says what the poet means. The French poet Valery put it like this:

> I seek a word
> A word which is feminine
> has two syllables
> contains 'p' or 'f'
> ends in a mute vowel
> is synonymous with the word 'brisure'
> which is not a learned or an unusual word.
> Six conditions at the very least.

So if it is so difficult why do they do it? Why not simply choose to write unrhymed or free verse? Or, to put it another way, what is the purpose of rhyme?

Structure

Rhyme helps to give the poem **shape** and **pattern**. The human mind appreciates pattern. Perhaps you can even say we are genetically programmed to do so by the symmetry of our bodies. Certainly we quickly learn to respond to shape and pattern. Our lives follow a pattern of days and nights, of weeks, months and years. In all probability the room you are sitting in contains many patterns – on the walls or floor, in the arrangement of the furniture.

Rhyme appeals to this love of pattern. It gives a structure to the poet's thoughts and ideas by arranging them in lines and stanzas. After we have read the first stanza of a poem our ear knows what to expect. We read with the expectation of the rhymes coming again in the same places in the following stanzas. To have this expectation satisfied is pleasurable in itself. If the poet is using an odd or unusual rhyme scheme that may give an added pleasure.

Of course not all poets want this kind of structure to their verse. They may find it too rigid. They may want to sound more conversational.

Prominence

When the reader is expecting a rhyming word it gives that word extra **prominence**. Because we are waiting for the rhyme to end the line, we notice it much more strongly. Rhyme also enables us to remember words much more easily. The poem can take advantage of the ability of rhyme to get words noticed by using them to carry important ideas. In some poems you can get a good idea of the meaning of a stanza just by looking at the rhymes, because the poet has used the rhymes so forcefully. It is as though the rhymes are a summary or a memory aid for the meaning of the whole line.

Bringing together

Because they sound the same, rhyming words are *brought together* as a pair. In a poem this pair of words may be separated by two or even more lines but we still hear them as a pair. The sound, which pairs them, also makes us think of their meaning together. Some rhyme pairs seem to go together very naturally, like defend/friend. We would defend a friend; someone who defends us would be a friend. Some rhyme pairs make a very strong contrast, like death/breath. Breath can be thought of as the essence of life; death is the absence of life and breath. Hence the contrast. Poets sometimes use rhymes to introduce or emphasize points of association, comparison or contrast like these. Some have been used so often, like trees/breeze, that the connection seems very stale and adds little to the poem. Other rhyme pairs are original, and make us think carefully about the words and their meanings. Andrew Marvell, writing about a little girl in a garden, says:

> And there with her fair aspect tames
> The wilder flowers, and gives them names.
> ('A Picture of Little T.C. in a Prospect of Flowers')

This is an affectionate picture of a small child inventing her own names for the flowers. This is how she makes them familiar to herself or 'tames' them as the poet puts it. In fact, when we think about it, the comparison between taming and naming is valid in all sorts of ways. Once something has a name we feel safer and more at ease with it. But it is a connection we might not have thought about until the poet's rhyme drew our attention to it.

A rhyme pair might direct us to a meaning which is stated nowhere else in the poem. Here is a simple example from Thomas Hardy's 'The Darkling Thrush':

> I leant upon a coppice gate,
> When frost was spectre-gray,
> And Winter's dregs made desolate,
> The weakening eye of day.

The poem tells us that everything is covered with a gray frost. The rhyme gray/day adds to this. Without having to take the time actually to say so the poet tells us that the whole day has been gray. Because we associate the two words through sound, we also associate their meaning. Gray can mean 'sunless' or 'depressing'. We realize from the context of the poem that the day has been both.

Humour

We must not forget that poets use rhymes for *fun*. Here Lord Byron is poking fun at a contemporary:

> Shut up the bald coot bully Alexander,
> Ship off the holy three to Senegal,
> Teach them that sauce for goose is sauce for gander
> And ask them how they like to be in thrall.
> ('Don Juan')

We know that Byron is going to have a go at Alexander when he calls him a 'bald coot'. The rhyme adds to this humour because it seems to compare Alexander with a gander.

Always ask yourself what the purpose of the rhymes are. Are they to give pattern and structure? Do they give prominence to certain words and show the connections between them? Are they for fun?

▷ Types of rhyme   Masculine rhyme

The simplest form of rhymes are words of one syllable, like rang/sang or mad/bad/sad. You will immediately be able to think of dozens of examples like this. These rhymes, called **masculine** rhymes, give a clean, definite ending to a line.

Feminine rhyme

Less numerous are words rhyming on two syllables, like pester/fester or gory/story. These are called **feminine** rhymes and give a lighter ending to the line or a sense of continuing, of something more to come.

Triple rhyme

A rhyme on three syllables, or **triple** rhyme, is quite unusual but you do find it used occasionally. Thomas Hardy uses it extensively in 'The Going of the Battery', often splitting the rhyme between two words, as in gleaming there/seeming there.

If you have a passion for labelling things you can use these names. If they confuse you, do not worry. Much more important than knowing the names is knowing what rhymes do, and being able to write about their effect.

There are three other types of rhyme which you should be able to recognize.

Eye rhyme

These are words which look as though they should rhyme from their spelling but in fact are pronounced differently like love/move or through/bough.

Half rhyme (or pararhyme)

The vowels in the middle of the rhyme words are different but the opening and closing consonants are the same, like stroked/streaked, battle/bottle or cope/cape.

The use of eye rhyme in a poem may indicate that the poet has given up the search for a perfect rhyme. On the other hand it may be used deliberately to disturb the perfect harmony of the rhyme and give a sense of discord or roughness in the sound. Half rhyme is also used for this purpose.

Internal rhyme

All the rhymes we have been discussing so far have been identified by their *sound*. **Internal rhyme** is distinguished by its position. It occurs in the middle of a line rather than at the end. When the lines are very long, as in the following example, it almost has the effect of cutting the line in half:

> Thou hast conquered O pale Galilean, the world has grown grey with thy breath,
> We have drunken of things Lethean, and fed on the fullness of death.

Why, we might ask, does the poet not turn this into a quatrain of four short lines instead of a couplet of two long ones? The answer must be that he wants two points of emphasis – the rhyme in the middle and the rhyme at the end. He saves for the end rhyme two words that are very important to his meaning. He also wants the longer unfolding, the expansiveness, the greater span for the rhythm to push forward, that the long line allows. A short line would be much more clipped and constrained.

Look at the *types* of rhyme the poet uses. Do they relate to the mood or meaning of the poem?

▷ **Patterns of rhyme**

When writing in rhyme a poet is committed to writing to a pattern, which gives the poem a shape. We describe these rhyme schemes by using letters of the alphabet – A for the first rhyme, B for the second and so on, with a new letter for every new rhyming sound until we come to the end of the stanza. At the beginning of each stanza we go back to A.

There is no point at all in writing about a rhyme scheme unless you can say something about its purpose or effect.

Couplets

The simplest rhyme scheme is two lines rhyming, or **couplets**, like this one by Ogden Nash:

> Tell me O octopus I begs   A
> Is those things arms, or is they legs.   A

Couplets are very useful for wrapping up a thought neatly and concisely in a tidy package. They are often used at the end of a stanza or a poem or even scenes in plays to give a sense of finality. But they also lend themselves to being added to indefinitely – AABBCCDD and so on, as long as the poet wishes. Many long poems are written in couplets.

Quatrains

Four line stanzas, **quatrains**, are probably the most common in English poetry. A quatrain may be two couplets, AABB, or it may be alternate rhyme, ABAB:

> Love seeketh not itself to please   A
> Nor for itself has any care,   B
> But for another gives it ease   A
> And builds a Heaven in Hell's despair.   B
>
> (William Blake)

Notice how this stanza is also a complete sentence, but the use of four lines allows complications in the thought to be introduced – the words at the beginning of the lines show this. Each line begins a new clause. Notice too how the stanza is divided into two halves by the rhyme. The first two lines tell of what love does, or rather does not do for itself. The second two lines tell of what love does for another, the loved one. The poet has built his sentence around the pattern of the rhyme. This is one of the important uses of rhyme: to clarify an idea by making the structure of the expression clear.

A quatrain may be in the form of a couplet enclosed between another rhyme, like this:

Practise your beauty, blue girls, before it fail;	A
And I will cry with my loud lips and publish	B
Beauty which all our power shall never establish,	B
It is so frail.	A

John Crowe Ransom, who wrote this stanza, follows the rhyme structure with his sentence structure. The two inner lines go together and are not broken by punctuation. The two outer lines are brought together by the sound of the rhyme, making us link 'fail' and 'frail'.

Poets do not always link rhyme structure with sentence structure. It would be monotonous if they did. One of the ways in which they bring variety into their poems is by making the sentence structure follow the rhyme scheme sometimes and at other times compete with it.

A quatrain may also follow the pattern ABCB, as in this anonymous poem:

Western wind when wilt thou blow	A
The small rain down can rain.	B
Christ that my love were in my arms,	C
And I in my bed again.	B

Ballads are often written in this way, as in the following example:

The king sate in Dumfermline town
Drinking the blude-red wine;
'O whare will I get a skeely skipper
To sail this new ship o'mine?'

Other stanza forms

There are many other stanza forms which are less frequently used, some of which have names. **Rime Royal** has seven lines rhyming ABABBCC. **Ottava rima** has eight lines rhyming ABABABCC. Of course poets do not have to stick to any previously used pattern, they can invent their own. However, over time every conceivable rhyme scheme has been used, making it difficult to devise a pattern that had not been used at sometime by someone.

Sonnet

This is one of the most widely used forms in poetry. It is such an important form and can show us so much about the workings of rhyme schemes that we must look at it in some detail. It has 14 lines and there are two traditional rhyme schemes, called after poets who used them.

The Petrarchan Sonnet
ABBAABBACDECDE. Milton, who often adopted this scheme, used it in 'On His Blindness':

When I consider how my light is spent,	A
Ere half my days in this dark world and wide,	B
And that one talent which is death to hide	B
Lodged with me useless, though my soul more bent	A
To serve therewith my maker and present	A
My true account, lest he, returning chide.	B
'Doth God exact day-labour, light denied?'	B
I fondly ask. But patience to prevent	A
That murmur, soon replies: 'God doth not need	C
Either man's work or his own gifts; who best	D
Bear his mild yoke, they serve him best. His state	E
Is kingly: thousands at his bidding speed,	C
And post o'er land and ocean without rest;	D
They also serve who only stand and wait.	E

'Note where the poet ends his sentences and where the pauses are. It is better to use the words "pause" and "sentence structure" in your writing, than to talk about commas and full stops.'

Look at how the rhyme scheme divides the sonnet into two parts. The first eight lines, or octave, uses two rhyming sounds, A and B. The last six lines, or sestet, uses three more rhymes, C, D, E. Now look at the meaning.

Milton spends the first part of the poem musing on his own blindness, his inability to use the one talent God has given him, and wondering what God expects of him. In the second part he answers himself. The transition in the argument can be seen quite clearly in 'patience to prevent That murmur, soon replies' (lines 8–9). The poet has used the rhyme scheme to organize the argument of his poem.

The Shakespearian Sonnet
ABABCDCDEFEFGG. There are more rhyming sounds used in this type, which divide it into three quatrains and a couplet:

Like as the waves make towards the pebbled shore,	A
So do our minutes hasten towards their end;	B
Each changing place with that which went before,	A
In sequent toil all forward do contend.	B
Nativity, once in the main of light,	C
Crawls to maturity, wherewith being crown'd,	D
Crooked eclipses 'gainst his glory fight,	C
And Time that gave doth now his gift confound.	D
Time doth transfix the flourish set on youth	E
And delves the parallels in beauty's brow,	F
Feeds on the rarities of nature's truth,	E
And nothing stands but for his scythe to mow:	F
And yet to times in hope my verse shall stand,	G
Praising thy worth, despite his cruel hand.	G

The opening quatrain tells us that the subject is time. It compares the inevitable progress of our lives towards death with the inevitability of the incoming tide. Each quatrain advances the argument a stage further. The second tells how Time gives, as Man grows to maturity, and then begins to take back those gifts. The third gives examples of the way Time works. The final couplet concludes the argument with a twist: despite the cruel work of Time Shakespeare's verse will survive. A proud boast – but one that has been justified! Once again we can see how the poet uses the rhyme scheme to support the development of his ideas.

The sonnet has proved to be so effective a form that poets have gone on using it for centuries and still do so. Sometimes the form is changed a little. For instance by using ABABABABCDCDEE the poet can have the advantage of an octave, as in the Milton sonnet, change the argument when the rhyme changes to CDCD and still have the benefit of a clinching couplet at the end.

The rhyme scheme the poet chooses allows the ideas to unfold in a particular way. When you work out the rhyme scheme of a poem look at the way it gives an outline or structure for the poet's thoughts.

▷ **Additional examples**   Use these examples as exercises to see if you have understood the chapter so far. Work them out yourself first before looking at the key at the end. For each poem write down the rhyme scheme and types of rhymes used then try to say what their purpose, or effect, is. Look back at the previous section if you have any difficulties.

1 When Molly smiles beneath her cow,
   I feel my heart, I can't tell how;
   When Molly is on Sunday dressed,
   On Sundays I can take no rest.

   What can I do? On working days
   I leave my work on her to gaze.
   What shall I say? At sermons I
   Forget the text when Molly's by.

Good master curate teach me how
To mind your preaching and my plough:
And if for this you'll raise a spell,
A good fat goose shall thank you well.

2 I doubt not God is good, well-meaning, kind.
And did he stoop to quibble could tell why
The little buried mole continues blind,
Why flesh that mirrors Him must someday die,
Make plain the reason tortured Tantalus*
Is baited by the fickle fruit, declare
If merely brute caprice dooms Sisyphus*
To struggle up a never ending stair.
Inscrutable His ways are, and immune
To catechism by a mind too strewn
With petty cares to slightly understand
What awful brain compels His awful hand
Yet I do marvel at this curious thing:
To make a poet black, and bid him sing!

('Countee Cullen')

* These are figures from Greek mythology. Sisyphus was doomed always to push a boulder up a hill. Tantalus was doomed to try, but fail, to reach some fruit which dangled 'tantalizingly' just out of reach.

3 Oh it was sad enough, weak enough, mad enough,
Light in their loving as soldiers can be –
First to risk choosing them, leave alone losing them
Now, in far battle, beyond the South Sea!

('The Going of the Battery')

Key to the examples

1 Rhyme scheme: Quatrains rhyming AABB. Types: All masculine. Purpose: The anonymous poet uses each couplet in stanzas 1 and 3 for a single statement. This is varied in stanza 2 where each couplet contains a question and explanation. (If you look at the punctuation you will see how each couplet ends in a full stop, semicolon or colon.) Each stanza concentrates on a different aspect of the subject: Molly herself, the speaker of the poem, the curate. Thus we can say that the purpose of the rhyme scheme is structural. But there are also several rhymes which emphasize the meaning of the lines: 'days/gaze' sums up the way in which he spends his days gazing at Molly; 'how/plough' sums up the speaker's plea to the curate to tell him how to keep his mind on the things he should be doing rather than on Molly.

2 Rhyme Scheme: Sonnet, ABABCDCDEEFFGG. Types: Masculine except for Tantalus/Sisyphus which is triple rhyme and also half rhyme. Purpose: The rhyme scheme divides the sonnet into two parts. The octave uses alternate rhyme and the sestet uses couplets. The subject of the octave is to suggest that God must have reasons for all the pain that man and animals have to endure. The sestet says that man cannot hope to understand the marvellous ways of God. The final couplet declares that of all the marvels the most difficult to understand is how God expects anyone who is black to overcome the difficulties of their life and write poetry. This sonnet uses the rhyme scheme to organize the thought but not as closely as the other sonnets we have looked at. The effect of the half rhyme Tantalus/Sisyphus is to introduce a note of discord or difficulty which is appropriate to the trials of Tantalus and Sisyphus.

3 Rhyme Scheme: ABAB. Types: mad enough/sad enough is internal rhyme and also triple rhyme; be/sea is masculine; choosing them/losing them is also internal triple rhyme. Purpose: The poet, Thomas Hardy, uses the contrast between the masculine rhymes and the triple rhymes as one of the ways of showing the contrast between the men and women in the poem. The lines which talk about soldiers and battle end on the firm masculine rhymes. The rest have unstressed endings appropriate to the feminine speakers of the poem. The choosing/losing rhyme brings out a contrast which the women feel. When a woman chooses a husband it should be for life but they are losing their husbands prematurely.

SUGGESTIONS FOR COURSEWORK

1   Compare the rhyme schemes used in two poems of your choice. Indicate what the use of rhyme adds to the poems. Possible suggestions: Robert Frost's 'Stopping by Woods on a Snowy Evening', Robert Graves' 'The Twin of Sleep', W.B. Yeats' 'Death', Linton Kwesi Johnson's 'Inglan Is a Bitch'.

2   Write about the use of rhyme in the work of one poet of your choice.

3   Re-write a favourite poem, changing the rhymes. Write an essay on the differences between the two versions.

4   Make a comparative study of two poems, one in rhyme and the other in blank verse.

5   Imagine you have been given the opportunity to interview a famous poet. Write the interview entirely in rhyme.

▷ **Coursework task**   Re-write a favourite poem, changing the rhymes. Write an essay on the difference between the two versions.

▷ **Suggested answer**   The poem I have chosen to alter is 'The Lake Isle of Innisfree' by W.B. Yeats.

I will arise and go now, and go to Innisfree,
And a small cabin build there, of clay and wattles made;
Nine bean-rows will I have there, a hive for the honey-bee,
And live alone in the bee-loud glade.

And I shall have some peace there, for peace comes dropping slow,
Dropping from the veils of the morning to where the cricket sings;
There midnight's all a-glimmer, and noon a purple glow,
And evening full of the cricket's wings.

I will arise and go now, for always night and day
I hear lake waters lapping with low sounds by the shore;
While I stand on the roadway, or on the pavements gray,
I hear it in the deep heart's core.

My version

I will arise and go now, and go to Innisfree,
And a small cabin build there of clay and wattles frail;
Nine bean-rows will I have there, a hive for the honey-bee,
And live alone in the bee-loud dale.

And I shall have some peace there, for peace comes, a dropping stream,
Dropping from the veils of the morning to where the cricket longs;
There midnight's all a glimmer and noon a purple dream,
And evening full of the linnet's songs.

I will arise and go now, for always night and morn
I hear lake waters lapping with low sounds on the sands;
While I stand on the roadway, or on the pavements worn,
I hear it in the deep heart's lands.

I found this a very difficult exercise. Every time I tried to alter a word I found Yeats' version forcing my word out. Because I knew the poem so well it seemed like rock that would not budge.

So I started searching for words in *Roget's Thesaurus*. This was not ideal, but it did get me started. Even so, I had to make sure that my choice of words did not alter the meaning of the poem completely. As you can see, I have left the first and third lines as they were, since the poem is about Innisfree and the only things that live in hives are bees!

The new rhymes in the first stanza – 'frail' and 'dale' – make a slight shift in meaning. 'Dale' is a more everyday word than 'glade' so it brings in a touch of reality, like 'pavements'. 'Frail' shows how his cabin is not made to last. It probably says something about his hopes.

In order to make the first and third lines of stanza two rhyme, I had to tinker with the end of the first line. The 'stream' makes the peace more like water. 'Dream' fits in with the general feeling of the poem. I think the cricket is longing as much as the poet who wants so much to return. 'Linnet's songs' sound a bit ordinary, but linnets do sing!

In the final stanza, 'morn' is rather poetic, though many of Yeats' original choices are rather artificial – 'glade' and 'glimmer'. The 'worn' pavements suggest the number of people who walk the city's streets. 'Sands' seems as good a choice as 'shore'. 'Lands' does alter the meaning quite a lot. The original choice, 'core', takes you into the centre of the heart. 'Lands' suggests that inside the heart there is a huge space, whole countries, in fact.

I do not think that my version is better. Nevertheless, I found that it was an interesting exercise. Every time I tried to find a new rhyme I really had to ask why Yeats had chosen the words he had. It became clear that rhyming words are not just stuck on to the ends of lines, but form an essential part of a poem's meaning.

▷ EXAMINATION QUESTIONS

It is unlikely that you will be asked in an examination to comment specifically on the rhyme. As in the previous chapter on figurative language, a response to a poet's use of rhyme would be included in an answer to a bullet point on the writer's method.

Questions on language and form will give you an opportunity both to use the skills you have learnt concerning rhyme and comment on any interesting aspect of rhyme which you may have discovered in studying poems.

Rhyme schemes are part of the form of a poem and also part of its poetic qualities. Whenever you are asked about these things, or about the way a poem is written, or what you think of a poem, you can include comments on rhyme.

In Question 1 you are asked to write about the method the poet uses to convey his meaning effectively. For the purpose of this particular exercise, concentrate on the poet's use of rhyme.

▷ **Question 1**

'MEG anthology. Higher or Foundation Tier.'

Show how effectively John Betjeman conveys his meaning in 'Slough'.

Slough

Come, friendly bombs and fall on Slough
It isn't fit for humans now,
There isn't grass to graze a cow
Swarm over, Death!

Come, bombs, and blow to smithereens
Those air-conditioned, bright canteens,
Tinned fruit, tinned meat, tinned milk, tinned beans
Tinned minds, tinned breath.

Mess up the mess they call a town –
A house for ninety-seven down
And once a week a half-a-crown
For twenty years.

And get that man with double chin
Who'll always cheat and always win,
Who washes his repulsive skin
In women's tears.

And smash his desk of polished oak
And smash his hands, so used to stroke
And stop his boring dirty joke
And make him yell.

But spare the bald young clerks who add
The profits of the stinking cad;
It's not their fault that they are mad,
They've tasted Hell.

It's not their fault they do not know
The birdsong from the radio,
It's not their fault they often go
To Maidenhead

And talk of sports amd makes of cars
In various bogus Tudor bars
And daren't look up and see the stars
But belch instead.

In labour-saving homes, with care
Their wives frizz out peroxide hair
And dry it in synthetic air
And paint their nails.

Come, friendly bombs, and fall on Slough
To get it ready for the plough.
The cabbages are coming now;
The earth exhales.

▷ **Question 2**   Show how the use of rhyme helps the poet to convey her meaning in 'Human Interest'.
'WJEC Anthology.'

Human Interest

Fifteen years minimum, banged up inside
for what took thirty seconds to complete.
She turned away. I stabbed. I felt this heat
burn through my skull until reason had died.

I'd slogged my guts out for her, but she lied
when I knew different. She used to meet
some prick after work. She stank of deceit.

I loved her. When I accused her, she cried
and denied it. Straight up, she tore me apart.
On the Monday, I found the other bloke
had bought her a chain with a silver heart.

When I think about her now, I near choke
with grief. My baby. She wasn't a tart
or nothing. I wouldn't harm a fly, no joke.

(Carol Ann Duffy)

▶ EXAMINATION ANSWERS

▷ **Question 1**   *Notes and tutor's answer*

Read these notes and then write your own answer to the question before reading the answer below.

Notes

This kind of a question rarely appears on its own. You are more likely to come across it in the form of a bullet point, as part of a much bigger question.

1 The first stage in any work on poetry is to understand the meaning of the poem.
2 Decide on the tone – is the tone serious or comic? What is the author's intention?
3 Consider the figurative language and show how its use adds to the meaning of the poem.
4 Work out the rhyme scheme. Look at the types of rhyme used. As with tone and figurative language ask yourself how the rhymes help the poet to convey his message. NB It is not enough to work out the rhyme scheme and leave it at that. If you write 'The poet uses an ABAB rhyme scheme' this is meaningless without some attempt to relate it to the poet's purpose.

Suggested answer

Notes
Rhyme Scheme:
AAAB   CCCB   DDDE   FFFE   GGGH   IIIH   JJJK   LLLK   MMMN   AAAN

Answer

'Recognizes the significance of the rhyme scheme.'

The poet uses an unusual rhyme scheme. Each quatrain contains three lines which possess an identical rhyme. The fourth line does not rhyme with any of the preceding lines. This produces a jarring effect. The first three lines proceed in the same repetitive way: 'Slough', 'now', cow'. The repetition emphasizes the monotony of the people's lives.

The final word in the fourth line of one stanza rhymes with the final word of the next stanza. This has an interesting effect. It serves to link the stanzas together, rather like the links in a chain. So 'death' is linked with 'breath'. The tinned breath is like the last breath of a dying person. 'Years' are linked with 'tears' as though the unhappiness of the people's lives has been lasting a long time. There is next the 'yell' in 'Hell'. In this way the poet combines different stages of his argument across the stanzas.

'Rhyme used to link and develop argument.'

The poet repeats a word to emphasize his sense of anger. He is clearly enraged by the artificial life of this town and its inhabitants' way of life. To reinforce his feelings he uses repetition to hammer home his message. By repeating 'tinned' in the second stanza he produces a kind of metallic rhythm, almost as if he were banging a tin can on the table. Similarly the repetition of the sounds 'mess' and 'smash' and the repetition of phrases produces a sort of internal rhyme: 'It's not their fault' conveys his strong feelings. He concludes his poem by repeating the first line of the poem in the final stanza. With the exception of the final line, he also maintains the same rhyme. In this way he returns to the feelings of monotony expressed in the opening.

'Rounds off the rhyme.'

'Neat conclusion.'

With his effective use of rhyme the poet manages to convey the monotonous lives of the people of Slough and his own mounting sense of anger.

This answer does two things. First, it identifies the rhyme scheme. More importantly, it shows how it helps to convey the poet's meaning.

▷ Question 2   *Student's answer – examiner's comment*

'Useful summary of content.'

The poem is a monologue spoken by a man imprisoned for killing a woman. The murder had been committed in a fit of rage. The man speaks in a very ordinary down-to-earth manner. The title of the poem, 'Human Interest', suggests a human interest story as reported in a tabloid newspaper.

The rhyme scheme is interesting. The poem contains four stanzas with an interesting rhyme scheme:

ABBA   ABB   ACDC   DCD

In the first stanza the rhyme scheme is quite balanced, like the man's story. The man is obviously angry, but the anger is controlled. By the third stanza the reason for the man's jealousy is given ('the other bloke'). Here the rhyme scheme is more uneven, perhaps hinting at the man's loss of control. By introducing new rhymes it prepares the reader for the rhyming of the final stanza. So, the third stanza is a kind of turning point of the poem.

'Very perceptive.'

'Important point which is not developed.'
'Nothing made of good observation.'

The use of rhyming words across the stanzas provides a kind of link, joining the threads together. It's odd that the poet chose to use rhyme when the poem is written in a kind of slang.

The poet uses the word 'she' a lot in different lines.

'This answer is very much a mixed bag. It begins well, making both observations and significant comment. The answer, however, tails off. The student fails to comment on the significance of the last two observations.'

Question	Assessment Objective(s)	Pre-20th century	20th century
Coursework task – W.B. Yeats	1, 2, 3	✓	
1 'Slough'	1, 2		✓
2 'Human Interest'	1, 2		✓

SUMMARY

▷ The purpose of rhyme is:

  – to give a structure to the poet's thoughts;

  – to give prominence to important words;

  – to show connections between words, lines and ideas;

  – to provide humour.

▷ Different types of rhyme give a different character to the line endings and can relate to mood and meaning.

▷ Different rhyme schemes, like the couplet, quatrain and the sonnet, can show the unfolding of the poet's ideas in different ways.

Rhythm

▷
GETTING STARTED

When you are asked to comment on the rhythm of a poem it is usually in the form of a comment on the writer's method. The form of a poem includes the rhythm, rhyme and the way the poem is divided into lines and stanzas. All these aspects can also be included in coursework writing. Rhythm makes such an enormous contribution to poetry that the more you understand about it the better you will be able to appreciate the poems you are studying. Like rhyme (see Chapter 5) it is a technical matter and so you need to become familiar with poetry that uses it. Therefore, if you are not used to reading poetry that has a fixed rhythm, accustom your ear by reading as much rhythmic poetry as possible.

There is a lot of technical vocabulary to do with rhythm. But this vocabulary is only important and useful if it helps you to recognize how a poem works. There is no merit in simply being able to slap the right labels on in the right places. We learn the technical words solely in order to show how the poet has used rhythm to increase the poem's effect. We can then say what is interesting or exciting about the rhythm used.

The topics covered in this chapter are applicable to all exam boards.

MEG	NEAB	NICCEA	SEG	LONDON	WJEC	IGCSE	TOPIC	STUDY	REVISION I	REVISION 2
✓	✓	✓	✓	✓	✓	✓	Rhythm, metre and free verse			
✓	✓	✓	✓	✓	✓	✓	Syllables			
✓	✓	✓	✓	✓	✓	✓	Stress			
✓	✓	✓	✓	✓	✓	✓	Feet and metres			
✓	✓	✓	✓	✓	✓	✓	Terminology			
✓	✓	✓	✓	✓	✓	✓	Pause			

WHAT YOU NEED TO KNOW

> **Rhythm, metre and free verse**
>
> 'Note the spelling of rhythm. Are you confusing rhyme and rhythm? This is a common mistake.'

In poetry we use the word **rhythm** to mean the sense of movement in the verse. When this is strong and regular, like a beat, it is called **metre**. The line:

> When the bell began to ring

has a regular metre. Very few poems have an absolutely regular metre.

When we talk about the rhythm of a poem we mean the regular beat of the metre and the way this beat varies, as it does in speech. Some poems, especially modern ones, are not written with a regular metre at all. Poetry that has no metre and no rhyme is called **free verse**. Free verse has no fixed metre but it still has rhythm, like the beginning of this poem by T.S. Eliot:

> The river's tent is broken: the last fingers of leaf
> Clutch and sink into the wet bank. The wind
> Crosses the brown land, unheard.
>
> (The Waste Land)

> **Syllables**

To understand and talk about rhythm you first need to know how to divide a word into syllables:

> *Caught* is a monosyllable. It cannot be divided.
> *Today* can be divided into two syllables – *to/day*.
> *Property* divides into three syllables – *pro/per/ty*.
> *Supersonic* has four syllables – *su/per/son/ic*.

If you have already had practice in dividing words into syllables, this will help your work on rhythm.

> **Stress**

You will have noticed how when pronouncing words one syllable carries more weight than another. Thus we say 'toDAY' – putting more emphasis on the 'day' part of the word. We cannot say 'TOday'. It sounds wrong, as though we had a strange foreign accent. Similarly 'heavy' must have the emphasis on the first syllable. We call this emphasis **stress** and every word has a natural stress. In fact some words change their meaning depending on where the stress is placed:

> *DEfect* is a fault;
> *deFECT* means to change sides.

We mark the stress of a word by a line above the stressed syllable. An unstressed syllable is marked ˘

today, heavy, property, supersonic.

Poets who write in metre use the natural stress of words to make the rhythmic pattern, or metre. They deliberately choose words to fit the stress pattern they want. In this poem the poet has chosen to work with seven syllables in each line, in a pattern of alternating stressed and unstressed syllables:

Lay your sleeping head my love

Human on my faithless arm

(W.H. Auden, 'Lullaby')

He keeps up this metre throughout the verse. Here is a more usual metre of ten syllables:

So long as men can breathe and eyes can see

(William Shakespeare)

A great deal of English poetry has been written in that particular metre.

It is more important to be able to recognize stress than to know all the names of the different metres. You can talk about rhythm in poetry very well by just looking at the way poets use stress in a line. Stressed syllables are sometimes called **heavy** and unstressed syllables **light**.

▷ Feet and metres

'If you are unhappy with technical details, ignore this section and go on to the next. However, make sure that you understand "stress".'

This section is included for the sake of completeness and for those of you who enjoy technicalities. Sometimes having labels to put on things helps you to feel confident.

Read through this section. If you find it too detailed or confusing do not worry about it: *concentrate on stress*. The only term you really should know is **Iambic pentameter**, which is the metre of the previous Shakespeare quotation; that is ten syllables to the line arranged in a regular pattern of unstressed and stressed:

ˇ — ˇ — ˇ — ˇ — ˇ —

Once we have worked out the stresses of each line we can divide the line up into smaller units, or **feet**, each with the same number of stressed and unstressed syllables. Because we are dealing with syllables and not words sometimes a word is cut in two by a foot. This line would be divided like this:

Ĭt seēmed/thăt oūt/ŏf baˉ/ttle Īˇ/escāped.

There are four basic feet and three supplementary ones. The four basic feet are as follows:

i) ˇ —   Iambic foot, or iamb.
ii) — ˇ   Trochaic foot, or trochee.
iii) ˇ ˇ —   Anapaestic foot, or anapest.
iv) — ˇ ˇ   Dactylic foot, or dactyl.

Here are some examples:

Ĭf Ī/ shŏuld diē/ thĭnk onˇ/ly this /ŏf me, is **Iambic**.

Thoū thy /worˇldly /task hăs /done, is **Trochaic**.

Ō the goose/ ănd the gan/der walked o/ver the green, is **Anapaestic**.

This is the/forest prim/aeval, the/murmuring/pines and the/hemlocks, is **Dactylic**.

You will see that in the second of these lines there seems to be a spare syllable at the end of the line. You can think of this as a missing unstressed syllable, because the poet wants to end on a good strong beat. On other occasions there will be an extra unstressed syllable, for the opposite reason. It all depends on the effect that the poet wants. Later on you will find more examples of variations in rhythm with some suggestions on what effect they have.

Sometimes poets combine two of these metres in one line. Here is a mixture of Iambic and Anapaestic:

Thĕ moth/ĕr of months/ ĭn mead/ŏw ănd plain

The three supplementary, or occasional, feet are:

i) — —   Spondaic foot, or spondee.
ii) ˇ ˇ   Pyrrhic foot, or pyrrhic.
iii) ˇ — ˇ   Amphibrach.

These three feet can bring variety into the rhythm of a line, or shift the emphasis on to a certain word, but they are not used throughout a line.

Here is an amphibrach used in a line that is a mixture of iambs and anapests:

Whĕn the pre/sent hăs latched/ĭts postern/behind/my trem/ŭlous stay.

The effect of the extra unstressed syllable that makes an iamb into an amphibrach on the word 'its postern' is to make a pause in the middle of the line.

Once you have worked out what kind of foot, or feet, the poet is using you can work out the number of feet in a line:

Monometer has one foot in a line;
Dimeter has two feet in a line;
Trimeter has three feet in a line;
Tetrameter has four feet in a line;
Pentameter has five feet in a line;
Hexameter, also called Alexandrine, has six feet in a line;

Heptameter has seven feet in a line;
Octameter has eight feet in a line;

The most usual rhythm is the pentameter, and then the tetrameter and hexameter.

▷ **Using the terminology**

It is far less important to know all these terms than it is to be able to recognize stress and to say what effects it has. You will not get a good grade for just knowing the terms; you will get a good grade if you can point out something interesting about the rhythm of a poem. Simply writing 'this poem is written in Iambic pentameter', is a waste of time and effort unless you can say *why* the poet might have used it or point to an interesting variation.

Meaning

The first question to ask yourself is, 'Has the poet selected this particular metre because it is in some way appropriate to the meaning of the poem?' For instance, Robert Louis Stevenson's 'From a Railway Carriage' clearly intends to convey the rhythm of the train:

Faster than fairies, faster than witches,
Bridges and houses, hedges and ditches;

He uses a regular metre (of dactyls and trochees) for this purpose. When Kipling writes about men marching, his rhythm sounds like a march.

We're marchin' on relief over Injia's sunny plains
A little front of Christmas-time an' just be'ind the Rains

In the poem Thomas Hardy wrote about men marching away from their wives to go to war, which we looked at in the previous chapter, he uses a different but equally strong rhythm:

O it was sad enough, weak enough, mad enough,
Light in their loving as soldiers can be –
First to risk choosing them, leave alone losing them
Now, in far battle beyond the South Sea!

('The Going of the Battery')

He calls this poem 'The Wives' Lament' and writes it from the point of view of the women, trudging along beside the company of soldiers as they go to board their ship. This gives us a clue to the choice of rhythm. It must be strong and regular, because they are marching. But the women are sad and reluctant for the men to go. There is a hesitancy in their step which is conveyed by the two unstressed syllables between the stresses:

O it was sad enough, weak enough, mad enough,

Look back at the comments on the rhymes of this stanza and you will see how well the rhymes and the rhythm work together to create the effect of the difference between the men and the women and the women's sadness at parting.

This is not to say that this kind of rhythm (dactylic) is always sad. 'Merrily, merrily, shall I live now' is the same rhythm. A rhythm can fit the mood of the words, can be appropriate to the meaning of the poem, but it cannot have a mood or meaning in itself. Every poem has to be looked at separately to see what effects the poet is creating in that particular case.

Variation

The second question to ask is, 'Can I hear any variations in the basic metre?' This takes practice. If there are variations then we have to try and say what effect they have.

This poem, by Dylan Thomas, is basically Iambic, but it has several irregularities.

The force that through the green fuse drives the flower
Drives my green age; that blasts the roots of trees
Is my destroyer.
And I am dumb to tell the crooked rose
My youth is bent by the same wintry fever.

If the metre were completely regular it should look like this:

In fact it looks like this:

The irregularities come on 'green fuse drives' – there is a stress on 'fuse' where we do not expect one. This gives three stressed syllables in a row which makes the rhythm heavy and emphatic. At the beginning of the second line there is again a stress on 'Drives' where there is not one in the first line. Then there is an unexpected stress on 'green'. In both these lines the stresses are used to emphasize the force that drives youth inexorably onwards, towards old age and death.

Finally the rhythm of the last line is jumbled. The line talks about youth being 'bent'. After the word 'bent' there is a pause and two unstressed syllables, which throws a lot of emphasis on to 'bent'. It is as if the line itself is bent out of shape to mirror the meaning.

▷ **Pause** Poetry uses punctuation just as prose does: to show **pause**. The rhythm and rhyme also lead us to expect pauses at the end of lines but the poet often defies our expectations by omitting the pause at the end of a line or by putting a pause in the middle of a line. The first of these effects is called the **run-on line**, or **enjambment**. The second is called **caesura**. Both are important because they affect the rhythm and flow of the verse.

The run-on line (enjambment)

When there is no punctuation at the end of a line the sense is carried on without a break into the next line. W.B. Yeats uses the run-on line three times in this stanza:

> At the grey round of the hill
> Music of a lost kingdom
> Runs, runs, and is suddenly still.
> The winds out of Clare-Galway
> Carry it: suddenly it is still.

Here the line ends have broken phrases in two. Because the pause we expect at the end of the line does not happen, we get a sense of being carried forward. This fits very well with Yeats' subject.

If the rhythm is heavy and ponderous, an unexpectedly long unpunctuated phrase may give us a sense of something long and drawn out, even tedious:

> but evermore
> Most weary seemed the sea, weary the oar.

Here Tennyson uses the run-on line, together with extra stress, long vowels (see Chapter 7) and repetition to convey the sailors' utter inability to stir themselves into action.

There are no hard and fast rules. You cannot say what a run-on line is going to do *until* the poet has done it. It all depends upon the meaning of the poem. If you think about the words and the meaning of the poem you may be able to suggest why the poet used a run-on rather than an end-stopped line.

Caesura

Many lines of poetry have a definite pause somewhere in the middle of the line. This too breaks up the metre of the poem and brings variety:

> The day is past, and yet I saw no sun;
> And now I live, and now my life is done.
>
> (Chidiock Tichborne, 'Elegy for Himself')

Here the poet is using the caesura to point up a contrast and balance of ideas in each line. This kind of contrast is called **antithesis**. The pause is the point of balance.

You may find the caesura very near the beginning of the line to emphasize the opening word or phrase. Christina Rossetti emphasizes 'Yes' in this way:

> Yes, to the very end

and so does Matthew Arnold:

> Yes! in the sea of life enisled.

On another occasion Arnold puts the caesura near the end, just before the word 'we' which, as a result, is isolated at the end of the line and thus very prominent:

> it brought
> Into his mind the turbid ebb and flow
> Of human misery; we
> Find also in the sound a thought

Run-on lines and caesurae often go hand in hand.

If, as we have seen, rhythm can contribute to the mood of the poem, the use of pause can bring some fine-tuning to the tone or the mood. Think of the occasions when you might use a pause in conversation – to bring attention to a particular word, or to make something dramatic. It might be difficult to say something sad, or even exciting, and so you pause before it. A poet can do all these things with caesurae.

Here is a rather obvious piece of drama by A.E. Housman. A young man is waiting to be hanged:

> Strapped, noosed, nighing his hour,
> He stood and cursed his luck.
> And then the clock in the tower
> Gathered its strength – and struck.

The heavy caesura in the last line gives a dramatic pause, a stillness, before the final words when the fatal hour arrives. Those words, 'and struck', fall heavily, like the man swinging on the end of the rope. The caesura is even more effective for coming so late in the line, after the run-on from the previous line. We are kept waiting. The poet never actually tells us that the man is dead. He tells us the clock struck the hour, and leaves the rhythm to imply the rest.

▷ **Additional examples**

Use these examples to test your understanding of what you have read in this chapter. Work through them before looking at the key below.

1   What can you say about this rhythm? Can you suggest why it is used for this poem?

> Before the Roman came to Rye or out to Severn strode
> The rolling English drunkard made the rolling English road.
> A reeling road, a rolling road, that rambles round the shire,
> And after him the parson ran, the sexton and the squire.

2   The Frost performs its secret ministry
    Unhelped by any wind. The owlet's cry
    Came loud – and hark again! loud as before.

  i) What is the basic rhythm of these lines?
  ii) What is the effect of the long caesura, shown by a dash?
  iii) Suggest a reason why this line is so broken by pause.
  iv) Can you find an irregularity in the rhythm and suggest a reason for it?

> ### Key to the examples
>
> I   This is a good strong regular rhythm (Iambic heptameter) to suggest movement. It pushes forward purposefully, as though we are setting off down the road. The length of the lines also helps give this effect. But then it becomes broken up by pauses as the road twists and turns in typical English country manner.
>
> 2   i)   The basic rhythm is Iambic pentameter.
>   ii) The caesura imitates the action of listening, as though the poet is actually speaking to someone and pauses to listen to the owl before going on.
>   iii) The effect of the line being broken is to suggest disturbance. The quiet of the night is broken. The owlet's cry is strange, perhaps distressing.
>   iv) There is an unexpected stress on 'loud' in 'loud as before' (a trochee). Compare this line with the previous two lines and you will see the stress here is the opposite way round. This gives emphasis, showing the strength of the cry.

▷ **SUGGESTIONS FOR COURSEWORK**

1   Take two examples of war poetry. Show how by the use of rhythmical technique the poet(s) tries to influence the audience.
2   You have been asked to present a radio programme. Make a selection of poems that have a strong sense of rhythm. Write the script for the broadcast to introduce each poem to the listener.
3   Write a rap poem about a day in your life. Write a commentary at the end to show how much more effective rhythm is in this kind of writing.

▷ **Coursework task**   You have been asked to present a radio programme. Make a selection of poems that have a strong sense of rhythm. Write the script for the broadcast to introduce each poem to the listener.

▷ **Suggested answer**   Rhythm has always fascinated poets. It plays an important part in their writing and has been used in many different ways. Some poets have used it to make the description vivid. Robert Browning in his account of 'How They Brought the Good News from Ghent to Aix' tries to echo the galloping of the horses in the rhythm of the verse. Listen to the poem's opening lines:

> I sprang to the stirrup, and Joris and he;
> I galloped, Dirck galloped, we galloped all three;
> 'Good speed!' cried the watch, as the gate bolts undrew;
> 'Speed!' echoed the wall to us galloping through;
> Behind shut the postern, the lights sank to rest,
> And into the midnight we galloped abreast.

Did you hear how the rhythm of a galloping horse is kept up throughout? Browning makes good use of the amphibrach to give a kind of rocking rhythm. The rhythm is maintained not just where the word 'gallop' occurs, but even in the quieter moments, with the description of the lights, for instance.

Another poet who has captured movement in rhythm is W.H. Auden. In his poem 'Nightmail' he imitates the rhythm of the wheels of a train:

> This is the night mail crossing the border,
> Bringing the cheque and the postal order.
> Letters for the rich, letters for the poor,
> The shop at the corner and the girl next door.

The poem was written for a documentary film about the work of the post office. The overnight train takes the mail from London to Scotland. The shots of the express steaming through the night are given added movement in the rhythm of Auden's verse.

Some modern poets have been fascinated by children's games. They have written about them using the rhythm of the game. Alan Brownjohn has captured the movement well in his 'Skipping Rhyme':

> Páin óf the leáf, oné twó –
> Wórd óf the stóne, threé, foúr –
> Foót óf the dárk, pít óf the hánd,
> Heárt óf the cloúd, fivé, síx, and
> oút!
>   Skíp.
> Nóra shé had whíte eyés,
> Máry shé had bláck –
> Hélen loóked in Greý Mán's Woód and
> Néver cáme
> Báck!
>   Júmp!

The skipping rhythm helps you to picture the scene of the children playing. It makes you want to skip.

Another poet has been impressed by a rhythm used in school-days. Jacques Prevert uses the rhythm of children chanting in the classroom as the starting point for his poem 'Exercise Book'.

> Two and two four
> four and four eight
> eight and eight sixteen ...
> Once again! says the master
> Two and two four
> four and four eight
> eight and eight sixteen
> But look! the lyre bird
> high on the wing
> the child sees it
> the child hears it
> the child calls it
> Save me
> play with me
> bird!

We all recognize the scene and it is the well-known rhythm of the arithmetic lesson which takes the listener into the poem. We can all remember the nursery rhymes of our childhood, and many poets have used these memories of our early use of language to give added pleasure to their poems.

Another poet who uses the rhythm of everyday language is Peter Porter. But he uses it entirely differently. He has taken the voice of a radio announcement. In his poem 'Your Attention Please' you are listening to the flat rhythm of someone making an official announcement:

> YOUR ATTENTION PLEASE –
> The polar DEW has just warned that
> A nuclear rocket strike of
> At least one thousand megatons
> Has been launched by the enemy
> Directly at our major cities.
> This announcement will take
> Two and a quarter minutes to make,
> You therefore have a further
> Eight and a quarter minutes
> To comply with the shelter
> Requirements published in the Civil
> Defence Code – section Atomic attack.

The poem does have a regular rhythm. It is based on the Iambic metre. But the poem sounds more like prose. The choice of words makes the poem sound ordinary. The announcement is made in the flat tone of an official reading out rules and regulations. An atomic attack is expected, but there is no excitement in the voice. How effective do you think this is?

The rhythm is almost completely hidden. A direct contrast to the obvious use made by Browning and Auden. But no matter which metre a poet uses, rhythm is one of the most important ways of holding the listener's attention.

EXAMINATION QUESTIONS

You can use your knowledge of rhythm to answer more general questions on the poet's method. Your answer on the rhythm of a poem can be incorporated into responses on the language, rhyme and imagery.

▷ **Question I**

'London anthology.'

Comment on the use of rhythm in 'Prayer before Birth'.

Prayer before Birth

I am not yet born; O hear me.
Let not the bloodsucking bat or the rat or the stoat or the club-
footed ghoul come near me.

I am not yet born, console me.
I fear that the human race with tall walls wall me
    with strong drugs dope me, with wise lies lure me
        on black racks rack me, in blood-baths roll me.

I am not yet born; provide me
With water to dandle me, grass to grow for me, trees to talk
    to me, sky to sing to me, birds and a white light
        in the back of my mind to guide me.

I am not yet born; forgive me
For the sins that in me the world shall commit, my words
    when they speak me, my thoughts when they think me
        my treason engendered by traitors beyond me
            my life when they murder by means of my
                hands, my death when they live me.

I am not yet born; rehearse me
In the parts I must play and cues I must take when
old men lecture me, bureaucrats hector me, mountains
    frown at me, lovers laugh at me, the white
        waves call me to folly and the desert calls
            me to doom and the beggar refuses
                my gift and my children curse me.

I am not yet born; O hear me
Let not the man who is beast or who thinks he is God come near me.
I am not yet born; O fill me
With strength against those who would freeze my
    humanity, would dragoon me into a lethal automaton,
        would make me a cog in a machine, a thing with
            one face, a thing, and against all those
                who would dissipate my entirety, would
                    blow me like thistledown hither and
                        thither or hither and thither
                            like water held in the
                                hands would spill me.

Let them not make me a stone and let them not spill me.
Otherwise kill me.

(Louis MacNeice)

Question 2 Comment on the rhythm of Verse XLI of *The Eve of St Agnes*.

'Foundation Tier.'

EXAMINATION ANSWERS

▷ **Question 1** *Notes and tutor's answer*

Notes

1 Look at the shape of the poem. What does it tell you about the rhythm?
2 Notice any rhythmical patterns in the poem.
3 How is the caesura used?
4 Are there any other features which serve to emphasize the rhythm?
5 What do you think the poet has based his rhythmical pattern on?

Suggested answer

The poet is writing a poem about his own birth. He imagines himself speaking before the actual birth. In the poem he describes the dangers that will face him in his life. He ends by stating that if others are going to make him into an automaton, a person who obeys without question, he might as well be killed now.

'Establishes a key theme.'

The poem is in the form of a prayer as the title indicates. Much of the rhythm is based on the language of a prayer. The speaker cries out in the form of prayer: 'O hear me', 'O fill me'. The poet uses the formal rhythm of a prayer: 'I am not yet born'. The caesura is placed in the middle of the line to emphasize this: 'I am not yet born; O hear me.' This draws the reader's attention to the opening phrase and prepares you for the opening of the prayer: 'O hear me.'

'Recognizes the significance of technique.'

The content of this prayer, however, is unlike the type of prayer usually heard in church. The tone is bitter. When the poet is describing the dangers of his life after birth he repeats phrases with a similar rhythmical pattern:

'Recognizes rhythmical pattern and its purpose.'

> old men lecture me, bureaucrats hector me, mountains
> frown at me, lovers laugh at me,

The rhythm is reinforced by the use of alliteration [see Chapter 7]. This constant repetition builds up a rhythm of its own. The points are hammered home. Some of the phrasing suggests the rhythm of a nursery rhyme or a child's tongue-twister:

> with wise lies lure me
> on black racks rack me,

'Points a crucial contrast.'

This rhythm of childhood gives the speaker of the poem a childlike character, which is entirely appropriate. It contrasts nicely with the adult subject matter. Thus the childlike pattern of the verse is used as an effective contrast to the seriousness of the subject matter. This is a similar technique to the one used by Blake in:

> My mother groan'd! My father wept
> Into the dangerous world I leapt: [Getting Started, Chapter 5]

'The essay is effective because it highlights the purpose of the rhythm. It goes beyond mere recognition and identification.'

▷ **Question 2** *Student's answer – examiner's comments*

'Good. States the basic rhythm and then makes careful observations of the variation. This continues throughout.'

> *The poem is basically written in Iambic pentameter, with variations to relate rhythm to the meaning. In the first line, two stressed syllables on the words 'wide hall' evoke an image of a large spacious area, and the word 'Phantoms' indicates the lovers gliding swiftly through the empty hall. A sense of urgency is added when three hurried syllables 'to the iron porch' indicate a sense of urgency in the lovers' flight. A slightly awkward*

(continued)

(continued)

three short beats in line three on the words 'uneasy sprawl' emphasize the porter's awkward position. In the following line, the words 'huge' and 'empty' are stressed, to indicate the large quantity of wine that the porter has drunk.

The next two lines are written in regular Iambic pentameter, without any particular rhythm inflections to highlight and add meaning. The next line begins with the words 'By one, and one' to emphasize slow, cautious pulling back of the bolts, 'full, easy slide' are emphasized to show the slowness of each bolt as it is drawn back. Three unstressed syllables in the penultimate line have no particular importance to the meaning of the poem. The last line is known as an Alexandrine line, and is two syllables longer than the rest of the lines in this verse. Keats often used Alexandrine lines. The pause after 'The key turns' is called a caesura, and is pregnant with suspense, and the final word 'groans' is stressed to emphasize its drawn-out sound in the silence.

'Good. Relates the variations in the rhythm to the meaning of the words in this, and the next, paragraph.'

'There is no need to spend time pointing out a variation if there is nothing to say about its effect.'

'Notices the use of the caesura and comments on the effect of the pause.'

'A well-written comment on the rhythm of the stanza. Variations in the basic rhythm noticed and related to the meaning of the words. On occasions the answer omits to say which words carry the extra stress and which would be stressed in any case by the metre.'

Question	Assessment Objective(s)	Pre-20th century	20th century
Coursework task – rhythm	1, 2, 3	✓	✓
1 'Prayer before Birth'	1, 2		✓
2 *On the Eve of St Agnes*	1, 2	✓	

SUMMARY

▷ When we speak, some syllables of our words are stressed and some are not.

▷ Poets use the natural stress of words to give rhythm, sometimes, but not always, in a regular metre.

▷ Variations in the metre are often connected with meaning or mood.

▷ Pauses at the end of lines, or in the middle (caesura), also affect the rhythm and pace of the verse.

Patterns of sound

▷ **GETTING STARTED**

In an examination question on poetry there is often an opportunity to comment on the way a poem is written. The question is usually in the form of a bullet-point guide to the method adopted by the poet. Sometimes it takes the form of an invitation to write about words or phrases you find interesting. What the examiner is looking for is the ability to discuss the language and techniques of poetry.

One of the important aspects of language is the poet's use of **sound**. Sound patterns are important in poetry because they give the poet an extra dimension to work with, an additional way of saying things. It is as if the poet has some of the resources of music at his disposal, as well as the power of words. One way to become sensitive to the sound of poetry is to read it aloud as much as possible, and certainly it is essential to read aloud all the poetry you intend to answer questions on, not just once but several times.

The topics covered in this chapter are applicable to all exam boards.

MEG	NEAB	NICCEA	SEG	LONDON	WJEC	IGCSE	TOPIC	STUDY	REVISION 1	REVISION 2
✓	✓	✓	✓	✓	✓	✓	Onomatopoeia			
✓	✓	✓	✓	✓	✓	✓	Individual sounds			
✓	✓	✓	✓	✓	✓	✓	Alliteration			
✓	✓	✓	✓	✓	✓	✓	Assonance			
✓	✓	✓	✓	✓	✓	✓	The purpose of sound patterns			

WHAT YOU NEED TO KNOW

▷ **Onomatopoeia**   The first task is to identify these patterns. This is easily done once you have learned to recognize the following techniques.

Onomatopoeia depends on the ability of sounds to echo the sense of a word, for example swish, or plop. Strict onomatopoeia is confined to those words whose meaning has something to do with sound:

> Only a cock stood on the rooftree
> Co co rico co co rico

You will find such words used occasionally by poets, as in this example, but much more frequently onomatopoeia is interpreted in a rather wider sense of mimicry or imitation as in this piece of children's verse:

> The dove said 'Coo
> What shall I do
> I can hardly maintain my two.'

The poet is clearly trying to imitate the sound made by a dove by using 'Coo', which echoes the dove's peculiar noise, and then repeating the sound in 'do' and 'two'. Neither of these words is onomatopoeic in itself, but because they repeat the dove's cooing sound in the same way that doves continually repeat their noise they appear to be imitating the dove's call.

Here is another way poets can imitate sounds:

> Faster than fairies, faster than witches
> Bridges and houses, hedges and ditches,

If you read this aloud you can hear that the poet has organized the rhythm to give the sound of wheels going over a railway track.

Very rarely is onomatopoeia employed throughout a poem but the following poem by Thomas Hardy was deliberately built around the technique, and 'Onomatopoeic' is its subtitle.

> Reticulations creep upon the slack stream's face
> When the wind skims irritably past,
> The current clucks smartly into each hollow place
> That years of flood have scrabbled in the pier's sodden base;
> The floating lily leaves rot fast.

The onomatopoeic qualities are these:

▷ There are two words that echo sense, 'clucks' and 'scrabbled'.
▷ The rhythm, which is not smooth and regular, tries to imitate the flow of the water, sometimes rapid, in other places slower.
▷ Hardy uses a lot of consonants like 't', 'c', 'p' and 'b' to give the sound of the water slapping against the bank and the bridge.
▷ The phrase 'When the wind skims' uses the sounds 'w' and 's' to help suggest the blowing of the wind.

Look at the poems you are studying and identify any occasions where the meaning is echoed in the sound.

▷ **Individual sounds**   Try to be alive to the individual sounds in words. These frequently assist the meaning of a word by reminding us of other words with similar meanings, or by the way in which the sound is formed.

There are two kinds of sounds, vowels and consonants. When we form a consonant we stop, or half-stop, the breath somewhere in the mouth or throat. When we form a vowel the breath is not stopped.

Some consonants can be very forceful, because the sound is dammed up, behind the lips or teeth or in the throat, and then let out suddenly in a small explosion. These consonants, 'p' and 'b', 't' and 'd', 'k' and 'g', are often called 'hard'. When they occur in words and phrases with a strong, hard or forceful meaning they seem to intensify that meaning. The sounds of 'bitter' and 'batter' add to the harshness of their meaning. Lines like John Donne's, 'Batter my heart three person'd God', and 'Death thou shalt die' use this quality of hard consonants to increase the impact of the line.

Other consonants, like 'm', 'n', 's', 'l' and 'w', are much softer. These sounds have a lot of soft or quiet associations from words in which they are found: 'slumber', 'sleep', 'lullaby', 'slowly', 'mellow', 'wistful' – you will be able to think of many more. Consequently John Keats' line, 'Season of mists and mellow fruitfulness', which uses a lot of these sounds, has a feeling of mellow softness. He has matched the sound to the meaning.

The particular quality of vowels is that they can be sustained like a held note in music, some more easily than others. So we talk about short vowels, like the sounds in 'pig', 'hot' and 'met', or long vowels, like the sounds in 'stream', 'low', 'moon' and 'star'. The kind of vowels used can affect the pace of a line. The line from Keats just quoted uses a number of long vowels which helps to make it slow and calm.

You must not think that vowels and consonants have meaning in themselves. You should, however, notice when they fit the meaning of the words or line in which they occur.

▷ Alliteration

Alliteration is the repetition of *consonants* at the beginning of words or syllables. For instance in the following line:

> In a coign of a cliff between lowland and highland

the poet uses two different sets of alliteration. First there is the use of 'c' in 'coign of a cliff'. Secondly there is the use of 'l' in 'lowland and highland'. Notice that the 'l' appears twice at the beginning of a syllable (land) rather than a word. It is also necessary to remember that it is the sound that is important, not the spelling, so whether the poet writes 'Kiss me Kate' or 'Kiss me Catherine' makes no difference. Both are alliteration because both 'c' and 'k' have the same *pronunciation*. This is one of the reasons why it is so essential to read poems *aloud*; reading with the eyes just does not have the same effect. One further point: the repetition must occur in words that are fairly close together, perhaps in the same line, perhaps near the end of one line and the beginning of another.

In the following poem the poet uses alliteration a number of times. The instances in the first two lines are underlined; there are two more examples in the following two lines:

> On <u>W</u>enlock Edge the <u>w</u>ood's in trouble;
> His <u>f</u>orest <u>f</u>leece the Wrekin heaves;
> The gale it plies the saplings double,
> And thick on Severn snow the leaves.

▷ Assonance

Assonance works on the same principle as alliteration, but now we are looking for repeated *vowel* sounds. The rule about sound rather than spelling is even more important when considering vowels because of some of the extraordinary spellings that have come about in English: these look the same but are pronounced quite differently – so be warned. You are already familiar with assonance of a particular type: when it occurs at the end of a line we call it rhyme. Assonance, then, is rhyme anywhere else in the line. The poet uses two sets of assonance in the following line:

> And the May month flaps its glad green leaves like wings

'Flaps' rhymes with 'glad' and 'green' with 'leaves'. You might perhaps have noticed that 'its' and 'wings' also have the same vowel sound, but this is not counted here as an instance of assonance, not because they are too far apart but because 'its' is not a sufficiently prominent word in this line. When we read it we glide over it without noticing because it is not a stressed syllable. Keats was very adept at using assonance, as you can hear in this stanza. Again the first few lines are marked and the rest left for you.

> Thou <u>still</u> unrav<u>ish</u>ed <u>Bride</u> of <u>quiet</u>ness
> Thou foster <u>child</u> of <u>si</u>lence and slow <u>Time</u>,
> <u>Sy</u>lvan <u>hi</u>storian, who canst thus express
> A flowery tale more <u>sweetly</u> than our rhyme:
> What <u>leaf</u>-fringed legend haunts about thy shape
> Of deities or mortals, or of both,
> In Tempe or the dales of Arkady?

What men or gods are these? What maidens loath?
What mad pursuit? What struggle to escape?
What pipes and timbrels? What wild ecstasy?

▷ The purpose of sound patterns

Collecting the evidence as we have been doing is relatively easy; deciding what to say about it is more difficult. To do that we have to decide what the poet achieves by using these effects. There is no point in listing them unless we can say why they are there.

Alliteration and assonance

Alliteration and assonance are very good at *bringing words together* and making or emphasizing a connection between them. Among our examples we found 'green leaves'. We know, of course, the connection between green and leaves but the assonance makes it even firmer, as though greenness and leaves were interchangeable. Alliteration performs the same trick with 'green grass', and Dylan Thomas used this to marvellous effect in 'Fern Hill' when he wrote 'Fire green as grass'. Sometimes the bringing together is to show contrast, as in 'Bluish mid the burning water'. An interesting exercise is to jot down all the pairs of words which are often found together and which use alliteration or assonance like 'hearth and home' or 'high and dry'. It is not only poets who know how to use sounds to bind words together, it seems to be built into the language.

Effects of consonants and vowels

The particular *kind of consonants and vowels used* give different effects. Ask yourself what there is in the *meaning* of the poem which makes the poet want to use hard or soft sounds. We have already seen how Keats uses a predominance of soft sounds to create the picture of an autumn day, with all the outlines of the landscape blurred by mist and the fruit ripened to softness. On the other hand Wilfred Owen, writing of the First World War, uses a high proportion of hard sounds to help create the noise of the guns:

> Only the stuttering rifles' rapid rattle
> Can patter out their hasty orisons.
> > ('Anthem for Doomed Youth')

In both cases the poets help the consonants by using appropriate vowel sounds: long, sustained vowels in Keats, like 'Season', 'mellow' and 'fruitfulness'; short, abrupt ones in Owen, like 'rifle', 'rapid', 'rattle'.

Sound patterns

The least definite effect, but still an important one, is to give the poem a *beautiful* or an *interesting sound*, which gives pleasure for itself just as music does. Melodiousness is generally thought of as being created by long vowels like 'oo', 'ee' etc. and gentle consonants, as in this example from Tennyson's *The Lotos-Eaters*.

> How sweet it were, hearing the downward stream,
> With half-shut eyes ever to seem
> Falling asleep in a half-dream!

But there is also a more vigorous music, created by the use of harder consonants and fewer long vowels, which can be just as pleasing, as in Browning's 'Home Thoughts from the Sea'.

> Nobly, nobly, Cape Saint Vincent to the North-west died away
> Sunset ran, one glorious blood-red, reeking into Cadiz Bay;
> Bluish 'mid the burning water, full in face Trafalgar lay;
> In the dimmest North-east distance dawned Gibraltar grand and gray.

▷ Additional examples

Use these examples as exercises to test your understanding of what you have read in this chapter. What can you say about the way these poets are using sounds? Work out your answers before looking at the key below.

1 And the afternoon, the evening, sleeps so peacefully!

2 There was a whispering in my hearth
  A sigh of coal,

3 He does not die a death of shame
  On a day of dark disgrace,

Key to the examples

1 T.S. Eliot is using the assonance of a long vowel in 'evening', 'sleeps' and 'peacefully'. This has the effect of slowing the line, emphasizing the connection between the three words and so intensifying its meaning.

2 Wilfred Owen uses two onomatopoeic words, 'whispering' and 'sigh', which imitate the sound of the coal burning. Only if you have listened to a coal fire burning can you know how accurate these words are for some of the little sounds a fire makes.

3 Oscar Wilde uses alliteration of hard consonants. This is appropriate to the harshness of his subject in these lines.

▷ SUGGESTIONS FOR COURSEWORK

1 Choose a number of poems to read aloud as a class or group performance. Write a record of the performance, examining how successful the choice of poems was and how well the poems went down with the audience. You may find it helpful to tape the performance and the ensuing discussion.

2 Write a review of a poetry reading on the radio, or one given live in your area. (Tape recorder essential here.)

3 Make a list of different sounds. You might listen to some of the various tapes available (steam trains, tropical rain forests, broadcasting sound effects). Describe each sound in your own words. You may wish to use onomatopoeic words, both well-known ones and ones of your own making. Write a poem about the sounds.

▷ **Coursework task** Make a list of different sounds. You might listen to some of the various tapes available (steam trains, tropical rain forests, broadcasting sound effects). Describe each sound in your own words. You may wish to use onomatopoeic words, both well-known ones and ones of your own making. Write a poem about the sounds.

▷ **Suggested answer** I first chose onomatopoeic words of noise:

clatter, smash, bang, boom, snap, rattle.

Then I made a list of words of similar sound:

clatter: batter fatter hatter latter matter natter patter ratter

smash: bash cash dash fashion gnash hash lash mash rash sash

bang: fang gang hang lang pang rang sang tang

boom: doom loom room tomb womb zoom

snap: cap flap gap hap lap map nap pap rap sap tap zap

rattle: battle cattle prattle tattle

I decided to write a poem about noise without using the first word in each list.
I started by putting words in pairs in a random way. For example, I wrote down:

prattling room
rap tomb

zoom sang
lang loom
cattle fashion
battle patter
fatter cash
lash gang
doom rash
sash pang
mash womb
lap tang
flap hang
pap prattle
sap fang
zap tattle

As I wrote them down, some of the phrases started to suggest ideas for a poem:

I entered the prattling room
With nattering tattle racketing
Along the zapping walls
Chattering of pattering battles
Bloodied sapping cattle
Dead men resting in zapped tombs
Tinkering and fashioning
Ideas of the salt tang
And zoom of life
Far away from this womb of a tomb.

When I had finished, I noticed that some of the sound effects were similar to those used by Wilfred Owen in his poem 'Anthem for Doomed Youth'. Where Owen had written: 'Only the stuttering rifles' rapid rattle' I had written:

I entered the prattling room
With nattering tattle racketing

In Owen's poem the 'stuttering' represents the sound of rifle fire; whereas in mine I have suggested the noise made by people chattering in a room. Owen uses an onomatopoeic technique to give a sound picture of a battlefield. I have tried to show the nervousness of people gossiping. But, strangely, my version also conveys the sound of gunfire. The people, who are not involved in the fighting, are talking about 'pattering battles' and 'sapping cattle'. Owen writes about men 'who die as cattle'.

The similarities between Owen's poem and mine came about by accident. I started to write a poem by thinking about sounds. Now that I have compared the two, I have begun to wonder where Owen got his inspiration from. Which came first, his thoughts about the war he was involved in or the sounds he heard in the trenches? Obviously mine does not make complete sense as his does, but there is some meaning in my poem which has been produced simply by experimenting with the sounds which words make.

EXAMINATION QUESTIONS

▷ **Question 1**   You can use what you have learnt in this chapter to respond to any instruction about the language of a poem. Read the poem printed below and answer the question.

Comment on the use of language in this extract from 'The Lotos-Eaters'.

The Lotos-Eaters

'Courage!' he said, and pointed toward the land,
'This mounting wave will roll us shoreward soon.'
In the afternoon they came unto a land
In which it seemed always afternoon.
All round the coast the languid air did swoon,

Breathing like one that hath a weary dream.
Full-faced above the valley stood the moon;
And like a downward smoke, the slender stream
Along the cliff to fall and pause and fall did seem.

A land of streams! some like a downward smoke,
Slow dropping veils of thinnest lawn, did go;
And some thro' wavering lights and shadows broke,
Rolling a slumbrous sheet of foam below.
They saw the gleaming river seaward flow
From the inner land: far-off, three mountain tops,
Three silent pinnacles of aged snow,
Stood sunset-flushed: and dew'd with showery drops,
Up-clomb the shadowy pine above the woven copse.

(Alfred Tennyson)

▷ **Question 2**
'Foundation or Higher Tier.'

Referring to one or more texts you have studied consider whether the words are effective in their sounds, meanings and suggestions.

▷ **Question 3**
'Foundation or Higher Tier.'

Write about the poem 'To Autumn'. What is the poet saying about the season? How does he create a picture of the season and its atmosphere? Does the atmosphere change during the poem?

EXAMINATION ANSWERS

▷ **Question 1**   *Notes and tutor's answer*

Notes

1   Make a list of some examples of alliteration, assonance and onomatopoeia (some, because if you wrote out every example from this extract you would end up copying out the whole poem!).
2   Try to say something about the effect they have. To do this, look carefully at the content of the poem. What is the poet describing? When you have decided this, how do the examples in Note 1 help the poet?
3   Try to write a short answer to the question, linking the points in 2 with those noted in 1. NB Do not simply copy out the examples! It is worthless to write: 'There is an example of alliteration in line 2.' The examiner's reaction to such a remark is likely to be: 'So what!'

When you have written your version, read the suggested answer below.

Suggested answer

Notes

Alliteration:	shoreward soon
	the slender stream
	a slumbrous sheet
	Stood sunset-flushed

Assonance:	weary dream
	Rolling a slumbrous sheet of foam below
	gleaming river seaward flow

Onomatopoeia:	swoon

Content:	people in a drugged state, atmosphere of drowsiness

Answer
The poet is attempting to describe a group of people who have come ashore in the land of the Lotos Eaters. The poet is describing them living in a semi-drugged state. It is, as the poet writes, a place where it always seems afternoon.

'Establishes the scene.'

The use of language emphasizes this state of being half-asleep. Most of the sounds are soft. The gentle alliteration of 'roll us shoreward soon' and 'slender stream' with its repeated 's' produces a dreamy atmosphere. There are very few harsh consonants. The occasional ones ('cliff' and 'copse') give a hint of the harsh world outside.

'*Discusses the texture of the language.*'

The poet's use of assonance helps to extend this sleepy atmosphere. Most of the vowel sounds are long: 'weary dream', 'slumbrous sheet of foam below'. Line-endings particularly contain long vowel sounds which help to prolong this feeling of drowsiness ('woven copse', 'swoon'). The rhymes extend this feeling of drowsiness ('soon', 'afternoon', 'swoon' and 'moon').

'*Describes the effect of assonance.*'

The real skill of the poet is to be seen in the use he makes of the assonance. In many of the lines he uses vowel sounds which are not precise assonance. The vowels are close in sound to one another but not exact repetition. For example, in 'Stood sunset-flushed' the vowel sounds glide into each other. There are other examples: 'above the woven copse', for instance. These gentle gliding sounds help to create a picture of drowsiness. It is as if the people are floating on a gently moving sea. There are no harsh sounds to wake everybody up!

'*Develops the significance of the assonance.*'

This is a *suggested* answer to the question. There is no right answer, and if you have made roughly the same points, but expressed them differently, there is no need to worry.

If you have not been so successful, try again, using some different examples from 'The Lotos-Eaters'. Remember, the key to success in this work is, first, to find out what the poem is about, and then to relate the poet's technique to the content.

▷ Question 2   *Student's answer – examiner's comment*

This is an extract from students' answers to the question asking for comments on the use of sound.

Doomed Youth

(a) '*Stuttering, rapid rattle, patter*' these words create the effect of rat tat tat – the firing of machine guns. This effect is onomatopoeia where these words sound like actual noise made by the firing of machine guns. It is created by using words that sound like the actual noise of the object being described which get one to imagine one is actually in the place at the time being described.

(b) Choirs of of wailing shells (line 7)
The noise of shells (bombs) or bullets tearing through the air created a series of high-pitched noises sounding like high notes. The different timing of when the shells were dropped created an effect of a series of notes which sounded like a group of people singing, therefore a choir of wailing shells.

'*Good. Correctly identifies onomatopoeia and describes how the words used make their effect.*'
'*Good. Does not fall into the trap of thinking this line sounds like a choir. Correctly identifies its effect as being due to the simile.*'

▷ Question 3   *Student's answer – examiner's comments*

To Autumn

The poet is saying that one season is happening now, it is all warm and the bees have made their honey, and it is overflowing, but soon one season will change and another one will come. The season was very hot, and lots of flowers came into trees, which bend with the weight of the heavy apples. Also all the fruit is ripe, and the sun is ripening all the time; to become hotter and hotter. A picture of the season and its atmosphere is created by lots of descriptive words, and on long words, there are long ending letters, a bit like (ness), (ow), (sts) and (bosom). Most of the words have a lot of vowels in, which helps to bring the word, sound much more smooth. The poem is very slow, but also sounds very lazy, with all the descriptive words in it.

'In this comment on the poem "To Autumn" there are a number of strengths and weaknesses.

Strengths: 1 Notices that the descriptive words are important.
2 Points out that the vowels give the effect of slowness and laziness.

Weaknesses: 1 Does not choose particular words or sounds to comment on, so that the writing is too vague to gain many marks.
2 Although the student makes a great effort to say precisely what he/she means, the student does not have the vocabulary to talk about what is happening in the poem.'

Question	Assessment Objective(s)	Pre-20th century	20th century
Coursework task – sounds	1, 2, 4		✓
1 'The Lotos-Eaters'	1, 2	✓	
2 Sounds	1, 2		✓
3 'To Autumn'	1, 2	✓	

SUMMARY

Individual sounds and patterns of sound (alliteration, assonance and onomatopoeia) have the following functions:

▷ To **bring words together** to emphasize a comparison or contrast in meaning.

▷ To **imitate** or **enact the meaning** by using onomatopoeia or a particular type of sound (i.e. hard or soft consonants, long or short vowels).

▷ To **produce a 'melody'** which is pleasing to the ear.

Remember that sounds support meaning. Very rarely do they mean anything in themselves.

8

Reading to understand drama

▷ **GETTING STARTED**

Without a doubt, the greatest help in studying drama is seeing plays acted on the stage. The experience of watching a play in the theatre is very different from reading it or of seeing it on TV or video. Nowhere, except in the theatre, can you experience the relationship between the audience and live performers acting out the drama for you. Every performance is a unique occasion between that particular set of people on that particular night. You put yourself at a disadvantage if you have no idea of what goes on in a theatre. Ideally you should have paid several visits so that you are familiar with theatre techniques, and then go to see the play you are studying, after reading it first. If you are not lucky enough to find a performance of your chosen play any experience of theatre will be helpful in enabling you to bring the play to life as you read it.

The topics covered in this chapter are applicable to all exam boards.

MEG	NEAB	NICCEA	SEG	LONDON	WJEC	IGCSE	TOPIC	STUDY	REVISION 1	REVISION 2
✓	✓	✓	✓	✓	✓	✓	Bringing a play to life			
✓	✓	✓	✓	✓	✓	✓	Stage directions			
✓	✓	✓	✓	✓	✓	✓	Stage design			
✓	✓	✓	✓	✓	✓	✓	Setting			
✓	✓	✓	✓	✓	✓	✓	Costume			
✓	✓	✓	✓	✓	✓	✓	Playing the parts			
✓	✓	✓	✓	✓	✓	✓	Movement			
✓	✓	✓	✓	✓	✓	✓	Other effects			
✓	✓	✓	✓	✓	✓	✓	Radio and television			

WHAT YOU NEED TO KNOW

▷ **Lifting the play off the page**

A playscript is only a blueprint. Like a builder faced with an architect's drawing, or a conductor with a musical score, when you read a play you have to fill in all the details in your mind from the outline that the dramatist gives you. You have far more work to do in your **imagination** than you do when reading a novel. There, the author gives you descriptions of the places, the characters, their actions, their dress, their feelings. In a play text you have only the dialogue and the stage directions.

In fact, in reading the text you are being asked to do what the director in the theatre has to do: that is, to lift the words off the page and envisage the play as it would be when performed in the theatre. To do that you need to be able to imagine the stage, the setting, the costumes, the lighting, the actors and their voices and movements. You begin to do some of these things as soon as you begin to read. When the text says:

GREGSON   [*menacingly*] I shouldn't do that if I were you!

you imagine the line being spoken in a menacing way, as the bracketed stage direction instructs. As you go on reading you will gradually build up a more complete picture.

Your first task in studying a play is *to read it right through to the end.* Ideally you should try to do this in one sitting with a short break in the middle. In this way you imitate the experience of seeing the play in the theatre, in one stretch of time. Try to do your first reading on your own before any reading you are going to do in class. Do not worry too much about detail at this stage; just try to get a general impression.

The following paragraphs should help you with the imaginative work you should try to do when you go through the play for the second time.

▷ **Stage directions**

In a play text you only have two sources of information: the dialogue, that is the words the characters say, and the stage directions. The **stage directions** are vitally important because they tell you how the dramatist wants the characters to look and sound, where the action takes place, what the time is, what the weather is like – anything that the dramatist thinks is important for you to know. Some playwrights give very brief stage directions. Some, like Bernard Shaw, make them so long that we might be reading a novel. They are frequently found in the following places:

 i)   at the beginning of the scene, to tell us where the action is to take place;
 ii) when a new character enters, to tell us something about the appearance, voice, personality, dress, position of the character;
 iii) at the beginning of a speech, to tell the actor how it should be spoken.

These instructions must be read with at least the same attention as the dialogue. Often you will have to read them very slowly and carefully to work out exactly what a room or a character should look like.

▷ **The stage**

When we think of a stage we most probably think of it as being at one end of a hall, with rows of seats facing it and perhaps with a curtain to draw across to hide the 'picture'. This kind of stage, called an **end-stage**, for obvious reasons, is, however, not the only kind. At different periods of history plays have been written to be shown on different kinds of stage.

A **thrust stage** juts or thrusts out into the audience. The audience sits round three sides which brings them into much closer contact with the actors. This was the kind of stage for which Shakespeare wrote.

An **arena**, or theatre-in-the-round, has the audience sitting all round the stage. The actors enter and exit down gangways through the audience. This kind of stage has become quite popular in recent years. When you see a play staged in this way you feel very close to the action.

Clearly some plays are more suited to one kind of stage than others. For instance it is not possible to have a curtain around a thrust or an arena, which makes some scenes rather difficult to do. Large pieces of furniture are also impossible in an arena, because part of the stage would then be hidden for some of the audience.

End-stages are best for those plays that are written for big, fixed sets, such as rooms full of furniture. *Hobson's Choice*, which is set in a boot and shoe shop, is an example. This kind of set takes a lot of time and effort to move, so the curtain is usually dropped and the audience has an interval while the stage hands dash around heaving the furniture about. Since the audience will only want one or two intervals this means you can only have a big set change once or twice. If the dramatist wants more set changes they have to be done differently, and this is something the dramatist has to think about when writing the play.

Thrust stages and arenas can easily accommodate those plays which have a succession of scenes in different places where the setting is simply suggested, perhaps by something which the actors can bring on and take off with them, or perhaps by the audience being told in the words of the play. When a character strolls on and says:

> How sweet the moonlight sleeps upon this bank,

then the audience knows that it must imagine the character sitting on a bank in the moonlight, even though the stage may be completely bare. Because Shakespeare was writing for this kind of stage (with no lighting effects either) he had to use extremely vivid language to arouse the imagination of his audience.

When reading a play you would do well to decide what kind of theatre it could best be performed in and imagine yourself sitting in that theatre. Usually the opening stage directions will give you an idea.

▷ The setting

Once you have decided what kind of stage you are going to work on in your imagination you can then get on with setting the scene. This is really the work of the designer, but in this production which takes place in your head you are director, designer, actor, lighting technician and everything else. Once again you go back to the stage directions to see what the dramatist wants the set to be like. The instructions may be very precise:

> [*It is Mrs Higgins at home day. Nobody has yet arrived. Her drawing room, in a flat on the Chelsea embankment, has three windows looking on the river; and the ceiling is not so lofty as it would be in an older house of the same pretensions. The windows are open, giving access to a balcony with flowers in pots. If you stand with your face to the windows you have the fireplace on your left and the door in the right hand wall close to the corner nearest the windows. Mrs Higgins was brought up on Morris and Burne-Jones; and her room, which is very unlike her son's room in Wimpole Street, is not crowded with knick-knacks. In the middle of the room there is a big ottoman; and this, with the carpet, the Morris wallpapers, and the Morris chintz window curtains and brocade covers of the ottoman and its cushions, supply all the ornament, and are much too handsome to be hidden by odds and ends of useless things. A few good oil paintings from the exhibitions in the Grosvenor Gallery thirty years ago are on the walls. The only landscape is a Cecil Lawson on the scale of a Rubens. There is a portrait of Mrs Higgins as she was when she defied fashion in her youth in one of the beautiful Rossettian costumes ... In the corner diagonally opposite the door Mrs Higgins, now over sixty and long past the age of taking the trouble to dress out of fashion, sits writing at an elegantly simple writing table with a bell-button within reach of her hand. There is a Chippendale chair further back in the room between her and the window nearest her side. At the other side of the room, further forward, is an Elizabethan chair roughly carved in the taste of Inigo Jones. On the same side a piano in a decorated case. The corner between the fireplace and the windows is occupied by a divan cushioned in Morris chintz.*]* (Pygmalion)

Or they may be quite vague:

> [*Thunder and lightning. Enter three witches.*]

This opening stage direction from *Macbeth* makes deciding on the setting easy. The scene obviously has to be played on an empty stage, deserted except for the three figures. All we have to decide is whether to dress the stage at all, or just let Shakespeare's words do the work. We might decide to have something on the floor to suggest the roughness of the heath. But then again, remembering the later scenes in a palace we might reject such a notion. Possibly we could have some large stones jutting up near the back of the thrust stage for the witches conveniently to disappear behind. These could later be moved slightly and used as the palace gate, or battlements, or whatever. Shakespeare's stage would have been completely bare and the witches would probably have emerged on to it through a trap door.

Pygmalion is much more complicated. Shaw specifies some very elaborate furniture, in an elegant room, with a particular pattern of wallpaper and curtains and pictures by named artists. Shaw knew perfectly well that in practice such a set would not be possible, even in the most lavish of professional productions. What is interesting is the detail with which he imagined his character's surroundings. He was trying to give the designer and director an idea of the elegant kind of drawing room Mrs Higgins would have. Every production does not need to have a Chippendale chair and an Elizabethan chair carved in the taste of Inigo Jones, a painting by Cecil Lawson and so on. But the stage set must create the impression of a finely decorated and furnished room and we must try to create this in our imagination when reading.

The set is usually the first thing the audience sees and it should make a strong impression. It must not only give a sense of place but also suggest something of the mood or atmosphere of what is to come. When reading a play it is a good idea to have in our minds a setting as complete as the one Shaw imagined for his characters.

▷ Costume

Now on to our set walks a character. Or perhaps he or she is sitting there already. The way the character is *dressed* also contributes to the atmosphere of the play. The elegant ladies in evening dress waiting in the rain at the opening of *Pygmalion* give us certain expectations. So does the untidy old tramp who enters the room at the beginning of *The Caretaker*. More specifically a costume tells us something about the person who is wearing it. Although in real life we should never judge people by their clothes, in drama the impressions the costumes make on us add to our other impressions. Costume may, for example, tell us the period in which the drama is taking place, or the social class of the character (whether rich or poor) and something of the personality. Everything put on stage is there for the purpose of showing us something, giving information. Lady Bracknell appears in frills and furbelows, draped in furs and jewellery, with a huge decorated hat. She is richly and fussily overdressed because she is rich, fussy and overbearing. In *A Man for All Seasons* Sir Thomas More's plain, monk-like gown reflects the honest integrity of his nature.

In a similar way, dramatists may be very precise in their descriptions of characters' appearances. In practice they know that it may not be possible to dress the character exactly according to the instructions, to say nothing of finding actors who look the same as the descriptions. What matters is fulfilling the spirit of the dramatist's instructions, and having the actor give the correct impression.

As long as we are working in imagination, though, these difficulties do not arise. We can create the character in our mind's eye exactly as the dramatist would wish. A little research in a costume book or an illustrated history will enable us to imagine the correct dress.

▷ Playing the part

It sometimes helps you to 'see' the characters and 'hear' the words they say in your mind if you *imagine* the play being performed by actors you have seen on stage, film or television. You can choose your cast from international stars, expense no object. Alternatively you can see and hear yourself playing all the different parts, becoming appropriately older or younger, thinner or fatter, taller or shorter, as the part dictates. As with costume, looks are important because the audience must receive the right impression. In *Hobson's Choice* Maggie Hobson must look older than her sisters, otherwise we will not believe she is in danger of becoming an old maid. In *Romeo and Juliet* Juliet must look very young because the Nurse says she is not yet fourteen.

Once again the stage directions often provide the character details the dramatist wants to give. Even so, we are sometimes given very little to go on, especially in older plays. For example, in *She Stoops to Conquer* it is the text of the play which provides our information about the heroine. Her father tells us at the beginning that she is decked out in silks as usual, and a little later notes that she has changed into a plainer dress to please him. Not until Act 3 do we find any further clues to her appearance, when her suitor says, 'I vow, child, you are vastly handsome . . . Never saw a more sprightly malicious eye.' In cases like this, when the stage directions are little help and there is very little in the text, we begin to form our idea of appearance from the character's behaviour, which shows how closely the two are connected in drama.

Even more important is the actor's voice. First, it has to be suitable for the character: it is no use having Billy Liar's father ranting and raving in a thin little wheeze, or Juliet booming like a foghorn. Secondly, every change in the character's feeling has to be expressed in the way the dialogue is spoken. When we are reading the dialogue we have to hear these changes in our minds so that the feeling becomes real for us. When Macbeth's mind is filled with horrible imaginings his voice shakes with fear. When Beatie Bryant, at the end of *Roots*, finds herself speaking her own mind instead of parroting her boyfriend's thoughts, she shouts for joy, her voice full of wonder at her own achievement.

When we are in the theatre we hear all these things; when we are reading at home we only have lifeless words in front of us until we lift them off the page through the strength of our imaginations and hear them in our inward ear.

▷ Movement

Everything that has just been said about the need for an appropriate voice also applies to the way each character *moves*. We should *see* Harold Pinter's tramp, Davies, moving with the uncertain clumsiness of an unsure old man: he shuffles or lurches across the stage in *The Caretaker*. Rita, in *Educating Rita*, might begin by slouching and lolling around in an ungainly fashion, but by the end of the play when she is more aware of herself her posture will have changed and she will be more restrained.

There is also the movement, or positioning of characters in relation to each other, to consider. What we see onstage are moving pictures which tell us about relationships. The king enters at the head of a procession. He takes his seat on a raised throne. The court stands humbly round at a respectful distance, all facing him attentively. We know he is an important man before he speaks, even if he has no crown on his head. Bernard Shaw illustrates this idea in *St Joan* when the Dauphin hides in the crowd and an imposter is placed on the throne to fool Joan. Her ability to see through what she is first presented with is taken as a mark of God's hand upon her.

When we are presented with pictures in the theatre we respond without having to think. A crowd on one side of the stage, and a solitary man on the other, means this character is in some way special – a stranger or an outsider, a rebel or an enemy, someone different from the others. In *An Enemy of the People* when Dr Stockman confronts a crowd of his fellow towns-people alone we see what they think of him even before we hear them call him 'an enemy of the people'. The difficulty that Romeo has in reaching Juliet on her balcony is a visual parallel to the difficulty of their relationship because of the feud between their two families.

Every movement and every grouping onstage has a message in this way, though not always as clearly as in these examples. If we are simply reading the play we are robbed of these pictures and have to do our best to provide them for ourselves.

▷ Other effects

Lighting

Another important tool in the theatre is **lighting**. The director can use it realistically, for instance to show night falling, or the red glow in the sky produced by burning buildings. Or it can be used to produce atmosphere. The murder of Thomas Becket in Canterbury cathedral might be accompanied by a red light flooding the stage, not because the cathedral is on fire, but to symbolize the blood that has been spilt. Sometimes such effects are written into the play, particularly in Shakespeare. The language of *Macbeth* is full of references to darkness, blackness and night, to create the atmosphere of evil and the guilt-tormented mind of Macbeth, as he pursues his murderous course. Shakespeare's theatre had no lighting and his plays were performed in daylight. Therefore it was the imagery of his poetry alone which had to work on the imagination of his audience, exactly what it has to do for a reader today.

Sound effects

These are almost always used realistically. We *hear* the clank of chains offstage as Elizabeth Proctor is arrested in *The Crucible*; we *hear* Willy Loman's son knocking and knocking on the door of his father's hotel room while Willy frantically tries to get rid of the woman he has there (*Death of a Salesman*). Like seeing things happen, hearing them as you read brings the events of the play vividly to life. There is no reason why sound effects should not also be used atmospherically. If you have imagined thunder rumbling in the distance while the murderer stalks his victim, or lovers plighting their troth to the song of skylarks, you may have had a directorial stroke of genius that no one has thought of yet.

▷ Radio and television

Most, but not all, of the plays we read have been written for the theatre. Some very fine plays have been written for radio, for example those by Giles Cooper and Dylan Thomas, and an increasing number of good plays are being written for television. When writing for these media the dramatist both knows the limitations of the form he has chosen, and makes the fullest use of its advantages. The advantage for us is that we can see and hear these plays on tape just as they were intended to be experienced.

A radio dramatist has to take into account the fact that all the information he wants to convey has to be through sound. Sound has to create the whole environment. The actors have to do much more work with their voices because their actions and feelings cannot be seen. If a character is called on to lift something heavy the audience has to hear it through the strain in his voice. If a character is sad it is no good weeping silently: the emotion has to be heard. Knowing this, the dramatist tries to make everything clear through the dialogue.

These limitations might be thought of as disadvantages when compared to the theatre. On the other hand, a radio play is not restricted to a particular space represented by the stage. Radio drama can jump from place to place at will. It can happen in the most strange and extraordinary locations. Fantasy is no difficulty when the listeners are providing their own visual imaginings. It can travel through time with ease. And it is particularly good at exploring characters' thoughts.

Television shares some of this freedom with radio. It too can easily move from place to place and even contrive to allow the audience to see two places at once. Because we see things on TV in clear photographic detail and close-up it is a medium where realistic drama can be done very well. Because the camera can play visual tricks television is also a medium which can explore fantasy.

▷ **Additional examples**

Use the following examples as exercises to test your understanding of what you have read in this chapter. This kind of work will help you to visualize the plays you are studying. It will also give you good material for revision or for writing a coursework unit. Work through the examples and then read the key at the end.

'You can do the exercise on the first passage even if you have not read the play, because it comes from the opening.

You will find the second passage difficult if you have not read *Romeo and Juliet* or some other plays by Shakespeare.'

1   Read the following stage directions and opening lines of *A Taste of Honey*. Then describe how you might set the stage and how you imagine the looks and dress of the characters. The play was written in 1957 but could equally well take place in the 1990s.

[*The stage represents a comfortless flat in Manchester and the street outside. Jazz music. Enter Helen, a semi-whore, and her daughter Jo. They are loaded with baggage.*]

HELEN   Well! This is the place.

JO   And I don't like it.

HELEN   When I find somewhere for us to live I have to consider something much more important than your feelings … the rent. It's all I can afford.

JO   You can afford something better than this old ruin.

HELEN   When you start earning you can start moaning.

JO   Can't be soon enough for me. I'm cold and my shoes let water … what a place … and we're supposed to be living off her immoral earnings.

HELEN   I'm careful. Anyway what's wrong with this place? Everything in it's falling apart it's true, and we've no heating – but there's a lovely view of the gasworks, we share a bathroom with the community and this wallpaper's contemporary. What more do you want? Anyway it'll do for us. Pass me a glass Jo.

2   Read the following short scene from *Romeo and Juliet* (III. i. 34–89). Describe how you see the characters: their dress, their actions and how they stand and move on stage. What kind of lighting or other effects could be used in this scene?

BENVOLIO   By my head, here comes the Capulets.

MERCUTIO   By my heel, I care not.

TYBALT   [*to Petruccio and the others*] Follow me close, for I will speak with them.
[*to the Montagues*] Gentlemen, good e'en. A word with one of you.

MERCUTIO   An but one word with one of us? Couple it with something. Make it a word and a blow.

TYBALT   You shall find me apt enough to that, sir, an you will give me occasion.

MERCUTIO   Could you not take some occasion without the giving?

TYBALT   Mercutio, thou consort'st with Romeo.

MERCUTIO   'Consort'? What dost thou make us minstels? An thou make minstrels of us, look to hear nothing but discords. [*touching his rapier*] Here's my fiddlestick; here's that shall make you dance. Zounds – 'Consort'!

BENVOLIO	We talk here in the public haunt of men.
	Either withdraw unto some private place,
	Or reason coldly of your grievances,
	Or else depart. Here all eyes gaze on us.
MERCUTIO	Men's eyes were made to look, and let them gaze.
	I will not budge for no man's pleasure, I.
	[*Enter Romeo.*]
TYBALT	Well peace be with you, sir. Here comes my man.
MERCUTIO	But I'll be hanged, sir, if he wear your livery.
	Marry, go before to field, he'll be your follower.
	Your worship in that sense may call him 'man'.
TYBALT	Romeo, the love I bear thee can afford
	No better term than this: thou art a villain.
ROMEO	Tybalt, the reason that I have to love thee
	Doth much excuse the appertaining rage
	To such a greeting. Villain am I none.
	Therefore, farewell. I see thou knowest me not.
TYBALT	Boy, this shall not excuse the injuries
	That thou hast done me. Therefore turn and draw.
ROMEO	I do protest I never injured thee,
	But love thee better than thou can'st devise
	Till thou shalt know the reason of my love.
	And so, good Capulet – which name I tender
	As dearly as my own – be satisfied.
MERCUTIO	[*drawing*] O calm, dishonourable, vile submission!
	Alla stoccado carried it away.
	Tybalt, you ratcatcher, come, will you walk?
TYBALT	What would'st thou have with me?
MERCUTIO	Good King of Cats, nothing but one of your nine lives. That I mean to make bold withal, and, as you shall use me hereafter, dry-beat the rest of the eight. Will you pluck your sword out of his pilcher by the ears? Make haste, lest mine be about your ears ere it be out.
TYBALT	[*drawing*] I am for you.
ROMEO	Gentle Mercutio, put thy rapier up.
MERCUTIO	[*to Mercutio*] Come sir, your *passado*.
	[*They fight.*]
ROMEO	[*drawing*] Draw Benvolio. Beat down their weapons.
	Gentlemen for shame, forbear this outrage.
	Tybalt, Mercutio, the Prince expressly hath
	Forbid this bandying in Verona streets.
	Hold Tybalt, good Mercutio.
	[*Romeo beats down their points and rushes between them. Tybalt under Romeo's arm thrusts Mercutio in.*]
PETRUCCIO	Away Tybalt!
	[*Exeunt Tybalt, Petruccio and followers.*]

Key to the Examples

I The following suggestions are only *one* way of setting the stage and dressing the characters. What is important is to convey the depressing atmosphere of squalor in the surroundings and the lack of care that Helen takes of her daughter, even though she spends time and money decking herself up. I see the play taking place on an end- or thrust stage. Your ideas may be quite different: what is important is that you should create a definite visual impression of your own.

The stage directions give us two important indications as to how the stage must look. The first is the word 'comfortless'. The second is that part of the stage represents the street outside. The front strip of the stage could represent the street. The rest of the stage could be at a slightly higher level with a few steps leading up to an imaginary front door. The way the characters talk about the flat shows how dreary and broken down it is.

(continued)

(continued)

The wallpaper is garishly bright and modern but is streaked with damp and peeling in places. The furniture is the kind you see on the pavement outside junk shops: a square table painted with dark brown varnish, two straight chairs in a similar colour, their seat bottoms hastily covered in cheap plastic; an ancient sofa in an indeterminate dirty green material with a large stain across the back. It has been split along the seat, a long cut, probably made by a knife, so that the stuffing and springs are bursting out. Against one wall stands an old sideboard, its doors hanging crookedly from wrenched hinges. Papers, plastic bags and a couple of empty jars have been left littering the floor in front of it. The curtains are torn and in one corner a scattered pile of mouldy garments might be forgotten dirty washing. A bare electric light bulb hangs from the ceiling.

Helen, a short woman, is plumper than she likes to admit. Her bright yellow coat is too tight for her. She wears black lacy stockings and very high heels. Her hair is dyed bright auburn and her make-up is far too thick. Jo seems to be in a sort of school uniform, the only clothes she has: a dark navy skirt, rather stained and creased, a whitish blouse, button missing at the neck and a threadbare blazer, the sleeves far too short. Her shoes are clearly worn out.

2   These characters should be dressed in Elizabethan costume of bright colours. The stage is bare so the costume needs to provide visual interest and also give a sense of the Italian heat – reds, yellows and oranges will do this. The scene takes place in a street on a hot afternoon. Mercutio strolls lazily across and leans on a pillar, followed reluctantly by Benvolio who wants to go indoors. But he suddenly jerks to attention when he sees Tybalt coming. Mercutio ostentatiously ignores Tybalt and his friends. The animosity between the two groups is apparent: they cluster on opposite sides of the stage until Tybalt marches stiffly across and challenges Mercutio. The derision Mercutio feels is shown by his lazy, unhurried response. When Tybalt persists, Mercutio's attitude changes: he leaps up, his hand going for his sword. At this Benvolio, who has been hanging back, comes towards them and tries to calm them down or at least agree to go to a more private place, but Mercutio stands firm.

The arrival of Romeo causes Tybalt to bow stiffly to Mercutio and turn his attention to Romeo. As Tybalt walks across to challenge Romeo, Mercutio calls tauntingly after him. Everyone now expects a fight; they stand back watching, very quiet and still. Contrary to expectations Romeo listens quietly to Tybalt's insults and then gently puts out his hand. Mercutio cannot stand this. He draws his rapier. Tybalt swings round and Mercutio circles him, taunting him with little thrusts of his extended sword. When Tybalt also draws his sword Romeo holds Mercutio's arm, trying to prevent the fight. Mercutio only shakes him off, his eyes concentrating on Tybalt. They lunge furiously from side to side of the stage.

Tybalt fights very properly and precisely but Mercutio has the superior skill and teases Tybalt. Romeo, who has been hovering around shouting in vain for them to stop, finally rushes between them. Tybalt, taking advantage of the fact that Mercutio can no longer fully see him, thrusts his rapier under Romeo's arm into Mercutio's body, and quickly rushes out with his followers.

The lights should give a bright golden glow, as if it were a sunny afternoon, at the beginning of the scene. Little peaceable domestic noises could accompany the opening: someone softly whistling, a child calling in the distance. All sounds would cease as the men started to quarrel.

Do not think that you have to write about each scene in this amount of detail, but you should imagine them in detail. Writing everything down for a few key scenes helps to get the imagination working on the rest of the play.

▶ SUGGESTIONS FOR COURSEWORK

1   Take a scene from a play you have studied. Write about how you would direct it, showing the kind of stage you would choose, the set, costumes, lighting and sound effects, and the instructions you would give to the actors.

2   Write about a production of a play you have seen. Write a review pointing out both the good and bad points of the production. You could write about the characters, the set, the actors' portrayal of their roles, any effects you found outstanding, the director's idea of the play.

3   Choose a scene from a play which you find interesting or exciting. Re-write it as a chapter from a novel. Describe the characters' appearance, their surroundings, their thoughts and behaviour. You may wish to adapt or edit some of the dialogue from the play.

▷ **Coursework task**   Imagine you are going to perform one of the parts in a play you have read. Explain what the character is like, how he or she would speak and behave, how he or she thinks and feels. Don't forget to look at the stage directions as well as the characters' words.

▷ **Suggested answer**   I have chosen the character Eliza Doolittle from G.B. Shaw's play *Pygmalion*.

On my first appearance as Eliza I would be bedraggled, dirty and obviously poor. However, despite the rain I am cheerful and determinedly getting on with the business of earning my living by selling a few flowers. To do this I have to appear friendly to all the passers-by, calling them 'Freddie ' or 'Charlie' even when I don't know them and pushing myself forward to attract the attention of anyone likely to buy. I am quite aware that sometimes people buy out of sympathy so I frequently refer to myself as 'a poor girl'. Even so, in acting Eliza, I would be careful not to make her too downtrodden. My response to Freddie's clumsiness in over-turning my flowers is quite challenging to his mother and although I am 'terrified' and 'dis-traught' at the thought of having my words noted down, because it could mean I was 'driven off the streets', I recover quite quickly and am even 'tickled by the performance' when Higgins imitates me, and begin to laugh. I'm even prepared to shout and throw my basket at him when he seems mean. At the end of the scene I show my pride and ambition by sailing off in a taxi cab.

Throughout this scene the dramatist gives the actress an obvious way of showing Eliza's inferior social position and education: the way in which she talks. Since this is central to the play I would have to adopt a convincing cockney accent. This accent continues very strongly in the scene where Eliza arrives at Higgins' flat in Wimpole Street. However there are already new facets of Eliza's character that I would attempt to portray. Mrs Pearce describes Eliza as 'very common indeed', but my costume has already changed as I try to put on airs and graces in a rather pathetic way. I would try to show that I am determined to better myself, although the situation becomes too much for me again when Higgins bullies me. Although my ideas are limited I react very strongly against anything improper such as having my clothes taken away and burnt and I'm quite prepared to give up the whole scheme when Higgins appears to be 'off his chump'. Yet I am so flattered by Pickering's courteous behaviour and react almost like a child to Higgins' bribes of chocolates and taxi rides. By the end of the scene when I appear bathed, clean and clad in a kimono I must already seem to be becoming more sensible. Despite being prudish about nakedness in front of mirrors I would try to show Eliza's appreciation of new-found comforts such as hot water and clean towels. Even though I still shout 'Aw-ow-oo-ooh' and rush off to see my fashionable new clothes I should give a sense that my education has already begun.

The next scene in which Eliza appears, at Mrs Higgins' 'at home' is very clever because it shows her education half-complete. There are two dramatic changes which the actress must show. First she must speak perfectly; secondly she must move and carry herself like an elegant lady. The stage direction says that Eliza '*produces an impression of such remarkable distinc-tion and beauty as she enters that they all rise*', and that she '*speaks with pedantic correctness and great beauty of tone*'. Higgins has taught Eliza to speak perfectly even though she does not yet know the right things to say. Fortunately Eliza is blissfully unaware of the mistakes she is making. Throughout this scene I would try to give this impression by sitting very straight, moving slowly and smiling serenely through each blunder that I made until I make my elegant and graceful exit while perfectly pronouncing, 'Not bloody likely, I'm going in a taxi.'

By Act 4 Eliza's transformation is complete. We do not see her triumph, only its aftermath. This is a difficult scene for the actress playing Eliza. Behaving and speaking beautifully must now appear to have become habitual. Now Eliza's mood and feelings have become more important. Her first feeling is weariness: the great task is accomplished. Her '*expression is almost tragic*' and her beauty '*murderous*'. The feeling underlying her actions is a sense of exploitation, that she has been picked up and is now to be dropped like a used toy. She does not know what to do. Above all she wants some reaction from Higgins, wants to be noticed for herself. As an actress I would try to convey the feelings and needs behind Eliza's initial control, her furious outburst at Higgins and then her dignified assumption of inferiority when she calls him 'Sir' and asks which of her clothes belongs to her. This last tack is obviously a ploy and must clearly be shown as such. When her nagging finally provokes a display of emotion from Higgins she drinks it in '*like nectar*'.

Eliza's last scene is her most important. It is during this scene that she becomes an inde-pendent person. In my opinion she should appear sincere when she says she would not marry

Higgins if he asked her and I would not play this scene as though she were really in love with Higgins. She wants respect, friendliness and 'a little kindness'. Although under control at the beginning of the scene and determined to teach Higgins a lesson by very pointed comparisons with Pickering I would still show Eliza as feeling at a disadvantage. The restless movement on to the balcony and back into the room in order to avoid Higgins portrays this. But a point comes when she realizes that in teaching her Higgins has passed on an inestimable gift; she really is now independent and can behave like an equal. She may, as Higgins expects, go back to Wimpole Street, but it will be a free choice. She has alternatives. The first step is her idea of offering herself as assistant to Professor Nepean, which reduces Higgins to fury. Eliza quickly passes on to the realization that she herself could earn a thousand guineas a time teaching others what Higgins has taught her. This speech should be delivered with a mounting conviction and excitement in her own strength, sufficient to draw admiration from Higgins. I would play Eliza at the end as triumphant for I believe that Higgins' self-satisfaction springs, at least in part, from the knowledge of having created a 'consort battleship' rather than a mere fetcher of slippers.

 EXAMINATION QUESTIONS

This chapter describes very important techniques of reading a play. These techniques will enable you to answer well the kinds of questions which ask you to select a scene from the play and write about it. Some questions will specifically ask about stage directions.

Many questions ask you to envisage how a play would look on the stage, how it might be performed or how the audience might react. Some questions will specifically remind you to look at the stage directions. Others will assume that you understand their importance and that you will refer to them in your answer without a reminder.

▷ **Question 1**
'SEG. Foundation Tier.'

Read the following extract from *The Crucible*. Describe the setting and atmosphere in this extract. Compare the atmosphere here with one other episode in the play.

DANFORTH	[*sharply to Parris*] Bring her out! And tell her not one word of what's been spoken here. And let you knock before you enter. [*Parris goes out.*] Now we shall touch the bottom of this swamp. [*to Proctor*] Your wife, you say, is an honest woman.
PROCTOR	In her life, sir, she has never lied. There are them that cannot sing, and them that cannot weep – my wife cannot lie. I have paid much to learn it, sir.
DANFORTH	And when she put this girl out of your house, she put her out for a harlot?
PROCTOR	Aye, sir.
DANFORTH	And knew her for a harlot?
PROCTOR	Aye, sir, she knew her for a harlot.
DANFORTH	Good then. [*to Abigail*] And if she tell me, child, it were for harlotry, may God spread His mercy on you! [*There is a knock. He calls to the door.*] Hold! [*to Abigail*] Turn your back. Turn your back. [*to Proctor*] Do likewise. [*Both turn their back – Abigail with indignant slowness.*] Now let neither of you turn to face Goody Proctor. No one in this room is to speak one word, or raise a gesture aye or nay. [*He turns toward the door, calls.*] Enter! [*The door opens. Elizabeth enters with Parris. Parris leaves her. She stands alone, her eyes looking for Proctor.*] Mr Cheever, report this testimony in all exactness. Are you ready?
CHEEVER	Ready, sir.
DANFORTH	Come here, woman. [*Elizabeth comes to him, glancing at Proctor's back.*] Look at me only, not at your husband. In my eyes only.
ELIZABETH	[*faintly*] Good, sir.
DANFORTH	We are given to understand that at one time you dismissed your servant, Abigail Williams.
ELIZABETH	That is true, sir.
DANFORTH	For what cause did you dismiss her? [*Slight pause. Then Elizabeth tries to glance at Proctor.*] You will look in my eyes only and not at your husband. The answer is in your memory and you need no help to give it to me. Why did you dismiss Abigail Williams?
ELIZABETH	[*not knowing what to say, sensing a situation, wetting her lips to stall for time*] She – dissatisfied me. [*pause*] And my husband.
DANFORTH	In what way dissatisfied you?

ELIZABETH	She were – [*She glances at Proctor for a cue.*]
DANFORTH	Woman, look at me! [*Elizabeth does.*] Were she slovenly? Lazy? What disturbance did she cause?
ELIZABETH	Your Honour, I – in that time I were sick. And I – my husband is a good and righteous man. He is never drunk as some are, nor wastin' his time at the shovelboard, but always at his work. But in my sickness – you see, sir, I were a long time sick after my last baby, and I thought I saw my husband somewhat turning from me. And this girl – [*she turns to Abigail*].
DANFORTH	Look at me.
ELIZABETH	Aye, sir. Abigail Williams – [*She breaks off.*]
DANFORTH	What of Abigail Williams?
ELIZABETH	I came to think he fancied her. And so one night I lost my wits, I think, and put her out on the highroad.
DANFORTH	Your husband – did he indeed turn from you?
ELIZABETH	[*in agony*] My husband – is a goodly man, sir.
DANFORTH	Then he did not turn from you.
ELIZABETH	[*starting to glance at Proctor*] He –
DANFORTH	[*reaches out and holds her face, then*] Look at me! To your own knowledge, has John Proctor ever committed the crime of lechery! [*In a crisis of indecision she cannot speak.*] Answer my question! Is your husband a lecher!
ELIZABETH	[*faintly*] No, sir.
DANFORTH	Remove her, Marshal.
PROCTOR	Elizabeth, tell the truth!
DANFORTH	She has spoken. Remove her!
PROCTOR	[*crying out*] Elizabeth, I have confessed it!
ELIZABETH	Oh, God! [*The door closes behind her.*]
PROCTOR	She only thought to save my name!

▷ **Question 2**
'SEG. Foundation Tier.'

The Long and the Short and the Tall. Read the following passage and answer the questions printed beneath it.

WHITAKER	[*notices the radio which is still standing on the table*] Sarge! The set!
MITCHEM	O God, lad! Get it! Quick! [*Whitaker moves as if to cross to table, but changes his mind and hugs wall in terror.*] Get the set! [*Whitaker is still afraid to move. Smith is about to fetch the radio when we hear the sound of feet on the wooden veranda.*] Too late!

[*The members of the patrol squeeze up against the wall as Mitchem edges away from the window out of sight. Johnstone tenses himself. The Japanese soldier can be heard clattering on the veranda for several seconds before he appears at the left hand window. He peers into the room but fails to see the patrol and is just about to turn away when he notices the radio on the table. He stares at it for a short while and then moves out of sight as he crosses along the veranda towards the door. A further short pause, Johnstone raises his hands in readiness. The door opens and the Japanese soldier enters. As he steps into the room Johnstone lunges forward and grabs the Japanese, putting an arm round his throat and his free hand over the soldier's mouth. Mitchem, holding the sten at his hip, darts out of the door and covers the jungle from the veranda. Johnstone and the Prisoner struggle in the room.*]

JOHNSTONE	Come on then, one of you! Get him! Quick! . . . Evans! Do for him! [*Evans crosses and raises his rifle, releasing the safety catch.*] No you burk! You want to do for me as well? Come on lad! Use your bayonet! In his guts! You'll have to give it hump. [*Evans unsheathes his bayonet and approaches the struggling figures.*] Sharp then lad! Come on! Come on! You want it in between his ribs. [*Evans raises the bayonet to stab the Prisoner who squirms in terror.*] Not that way lad! You'll only bust a bone. Feel for it first, then ram it in. Now, come on, quick! [*Evans places his bayonet point on the chest of the Prisoner, who has now stopped struggling and is cringing in the grip of Johnstone.*] Come on! Come on! I can't hold on to him forever! Will you ram it in!
EVANS	[*steps back*] I . . . I can't do it, Corp.
JOHNSTONE	Stick it in! Don't stand there tossing up the odds! Just close your eyes and whoof it in!
EVANS	I can't! I can't! Corp, I can't.
MACLEISH	Not me!
JOHNSTONE	Smith! Take the bayonet! Don't stand there gawping. Do the job!

SMITH	For God's sake do it Taff. Put the poor bastard out of his misery.
EVANS	[*proffering the bayonet to Smith*] You!
BAMFORTH	[*crossing and snatching the bayonet from Evans*] Here. Give me hold. It's only the same as carving up a pig. Hold him still. [*Bamforth raises the bayonet and is about to thrust it into the chest of the Prisoner as Mitchem enters, closing the door behind him.*]
MITCHEM	Bamforth! Hold it!
BAMFORTH	[*hesitates, then moves away*] I'm only doing what I'm told.

What does this passage tell you of Johnstone's character? What do you learn from this passage about all the other members of the patrol who appear in it?

 Question 3   Write a review of a play you have seen.

EXAMINATION ANSWERS

Question 1   *Notes and tutor's answer*

Notes

1 Your study of the play should have made you acquainted with the sevententh-century background. You should know how the characters dressed and what their houses and buildings were like. Describe as clearly as you can how you believe the scene should look on the stage.
2 Try to identify what creates the atmosphere, and how and why the atmosphere changes.
3 Make your description of the characters' behaviour and reactions as vivid and lively as you can, as if you had seen it on stage.

Suggested answer

The waiting room outside the court at Salem, to which John Proctor has come to try to prove his wife's innocence, is austerely bare. The plain wooden structure suggests the simple farming life of the men who built it. The men gathered here, come like John to save their wives from hanging, are simply and plainly dressed even though they have put on their Sunday best in deference to the court. The court officials, even the Deputy Governor Danforth, are hardly more grand, though their black coats and breeches are of the best quality. The girls, whose words can condemn the most respectable woman as a witch, are also in the same black and browns, only their wide, white Puritan collars bringing any relief to the severity of the scene.

The atmosphere in the room is tense with subdued shock: in a burst of anger Proctor has confessed that he has slept with Abigail. This is the reason she now accuses Elizabeth of witchcraft because she hopes to take her place as Proctor's wife. Danforth is disturbed. His authority and the authority of the court are in question. Abigail haughtily refuses to confirm or deny Proctor's assertion and Danforth does not know who to believe. He sends for Elizabeth in order to confirm Proctor's story: if she answers truthfully Abigail will be exposed and the whole basis of the trials will be swept away.

Elizabeth is led into a room which is breathlessly hushed. The nervousness of everyone present is palpable because what she says will have consequences for everyone. Danforth's order that Proctor and Abigail turn their backs means that Elizabeth has no help. She is a good, honest woman and she loves her husband. In the face of Danforth's questions she is uncertain what to do. She can feel the tension in the atmosphere but she cannot judge what has gone before. What has Abigail said? What has John said? We are held in suspense as we hear her trying to explain why she dismissed Abigail, trying to feel her way to the right answer. She seems in her replies to be creeping towards the truth and we hope desperately that she will remain true to her character and not lie. But her wavering fills us with doubt. She can read nothing from the backs of Abigail and Proctor and we sense her desperation as she casts about for guidance. There is no softening in Danforth: fiercely he drives her to answer the question directly. Faced with the public betrayal of her husband her courage fails and she speaks the lie that cannot be retracted.

The suspense is over, the tension drops, to be replaced by a bleak despair. What now can Proctor do? He has exposed his own sinful weakness to no avail. He has no weapons left against the hard, unrelenting narrowness of the authority under which he lives.

Later on in the play John and Elizabeth meet again. They have both been in prison for three months, but while Elizabeth has been granted a stay of execution because she is pregnant John is condemned to hang that morning for being in league with the devil and sending out his spirit upon Mary Warren.

They meet in a cell: bare, dark and gloomy. Through the barred window the moon grows pale as dawn begins to lighten the sky; when the sun comes up John must die if he will not confess his guilt. They have left Elizabeth alone with him in the hope that she can persuade him to confess. As they face each other in the empty cell the atmosphere is intense. The feeling flowing between them is strong with love and longing. As they quietly question each other about their sons, their situation, the fate of their friends, they seem as if suspended in time. It is love of Elizabeth that makes Proctor wish to confess. He cannot feel himself to be a good person, like Rebecca Nurse, and go to the gallows like a saint, for he has the weight of his adultery upon him. And when Elizabeth acknowledges her own faults and asks his forgiveness Proctor is galvanized by his desire to live.

In a frenetic scene Proctor first signs and then retracts his confession. When he first signs the mood on stage is an anguished mingling of doubt and relief, and not just in Proctor. There is also the relief of Danforth and Parris as they take down the confession, for they fear the consequences of the death of such a one as John Proctor; there is the doubt of Rebecca Nurse for she believes it is a lie and she sorrows that John should bring himself to it. In Elizabeth there is both relief and doubt for she would have him live and yet believes he damns his immortal soul, but she will not judge him. We must surely share Elizabeth's emotions for we see a decent man caught in a dilemma which must bring either his death or his shame. Yet as Danforth's demands for his confession to be made public become clear Proctor's anger and desperation grow. He cannot give this lie. There is a frenzied mood of conflict, truly a conflict between good and evil, as Proctor wrestles with his conscience. When he tears up his confession the atmosphere is electric. He will go to the gallows like a saint. The fanatic ideology of the court is defeated; Proctor triumphs over himself and over the power of theocracy*. In the audience we have that sense, which all true tragedy brings, of being for some short time made nobler ourselves by example.

* theocracy: a system of government directed by religious belief, in which the laws are taken from God.

▷ Question 2   *Notes and tutor's answer*

Notes

1   In this passage the characters emerge as much from the stage directions which describe the action as from the words. Therefore when you are reading through the passage you must envisage the characters in action.
2   Go through the stage directions underlining all Johnstone's actions.
3   Read Johnstone's speeches again and jot down a few adjectives to describe his behaviour here (e.g. experienced, brutal).
4   Write a paragraph about Johnstone's character as shown by his behaviour here.
5   Make a list of all the other members of the patrol. Go through the passage identifying what each one does and jotting down adjectives alongside their names.
6   Write a second, longer paragraph about the others.

Suggested answer

'Have you supported all your character points with evidence from the passage?'

Johnstone is an experienced and hardened soldier. The stage directions show he has positioned himself ready to attack the Japanese soldier if he enters the room and he waits, tense, ready for action, when the door opens. He knows how to capture and silence the man effectively by 'putting an arm round his throat and his free hand over the soldier's mouth'.

He has no hesitation in ordering his subordinates to kill the Japanese. He realizes the method necessary in this situation is bayoneting, a most brutal and vicious way of killing a man. While the other soldiers quail at the act, he has no qualms. His only concern seems to be that they should do it in the right place and make a good job of it. He even appears to relish it, urging them on with vigour:

> In his guts. You'll have to give it hump.

He shows no sympathy for the Japanese and no humanity.

Whitaker has sufficient wits about him to realize that the radio set will give their presence away but is too frightened to move away from the wall and pull it out of sight.

Smith has the courage to risk moving to fetch the set but he is too late. Later Smith shows some pity for the Prisoner by wanting to get the horrible performance with the bayonet over as quickly as possible, though he will not contradict his superior officer.

Both Evans and Macleish also show their revulsion for killing the Japanese. Evans does try to respond to the order from Johnstone but the sight of the helpless man, reduced to immobile terror, arouses his sympathy. Macleish refuses point blank.

Only Bamforth equals Johnstone in ruthlessness. He deliberately hardens himself against the Japanese by speaking of him as an animal rather than a human being. His response is unthinking, that of a man who is unused to using his imagination to put himself in another man's shoes. Later he will react equally unthinkingly in defence of the Japanese.

Mitchem's authoritative command saves the man. He has the stature to command his men. He thinks clearly and acts decisively in an emotional situation.

▷ **Question 3**   *Student's answer – examiner's comments*

I have been to see a production of A Midsummer Night's Dream. *The director's intention in the play was to relate to dreams as he saw them and clearly state the difference between the immortals and the mortals.*

The set was basic in the way that there was not much on stage, and it was composite, because in order to let the words and lighting do the rest they could not clutter the stage. The lighting played a central part in re-enforcing the main intention. For example during the dream the mortals were lit only from the front so they appeared two dimensional and very specific, whereas the immortals were lit from the back and sides giving them an ethereal quality and creating a mystical atmosphere. Also when the mechanicals had torches they were lit by an orange light. This re-enforced the darkness around and gave a warmer atmosphere which went well with the characters. The sound also re-enforced the atmosphere of a scene. For instance, at the beginning the mortals seemed to have finished dinner as there was soft piano music in the background. This also brought out the formality of what had just happened and set the mood. When Helena was alone in the wood there were dull noises and 'spooky' sounds which enhanced the tension and the sense of waiting for something to happen.

The movement also contributed to the main intention. For example the mortals used direct movements whereas the immortals had soft but flickering movements, which again differentiated them as strange beings. The choreography added more interest to the play but Oberon and Titania's dance was unfortunately wrong: it looked as if he could not remember how to do it. It spoilt the atmosphere of their dance as a natural part of their fun.

The costumes were in the period of the 1920s, but in my opinion this was not very successful. Throughout the play I could not work out when it was set because the formal dress seemed much older than the informal. There was too great a contrast and that became confusing. What is more the language was obviously not of the same period. I understood the director's intention of giving the play a wider period of reference but it did not seem to work. This contrasted with another modern dress production I have seen, Romeo and Juliet, *where the actors seemed to believe so strongly in what they were saying that you forgot that it was in Shakespearean language and could relate to it directly.*

'In this answer there is nothing to tell the reader what the play is about, or who the characters are. Somewhere in the answer you need to show your knowledge of the plot and the characters.

The comments on the set are confused and difficult to understand. This is a pity because a good point is being made about the bare, uncluttered stage. The word "composite" is a good one, but needs explaining.

The comments on the lighting are good, demonstrating an understanding of how this technique can be used to express the themes of the play. There are similarly good comments on the sound effects, recognizing the atmosphere of the play, and on the movement.

The conclusion gives a clear opinion and a reasoned judgement for it.

This student obviously understands the theatre and has a strong feeling for it: the answer conveys a great involvement in the production. The student probably also has a good knowledge and understanding of the play's plot, character and themes, but the answer seems to take these things for granted. You must take the opportunity to show what you know.'

Question	Assessment Objective(s)	Pre-20th century	20th century
Coursework task – *Pygmalion*	1, 2		✓
1 *The Crucible*	1, 4		✓
2 *The Long and the Short and the Tall*	1, 2		✓
3 *A Midsummer Night's Dream*	1, 4	✓	

SUMMARY

▷ Whenever possible **go and see the play** you are studying.

▷ The script is only an outline; **you must fill in all the details** when reading.

▷ The **stage directions** are an important source of information for everything you would see in a performance.

▷ **Imagining** the stage performance (stage, costume, sets, lighting) gives atmosphere and brings to life the situation and the characters.

▷ **Imagining** the actors' appearances, voices and movements helps us to understand the characters' feelings and relationships.

Chapter

9

The conventions of drama

GETTING STARTED

When we go to the theatre or watch a play on television, listen to the radio or go to the cinema, we have to accept that things are going to be presented to us in a particular way. Often this way is not realistic but the audience accepts what is happening because they are used to seeing it done in this way. Such methods or techniques of presentation are called *conventions*. For instance it used to be the convention in films always to have music in the background at moments of high drama or emotion. The audience did not imagine there was a full orchestra playing behind the sitting-room curtains when the hero took the heroine in his arms. The soaring violins were accepted as mood music, showing the strength of the characters' feelings. If we are used to watching plays frequently we accept conventions such as this and do not think about them.

To understand and appreciate what the dramatist is doing we should be able to recognize conventions and know what effects they have. This chapter helps you to do that and shows you how to use your knowledge.

The topics covered in this chapter are applicable to all exam boards.

MEG	NEAB	NICCEA	SEG	LONDON	WJEC	IGCSE	TOPIC	STUDY	REVISION I	REVISION 2
✓	✓	✓	✓	✓	✓	✓	Acts and scenes			
✓	✓	✓	✓	✓	✓	✓	Time			
✓	✓	✓	✓	✓	✓	✓	Chorus			
✓	✓	✓	✓	✓	✓	✓	Disguise			
✓	✓	✓	✓	✓	✓	✓	The soliloquy			
✓	✓	✓	✓	✓	✓	✓	The aside			
✓	✓	✓	✓	✓	✓	✓	The supernatural			
✓	✓	✓	✓	✓	✓	✓	Battles			
✓	✓	✓	✓	✓	✓	✓	Radio conventions			
✓	✓	✓	✓	✓	✓	✓	Film and TV conventions			

WHAT YOU NEED TO KNOW

▷ **Acts and scenes**
The first convention we notice when reading, rather than watching a play is that it is divided into acts and scenes which break up the action in the same way that chapters do in a novel. The practice in Shakespeare's time was to divide the play into five **acts**. Later on it became three acts. Modern plays are often divided into only two acts and some do not have acts at all, simply a succession of **scenes**.

A scene generally marks off a piece of action which happens in one place, in one continuous stretch of time. When the action moves to another place, or the dramatist wants a gap in time, then the scene ends and another one begins. The first four scenes of *Macbeth* take place on a heath in Scotland. We first see the witches, then the king and his nobles. We go back to the witches, and then move once again to the king's camp. With each move we start a new scene to denote a change of place. Shakespeare could use short scenes and move the action freely from place to place like this because he had no scenery to move.

Bernard Shaw writes in a different style. *The Devil's Disciple* opens with Mrs Dudgeon sitting up in the kitchen in the middle of the night with Essie. Characters come and go, but the whole of the action takes place continuously in the kitchen until the end of Act 1. Therefore, the act is not divided into scenes.

Another play written in this century, *Journey's End* (R.C. Sheriff), all takes place in a dug-out in the British trenches in the First World War. The divisions are these:

Act I: Evening on Monday 18 March 1918
Act II: Scene 1 – Tuesday morning
            Scene 2 – Tuesday afternoon
Act III: Scene 1 – Wednesday afternoon
            Scene 2 – Wednesday night
            Scene 3 – Thursday, towards dawn.

The location never changes, but the advancing time is important. The gaps in time represented by these scene divisions are often shown on stage by dimming the lights.

There is a dramatic purpose to scene divisions. The way in which the dramatist divides the action into scenes affects the pace and tension of a play. A series of short scenes gives the sense of rapidly advancing action, perhaps of events becoming beyond the control of a character. Shakespeare's battles are often constructed of a series of very short scenes. Long scenes are needed to give cohesion and the development of relationships, feelings and ideas. Trial scenes, like those in *The Crucible* (Arthur Miller) and *St Joan* (Bernard Shaw), are long for this reason. Notice the act and scene divisions in the plays you are studying and ask yourself what is achieved by them and what effect they have on stage.

▷ **Time**
As well as having to show gaps in the passage of **time** by scene changes, the dramatist has to manipulate time in other ways. Shakespeare talks about 'the two hours traffic of our stage'. But during the time that the play takes to perform we understand that we may see days, even years, passing. The dramatist has to concentrate all the important events of the story into two or three hours.

Most of these events will have to be telescoped into a far shorter time than they would take in reality. In Thornton Wilder's short play *A Happy Journey to Trenton and Camden* a family travels 70 miles by car in 20 minutes of stage time. Love scenes or quarrels come to a head much faster on stage than they would in real life. Algernon and John Worthing would have to gobble their muffins and teacakes to get through them in the time allowed for tea in *The Importance of Being Earnest* (Oscar Wilde).

Another favourite dramatic trick with time is the **flashback**. Arthur Miller uses this convention in *Death of a Salesman*. Willy Loman is approaching the crisis of his life which leads to his suicide. In a series of flashbacks we are shown how the events of his life have led him to this. Each scene from the past gives us a deeper understanding of his character and relationships with his family and we slowly learn how his long-standing inability to see things as they really are has led him to despair. The value of seeing the ageing Willy enacting the scenes from earlier, happier times in flashback is that it makes his failure all the more poignant and the happy scenes all the more painful.

In *The Skin of Our Teeth* Thornton Wilder uses time in yet another way. The audience sees two eras at once. The Antrobus family lives both in prehistoric times and in modern

America. The dramatist here is trying to set the daily events of his play in a greater perspective.

Whenever a dramatist uses time differently from actual time we must consider what the dramatic purpose is.

▷ **Chorus**   Generally we learn of events from what characters say or what we see them do. Occasionally, however, when the dramatist wants to give the audience a lot of information in a hurry, a **Chorus** can be used.

Originally, in Greek drama, a Chorus was a group of people who watched the actions of the main characters and then commented on them and gave their reactions. They could not affect the actions of the play, only voice their hopes and fears. This kind of group Chorus has been little used since the Greeks, but there is one modern play, T.S. Eliot's *Murder in the Cathedral*, where it is used very successfully. A group of the women of Canterbury wait for Thomas, the Archbishop, to return to his cathedral. They are filled with an awful sense of doom. Their speeches express fear and helplessness and, after Thomas' murder, horror, guilt and finally submission to the will of God. Their role is to stand for the ordinary people.

It is much more usual to have a single person as Chorus, but the function can remain the same. In *A Man for All Seasons* Robert Bolt uses a character called the Common Man: his name states clearly whom he represents. He slips in and out of the scenes, sometimes commenting on them, sometimes taking part as a boatman or steward, or whatever is needed.

Shakespeare occasionally uses a Chorus figure. In *Henry V* his purpose is to introduce each act and to set the scene. He rouses the imagination with descriptions of the horses 'printing their proud hooves in the receiving earth' and reminds the audience of details of who is treacherous and who is true. In *The Winter's Tale* his purpose is to describe the lapse of sixteen years between Acts III and IV.

A Chorus acts as a kind of intermediary between the audience and the play. Because he speaks directly to the audience as commentator or narrator he forcefully reminds us we are sitting in a theatre listening to an actor. We cannot get carried away by the spell of a story and begin to believe the characters are real people with lives that continue beyond the end of the play. Some dramatists, like Bertolt Brecht, very deliberately use Chorus and narrator figures to prevent the audience being carried away on a wave of sympathy for the characters. In *The Caucasian Chalk Circle* Brecht uses the Singer to break up the action with songs and snatches of narrative. He does not want the audience simply to feel for Grusha and the child she has rescued; he wants them to think about what their story means for society as a whole.

If there is a Chorus in a play, try to determine what function it fulfils.

▷ **Disguise**   Disguise is used a great deal in drama. This sometimes worries those who are not used to this convention because it does not seem believable. In *Twelfth Night* a pair of twins, separated in a shipwreck, are both washed up in Illyria. The girl dresses up as a boy and we are asked to believe first that no one notices she is not a man – so much so that a woman falls in love with her – and secondly no one can tell her apart from her brother. Of course, Shakespeare had a particular reason for wanting to get his heroines disguised as young men, as quickly as possible, because they were all acted by boys. There were no actresses. But this does not help our sense of the reality of the action. The answer is not to worry about realism, any more than we would with *ET* or *Superman*.

Disguise allows a dramatist to construct extraordinary situations, to confront the characters with situations which they might never otherwise see and know of. In *Twelfth Night* Olivia is made to fall in love with a disguised woman so that she can learn something about her own nature and the nature of love.

When a character assumes a disguise ask yourself what it allows the dramatist to do with him or her that could not otherwise be done.

▷ **The soliloquy**   The soliloquy is a way of letting the audience know what a character is thinking. Almost everyone knows Hamlet's famous words 'To be or not to be'. It is the beginning of a speech in which he debates with himself about suicide. We are to suppose that these are the thoughts going round in his brain. The convention allows us to get inside his head. Another, perhaps equally famous soliloquy is Macbeth's 'Is this a dagger that I see before me'. Very frequently the character is alone on stage with his thoughts, but not always. The fact that we, the audience, can hear, but the rest of the characters onstage cannot, is not a problem because the soliloquy is not intended to represent someone talking to himself, but his unspoken thoughts.

There is a second kind of soliloquy, not of unspoken thoughts but of the character very directly addressing the audience and telling them what he is up to. When Launcelot Gobbo has a tussle with his conscience about leaving the Jew, his master, in *The Merchant of Venice*, he discusses all the pros and cons with the audience and confidentially makes them a party to his decision to run away.

▷ The aside

Another means of communicating directly with the audience is the **aside**. A character turns aside from the action onstage and speaks to the audience. The difference between this and the soliloquy is that the aside is usually very short and, although there are other people onstage, the convention is that they do not hear what the audience is told.

ABSOLUTE   [*aside*] So much thought bodes me no good. – [*to her*] So grave Lydia!

LYDIA   Sir!

ABSOLUTE   [*aside*] So! Egad I thought as much! – that damned monosyllable has froze me! – [*to her*] What Lydia, now that we are happy in our friends' consent, as in our mutual vows –

LYDIA   Friends' consent indeed!

(Richard Sheridan, *The Rivals*)

Absolute, commenting to the audience on his mistress' silence, and then her monosyllabic reply, makes the audience feel like a friend and confidante. An aside can give the audience more knowledge than characters onstage. It is often used for comic effect.

▷ The supernatural

Witches, ghosts and spirits are frequently portrayed on the stage. They can be given knowledge that ordinary mortals do not possess. We have to remember that in previous centuries many people believed in the **supernatural** much more literally than we do now. The spirits that were thought of as agents of the devil, as many were, were usually given a hideous appearance. The witches in *Macbeth* are called 'secret, black and midnight hags' to show that they are evil creatures. The devil's henchman, Mephistopheles, is so ugly on his first appearance in *Doctor Faustus* (Marlowe) that he is sent away to assume a more acceptable shape. Ghosts are dangerous beings whose credentials have to be established. They, too, may come from the devil and so must not be immediately trusted.

There are also good and benevolent spirits. Shakespeare brings on the god of marriage, Hymen, to bless the couples at the end of *As You Like It*, and a trio of goddesses appears to sing and dance in *The Tempest*.

The theatre Shakespeare worked in had special winching gear by which actors playing gods and good spirits could be lowered from the roof on to the stage, as though descending from the heavens. Evil spirits rose through a trapdoor in the stage as though coming up from the bowels of the earth. In modern productions they are more likely to appear and disappear in a cloud of dry ice.

In more modern plays ghosts can be treated comically because the audience is no longer very frightened by the thought of them. In *Blithe Spirit* Noel Coward allows a man to be plagued by the ghost of his dead wife because she is jealous of his second wife. The pranks she gets up to are mischievous rather than frightening and create comic situations.

When ghosts, gods or spirits appear in a play you are reading consider what use the dramatist is making of them. Think too of what their appearance should be and how they can be got on and off the stage.

▷ Battles

Many of Shakespeare's plays, notably the history plays, include **battles**. Film has many advantages over the stage in the representation of battles. The film of *Richard III* can use hundreds of extras carrying spears and dozens of horses. The armies confronting each other look like real armies. Looked at objectively, battles on stage are often quite farcical. All the male members of the cast run on and off stage several times, pausing only to shout instructions or give a brief report of somebody's friend or son dying bravely; several people have duels; a lot of trumpets are blown, usually offstage. Finally somebody staggers to the front, declares that he has won, and everybody cheers.

We accept the convention that the noise and confusion represents the real battle, and the duels stand for all the fighting. If we insist on seeing these realistically we destroy the play. We have to accept the convention for the drama to work.

▷ Radio conventions

Radio has a set of conventions quite different from the stage, which have to be understood in order to grasp what is going on. Since everything has to be conveyed through sound, the silences are very important. Through silence the dramatist shows the passing of time, or a change of place: the sound of birds fades, then after a short silence we hear a lot of traffic, so we know that we have moved from the country to the town.

When radio wishes to convey a character's thoughts it, too, can use soliloquy. A quiet voice close to the microphone can show that this is the character thinking; the same voice, louder and more distant, is the character speaking aloud. One of the advantages of radio is that it can switch instantly from one to the other, or even have both thought and voice speaking at the same time. Dylan Thomas does this in *Under Milk Wood*. Blind Captain Cat hears Polly Garter with her bucket and mop. His thoughts about her are spoken quietly, then he calls to her, 'Hello Polly.' This is said loudly. Her reply is distant from the microphone to show that she is down in the street outside his window.

▷ Film and television conventions

Yet another set of conventions applies to films or plays on television. Change of time or place is conveyed by the picture fading or being cut. As with radio techniques, this means that moving from scene to scene can be very quick. Inner thoughts can be conveyed by a technique called the voice over. The picture on the screen may show the view from a window, while the character talks about her feelings, or her past life, or what she is going to do next. Like radio, television can travel in time with enormous ease: flashbacks are a common technique. It can also 'crosscut' to show things going on at the same time in different places. The screen picture moves rapidly back and forth between the two places. The screen can also be split in two, for instance to show the reactions of both speakers in a telephone conversation. We are so familiar with these conventions, which are used all the time in soap operas or sitcoms like *EastEnders* or *Keeping Up Appearances*, that we forget that these are things which the medium of film can do which other media cannot do.

One of the best TV dramatists, who used the medium creatively, was Dennis Potter. *The Singing Detective* is about a man lying in hospital recovering from a skin disease and thinking about his life and about a detective story he once wrote. We see what happens to him in the hospital, are shown his thoughts and fears about his past life and relationships, and we are told the detective story as well. The scenes flash between the present and his memories and the fictional thriller in the same way that ideas flit in and out of our minds, especially when we are feeling ill. The conventions of the TV drama allow the action to progress on all three levels at once.

▷ Additional examples

The following passages illustrate some of the techniques discussed in this chapter. You can test your understanding of what you have read by answering the questions on them. Write down your ideas before reading the key below.

'Are you seeing this scene in your mind's eye? If not you will have difficulty answering questions on it.'

1   For what purpose does the dramatist use the character of the Stage Manager in the following extract?

STAGE MANAGER   In our town we like to know the facts about everybody. There's Mrs Webb, coming downstairs to get her breakfast, too – That's Doc. Gibbs. Got that call at half-past-one this morning. And there comes Joe Crowell Junior, delivering Mr Webb's *Sentinel*.

[*Dr Gibbs has been coming along Main Street from the left. At the point where he would turn to approach his house he sets down his – imaginary – black bag, takes off his hat and rubs his face with fatigue, using an enormous handkerchief. Mrs Webb, a thin, serious, crisp woman, has entered her kitchen, left, tying on her apron. She goes through the motions of putting wood on the stove, lighting it and preparing breakfast. Suddenly, Joe Crowell, eleven, starts down Main Street from the right, hurling imaginary newspapers into the doorways.*]

JOE CROWELL	Morning, Doc. Gibbs.
DR GIBBS	Morning, Joe.
JOE CROWELL	Somebody been sick, Doc.?
DR GIBBS	No. Just some twins born over in Polish town.
JOE CROWELL	Do you want your paper now?
DR GIBBS	Yes I'll take it – Anything serious goin' on in the world since Wednesday?
JOE CROWELL	Yessir. My schoolteacher, Miss Foster's, getting married to a fella over in Concord.
DR GIBBS	I declare – How do you boys feel about that?
JOE CROWELL	Well, of course, it's none of my business – but I think if a person starts out a teacher, she ought to stay one.
DR GIBBS	How's your knee, Joe?
JOE CROWELL	Fine, Doc. I never think about it at all. Only like you said, it always tells me when it's going to rain.
DR GIBBS	What's it telling you today? Goin' to rain?
JOE CROWELL	No sir.
DR GIBBS	Sure?
JOE CROWELL	Yessir.
DR GIBBS	Knee ever made a mistake?
JOE CROWELL	No sir. [*Joe goes off. Dr Gibbs stands reading his paper.*]
STAGE MANAGER	Want to tell you something about that boy Joe Crowell there. Joe was awful bright – graduated from high school here, head of his class. So he got a scholarship to Massachusetts Tech. Graduated head of his class there, too. It was all wrote up in the Boston paper at the time. Goin' to be a great engineer Joe was. But the war broke out and he died in France – All that education for nothing.

(Thornton Wilder, *Our Town*)

2   What is achieved by the use of asides in the following scene? This scene is the first meeting between the hero and the heroine. She already knows that he has a reputation for being forward, but only with lower-class women.

MARLOW	It's a disease of the mind madam. In the variety of tastes there must be some who, wanting a relish for um – a – um –
MISS HARDCASTLE	I understand you sir. There must be some who, wanting a relish for refined pleasures, pretend to despise what they are incapable of tasting.
MARLOW	My meaning madam, but infinitely better expressed. And I can't help observing – a –
MISS HARDCASTLE	[*aside*] Who could ever suppose this fellow impudent upon some occasions. [*to him*] You were going to observe, sir –
MARLOW	I was observing Madam, – I protest, madam, I forget what I was going to observe.
MISS HARDCASTLE	[*aside*] I vow and so do I. [*to him*] You were observing, sir, that in this age of hypocrisy – something about hypocrisy, sir.
MARLOW	Yes, madam. In this age of hypocrisy, there are few who upon strict inquiry do not – a – a – a –
MISS HARDCASTLE	I understand you perfectly, sir.
MARLOW	[*aside*] Egad! and that's more than I do myself!

(Oliver Goldsmith, *She Stoops to Conquer*)

3   In the following scene the audience knows that Sebastian is Viola's twin brother but because Viola has disguised herself as a man and taken a man's name, Cesario, the characters onstage think Sebastian is Cesario. Olivia has fallen in love with Cesario, and Sir Andrew has challenged him to a duel in the sure belief he is a coward who cannot use a sword. Now read on!

SIR ANDREW	[*to Sebastian*] Now, sir, have I met you again? [*striking him*] There's for you.
SEBASTIAN	[*striking Sir Andrew with his dagger*] Why there's for thee, and there, and there. Are all the people mad?
SIR TOBY	[*to Sebastian, holding him back*] Hold sir, or I'll throw your dagger o'er the house.
FESTE	This I will tell my lady straight, I would not be in some of your coats for twopence. [*Exit.*]
SIR TOBY	Come on, sir, hold.
SIR ANDREW	Nay, let him alone, I'll go another way to work with him. I'll have an action of battery against him if there be any law in Illyria. Though I struck him first, yet it's no matter for that.

SEBASTIAN	Let go thy hand.
SIR TOBY	Come sir, I will not let you go. Come my young soldier, put up your iron. You are well fleshed. Come on.
SEBASTIAN	[*freeing himself*] I will be free from thee. What would'st thou now?
	If thou dar'st tempt me further, draw thy sword.
SIR TOBY	What, what? Nay then I must have an ounce or two of this malapert blood from you.
	[*Sir Toby and Sebastian draw their swords. Enter Olivia.*]
OLIVIA	Hold, Toby, on thy life I charge thee hold.
SIR TOBY	Madam.
OLIVIA	Will it be ever thus? Ungracious wretch,
	Fit for the mountains and the barbarous caves,
	Where manners ne'er were preached – out of my sight!
	Be not offended, dear Cesario.
	[*to Sir Toby*] Rudesby, be gone. [*Exeunt Sir Toby and Sir Andrew.*]
	Let thy fair wisdom, not thy passion sway
	In this uncivil and unjust extent
	Against thy peace. Go with me to my house,
	And hear thou there how many fruitless pranks
	This ruffian hath botched up, that thou thereby
	May'st smile at this. Thou shalt not choose but go.
	Do not deny. Beshrew his soul for me,
	He started one poor heart of mine in thee.
SEBASTIAN	What relish is in this? How runs this stream?
	Or am I mad, or else is this a dream?
	Let fancy still my sense in Lethe steep
	If it be thus to dream, still let me sleep.
OLIVIA	Nay come, I prithee, would thou'dst be ruled by me.
SEBASTIAN	Madam, I will.
OLIVIA	O, say so, and so be.

(*Twelfth Night*: IV i. 23–64)

What does Shakespeare achieve through the use of disguise in this scene?

4   How would you expect the following scene to look onstage? It was written by Christopher Marlowe in about 1592 and is usually, but not always, acted in Elizabethan or medieval costume. Doctor Faustus has sold his soul to the devil, but is now regretting and repenting of it.

FAUSTUS	Ay go, accursed spirit, to ugly hell!
	Tis thou hast damned distressed Faustus' soul
	Is't not too late?
	[*Re-enter the Good Angel and Evil Angel.*]
EVIL ANGEL	Too late.
GOOD ANGEL	Never too late if Faustus can repent.
EVIL ANGEL	If thou repent, devils shall tear thee in pieces.
GOOD ANGEL	Repent, and they shall never raze thy skin [*Exeunt Angels.*]
FAUSTUS	Ah, Christ, my Saviour,
	Seek to save distressed Faustus' soul!
	[*Enter Lucifer, Belzebub and Mephistopheles.*]
LUCIFER	Christ cannot save thy soul, for he is just:
	There's none but I have interest in the same.
FAUSTUS	Oh who art thou that lookst so terrible?
LUCIFER	I am Lucifer,
	And this is my companion prince in hell.
FAUSTUS	O, Faustus, they are come to fetch away thy soul!
LUCIFER	We come to tell thee thou dost injure us;
	Thou talkst of Christ, contrary to thy promise:
	Thou should not think of God, think of the devil,
	And of his dam too.

FAUSTUS	Nor will I henceforth: pardon me in this And Faustus vows never to look to heaven, Never to name God, or to pray to him, To burn his Scriptures, slay his ministers, And make my spirits pull his churches down.
LUCIFER	Do so, and we will highly gratify thee. Faustus we are come from hell to show thee some pastime: sit down and thou shalt see all the Seven Deadly Sins appear in their proper shapes.
FAUSTUS	That sight will be as pleasing unto me, As Paradise was to Adam the first day Of his creation.
LUCIFER	Talk not of Paradise nor creation; but mark this show: talk of the devil, and nothing else. – Come away!

[*Enter the Seven Deadly Sins.*]

Now Faustus, examine them of their several names and dispositions.

FAUSTUS	What art thou, the first?
PRIDE	I am Pride. I disdain to have any parents. I am like to Ovid's flea; I can creep into every corner of a wench; sometimes like a periwig I sit upon her brow; or, like a fan of feathers, I kiss her lips; indeed I do – what do I not? But fie, what a scent is here! I'll not speak another word, except the ground were perfumed and covered with a cloth of arras.
FAUSTUS	What art thou the second?
COVETOUSNESS	I am Covetousness . . .

[*The rest of the Seven Deadly Sins follow in a procession – Wrath, Envy, Gluttony, Sloth and Lechery. They describe the sin they represent to Faustus as they pass.*]

Key to the examples

1 The dramatist uses the Stage Manager as a Chorus and narrator. He introduces the characters to the audience and tells us a little of their background. In this way the audience gets a lot of information that couldn't be shown onstage in this scene. His manner of speaking to the audience is the chatty, gossipy way in which people talk to each other in the street, which helps to give the small town atmosphere and make the audience feel part of it. When Joe goes off, the Stage Manager tells his story up to his death (that is, he moves us into the future). Joe is only a very minor character. Knowing what eventually happens to him gives a sense of a community all leading their lives around the main characters which the play concentrates on. When the Stage Manager concludes 'All that education for nothing' it is a moral comment on the waste of war in the traditional manner of a Chorus. The Stage Manager acts as a guide around the town and a commentator. His presence, along with other techniques such as having only an imaginary black bag and newspapers rather than real ones, means that the audience is continually reminded that they are watching a play. They are not expected to be carried away by the illusion or imagine that the scene on the stage is real.

2 Marlow is incredibly shy. Miss Hardcastle's asides express her astonishment because she has been told that he can be impudent, yet he seems absolutely tongue-tied and she has to finish his sentences for him. She has to keep up a polite, smiling conversation with him but she is really wondering what sort of person he could possibly be. He speaks in a very formal, stilted way and doesn't seem to be able to keep an idea in his head. The asides allow her to show her perplexity and amusement to the audience, while keeping up her polite façade to Marlow. Marlow's aside shows that he knows he is making a fool of himself by being so incapable of conversation. He is able to talk quite normally and naturally to the audience, but not to Miss Hardcastle.

3 Sebastian is mistaken for Cesario by Sir Andrew, who strikes him. Instead of the weakling that he expected he finds a vigorous young swordsman, more than ready to defend himself. In this case the disguise is used to create a humorous situation. The tables are turned. Sir Andrew retreats in alarm and bewilderment at the change and Sir Toby has to defend his friend's honour by taking up the fight. Part of the humour is created by Sebastian not knowing why on earth this person, who seems to think he knows him, should suddenly come up and strike him.

(continued)

(continued)

Olivia also mistakes Sebastian for Cesario. On previous occasions Cesario would not respond at all to Olivia (naturally, since Cesario is really Viola, and a woman). Sebastian behaves quite differently. He can't believe his luck when a beautiful, young and apparently rich woman throws herself at him. He responds with enthusiasm, although he wonders if it is himself or everybody else who has suddenly gone mad. Now it is Olivia's turn to be astonished and delighted. The humour is still in the reactions of the characters to the situation which the disguise has created.

There is another more serious purpose in the use of these disguises. Olivia does not really know what love means. At the beginning of the play she declares that she will mourn for her brother for seven years because she loved him so much, but she falls in love simply with the appearance of Cesario. She has to wait until Sebastian appears for the reality of love. Viola, through her disguise, is able to teach Olivia and other characters in the play the difference between appearance and reality. Disguise is a very convenient technique for the dramatist to use to make this point.

This kind of comedy of situation depends on the audience knowing more than the characters do themselves. This is called **dramatic irony**.

4 The Good Angel and the Evil Angel should be dressed to show their opposing characters – white and black are the obvious colours. They should enter from opposite sides of the stage – the Elizabethans would have put the good one on the right and the bad one on the left (or sinister) side. When Lucifer appears Faustus is terrified, therefore Lucifer must look terrifying, perhaps wearing a mask, or painting his face in lurid colours. He could wear built-up shoes, a high head-dress and hugely padded shoulders, with a long swirling black cloak, to make him seem bigger and taller. He should really come up from below the stage in an explosion of fireworks or smoke. This is how the Elizabethans would have done it: modern productions could use lights and dry ice to get the effect of coming up out of hell. Lucifer and Belzebub are representations of evil and are intended to arouse fear in the audience so that they understand and appreciate Faustus' plight.

The Seven Deadly Sins are conjured up to entertain Faustus. They are agents of the devil and so have to appear exotic and strange but also corrupted and dangerous. They too would have appeared through the trapdoor in a procession, moved around the stage and disappeared again through the trap. Each character passing in front of Faustus should appear repugnant in an appropriate way. Pride might not be disgusting to look at, indeed might be quite dazzlingly dressed, but must be so haughty and arrogant in his manner that the audience despises him. Gluttony, who comes later, could be incredibly fat and all the time he is onstage be stuffing food into his mouth and spilling it down his clothes. Marlowe expected his audience to be fascinated and disgusted. The purpose of showing the spirits of the Seven Deadly Sins was to teach a moral lesson. They are the embodiment of evil, sin personified, to teach the audience to shun evil ways.

▷ SUGGESTIONS FOR COURSEWORK

1 Make a study of one of the following conventions as it is used in a play (or plays) of your choice: disguise, the supernatural, the use of time, the use of Chorus.

2 Compare the ending of a novel with the film or television version. For example, in *Kes* look carefully at the last section where Billy bursts in to confront Jud. Why do you think this is not included in the film? Give reasons for the different emphasis in the film version.

3 Look at the opening of a film version of a novel or play, for example *Great Expectations*, *Henry V*, *Romeo and Juliet*. What do the film versions add to the printed text, and how successful are they in interpreting the originals?

4 Write about a video or stage performance of a play you are studying. Describe what pleased or disappointed you about the performance.

▷ **Coursework task**   Write a review of the BBC video production of *Twelfth Night*.

▷ **Suggested answer**   It is always helpful to see a performance of a play because it brings the text to life. While the BBC production of *Twelfth Night* helped me to understand the nature of the characters and their relationships, I did not find it as exciting or as illuminating as I had hoped.

The costumes were of the late Elizabethan or Jacobean period and the setting was an Elizabethan house and garden. Thus we saw Orsino in the opening scene musing disconsolately in what appeared to be a real room filled with furniture of the period. Similarly we saw Olivia interview Viola in a chamber of the same style and gaze longingly after her through a very real leaded window. These features of the setting encouraged us to regard the action as realistic which, in my opinion, created difficulties because *Twelfth Night* is not a realistic play and we cannot hope to enjoy it if we expect realism. The director had made a great effort to find a suitable actor and actress to play Sebastian and Viola: they really did look as if they might be brother and sister. And yet throughout there was no doubt that Viola was indeed a woman and it was not credible that any of the other characters should truly take her as a man. But of course we are not really expected to believe that she can pass as a man, any more than Shakespeare's audience would really believe that his boy actors were women. We simply accept the dramatic convention of disguise. However, by emphasizing realism in the setting, costume and casting the director made the audience's task of accepting the convention more, not less, difficult.

When it came to the interpretation of the characters I was again somewhat disappointed. The actor playing Orsino gave a convincing portrayal of a self-involved, self-deceiving egoist indulging his own romantic notions but nevertheless someone of sufficient stature to recognize his own errors at the end of the play. Olivia commanded her household as the text suggests and seemed genuinely led from a foolish infatuation with Viola to a substantial love of Sebastian. Yet while these two characters are very prominent in the working out of the plot and the themes of love and deception in the play, they are not as important as Viola or Malvolio, both of whom seemed to me to be inadequate. Viola was played as if everything were a jolly game: after the initial scene when she mourned the death of her brother there was no sense of the difficulties which her love for Orsino gave her and no depth in her sympathy for Olivia. The knot of relationships which she feels is too hard to untie seems to be shrugged off with a smile. This is not Shakespeare's Viola who can educate the other characters into a real understanding of love. Malvolio is equally disappointing. This is a character who should inspire so much dislike and resentment in others that they are prepared to play really destructive tricks on him. His overweening pride and overbearing behaviour must be such that the other characters are cowed by him. We should sympathize at first with their rebellion, as we do when an unjust domination is overthrown. The humour of Malvolio's appearance in yellow stockings and cross gartered is in seeing the proud man made ridiculous. In this production Malvolio at no time appears to have sufficient power or status to excite the reactions from Sir Toby and Maria, Fabian and Feste that are demanded by the text.

▶ EXAMINATION QUESTIONS

If a dramatist uses a particular convention you may find a question on it in the exam. For instance the use of the Chorus in *Henry V* is a notable feature of the play so you could be asked to comment on its role and function. Similar questions could be asked about the Singer in *The Caucasian Chalk Circle* or the Common Man in *A Man for All Seasons*. If there are supernatural characters, such as the witches in *Macbeth*, you could be asked about their effectiveness, or how you would make them convincing on stage. A question on asides, such as those spoken by Puck, might appear as part of a bulleted list. If you are studying a television play, such as *Our Day Out*, or a radio play like *Under Milk Wood* you should expect questions on how effectively the dramatist uses the medium of television or radio.

The following question is about Arthur Miller's use of flashback in *Death of a Salesman*. The extract is a long one, about the length of extract you would be expected to read in an open-book exam. The present-day scene is taking place in a restaurant, where Biff and Happy have gone with their father, Willy, but scenes from the past continually keep interrupting. The first character to speak is someone from the past.

▶ **Question 1**

'MEG. Higher Tier.'

Miller often uses flashback in this play for dramatic effect. How well does it work here for you? Support your viewpoint in detail from the passage.

[*The light of green leaves stains the house, which holds the air of night and a dream. Young Bernard enters and knocks on the door of the house.*]

'When you have read the passage go back and underline or highlight those speeches which are "flashbacks".'

YOUNG BERNARD	[*frantically*] Mrs Loman, Mrs Loman!
HAPPY	Tell him what happened!
BIFF	[*to Happy*] Shut up and leave me alone.
WILLY	No, No! You had to go and flunk math!
BIFF	What math? What are you talking about?
YOUNG BERNARD	Mrs Loman, Mrs Loman! [*Linda appears in the house, as of old.*]
WILLY	[*wildly*] Math, math, math!
BIFF	Take it easy, Pop!
YOUNG BERNARD	Mrs Loman!
WILLY	[*furiously*] If you hadn't flunked you'd've been set by now!
BIFF	Now, look, I'm gonna tell you what happened and you're going to listen to me.
YOUNG BERNARD	Mrs Loman!
BIFF	I waited six hours –
HAPPY	What the hell are you saying?
BIFF	I kept sending in my name but he wouldn't see me. So finally he . . . [*He continues as the light fades low on the restaurant.*]
YOUNG BERNARD	Biff flunked math!
LINDA	No!
YOUNG BERNARD	Birnbaum flunked him! They won't graduate him!
LINDA	But they have to. He's gotta go to university. Where is he? Biff! Biff!
YOUNG BERNARD	No, he left. He went to Grand Central.
LINDA	Grand – You mean he went to Boston!
YOUNG BERNARD	Is Uncle Willy in Boston?
LINDA	Maybe Willy can talk to the teacher. Oh the poor, poor boy! [*Light on house area snaps out.*]
BIFF	[*at the table, now audible, holding up a gold fountain pen*] . . . so I'm washed up with Oliver, you understand? Are you listening to me?
WILLY	[*at a loss*] Yeah, sure. If you hadn't flunked –
BIFF	Flunked what? What are you talking about?
WILLY	Don't blame everything on me! I didn't flunk math – you did! What pen?
HAPPY	That was awful dumb, Biff, a pen like that is worth –
WILLY	[*seeing the pen for the first time*] You took Oliver's pen?
BIFF	[*weakening*] Dad I just explained it to you.
WILLY	You stole Bill Oliver's fountain pen!
BIFF	I didn't exactly steal it! That's just what I've been explaining to you!
HAPPY	He had it in his hand and just then Oliver walked in, so he got nervous and stuck it in his pocket!
WILLY	My God, Biff!
BIFF	I never intended to do it, Dad!
OPERATOR'S VOICE	Standish Arms, good evening!
WILLY	[*shouting*] I'm not in my room!
BIFF	[*frightened*] Dad what's the matter? [*He and Happy stand up.*]
OPERATOR	Ringing Mr Loman for you!
WILLY	I'm not there, stop it!
BIFF	[*horrified, gets down on one knee before Willy*] Dad I'll make good, I'll make good. [*Willy tries to get to his feet. Biff holds him down.*] Sit down now.
WILLY	No, you're no good, you're no good for anything.
BIFF	I am Dad, I'll find something else you understand? Now don't you worry about anything. [*He holds up Willy's face.*] Talk to me Dad.
OPERATOR	Mr Loman does not answer. Shall I page him?
WILLY	[*attempting to stand, as though to rush and silence the operator*] No, No, no!
HAPPY	He'll strike something Pop.
WILLY	No, no . . .
BIFF	[*desperately, standing over Willy*] Pop, listen! Listen to me! I'm telling you something good. Oliver talked to his partner about the Florida idea. You listening? He – talked to his partner, and he came to me . . . I'm going to be all right, you hear? Dad, listen to me, he said it was just a question of the amount.
WILLY	Then you . . . got it?
HAPPY	He's gonna be terrific, Pop!
WILLY	[*trying to stand*] Then you got it haven't you? You got it! You got it!

BIFF	[*agonized*] No, no. Look, Pop. I'm supposed to have lunch with them tomorrow. I'm just telling you this so you know that I can still make an impression, Pop. And I'll make good somewhere, but I can't go tomorrow, see?
WILLY	Why not? You simply –
BIFF	But the pen, Pop.
WILLY	You give it to him and tell him it was an oversight!
HAPPY	Sure, have lunch tomorrow!
BIFF	I can't say that –
WILLY	You were doing a crossword puzzle and accidentally used his pen!
BIFF	Listen, kid, I took those balls years ago, now I walk in with his fountain pen? That clinches it, don't you see? I can't face him like that! I'll try elsewhere.
PAGE'S VOICE	Paging Mr Loman!
WILLY	Don't you want to be anything?
BIFF	Pop, how can I go back?
WILLY	You don't want to be anything, is that what's behind it?
BIFF	[*now angry at Willy for not crediting his sympathy*] Don't take it that way! You think it was easy walking into that office after what I'd done to him? A team of horses couldn't have dragged me back to Bill Oliver!
WILLY	Then why'd you go?
BIFF	Why did I go? Why did I go? Look at you. Look at what's become of you! [*Off left The woman laughs.*]
WILLY	Biff, you're going to that lunch tomorrow, or –
BIFF	I can't go. I've no appointment!
HAPPY	Biff for . . .!
WILLY	Are you spiting me?
BIFF	Don't take it that way! Goddammit!
WILLY	[*strikes Biff and falters away from the table.*] You rotten little louse! Are you spiting me?
THE WOMAN	Someone's at the door, Willy!
BIFF	I'm no good, can't you see what I am?
HAPPY	[*separating them*] Hey, you're in a restaurant! Now cut it out both of you! [*The girls enter.*] Hello girls, sit down. [*The woman laughs, off left.*]
MISS FORSYTHE	I guess we might as well. This is Letta.
THE WOMAN	Willy, are you going to wake up?
BIFF	[*ignoring Willy*] How're ya, miss, sit down. What do you drink?
MISS FORSYTHE	Letta might not be able to stay long.
LETTA	I gotta get up very early tomorrow. I got jury duty. I'm so excited! Were you fellows ever on a jury?
BIFF	No, but I been in front of them! [*the girls laugh.*] This is my father.
LETTA	Isn't he cute? Sit down with us, Pop.
HAPPY	Sit him down, Biff!
BIFF	[*going to him*] Come on, slugger, drink us under the table. To hell with it! Come on, sit down, pal. [*On Biff's insistence Willy is about to sit.*]
THE WOMAN	[*now urgently*] Willy are you going to answer the door! [*The woman's call pulls Willy back. He starts right, befuddled.*]
BIFF	Hey, where are you going?
WILLY	Open the door.
BIFF	The door?
WILLY	The washroom . . . the door . . . where's the door?
BIFF	[*leading Willy to the left*] Just go straight down. [*Willy moves left.*]
THE WOMAN	Willy, Willy, are you going to get up, get up, get up, get up? [*Willy exits left.*]
LETTA	I think it's sweet you bring your Daddy along.
MISS FORSYTHE	Oh, he isn't really your father!
BIFF	[*at left, turning to her resentfully*] Miss Forsythe, you've just seen a prince walk by. A fine and troubled prince. A hard-working unappreciated prince. A pal, you understand? A good companion. Always for his boys.
LETTA	That's so sweet.
HAPPY	Well, girls, what's the programme? We're wasting time. Come on Biff. Gather round. Where would you like to go?
BIFF	Why don't you do something for him?

HAPPY	Me!
BIFF	Don't you give a damn for him Hap?
HAPPY	What're talking about? I'm the one who –
BIFF	I sense it, you don't give a good goddam about him. [*He takes the rolled up hose from his pocket and puts it on the table in front of Happy.*] Look what I found in the cellar, for Christ's sake. How can you bear to let it go on?
HAPPY	Me? Who goes away? Who runs off and –
BIFF	Yeah, but he doesn't mean anything to you. You could help him – I can't. Don't you understand what I'm talking about? He's going to kill himself, don't you know that?
HAPPY	Don't I know it! Me!
BIFF	Hap, help him! Jesus … help him … Help me, help me, I can't bear to look at his face! [*Ready to weep, he hurries out, up right.*]
HAPPY	[*staring after him*] Where are you going?
MISS FORSYTHE	What's he so mad about?
HAPPY	Come on, girls, we'll catch up with him.
MISS FORSYTHE	Say, I don't like that temper of his!
HAPPY	He's just a little overstrung, he'll be all right!
WILLY	[*off left, as The woman laughs*] Don't answer! Don't answer.
LETTA	Don't you want to tell your father –
HAPPY	No, that's not my father, He's just a guy. Come on, we'll catch Biff, and, honey, we're going to paint this town! Stanley, where's the Check! Hey Stanley! [*They exit. Stanley looks toward left.*]
STANLEY	[*calling to Happy indignantly*] Mr Loman! Mr Loman!
	[*Stanley picks up a chair and follows them off. Knocking is heard off left. The woman enters laughing. Willy follows her. She is in a black slip; he is buttoning his shirt. Raw, sensuous music accompanies their speech.*]

 Question 2   This essay discusses how a character who is not 'real' can be presented on stage. It is based on J.B. Priestley's play *An Inspector Calls*.

What kind of a character is Inspector Goole?

EXAMINATION ANSWERS

Question 1   *Notes and tutor's answer*

Notes
1   Read the passage through carefully.
2   Make a list of the different people and events in the flashbacks.
3   Notice the way the past and present events are organized onstage.
4   Make a note of any relationships you can see between past and present events.
5   Decide what the effect of this technique is on the way we see Willy.

Suggested answer

In *Death of a Salesman* Arthur Miller uses the technique of flashback as far more than a means of providing the audience with information about the past. It becomes a device for exploring a character's mind and demonstrating how the past is always a part of the present. In this scene the past and the present are inextricably mixed. The effect is a confusion which shows the confusion in Willy's mind. The purpose is to show some of the causes of Willy and Biff's present relationship and show how their situation is influenced by past events. These events in themselves demonstrate the lifelong traits in Willy's personality which have led him to this crisis.

The scene is set in a restaurant where Willy has gone to meet his boys. Their outing is supposed to be a special treat but it is spoiled by Biff's difficulties with Bill Oliver. Willy feels guilty about Biff's failure to make his proper mark in the world. Scenes from the past arise in Willy's mind. Alongside the scene in the restaurant we see, bathed in green light as though in a dream, the young Bernard trying to tell Linda of Biff's failure in his maths exam. Willy's mind is taken over by these figures from the past who play out the news of the event that caused the division between Willy and Biff. The voices from the past intrude on the present, cutting across Biff's story of his attempt to see Oliver, as though Willy can no longer concentrate on

'Have you written an introduction explaining the purpose of the flashback technique? If not, it should be in your conclusion.'

reality. As Biff insists on telling of his failure with Oliver the past overwhelms the present in Willy's mind, and the figures of Linda and young Bernard take over the stage. Biff's past failure is equated with his present one, if he had not flunked maths everything would have been different.

As Willy struggles back into the present, the lights go out on Linda and Bernard. He has hardly heard what Biff has been saying but for a moment he concentrates on the awful fact that Biff has walked out with, stolen, Oliver's gold pen. His mind cannot hold on to it. As though every dire event in the present forces him deeper into the trauma of past events he now answers aloud the voice of the operator in his head. The progression in Willy's reaction is important in increasing the tension. His sudden inexplicable shout, 'I'm not in my room', forces a reaction from his startled sons, who think he is either ill or mad. Worried for his father Biff backs off from the truth and starts inventing the kind of lying, soothing story they have always told. As Willy becomes calmer in response to this new tale the past recedes and Willy begins to talk coherently, deceiving himself into hope for Biff's future.

Miller is using the flashback to make a clear connection between Willy's need for present optimism and his memory of past failure. The past can only be pushed aside if it seems as though Biff will succeed. Willy is prepared to go on lying to maintain the fiction necessary to keep himself going. Biff is not. When Biff insists on the truth, on reality, the voices return. As Biff turns on Willy the most painful visions begin to take over his mind. The woman's laugh signals the onset of his most dreadful, shameful memories. Her voice is so insistent in his head that it pulls him to his feet and he goes to answer her instruction to open the door. He leaves the stage to Biff, Happy and the visiting girls. The juxtaposition of the arrival of the girls in the present with the woman from the past points to another parallel. Happy too is a failure, a womanizer with no sense of direction. Happy's weakness is also a reflection of Willy's past misdeeds, exaggerated as if in a distorting mirror.

Willy does not hear Biff calling him 'a prince . . . A fine and troubled prince', does not see Biff's concern and love for him. He remains locked in the belief that Biff has thrown away his life for spite. The flashbacks enable Miller to display that troubled mind to us. They indicate that for Willy the past is painfully ever present. He has lived these scenes over and over again; he can no longer push them aside and his grip on reality is slipping. When he finally commits suicide we understand the process that has led him there.

▷ **Question 2**   *Student's answer – examiner's comment*

'Good. Points out the significance of the exact moment the Inspector appears and how this points to him being a non-naturalistic figure.'

'Good. Notices how everything onstage contributes to the effects, from the character's words to the lighting.'

At the beginning of the play Mr Birling is saying that a man should just take care of himself and his family and not other people:

> *A man has to look after himself and he won't come to any harm . . . community and all that nonsense.*

This is the first time we see what is wrong with these people. The Inspector arrives then so stopping him in the middle of this speech, this is significant – as if he just came to set that attitude right and teach them a lesson, this suggests that he wasn't a Police Inspector but had another, special purpose. Mr Birling had just been talking about 'the way these cranks talk', the Inspector could have been a 'crank' – at least in their eyes. Police Inspector Goole then involves the Birlings and Gerald in the murder of Eva Smith. From what we know of Priestley's plays, they all have a message to the whole of society, they criticize the social system, through Inspector Goole his message is effectively portrayed to us all. Priestley cleverly makes him different by what he says and how he acts; we cannot put a class to the Inspector, he acts in a way that creates an impression; he has a way of looking hard at people before he talks to them. Even in the lighting directions it says 'the lighting should be pink and intimate until the Inspector arrives and then it should be brighter and harder.' This shows the Inspector shatters their homely complacent lives.

(continued)

(continued)

Throughout the whole play he creates an atmosphere of strangeness and doubts; he has a cool way of talking and manages to get everything out of the person by not saying very much. They get annoyed with him because he asks questions which they would rather not answer and puts them on their guard with cutting replies. Birling says 'we were having a nice little family celebration tonight . . . and a nasty mess you've made of it now!'

The Inspector replies 'that's more or less what I was thinking at the Infirmary . . . A nice little promising life there, I thought, and a nasty mess someone has made of it.' So how do we answer exactly, the question, 'Who is Inspector Goole?' He doesn't act like a Police Inspector; they don't make moral speeches to the people they are inspecting. They actually found out in the end that he wasn't a real Police Inspector, but the older ones think of realistic alternatives like – he was a practical joker – trying to frame them and just pretending to be a police officer, a hoax, but the younger generation Eric and Sheila are more impressionable and susceptible to change, they sense that he may be something supernatural, they don't know where he comes from but are influenced by what he said. The others try to let themselves out of their responsibility – but there is still a girl dead.

I think we all know that Inspector Goole is not human, but just because of what the Birlings and Gerald did, it's still the same. As Eric said, 'Whoever that chap was, the fact remains that I did what I did . . . it's still the same rotten story whether it's been told to a Police Inspector or to someone else.' The young realize this and have been taught something by the Inspector. This shows the difference between young and old attitudes. Even when they find out that Eva Smith was not dead she could have been, they did the same things to her. The younger ones have learnt to care for everyone and they have responded to Priestley's message, they feel their conscience and guilt. Sheila said 'I behaved badly too. I knew I did. I'm ashamed of it. But now you're beginning all over again to pretend that nothing much has happened.'

'Good. Correctly identifies the dramatist's use of the supernatural connection to make a moral point.'

'This goes back to discussing the reactions of the various characters. It is better to group all points on one issue together, and discuss them in one place.'

Question	Assessment Objective(s)	Pre-20th century	20th century
Coursework task – *Twelfth Night*	1, 4	✓	
1 *Death of a Salesman*	1, 2		✓
2 *An Inspector Calls*	1, 2		✓

SUMMARY

▷ **Conventions** are accepted ways of presenting action, often non-realistically, as with battle scenes or the use of the supernatural.

▷ **Act** and **scene divisions** are used to denote changes in time and place.

▷ **Time** in plays is usually compressed. It can also move from present to past in flashback, or show the future.

▷ A **Chorus** is an accepted way of narrating or commenting on events.

▷ **Disguise** is often used as a way of developing situations.

▷ The **Soliloquy** and the **aside** are ways of letting the audience know what the character is thinking, without the other characters knowing.

▷ Radio and television have their own conventions. They enable the action to move quickly in time and from place to place.

Chapter

10

The plots of plays

GETTING STARTED

Plot is a good word because it suggests a plan, something carefully worked out, and this is exactly what the dramatist does. You have to remember that nothing happens by accident. Everything is the result of deliberate choice by the dramatist. In the world of the play the dramatist has the power of life and death, success and failure, over the characters. Every development, every turn of the plot could have gone the other way if the dramatist had chosen to make it do so. So every action has its function in the whole. This chapter will help you to understand the importance of these significant features of the plots of plays.

The topics covered in this chapter are applicable to all boards.

MEG	NEAB	NICCEA	SEG	LONDON	WJEC	IGCSE	TOPIC		STUDY	REVISION 1	REVISION 2
✓	✓	✓	✓	✓	✓	✓	Drama				
✓	✓	✓	✓	✓	✓	✓	Opening the action				
✓	✓	✓	✓	✓	✓	✓	Constructing the action				
✓	✓	✓	✓	✓	✓	✓	Guessing right and guessing wrong				
✓	✓	✓	✓	✓	✓	✓	Sub-plots				
✓	✓	✓	✓	✓	✓	✓	Humour				
✓	✓	✓	✓	✓	✓	✓	Climax				
✓	✓	✓	✓	✓	✓	✓	Endings				
✓	✓	✓	✓	✓	✓	✓	Themes				

WHAT YOU NEED TO KNOW

▷ **Drama** Think about the word 'drama' and the way we use it in ordinary speech. A man is standing on a ledge high up on a cathedral and threatening to jump. A priest is trying to talk him out of it. The cameras down in the street are trained on the man and a reporter describes the scene for the television news. We would call this a drama. The greatest all-round cricketer in the world comes on to bowl after a two-month suspension. He needs two wickets for the world record. Can he prove his critics wrong? He gets a wicket with his first ball. This too is called drama. Both these incidents, from real life, have the essential ingredients of **suspense, conflict** and **tension**. When studying a scene try to identify these elements so that you can then describe and explain them.

Suspense

The dramatist creates suspense by getting us involved and then keeping us waiting. At its mildest, suspense is wanting to know what happens next. The dramatist must create this level of interest or the audience will just stop watching, stop reading, or not go to see his next play. At its most acute, suspense brings the audience to the edge of their seats hoping that something will or will not happen. Most plays move between a low level of suspense for the greater part of the scenes and a high level at important moments.

Try to decide while you are reading or watching just what it is that the dramatist is doing that keeps the suspense going. One thing may be interest in the characters: this will be dealt with in the next chapter. Another is the situation. When Tony Lumpkin in *She Stoops to Conquer* pretends that his father's house is an inn and directs Marlow there, we know that an interesting situation will develop. We expect Marlow to behave in a quite inappropriate manner towards his future father-in-law because Tony has made him believe he is the landlord of this supposed inn. As expected Marlow behaves quite rudely. The situation creates suspense, in this case humorously, because we wait to see how it will develop and be resolved. Such suspense is not extreme or acute, so it cannot be expected to hold the audience's attention for long. New twists and complications have to be introduced to keep the interest going.

Acute suspense is created when the outcome is very serious and we are kept waiting, not knowing what will happen. Such a situation occurs at the end of *The Devil's Disciple*. Dick Dudgeon, the roguish hero, awaits execution. The rope is around his neck. The hour has begun to strike when his rescuer arrives. The dramatist, Bernard Shaw, has kept his audience waiting until the very last moment, with no clues as to where the rescue will come from.

Acute suspense must be used sparingly. An audience quickly gets tired of such tension. The screw has to be loosened before it can be tightened again, to be effective.

Work out the kind of suspense that the dramatist is using in the plays you are studying. Ask yourself these questions:

▷ Does the situation develop through a whole series of events which create some suspense, but not too much?
▷ Is the suspense acute? If so how long does the dramatist take to build it up?

Conflict

Every drama includes conflict of some sort. Sometimes it is of the literal, physical sort: duels are fought; families feud; battles are waged. Often these battles are expressions of strains or differences between characters which are the subject of the whole play. The subject of *Romeo and Juliet* is the destructive enmity between two clans which is only changed by the death of their children. The enmity is depicted in street brawls, arguments and duels, which are all signs of the conflict. The subject of conflict is so universal that it has been adapted to all sorts of environments. *Look Back in Anger* is about class conflict, but there is no fighting. The conflict takes the form of bitter rows between a husband and wife who come from different social classes.

The conflict need not be so obvious as an argument. Some struggles are silent. Some are so unequal that they seem over before they are begun. In *Hobson's Choice*, when Maggie Hobson decides she wants Will as her husband she sends Will's girlfriend packing in three or four sentences. Poor little Ada Figgins does not stand a chance. Nevertheless there has been a conflict. Some are internal struggles of the mind like John Proctor's in *The Crucible*. His fight is with his own conscience when faced with the choice between death with honour, or signing a false confession of witchcraft.

Whenever a difference of interest occurs between characters, a conflict follows. In **comedy** conflicts are resolved and there is a happy ending. In **tragedy** the conflicts are more difficult and serious and are frequently only resolved by death.

Look for the points of conflict in the plays you are studying, not just the obvious ones but all the subtle and minor ones too. Try to trace how they came about and what they show about the differences of interest between the characters. Ask yourself too if they represent ideas that the dramatist is trying to explore in the play.

Tension

Both suspense and conflict create tension. Tension mounts as we wait to see if Eliza Doolittle will manage to speak properly on her first outing in polite society. Professor Higgins has taught her the correct pronunciation; can she say the right things? It is not a serious scene and nothing vital depends on Eliza getting it right so the tension is not acute. Laughter relieves it at the end of the scene when Eliza sweeps out saying, 'Walk? Not bloody likely!'

Tension of a quite different quality is built up as Macbeth prepares to kill the king, Duncan. We see his reluctance and watch Lady Macbeth urging him on, overcoming his objections, making the plan. We see him again struggling with his conscience. Finally a bell rings, the signal for the murder, and he goes to do the deed. The suspense generated is intense because of the horror of the deed about to be committed. Even those who have never seen or read the play before realize the probable outcome, because of the witches' prophecy, but the enormity of the crime still creates great tension.

Pace

Another aid to tension is **pace**, or the speed at which things happen.

A series of events in swift succession gives a sense of excitement or one of things getting out of control. When Richard III is losing his grip on the country he is given no time to digest one piece of bad news before another messenger arrives telling of a second disaster. A third messenger of doom follows almost immediately.

The pace changes during a play according to the importance of the events, what kind of atmosphere is required, or perhaps what the dramatist wants to show us about the characters involved. A death or a marriage can happen quickly or slowly. Maggie Hobson courts and marries Will in *Hobson's Choice* and Kate is married to Petruchio in *The Taming of the Shrew*, both with relative speed. In neither case is the wedding the important event. After getting married the couples have to sort out their relationship. Kate is gradually tamed and Will is painstakingly taught a sense of his own worth. The pace of these events is much slower than the whirlwind courtships.

On the whole the pace of comedy is faster than that of tragedy. The grave events of tragedy have to be prepared for in long, serious scenes which convey the terrible importance of the events they record. If one dreadful event follows another too quickly we lose the sense of horror and may even begin to laugh.

When you are studying a play look at the way events are spaced out in individual scenes and throughout the play as a whole. Are they coming thick and fast at some points and at other times does it seem that not much is happening? Why is this? What is the effect of the pace on the atmosphere of the play? What does it tell you about the characters and themes of the play?

▷ **Opening the action**

The dramatist has a lot to do in the opening scene. This is the scene which has to catch the audience's attention and arouse interest in the characters and situation, and it has to set things moving so the audience has an idea of what is going to be important in the play.

Shakespeare often opens his plays with a couple of less important characters discussing something which we later realize is important to the theme of the play. *A Midsummer Night's*

Dream begins with Theseus and Hippolyta talking about their forthcoming marriage. Very quickly other characters enter and the conflict between Demetrius and Lysander for Hermia's hand in marriage is introduced. Clearly marriage, and the proper basis for love, is going to be a theme.

Occasionally Shakespeare opens with a piece of really strong dramatic action, like the witches appearing amid thunder and lightning in *Macbeth*, or the storm and shipwreck at the beginning of *The Tempest*. No trouble about catching the attention there.

Look at the opening scene of any play you are studying.

▶ How does it arouse your interest?
▶ Does it introduce major characters?
▶ What major themes does it introduce?

▷ Constructing the action

'If you have made summaries of each scene as you read the play, your own reactions will help you to assess the development of the plot, the use of suspense and the characters' consistency.'

Having set the situation in motion the dramatist now has to find ways of portraying his ideas through action. The more that can be shown in action rather than simply talked about in words the more essentially dramatic it will be. Every action on stage is a sign of something.

One scene must follow another logically so that the audience can see links with what has gone before. The more characters of importance that are involved the more difficult it is. The dramatist has to keep the audience up to date with what everybody is doing, thinking and feeling. Even when there are only two characters the dramatist has to construct his scenes carefully. *Educating Rita* plots the developing relationship between a girl and her Open University tutor. The scenes have to be organized to show the pair's changing behaviour and feelings in a believable and understandable way so that the audience does not lose sympathy with the characters. By the end of the play the girl has changed enormously, but we have seen her changing gradually, each scene charting the progress of her course, so that we understand how the change has come about.

When you are studying a play ask yourself these questions:

▶ Are there strong links between scenes?
▶ How do the links work?
▶ Are the scenes connected by events following on from the previous scene or by developments in feelings or relationships?

▷ Guessing right and guessing wrong

Suspense keeps an audience guessing. Will it happen or won't it? We feel a sense of satisfaction when we have guessed rightly and our expectations are confirmed. The dramatist can also keep our interest by *failing* to fulfil expectations. If we guess wrongly we are surprised and we want to know why we were wrong. We must be given good reasons when this happens or we will feel it is just a cheap trick. When Pastor Anderson rides in to rescue Dick Dudgeon from the gallows at the end of *The Devil's Disciple* it is not what we expect. He is a preacher and earlier in the play he had disappeared, apparently in fear of his life. But when we learn that he went to join the rebels and defeat the British at Springtown it seems consistent with what we know of his character and so we can accept the surprise.

Think about the plays you are studying. Has the dramatist ever surprised you with a development in the plot you didn't expect? If so did you feel it was justified when you thought about it?

▷ Sub-plots

Some plays tell more than one story. Once the main story is under way a second one will be introduced. This is often related thematically to the first. We saw, above, how *A Midsummer Night's Dream* opens with two sets of characters. There is also a third set, Oberon and Titania, who also contribute to the main plot. But then a quite different group appears – uneducated workmen who plan to produce a play for the Duke's wedding. All the other characters are involved in the main story of the lovers: these characters are not, so their story forms a **sub-plot**. A great deal of comedy arises from their efforts to rehearse and perform their play which provides a commentary on love, although they intend to present it seriously. They are also joined to the main plot through the exploits of Bottom, their leader, when Titania, under a spell, falls in love with him. In this way every thread of the story contributes to the central theme.

This degree of unity is unusual, however. Very few modern plays have sub-plots.

Look carefully at the plays you are studying. Do they have sub-plots? If so how are they related to the main plot? And how are they linked to the theme of the play?

▷ Humour

Humour is just as much a product of a developing situation in a play as it is of the words. Some humour is purely verbal but some of the best comedy comes from action. Farce is built completely on the humour of action: characters are discovered where they should not be and escape in the nick of time with their trousers round their ankles and so on. The humour of Titania and Bottom relies on the situation of a beautiful fairy ridiculously in love with an ass. When you are asked to explain or describe the humour in a scene look for the things which are out of place, the mistakes, the accidents in a situation as well as the characters and the language.

▷ Climax

The **climax** is the point towards which all the action moves. There can be several climaxes in a play, but one is usually more important than the others. It does not necessarily have to come at the end, though it frequently does. There is a sense in which the climax of *Macbeth* is the murder of Duncan and the rest of the play a consequence of that act. If you have read *Macbeth* try to decide whether you think Duncan's murder or the defeat and death of Macbeth is the greater climax, and why.

Bernard Shaw is particularly good at ending each act with a resounding dramatic climax. In *Caesar and Cleopatra* Act 1 ends with a terrified Cleopatra being forced to face Caesar for the first time, alone; Act 2 with Caesar rushing off to win a battle; Act 3 with Cleopatra being thrown into the sea; Act 4 with the murder of Cleopatra's nurse and Act 5 with the final parting of Caesar and Cleopatra. Each of these is a very decisive moment and three of them highly exciting and visually striking.

We tend to think of climax as always being of this nature – a very strong dramatic moment – but it is not always so. At the end of Tom Stoppard's *Rosencrantz and Guildenstern Are Dead* the two main characters stand talking about what has happened to them and the lights quietly go out on first one and then the other. Yet this is the climax of the action because it is the point towards which everything has been moving, the culmination of the theme of the play – their 'deaths'.

A climax should show how the situation or conflicts have been, or are going to be resolved. In a comedy the conflicts will be resolved happily. The characters will sort out their problems, the future will look rosy. In a tragedy the only way out of a situation is through suffering, and often death.

Where are the climaxes in the plays you are studying? What kind of climaxes are they?

▷ Endings

When the climax comes at the end of a play it makes a good, neat finish. When it comes before the end, though, what is the rest of the action supposed to do? Often it is used to show how the events of the play have changed those who witnessed them. *Romeo and Juliet* ends like this. The climax is the death of the lovers. The **ending** shows how the families are brought together by the lovers' deaths and how they repent of their previous foolish antagonisms.

At other times endings show how, despite everything that has happened, life is essentially the same. At the end of *A Taste of Honey* Helen comes back to her daughter's flat, kicks Jo's friend out and takes over again just as if she had not left. All that Jo has been through in the intervening months, and the fact that Helen left her to fend for herself, is just pushed aside. Often this point is made by the setting – it is just as it was at the start, showing that nothing has changed.

▷ Themes

The **theme** of a play can be brought out very strongly by the ending. But everything through-out the play can express the dramatist's ideas. The way the plot is shaped, and the way the characters are drawn, reveals the theme. Sometimes those views are so strong that the play gives a definite message. For instance Bertolt Brecht was a Marxist, and his plays are intended to change the audience's ideas about how society should be run.

Many exam questions which ask you about what happens in a play will also ask about ideas. As you read, try to think about what ideas the dramatist is trying to convey. If this seems a little difficult now, do not worry; Chapter 17 on themes and ideas in novels looks at this more closely.

▶ **Additional examples**   You can test your understanding of the ideas in this chapter by reading the passages below and answering the questions on them. This work will help you to answer exam questions. Write down your own ideas first then read the key below.

1   Why is this an effective opening scene?

> [*As the curtain rises Reverend Parris is kneeling beside a bed in prayer. His daughter, Betty Parris, aged ten is lying on the bed, inert ...The door opens, and his Negro slave enters.*]

TITUBA   My Betty be hearty soon?

PARRIS   Out of here!

TITUBA   My Betty not goin' die ...

PARRIS   [*scrambling to his feet in a fury*] Out of my sight! [*She is gone.*] Out of my – [*He is overcome with sobs. He clamps his teeth against them and closes the door and leans against it exhausted.*] Oh my God! [*Quaking with fear, mumbling to himself through his sobs, he goes to the bed and gently takes Betty's hand.*] Betty child, dear child. Will you wake, will you open your eyes! Betty, little one ...

> [*He is bending to kneel again when his niece, Abigail Williams, 17, enters – a strikingly beautiful girl, an orphan with an endless capacity for dissembling. Now she is all worry and apprehension and propriety.*]

ABIGAIL   Uncle? [*He looks at her.*] Susanna Walcott's here from Dr Griggs.

PARRIS   Oh? Let her come, let her come.

ABIGAIL   [*leaning out the door to call to Susanna, who is down the hall a few steps*] Come in Susanna. [*Susanna Walcott, a little younger than Abigail, a nervous, hurried girl, enters.*]

PARRIS   [*eagerly*] What does the doctor say, child?

SUSANNA   [*craning round Parris to get a look at Betty*] He bid me come and tell you, reverend sir, that he cannot discover no medicine for it in his books.

PARRIS   Then he must search on.

SUSANNA   Aye, sir, he have been searchin' his books since he left you, sir. But he bid me tell you, that you might look to unnatural things for the cause of it.

PARRIS   [*his eyes going wide*] No – no. There be no unnatural cause here. Tell him I have sent for Reverend Hale of Beverly, and Mr Hale will surely confirm that. Let him look to medicine and put out all thought of unnatural causes here. There be none.

SUSANNA   Aye, sir. He bid me tell you. [*She turns to go.*]

ABIGAIL   Speak nothin' of it in the village, Susanna.

PARRIS   Go directly home and speak nothing of unnatural causes.

SUSANNA   Aye, sir. I pray for her. [*She goes out.*]

ABIGAIL   Uncle, the rumour of witchcraft is all about; I think you'd best go down and deny it yourself. The parlour's packed with people, sir. I'll sit with her.

PARRIS   [*pressed, turns on her*] And what shall I say to them? That my daughter and my niece I discovered dancing like heathen in the forest?

ABIGAIL   Uncle, we did dance; let you tell them I confessed it – and I'll be whipped if I must be. But they're speakin' of witchcraft. Betty's not witched.

PARRIS   Abigail, I cannot go before the congregation when I know you have not opened with me. What did you do with her in the forest?

ABIGAIL   We did dance, uncle, and when you leaped out of the bush so suddenly, Betty was frightened and then she fainted. And there's the whole of it.

PARRIS   Child, sit you down.

ABIGAIL   [*quavering as she sits*] I would never hurt Betty. I love her dearly.

PARRIS   Now look you, child, your punishment will come in its time. But if you trafficked with spirits in the forest I must know it now, for surely my enemies will, and they will ruin me with it.

'When asked about "dramatic interest" look for conflict, suspense, tension, climax and interesting points about character.'

| ABIGAIL | But we never conjured spirits. |
| PARRIS | Then why can she not move herself since midnight? This child is desperate! |

(Arthur Miller, *The Crucible*)

2   What would you say is the dramatic interest in the following scene?

GRUSHA	I won't give him away. I've brought him up and he knows me. [*Enter Shauva with the child.*]
THE GOVERNOR'S WIFE	It's in rags!
GRUSHA	That's not true. I wasn't given the time to put on his good shirt.
THE GOVERNOR'S WIFE	It's been in a pigsty.
GRUSHA	[*furious*] I'm no pig, but there are others who are. Where did you leave your child?
THE GOVERNOR'S WIFE	I'll let you have it, you vulgar person. [*She is about to throw herself on Grusha, but is restrained by her lawyers.*] She's a criminal! She must be whipped!
THE SECOND LAWYER	[*holding his hand over her mouth*] Most gracious Natella Abashvili, you promised . . . Your worship, the plaintiff's nerves . . .
AZDAK	Plaintiff and defendant! The court has listened to your case, and has come to no decision as to who the real mother of the child is. I as judge have the duty of choosing a mother for the child. I'll make a test. Shauva get a piece of chalk and draw a circle on the floor. [*Shauva does so.*] Now place the child in the centre. [*Shauva puts Michael, who smiles at Grusha, in the centre of the circle.*] Stand near the circle, both of you. [*The Governor's Wife and Grusha step up to the circle.*] Now each of you take the child by the hand. The true mother is she who has the strength to pull the child out of the circle, towards herself.
THE SECOND LAWYER	[*quickly*] High court of justice, I protest! I object that the fate of the Abashvili estates, which are bound up with the child as the heir, should be made dependent on such a doubtful wrestling match. Moreover my client does not command the same physical strength as this person, who is accustomed to physical work.
AZDAK	She looks pretty well fed to me. Pull! [*The Governor's Wife pulls the child out of the circle to her side. Grusha has let it go and stands aghast.*]
THE FIRST LAWYER	[*congratulating the Governor's Wife*] What did I say! The bonds of blood!
AZDAK	[*to Grusha*] What's the matter with you? You didn't pull!
GRUSHA	I didn't hold on to him. [*She runs to Azdak.*] Your worship, I take back everything I said against you. I ask your forgiveness. If I could just keep him until he can speak properly. He only knows a few words.
AZDAK	Don't influence the court! I bet you only know twenty yourself. All right I'll do the test once more, to make certain.

[*The two women take up positions again.*]

| AZDAK | Pull! |

[*Again Grusha lets go the child.*]

| GRUSHA | [*in despair*] I've brought him up. Am I to tear him to pieces? I can't do it. |
| AZDAK | [*rising*] And in this manner the court has established the true mother. [*to Grusha*] Take your child and be off with it. I advise you not to stay in town with him. |

(Bertolt Brecht, *The Caucasian Chalk Circle*)

Key to the examples

1   The first task of an opening scene is to arouse interest. This scene does that by showing Betty motionless on the bed, with Parris and Tituba afraid that she might die. This raises one question in our minds but an even stronger question is posed by the reaction of the other characters to the nature of Betty's illness. They do not seem merely to be grieving but are in a panic. There is tremendous tension in Parris' fear: he calls on God, pleads with Betty to wake and almost strikes Tituba in his fury. What has happened to make him like this? When Susanna Walcott comes to say the doctor can discover no medicine for it in his books, some explanation for their fear is given, but further questions are raised when Susanna says they might have to look for unnatural causes.

(continued)

(continued)

> This seems to be the root of Parris' fear as he immediately denies the possibility of such a thing and Susanna is sworn to silence. Abigail makes clear that she is frightened of being accused of witchcraft and, when we learn that she and Betty have been discovered dancing in the forest, we begin to wonder what they have been up to and what the consequences will be.
>
> This is a very effective opening scene because it immediately creates suspense through the condition of Betty and the fear of Parris and Abigail. The mention of witchcraft, which excites our curiosity, introduces an issue of major importance in the play. It also introduces two major characters, Parris and Abigail, and shows us from the beginning Parris' fearful and intolerant nature. The scene is tense with the characters' strong emotions.
>
> 2   The dramatic interest in this scene lies chiefly in the conflict between the Governor's Wife and Grusha over the child. There is suspense as we wait to see the way the judge's decision will go. The test shows us the contrasting characters of the two sides, and this relates to the theme of the play.
>
> Any trial is a conflict, and here we see Grusha is determined to fight to keep the child. The battle is not just a legal one because the Governor's Wife insults Grusha and is about to attack her until she is restrained by her lawyers. When Azdak announces the test of the chalk circle – a surprising way of deciding the case – this seems to favour Grusha, but to our amazement she simply lets the child go and does not pull. Even with a second chance she cannot do it. It seems her case is lost. In another twist, Azdak declares that this has determined her to be the true mother, the one who cares most for the child. The Governor's Wife is rich, supercilious, surrounded by attendant lawyers who pamper her. They are clearly unscrupulous about how she secures her right to benefit from the great Abashvili estates that the child is heir to. Grusha, on the other hand, is poor but caring and straightforward. Our sympathy is with Grusha and our interest is maintained by the desire to see her win.
>
> The characters represent two classes of society and, in making Grusha the winner, the playwright brings the argument of his play to a conclusion and demonstrates the principle he believes in. Grusha gains the child because she is a properly caring person. This illustrates the theme that things must belong to those who are most fitted for them.

▷ SUGGESTIONS FOR COURSEWORK

1   Having studied a Shakespeare play, watch the animated version on television. Use the simplified version to make a step-by-step summary of the plot and a short list of the themes. Write down those parts of the play the animators have left out. Discuss whether or not they were right to do so.

2   Select a comic scene from a play you are studying. Make a list of the serious issues raised in the scene. Show how the comedy brings these serious issues home to the audience.

3   As a character in one of your chosen plays write a letter to a friend describing what happened in the final act or scene and your feelings about the way in which the play ended. Comment on how pleased or disappointed you were.

4   Write about conflict in a play, or plays, you are studying. Choose at least two scenes which include different kinds of conflict. Explain the nature of each conflict, the point of view of the characters involved, its significance for the rest of the play, where your sympathies lie.

5   Compare two plays with sub-plots and discuss how these relate to the main plot (see Coursework Task).

6   Some playwrights have written alternative endings to their plays, Arthur Miller in *A View from the Bridge* for example. Re-write the final scene of a play you are studying.

▷ **Coursework task A**

Compare the sub-plots of *The Merchant of Venice* and *A Midsummer Night's Dream*.

▷ **Outline answer**

1   **Introduction.** The sub-plot in *The Merchant of Venice* is the story of Jessica and Lorenzo, her lover. It is a parallel story to that of Portia and Bassanio and contributes to the themes of love and generosity which are developed in the play. Jessica also casts further light on the character of Shylock and gives an alternative picture of a Jew.

2   **Describe the scenes** which concern Jessica and Lorenzo, bringing out the following points:

Act 2 Scene 3. Jessica's criticism of her father; Launcelot's relationship with Jessica; Jessica's intention to marry Lorenzo and become a Christian.

Act 2 Scene 4. Lorenzo's feelings about Jessica and Shylock. Their plans.

Act 2 Scene 5. Shylock's treatment of Jessica.

Act 2 Scene 6. Jessica's flight. Lorenzo's description of her (wise, fair, true).

Act 3 Scene 1. Shylock's discovery; his feelings about his daughter and his ducats.

Act 3 Scene 4. The trust shown by Portia in Lorenzo and Jessica by leaving them in charge of Belmont.

Act 3 Scene 5. The views on Christians and Jews; the jesting comparison that Lorenzo makes between himself and Portia.

Act 5 Scene 1. The love between Lorenzo and Jessica and the sense of harmony and concord.

3   **Conclusion.** *The Merchant of Venice* is a play about giving and taking. Antonio gives to his friend Bassanio and risks his life. Bassanio understands that he must 'give and hazard all' he has in order to win Portia. Portia gives her all to Bassanio as well as giving him back his friend. Shylock, on the other hand, only lends out money at great interest for his own benefit and hates Antonio because he 'lends out money gratis'. He is even prepared to take Antonio's life. It is his mean-minded grasping hatred that makes him the villain of the play. The play states there are other Jews who are not like him and Jessica provides a contrast to Shylock. She puts her love of Lorenzo above everything. Her profligate spending of Shylock's wealth shows her contempt for his values. Her love is 'unthrifty': she, like Antonio, Bassanio and Portia, does not count the cost. Jessica and Lorenzo are rewarded with a love that brings them peace. They participate in, and contribute to the great scene of harmony at Belmont at the end of the play.

4   **Introduction.** *A Midsummer Night's Dream* has in fact three stories that are closely interwoven. The main story concerns the difficulties of two pairs of lovers. The sub-plot tells about the preparation of a play for performance at Theseus' wedding by a group of workmen. The third story, that of Oberon and Titania, king and queen of the fairies, affects the other two stories and links them together.

5   **Describe the scenes** in which Bottom and the mechanicals appear, bringing out the following points:

Act 1 Scene 2. The character of the mechanicals and the nature of the play they intend to perform.

Act 3 Scene 1. Their difficulties with the presentation of the play; Puck's spell on Bottom and Titania's reaction.

Act 4 Scene 1. Bottom's behaviour with the fairies; Titania's and then Bottom's reactions when awakening from the spell.

Act 5 Scene 1. The performance of the play, particularly the lovers Pyramus and Thisbe, and the reactions of the court.

6   **Conclusion.** One of the principal objects of this sub-plot is to create humour and it is able to do this through the character of the mechanicals, their difficulties in staging the play, their simplicity and directness in performance which contrasts with the sophistication of the court. At the same time the sub-plot contributes to the general themes of the play. Like the lovers Bottom is transformed by the power of Puck's spell and mistakenly becomes the object of Titania's love. Like them he feels on waking to have been subject to a strange bewitchment. The play of Pyramus and Thisbe is also a comic commentary on the other love stories. Just as the other lovers' difficulties are resolved by a little witchery and common sense so the tragedy of the deaths of Pyramus and Thisbe is cancelled by the comic presentation and Bottom's determination that nobody shall be upset by anything. Bottom earnestly insists that everyone must understand what is reality and what is only pretending.

7   **General conclusion.** In both these plays the sub-plots add an extra dimension which enriches the texture and broadens the argument. They are not simply additional stories for they deepen the discussion of the themes of each play by exploring further situations relevant to the central ideas of the main plots.

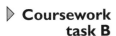 ▷ **Coursework task B**   *A Taste of Honey.* Imagine that Jo has had her baby and that several weeks have passed. Write a new ending to the play showing how the characters are coping with the situation.

▷ **Notes** This type of question gives an excellent opportunity to express a thorough knowledge and a sensitive understanding of the play:

i) by putting the characters in a situation that fits in with the original play;

ii) by giving them dialogue which the original characters might have used – look carefully at the play and try to imitate the language; and

iii) by allowing the scene to express the same ideas and themes as the original.

▷ **Suggested answer**

Act 2 Scene 3: *Blackout after Scene 2. Music – the fairground music of the earlier scene, slowed down so that it is sad and discordant. Slowly this is drowned by the sound of a baby crying, which becomes insistent as the lights go up. The stage is exactly the same as at the end of the last scene, except for a frilly pink cot sitting incongruously in the middle of the floor. Jo is still leaning against the doorpost, though clearly she is no longer pregnant. Helen is sitting on the couch, flicking through a magazine and smoking.*

HELEN Why don't you do something about that noise?

JO What do you suggest, suffocation?

HELEN You could feed her.

JO I've only just fed her. And patted her on the back two hundred times until she gave vent ...

HELEN She did what?

JO Gave vent to her feelings. Burped to you. Do you know the stomach used to be thought of as the seat of our emotions? Geoff told me that. [*The baby is still crying.*]

HELEN Oh did he now. Well it's a pity he didn't tell you how to stop a kid from bawling or I might have to give vent to *my* emotions. I don't believe it ever stops. At least not while I'm around. Perhaps it's cause and effect.

JO She doesn't like the smoke.

HELEN What?

JO Your cigarette smoke. She doesn't like it. She always starts to cry on the third cigarette.

HELEN Oh don't be ridiculous. I never had any bother when you were an infant.

JO No? I dare say I was drugged by the alcohol in your bloodstream. The only baby in Salford to be reared on whisky.

HELEN You're disgusting. In any case I hardly touched a drop in those days. I could do with one now though. [*She gets up and fetches the whisky bottle from the kitchen.*]

JO You've only just got back from the pub.

HELEN Right, and I'm likely to be going back there if you don't stop it wailing. I can't stand it. That noise goes right through me. Perhaps it needs its nappy changing.

JO [*going to the cot, which is an elaborate, swinging type, and giving it a little push*] I've just changed her. I've done everything a conscientious mother who's read all the right books could possibly think of.

HELEN Then rock her to sleep or something. The hand that rocks the cradle ...

JO Rules the world. Yes I know. Then *you'd* better rock her since you're the bossy one around here.

HELEN [*happier with the whisky*] I'll ignore that. I could sing her a lullaby [*singing loudly as she waltzes around*] Who's sorry now,

Who's sorry now,

Whose heart is aching

For breaking each vow. [*The baby roars.*]

JO [*screaming*] Shut up Helen. And put your cigarette out, or go and smoke on the landing like I do. [*A knock on the door finally makes itself heard. Jo opens it, revealing Geoff clutching a bunch of flowers.*]

HELEN Oh look what the cat brought in.

JO Geoff! Hello!

GEOF Hello. Are you all right? There was a lot of noise. Can I come in?

HELEN Why not. One more in this mad house won't make much difference and we're in need of a nursemaid.

GEOFF [*to Jo*] I just came to see if you and the baby were OK.

JO Mother and baby are both doing well, relatively. Only Grandma isn't too happy.

HELEN Don't call me Grandma. I've told you before.

GEOFF What sort is it? I mean is it a boy or a girl?

HELEN Well it's not one of your sort, you can be sure of that.

JO	It's a girl. Her name's Miranda.
GEOFF	That's pretty. [*He is standing by the cot gently rocking it.*]
HELEN	Miranda! Did you ever hear the like. She won't half get teased when she gets to school with a handle like that.
JO	[*to Geoff*] I got it out of a book. One of those you left.
GEOFF	[*taking a small parcel from his sack*] I didn't know what to bring her so I made her this. [*He unwraps a home-made mobile.*]
JO	What is it?
GEOFF	If you hang it up here she can watch it turning in the breeze. [*The baby, unremarked, has been quiet for some time.*]
HELEN	Oh my God, Doctor What's-his-name the Second! Well, since you two are so happy round the crib, I think I'll just pop off for a bit. Where's my hat?
JO	Where you left it. In the kitchen. [*Helen goes into the kitchen, returns with the hat and stands in front of the mirror carefully arranging her hair and applying her lipstick.*]
HELEN	There, how do I look? Not bad for a woman of thirty. [*Jo snorts.*]
JO	Where are you going?
HELEN	To see a man about a dog. [*She goes out.*]
JO	I've heard that before, but no dog ever materialized.
GEOFF	Will she be long?
JO	Who's to say? I'm not privy to Helen's affairs – and affairs is the right word. Would you like some tea?
GEOFF	I wouldn't mind. Shall I put the kettle on?
JO	Why not? You know where everything is.
GEOFF	[*going to and fro with tea things*] I brought some cake. [*He stops.*] Were you all right Jo?
JO	[*grinning*] Sure. Easy as swallowing an oyster.
GEOFF	I bet you've never had an oyster.
JO	You're right. It was all right though.
GEOFF	I told you it would be. [*They are sitting on the couch drinking tea.*]
JO	OK Mr Know-all. Have you finished your exams?
GEOFF	Yes, I've got a job in a photographer's until the beginning of next term.
JO	Touching up pictures of naked ladies.
GEOFF	Don't be silly Jo. [*silence*] Is it all right then if I stop for a bit?
JO	How long do you have in mind?
GEOFF	Till Helen gets back.
JO	Judging from past performance that might be some time.
GEOFF	So is it all right?
JO	I don't mind.

▷ EXAMINATION QUESTIONS

You may be asked a question about:

▶ an opening or closing scene;
▶ dramatic tension or climax;
▶ or simply what makes a scene interesting or enjoyable.

You should always try to say how the actions of a scene bring out ideas important to the whole play.

Right from the beginning of most plays there are ideas and issues which become important later on. You may be asked about what expectations the early pages of a play set up for you and how these are developed later in the play. You could be asked about how tension is created by the use of a particular dramatic effect, such as darkness in *Macbeth*.

▷ **Question 1**
'Foundation Tier.'

Several scenes from *A Man for All Seasons* show Sir Thomas More with his family. Choose one of these scenes and say what it adds to your enjoyment of the play.

▷ **Question 2**
'Higher Tier.'

This question on *The Merchant of Venice* asks the student to look at the progress of the plot in order to discuss reaction to one character. 'In our feelings about Shylock we swing as the play progresses between sympathy and disgust; between dislike and admiration.' Drawing your evidence from as many occasions as possible, show clearly why and for what reasons your own feelings for Shylock vary.

EXAMINATION ANSWERS

▷ Question 1   *Notes and tutor's answer*

Notes

1 I have chosen to answer this question using the scene in which More's family visit him in jail.
2 There are numerous things which can make a scene enjoyable. Different people are likely to make different choices. The answer below is based on my own response to the scene. What is important is that you base your opinion firmly on what is happening in the text.
3 Jot down the important aspects of the scene which seem to you to make it enjoyable. Here are my notes:
    – contrast of characters;
    – argument with Meg – resolved;
    – uprightness of More;
    – conflict with Alice – resolved;
    – family affection.
4 As you write your answer use details from the scene to illustrate the enjoyable aspects you have chosen.

Suggested answer

'Have you clearly stated in your introduction what it is that adds to your enjoyment? If not, it should be in your conclusion.'

The enjoyment of the scene in which More's family visit him in jail comes from the contrast in the characters of More, Meg and Alice, contrasts which cause tensions and conflict. Much of our pleasure derives from the interplay of the characters and the resolution of the conflicts, which represent the choices that More has to make.

Thomas is overjoyed to see his family, especially Meg, though briefly alarmed that she might have been imprisoned too. This is what he fears: that his family may suffer harm because of the stand he has taken. The conflict that we see in this scene is over the place of his family in his scale of values. First, however, he has to combat Meg's arguments.

Meg, who is under oath to try to persuade More to swear to the Act of Succession, is constrained as she unpacks the basket of food they have brought him. Her father is a formidable opponent in argument and she knows that she is setting herself against his most deeply held convictions. Nevertheless she feels bound to try to alter his mind: his life depends on it. It is the vital consequences that give this conversation between More and his daughter its dramatic tension. As she seeks to persuade him to speak the words of the oath but believe otherwise in her heart we sympathize with both his position and hers. She loves her father and desires him to live above all. He knows he cannot live with a bad conscience about a deed which would rob him of his self-respect. He must do what is right even at the risk of making himself a martyr or a hero.

Even in this most dire of circumstances, More enjoys wrestling intellectually with his daughter and is proud of her ability to advance compelling arguments. We share his enjoyment of this intellectual battle, and we derive satisfaction from More's victory. Meg concedes out of love for her father and admiration for the honour and truth of his position. If More had departed from that position we, the audience, would have been shocked and disappointed. Part of our pleasure is in the spectacle of a man who can stand out for what he believes is good and right against all the odds. We are ennobled by his nobility.

More's conflict with his wife, Alice, is of a different nature. She is stiff and hostile, refusing to understand why he leaves his family alone when a mere signature would return him to them. When More begins to compliment her on her cooking and her dress she bursts out in anger. She feels that he belittles her in thinking such things are important to her at such a time. More begs for her understanding of his refusal to sign but she refuses to lie about what she feels. Where Meg's appeal was through reason, Alice's is through feeling. More is heart-rent but will not yield. Having failed to move him Alice repents and goes to comfort her husband.

The intricacies of argument are beyond her, and do not interest her, but she knows that More is the best man she has ever met or is ever likely to. Her forgiveness means that More can go to his death, if necessary, more easily, assured of his family's love. The coming together of Alice and More is a very touching moment, especially because their affection has so far been hidden.

When the jailor comes to remove them the family is united. They have accepted More's instruction to flee the country – Alice with her usual truculence – and we are left with a sense of strong family affection and an increased admiration for the uprightness of Sir Thomas.

▷ **Question 2**   *Student's answer – examiner's comment*

'Good. Looks carefully at words used in the beginning of the play and states their effect on the audience. This begins to answer the question set.'

It is indeed true that as I progress through the play, The Merchant of Venice, *my feelings for Shylock vary tremendously. In parts it is portrayed he is, in fact, a humane man, like any other; whereas in other parts, one is forced to wonder how such a man could be classed as 'human'. Shylock's opening speech in the play immediately causes me to dislike him, for he deliberates purposely, on consenting to Bassanio's request, and he leads Bassanio to the point of begging for a loan of money. The word 'well', uttered several times in his speech, emphizes his deliberate hesitation:*

> *Three thousand ducats; well?*

He seemingly delights in seeing his enemy plead for his help. Then Antonio, the one who wishes to borrow some money, enters, and Shylock talks spitefully of him to himself; thus succeeding in increasing my dislike of him. He says:

> *I hate him for he is a Christian.*

'Good. Notes how Shakespeare shifts our sympathy, by giving Shylock's own point of view.'

However, this dislike gradually changes to an understanding of him, and then sympathy, as the reason for Shylock's spitefulness becomes clear. It is apparent that Antonio, as well as being unnecessarily unkind to Shylock, lends out money free of charge, and so destroys Shylock's business as a money lender. He also destroys Shylock's pride, when insulting his Jewish religion, so it is no wonder that Shylock bears a grudge against him. He says of Antonio:

> *You call me misbeliever, cut-throat dog,*
> *And spit upon my Jewish gaberdine,*

'Points to a second shift of sympathy, i.e. the essay is moving carefully through the plot, just as the question requires.'

The sympathy, therefore, arises when it can be understood that Shylock has a job to do that he cannot help but do, in order to earn a living: and he also has a religion which he takes great pride in, and I admire him for that. So it seems unjust that Antonio should destroy this and so treat him. However, this sympathy does not last long, for it can be perceived that Shylock is cunningly planning revenge towards the end of their meeting. Only Bassanio notices this, and says:

> *I like not fair terms and a villain's mind.*

'This is a major part of the action, but it is only mentioned briefly.'

'The discussion of Launcelot is confused. The question is leading the student to strain after points that are not really there.'

When Launcelot comes on the scene, he comically talks of leaving Shylock. Once again I feel sympathetic, that nobody likes Shylock. However, this feeling is almost immediately contrasted with dislike, for Launcelot then goes on to tell his father of how ill-treated he is in Shylock's service. He says:

> *I am famished in his services;*
> *You may tell every finger I have with my ribs.*

'This answer is incomplete. It does not cover the whole of the action. The rest of the answer should go on to discuss Shylock's reaction to Jessica's flight and, most importantly, the trial scene.'

Question	Assessment Objective(s)	Pre-20th century	20th century
Coursework task A – The Merchant of Venice/A Midsummer Night's Dream	1, 2, 3	✓	
Coursework task B – A Taste of Honey	1, 2, 4		✓
1 A Man for All Seasons	1		✓
2 The Merchant of Venice	1, 4	✓	

SUMMARY

▷   To hold the interest of the audience the dramatist uses **suspense**, **conflict** and **tension**.

▷   The **opening scene** should:

– catch the attention of the audience;

– introduce the characters;

– introduce the major themes of the play.

▷   As the action progresses the audience's attention is held by **developing relationships** or **situations** which express the underlying ideas.

▷   The **pace** at which events happen is important for atmosphere and theme.

▷   If a play contains a **sub-plot**, or second story, it usually contributes to the main theme of the play.

▷   **Humour** is a product of situation as much as of character or language.

▷   The **climax** is the critical point towards which the action moves.

▷   **Endings** show how things have changed or how they must remain the same.

Character in plays

▷ **GETTING STARTED**

More questions are asked about characters and their relationships than any other topic. A great deal of the material in the previous chapters is useful in helping you to understand character. This chapter will help you specifically to look for character points in what characters say and do and how they relate to each other. Always remember, though, that characters are not real people, although a good dramatist may make them seem so. They are inventions, and our knowledge of them is strictly limited to their words and actions in a few scenes. You should try to make notes on each major character as you read. If you do this from the beginning you will be able to record how your impressions of a character develop as the play progresses.

The topics in this chapter are applicable to all exam boards.

MEG	NEAB	NICCEA	SEG	LONDON	WJEC	IGCSE	**TOPIC**	STUDY	REVISION 1	REVISION 2
✓	✓	✓	✓	✓	✓	✓	Actions			
✓	✓	✓	✓	✓	✓	✓	What characters say			
✓	✓	✓	✓	✓	✓	✓	Character consistency			
✓	✓	✓	✓	✓	✓	✓	Characters of convenience			
✓	✓	✓	✓	✓	✓	✓	Symbolic characters			
✓	✓	✓	✓	✓	✓	✓	Characters' names			
✓	✓	✓	✓	✓	✓	✓	Contrasting characters			

WHAT YOU NEED TO KNOW

▷ **Actions**   Just as with real people, we know and understand characters through their actions. When we go to see a play we see how the characters behave. When we read the same play we have to imagine that behaviour from the stage directions. This is one of the reasons why it is so important to learn to read a play effectively, as Chapter 8 explained. A great deal of the character of Billy Fisher is portrayed in the action described in these stage directions from *Billy Liar*:

> [BILLY *hums to himself and then turns on the seat and takes up a garden cane. He toys with the cane for a moment, attempting to balance it on his fingers. His humming grows louder and he stands and conducts an imaginary orchestra using the cane as a baton. He is humming a military march and he suddenly breaks off as the garden cane becomes, in his imagination, a rifle. He shoulders the cane and marches briskly down the garden path.*)
>
> BILLY (*marching*)   Lef', ri', lef', ri', lef'-ri'-lef'! Halt! (*He halts.*) Order arms! (*He brings the cane down to the 'Order' position.*)
>
> *He pauses for a moment and the garden cane becomes, in his imagination, an officer's baton which he tucks under his arm, and then he marches smartly off to an imaginary saluting base a few paces away. He has become, in his imagination, a major-general.*

We know from this that Billy is a dreamy, imaginative person who can easily lose himself in his thoughts. The world inside his head is often more real than the world outside, so much so that he often confuses imagination with reality. We can see how this might lead to trouble for him. In his imaginary world he sees himself in important positions – a conductor or a major-general – so we understand how he would like to be important and not just a very ordinary young man in a humdrum job in a small town. What we learn here is strengthened throughout the play by other actions and by words.

Some actions which display character can be suggested by the dialogue, as in this scene at a critical moment when Macbeth faces the prospect of battle with the English army.

> MACBETH   Throw physic to the dogs; I'll none of it.
> [*to an attendant*] Come, put mine armour on. Give me my staff.
> Seyton, send out. Doctor, the thanes fly from me.
> [*to an attendant*] Come sir, dispatch. – If you could'st, Doctor, cast
> The water of my land, find her disease,
> And purge it to a sound and pristine health,
> I would applaud thee to the very echo,
> That should applaud again. [*to an attendant*] Pull't off, I say.
> [*to the doctor*] What rhubarb, senna, or what purgative drug
> Would scour these English hence? Hear'st thou of them?
> DOCTOR   Ay, my good lord. Your royal preparation
> Makes us hear something.
> MACBETH   [*to an attendant*]   Bring it after me.
> I will not be afraid of death and bane
> Till Birnam forest come to Dunsinane.

Macbeth instructs his servant to put on his armour. He is impatient, telling the servant to hurry when he says, 'Come, sir, dispatch.' A moment later he contradicts himself and tells the servant to pull it off. However he needs to be armed because as he goes out he tells the servant to bring the armour after him. All during these actions he is talking to the Doctor, half about his wife's illness and half about the English. He is clearly in a turmoil, abusing the Doctor, 'Throw physic to the dogs', speaking roughly to the servant and deciding first one thing and then another. His physical actions mirror his state of mind, unable to concentrate on one subject and prepare for the coming battle. It is a complete contrast to the picture we had of him at the beginning of the play.

Macbeth's actions, at this point in the play, add to the knowledge we have of him from other actions at other times. We build up our awareness of a character from his or her actions throughout the play.

When you have read a scene summarize the characters' actions. Then say what they tell you about the characters.

▷ **What characters say**

There are three ways in which we learn about characters from the dialogue of the play:

   i)   what they say about themselves;
   ii) what other characters say about them;
   iii) the kind of language they use.

True and false self-descriptions

What characters say about themselves need not necessarily be true. Just as with people we have to judge the characters' words alongside other evidence. When Owen Glendower says, in *Henry IV Part I*:

> I can call up spirits from the vasty deep

it shows that he believes himself to be a man endowed with unusual, mysterious powers. What he claims may not be true, in fact Hotspur obviously thinks it isn't because he answers:

> Ay, so can I and so can any man, but will they come when you call them?

Hotspur's speech also tells us something about himself: that he doesn't believe in spirits and he thinks that Glendower is talking pretentious poppycock.

Let us look at two occasions when Lady Macbeth speaks about herself. In the first, when she is persuading Macbeth to murder Duncan she says, about a baby at her breast:

> I would, when it was smiling in my face
> Have plucked my nipple from its boneless gums
> And dashed its brains out

She is characterizing herself as a most cruel and heartless woman. Are we to believe this? She certainly does organize a cruel and heartless deed – Duncan's murder. Later, however, she says:

> Had he not resembled
> My father as he slept, I had done it

She could batter a baby in her imagination, but could not in reality kill a man because he looked like her father. This suggests she cannot be quite as cruel as she at first described herself, not quite as heartless as it was necessary to be. It is not surprising that she later breaks down.

Remarks on each other

Characters make many remarks about each other. Again we have to decide whether to believe them on the basis of other evidence in the play.

In Bill Naughton's *Spring and Port Wine* Arthur turns on his future father-in-law:

ARTHUR   But you want to crush the spirit out of everybody who doesn't agree with you. You
           know what you are, Mr Crompton?
FLORENCE   Be quiet, Arthur.
ARTHUR   You're a bully.

We know this is true because we have just seen Mr Crompton bullying the son to the point where it brings on one of his fits, and the whole play grows out of his attempts to bully his daughter into eating a herring when she didn't want to. Arthur only puts into words what we already know.

In *A Taste of Honey* Jo says this about her mother:

JO   I won't set eyes on her for a week now. I know her when she's in the mood. What are you
     going to do about me, Peter? The snotty-nosed daughter? Don't you think I'm a bit young to
     be left on my own while you flit off with my old woman?

We have already seen enough of Helen's behaviour to believe that she is quite capable of neglecting her daughter to this extent. Jo's words tell us that Helen is a feckless and irresponsible person 'when she's in the mood'. We are not surprised when she goes off and leaves Jo to fend for herself and we are ready to believe that this has been a regular occurrence throughout Jo's life.

The truth but not the whole truth

Characters may tell the truth about each other but they cannot tell the whole truth. When Hamlet kills Polonius by mistake he calls him a 'wretched, rash, intruding fool'. Polonius is all those things, and Hamlet is particularly justified in saying them because Polonius was hiding behind a curtain, eavesdropping, in the bedroom of Hamlet's mother. Yet this judgement misses out other, better aspects of Polonius' character. For instance he is an affectionate father, loved by his children. We have to weigh up *all* the evidence.

Conflicting opinions

Sometimes a dramatist deliberately allows opinions about a character to conflict. Maggie Hobson's sisters think Will Mossop a poor specimen of a man. From what we see of him in the first act we would agree with them. Maggie disagrees: she sees Will's potential and by the end of the play it is her opinion which is shown to be right.

Lies

Characters may also lie about each other. This may be for their own devious reasons. In *Twelfth Night* Sir Toby lies to Viola when he tells her Sir Andrew is an excellent swordsman. He does it to goad Viola into a fight, not knowing she's really a woman in disguise and this is just the thing to put her off. The audience knows the truth about both characters. When characters lie the audience is usually told quite clearly: to mislead the audience is disorientating.

What have you learnt about the characters from their own and others' words?

Use of language

Every time characters speak, no matter what the subject, we are told something about them by the kind of language they use. A very simple example is Cliff in *Look Back in Anger*. The playwright makes him say 'boyo' from time to time, so we know he is a Welshman. What we find out about Cliff's friend Jimmy Porter from the way he talks is much more complicated. He boasts of his working-class origins but his language is anything but that of an ordinary working man. It is full of images and flights of imagination. Even the length of the sentences show the extent of his education and subtlety of his mind.

JIMMY   There is no limit to what the middle-aged mummy will do in the holy crusade against ruffians like me. Mummy and I took one quick look at each other, and, from then on, the age of chivalry was dead. I knew that to protect her innocent young, she wouldn't hesitate to cheat, lie, bully and blackmail. Threatened with me, a young man without money, background or even looks, she'd bellow like a rhinoceros in labour – enough to make every male rhino for miles turn white, and pledge himself to celibacy. But even I underestimated her strength. Mummy may look over-fed and a bit flabby on the outside, but don't let that well-bred guzzler fool you. Underneath all that, she's armour plated –

If we had no other information to go on we could tell from this speech that Jimmy was an aggressive young man, with a grievance against the middle class. This language is witty, sarcastic, colourful and deliberately vulgar. Jimmy uses it as a weapon.

The extent to which we judge character from speech is the whole basis of *Pygmalion*. Eliza Doolittle will remain a common flower-girl as long as she talks like this:

Ow, eez ye-ooa san, is e? Wal, fewd dan y'dooty bawmz a mather should, eed now bettern to spawl a pore gel's flahrzn than ran awy athaht pyin.

This is Bernard Shaw's way of representing Eliza's dialect. In other words: 'Oh he's your son, is he? Well, if you'd done your duty by him as a mother should, he'd know better than to spoil a poor girl's flowers and then run away without paying.' With Professor Higgins' help she learns to speak differently and becomes a lady. As her speech changes people begin to see her differently and treat her differently. It seems that it is not just her speech but her whole character that changes so that by the end of the play she is unable to return to her former life.

What is distinctive about the way the characters speak in the plays you are studying?

▷ **Character consistency**

Despite the fact that we see characters in only a few situations in a play we often come to feel we know them as real people. We forget they are inventions and begin to imagine what they would do in other situations. A good dramatist can do this because what the character is given to say and to do, as well as the manner of speech, all chime together as a believable whole. Everything Joan does and says in *St Joan*, for example, is consistent with her country origins and her simple, sincere courage. Her manner of speech is that of a blunt, country girl:

> Coom, Bluebeard! Thou canst not fool me. Where be Dauphin?

she says on her arrival at court. Everything else she says and does, however extraordinary, has the mark of a plain, uneducated girl applying her common sense to the situation. Therefore we believe in her.

This does not mean that characters do not surprise us with their words and actions. They do. Yet even as we are being surprised we must understand why the dramatist has made them do it and see clues to their behaviour in earlier scenes. At the end of *Spring and Port Wine* Mr Crompton suddenly stops bullying his family and starts letting them behave more as they please. However we are shown that he was far more aware of his family's feelings and desires all the time, and that it was elements of his own experience which prevented him from being softer on them.

When we cannot see the reasons behind a character's change of behaviour it seems unreal, a dramatist's failure or trick, and we criticize the playwright for not drawing consistent characters.

▷ **Characters of convenience**

Even great dramatists do not draw all their characters in depth. Some characters have different functions, within the scheme of the play. Some characters merely provide the right sense of place, situation or atmosphere. These can range from the spear-carriers in battle scenes to the townsfolk occupying the graveyard alongside Emily in *Our Town*, or those shouting abuse at Stockman in *An Enemy of the People*. Some are there simply to help the plot along, like messengers. Some have a single characteristic because they have only one function in the plot. Lady Macduff is characterized well but simply as a mother. She appears in the play just to be killed by Macbeth, to give us an example of Macbeth's cruelty and to give Macduff a personal motive for revenge.

If you remember that the dramatist brings in each character to do a job you will have fewer difficulties with characterization. Even major characters who have been skilfully drawn sometimes have to drop out of character and speak in a purely functional way because the dramatist has a piece of the plot that has to be got across to the audience.

▷ **Symbolic characters**

Some characters are never intended to be seen as realistic representations of people. They stand for ideas. The Seven Deadly Sins in *Doctor Faustus* are this kind of character. Few characters are so obviously symbolic as that, but they have a symbolic aspect. The Inspector in J. B. Priestley's *An Inspector Calls* is such a character. He is not a real police inspector, as the other characters realize by the end of the play; he has come to show them what their moral responsibilities are. He is a modern representation of conscience.

▷ **Characters' names**

The names given to characters sometimes show their dominant characteristic, or what they stand for. Here are a few examples of characters whose names give them away: Justice Shallow, Joseph Surface, Lydia Languish, Sir Antony Absolute, Tony Lumpkin. In modern plays such names are thought inappropriate. Nevertheless some names can be very apt, like Willy Loman in *Death of a Salesman*. He is just an ordinary, little man. This is what he finds so difficult to accept. He dreams of big success – the American Dream. (His brother, Ben, is another symbolic figure representing the fulfilment of those dreams.) Willy Loman is a very real, well-developed character but he has a symbolic aspect too, signalled by his name. He stands for every ordinary man.

Have you come across any symbolic characters or characters with significant names?

▷ **Contrasting characters**

Quite often you will find two characters in a play who form a deliberate contrast. Take Maggie and her sisters in *Hobson's Choice* or Kate and Bianca in *The Taming of the Shrew*.

Bianca is ladylike, sweet tempered and pliant, making Kate's tempestuous and uncontrollable nature seem worse by comparison. Maggie Hobson's firm, mature and decisive behaviour appears particularly outstanding beside her two rather ineffectual and conventional sisters. In both these cases the playwright has used contrast to highlight the character of his heroine. Shakespeare puts contrast to further use by turning the tables at the end: Kate becomes the contented wife, comparing favourably with her sister.

Contrasts need not last for the whole play. Similar characters can be shown reacting differently to certain situations. Macbeth and Banquo are initially shown as very similar in position and courage. The King praises them both for their bravery and loyalty. After the meeting with the witches they are seen to diverge. Banquo remains loyal; Macbeth becomes enmeshed in the evil consequences of his ambitions. Banquo is used first as a comparison and then a contrast to Macbeth, to show how he could and should have reacted to the witches' prophecies.

Character contrasts are usually made for a purpose: ask yourself what that purpose is. Usually they tell you something about the themes and ideas of the play.

▷ **Additional examples**

Use the passages below to test your understanding of what you have read in this chapter. Write down your own ideas before reading the key below.

What do we learn about the characters in the following extracts?

1   BIRLING   We shall be along in a minute now. Just finishing.

    INSPECTOR   I'm afraid not.

    BIRLING   [*abruptly*] There's nothing else y'know. I've just told you that.

    SHEILA   What's all this about?

    BIRLING   Nothing to do with you, Sheila. Run along.

    INSPECTOR   No, wait a minute, Miss Birling.

    BIRLING   [*angrily*] Look here, Inspector, I consider this uncalled for and officious. I've half a mind to report you. I've told you all I know – and it doesn't seem to me very important – and now there isn't the slightest reason why my daughter should be dragged into this unpleasant business.

    SHEILA   [*coming in further*] What business? What's happening?

    INSPECTOR   [*impressively*] I'm a police inspector, Miss Birling. This afternoon a young woman drank some disinfectant, and died, after several hours of agony, tonight in the Infirmary.

    SHEILA   Oh – how horrible! Was it an accident?

    INSPECTOR   No. She wanted to end her life. She felt she couldn't go on any longer.

    BIRLING   Well, don't tell me that's because I discharged her from my employment nearly two years ago.

    ERIC   That might have started it.

    SHEILA   Did you, Dad?

    BIRLING   Yes. The girl had been causing trouble at the Works. I was quite justified.

    GERALD   Yes, I think you were. I know we'd have done the same thing. Don't look like that, Sheila.

    SHEILA   [*rather distressed*] Sorry! I just can't help thinking about this girl – destroying herself so horribly – and I've been so happy tonight. Oh I wish you hadn't told me. What was she like? Quite young?

                    (J. B. Priestley, *An Inspector Calls*)

2   JACK   [*astounded*] Well . . . surely. You know that I love you, and you led me to believe, Miss Fairfax, that you were not absolutely indifferent to me.

    GWENDOLEN   I adore you. But you haven't proposed to me yet. Nothing has been said at all about marriage. The subject has not even been touched on.

    JACK   Well . . . may I propose now?

    GWENDOLEN   I think it would be an admirable opportunity. And to spare you any possible disappointment, Mr Worthing, I think it only fair to tell you quite frankly beforehand that I am fully determined to accept you.

    JACK   Gwendolen!

    GWENDOLEN   Yes, Mr Worthing, what have you got to say to me?

    JACK   You know what I have got to say to you.

    GWENDOLEN   Yes, but you don't say it.

    JACK   Gwendolen, will you marry me? [*goes on his knees*]

GWENDOLEN	Of course I will, darling. How long you have been about it! I'm afraid you have had very little experience in how to propose.
JACK	My own one, I have never loved anyone in the world but you.
GWENDOLEN	Yes, but men often propose for practice. I know my brother Gerald does. All my girl-friends tell me so. What wonderfully blue eyes you have, Ernest! They are quite, quite, blue. I hope you will always look at me just like that, especially when there are other people present.

[*Enter Lady Bracknell.*]

LADY BRACKNELL	Mr Worthing! Rise, sir from this semi-recumbent posture. It is most indecorous.
GWENDOLEN	Mamma! [*He tries to rise; she restrains him.*] I must beg you to retire. This is no place for you. Besides Mr Worthing has not quite finished yet.
LADY BRACKNELL	Finished what, may I ask?
GWENDOLEN	I am engaged to Mr Worthing, mamma. [*They rise together.*]
LADY BRACKNELL	Pardon me, you are not engaged to anyone. When you do become engaged to someone, I, or your father should his health permit him, will inform you of the fact. An engagement should come on a young girl as a surprise, pleasant or unpleasant, as the case may be. It is hardly a matter she could be allowed to arrange for herself . . . And now I have a few questions to put to you Mr Worthing. While I am making these enquiries, you, Gwendolen, will wait for me below in the carriage.
GWENDOLEN	[*reproachfully*] Mamma!
LADY BRACKNELL	In the carriage, Gwendolen! [*Gwendolen goes to the door. She and Jack blow kisses to each other behind Lady Bracknell's back. Lady Bracknell looks vaguely about as if she could not understand what the noise was. Finally turns round.*] Gwendolen, the carriage!
GWENDOLEN	Yes, mamma. [*She goes out, looking back at Jack.*]
LADY BRACKNELL	[*sitting down*] You can take a seat, Mr Worthing. [*looks in her pocket for notebook and pencil*]
JACK	Thank you, Lady Bracknell, I prefer standing.
LADY BRACKNELL	[*pencil and notebook in hand*] I feel bound to tell you that you are not down on my list of eligible young men, although I have the same list as the dear Duchess of Bolton has. We work together, in fact. However I am quite ready to enter your name, should your answers be what a really affectionate mother requires. Do you smoke?
JACK	Well, yes, I must admit I smoke.
LADY BRACKNELL	I am glad to hear it. A man should always have an occupation of some kind. There are far too many idle men in London as it is.

(Oscar Wilde, *The Importance of Being Earnest*)

Key to the examples

1   Mr Birling is a hard-nosed business man. He feels quite justified in sacking a young woman from his works because he sees her as a trouble-maker. He feels no responsibility for her welfare and totally rejects the suggestion that his action had any bearing on her later distress, or was in any way the cause of her suicide. The horrible nature of her death does not seem to affect him, or change his attitude in the least. He seems incapable of sympathy. His manner with the Inspector is overbearing and self-important. He loses his temper easily when it seems that his authority is questioned.

Birling is supported in his attitude by Gerald, who takes the same view of a worker and seems, at this point, to be just as unfeeling as Birling. However Sheila and Eric respond differently. Eric believes that his father's action in dismissing the girl might well have started her on the path to despair. By taking this view Eric shows he has a greater imaginative grasp of how things affect people, and a greater sense of social responsibility. Sheila is very upset by the appalling manner of the girl's death and immediately relates the girl's experience to her own. While Sheila was enjoying herself the girl was suffering. Sheila's question, 'What was she like? Quite young?' shows her immediate identification with the girl as somebody very like herself. Her sympathy is immediate and strongly felt. Her feelings are that, had things been different, it could have been herself in that position.

Throughout, the Inspector is calm, matter-of-fact, and totally in charge.

(continued)

(continued)

2   These characters are not naturalistic in the way that those in the previous passage are. The dramatist's purose is to present social types and manners in order to mock them. They are caricatures rather than characters.

Jack is the eligible young man about town, but serious, innocent and out of his depth with women. He is presented as devoted to Gwendolen, and is nervous, socially inept, and unsure of what to do in this situation. He speaks haltingly and has to be prompted into proposing. Gwendolen is a very assured young lady. She is determined to have a proper proposal, with Jack on his knees. She betrays no emotion, except satisfaction at the way Jack admires her, which she hopes will be publicly displayed. Her manner is brisk and businesslike.

The relationship between Jack and Gwendolen is not a naturalistic one. They do not behave like real lovers. Their courtship is a mockery of the conventional forms of courtship between men and women of their class at the time the play was written (1894). This is shown in the way that Gwendolen states quite openly that she intends to accept Jack, but nevertheless expects him to go through the performance of getting down on his knees. It is all an elaborate little game. People like her brother do it often for practice. There is a suggestion that Jack should have practised too. Gwendolen stands for all the fashionable young women of the time and Jack for all the rich young bachelors who allowed themselves to be bamboozled by them.

Similarly Lady Bracknell stands for the upper-class mother with a marriageable daughter, determined to acquire a husband of the right class for her. Gwendolen's desires are of no account. Lady Bracknell takes formidable command of the situation as she prepares to question Jack. It is in Lady Bracknell's remarks that Wilde's mockery of society is clearest because her statements are extreme, silly and comic. Wilde phrases them to be clever and funny rather than to sound as if a real person is speaking. No one in reality would say, 'Rise, sir, from this semi-recumbent posture' but it makes a wonderful line for an actress to bellow as she stands erect in exaggerated horror at the door. And no one would regard smoking as a man's 'occupation'. It is examples like this, throughout the speech of all the characters, which give this play its life and its point.

> 'Do not think that "caricature" is always bad and "real" is always good.'

▷ **SUGGESTIONS FOR COURSEWORK**

1   Choose two characters from a play, preferably 'paired' characters such as Macbeth and Lady Macbeth, Oberon and Titania, Jimmy Porter and Alison. Each character writes a letter to a friend, complaining about the behaviour and attitude of the other.

2   Write the conversation which two characters from different plays might have had if they had ever met. For example Yosser Hughes in *Boys from the Blackstuff* and Willie Mossop in *Hobson's Choice* or Jo in *A Taste of Honey* and Raina in *Arms and the Man*. Yosser and Willie could discuss the problems of employment while Jo and Raina could talk about their feelings about men.

3   Introduce a character of your own devising into a scene from a play you are studying. Rewrite that scene to include dialogue for your new character.

4   Write about a character you dislike in a particular play. Then *either*: discuss how that character could be removed from the play, showing the changes this would cause; *or*: describe the ways in which you could expand the character's role. Say what effect this would have on the play as a whole.

5   Make a study of a character as seen by two different dramatists, for example Joan in Bernard Shaw's *St Joan* and Jean Anouilh's *The Lark* or Shakespeare's *Henry VI*, where she is called La Pucelle; Cleopatra in Shaw's *Caesar and Cleopatra* and Shakespeare's *Antony and Cleopatra*. You could also compare Richard III in Shakespeare's play *Richard III* with the same character in Josephine Tey's detective novel *The Daughter of Time*.

6   Write a comparison of two similar characters in different plays; for example Maggie in *Hobson's Choice* and Fanny in *Hindle Wakes*.

7   Write the diary of a character.

▷ **Coursework task**   *The Importance of Being Earnest.* As we know Gwendolen keeps her diary with her in order to 'have something sensational to read on the train'. Write one or more extracts from Gwendolen's diary.

▷ **Notes**   1   Look at the scenes in which Gwendolen appears. Show your knowledge of the play by including appropriate details from these scenes.

2   Look at the kind of language given to Gwendolen and try to imitate it.

3   Show your understanding of the character by inventing details but do not stray too far from the original.

▷ **Suggested answer**

Thursday 5pm. To tea with cousin Algernon, where we unexpectedly found Mr Ernest Worthing. Mamma having withdrawn with Algernon to discuss the music for next Saturday's reception I took the occasion of a tête-à-tête with Mr Worthing to encourage him to make the declaration which I fully expected him to make by next Saturday at the latest. Since he began by talking about the weather I had to advise him to make haste and take advantage of Mamma's absence for she has an unfortunate habit of returning unexpectedly. I have been well aware of Mr Worthing's admiration for me ever since we met, although his behaviour in public has been somewhat disappointing, hardly leading anyone to notice and remark on the constancy of his devotion, though I am sure that can be remedied in future with a little instruction. My brother Gerald affords an admirable example of what is to be expected from a young man towards the beloved object of his affections. For my own part I was able to tell Mr Worthing of the irresistible fascination that I feel for him, and the fact that I was far from indifferent to him even before we met because he bears the name Ernest. The poor dear boy seemed quite amazed that his name could inspire such confidence and indeed he seems quite out of touch with the idealism of the times. In fact he inexplicably proposed 'Jack' as a suitable alternative, a horribly dull name in which I can find no thrill.

I am afraid my darling boy has very little experience in how to propose. He said quite suddenly that we must be married at once when the subject had not even been touched on in the proper manner. In order to spare him any disappointment I of course made it quite clear that I was intending to accept, yet it was fully a minute before he embarked on the correct procedures. Although it was unfortunate that Mamma interrupted before Mr Worthing was quite finished it was nevertheless gratifying that both she and Algernon should witness the end of our little scene and the outcome was very satisfactory. Ernest has wonderfully blue eyes and I shall insist that he always gazes at me in public in just the way that he did this afternoon.

Of course Mamma insisted that I go down and wait in the carriage while she interviewed dear Ernest. The story of his romantic origins that she relayed to me has stirred me deeply. Until today I was quite unaware of the wonderful mystery of his parentage, in fact his whole history reminds me of one of my favourite three volume novels. To be found in the cloakroom of Victoria Station displays quite amazing originality, particularly in one so young. And, although I am sure that Ernest, even as an infant, would never stoop to mere materialism, to choose as his benefactor a gentleman of such considerable means as Mr Cardew shows a perspicacity that augurs well for our future. Indeed Ernest grows more interesting by the minute. However I fear from Mamma's looks that Ernest and I may never be married. Whoever I do marry, and however many times I marry, I shall always be eternally devoted to Ernest. I am only thankful that we have an excellent postal service. I have his address in the country and shall communicate with him daily. The desperate steps which may be necessary to effect our union are already taking shape in my mind. I could, if the need arises, absent myself from the next lecture of the University Extension Scheme. There is, I believe, a good train service to Hertfordshire.

The weather today has been charming.

▷ EXAMINATION QUESTIONS

More questions are asked about character, development and relationships than any other type of question. If you have made proper notes on each scene as you have gone along you will find it much easier to revise and then to answer questions on the development of character and relationships. Other kinds of question that are asked about character include: what are their attitudes, what are their motives, whether you sympathize with them. You may be asked to put yourself in a character's shoes and write as though you were that character.

▷ **Question 1**

A View from the Bridge is written for the stage. Write an account of the events in the following passage as if it is an extract from a novel, so that you can bring out what the characters are thinking and feeling. You may write as one of the characters if you wish.

CATHERINE	[*flushed with revolt*] You wanna dance, Rodolpho?
	[*Eddie freezes.*]
RODOLPHO	[*in deference to Eddie*] No, I – I'm tired.
BEATRICE	Go ahead, dance, Rodolpho.
CATHERINE	Ah, come on. They got a beautiful quartet, these guys. Come.
	[*She has taken his hand and he stiffly rises, feeling Eddie's eyes on his back, and they dance.*]
EDDIE	[*to Catherine*] What's that, a new record?
CATHERINE	It's the same one. We bought it the other day.
BEATRICE	[*to Eddie*] They only bought three records. [*She watches them dance; Eddie turns his head away. Marco just sits there, waiting. Now Beatrice turns to Eddie.*] Must be nice to go all over in one of them fishin' boats. I would like that myself. See all them other countries?
EDDIE	Yeah.
BEATRICE	[*to Marco*] But the women don't go along, I bet.
MARCO	No, not on the boats. Hard work.
BEATRICE	What've you got, a regular kitchen and everything?
MARCO	Yes, we eat very good on the boats – especially when Rodolpho comes along; everybody gets fat.
BEATRICE	Oh, he cooks?
MARCO	Sure, very good cook. Rice, pasta, fish, everything.
	[*Eddie lowers his paper.*]
EDDIE	He's a cook, too! [*looking at Rodolpho*] He sings, he cooks ...
	[*Rodolpho smiles thankfully.*]
BEATRICE	Well it's good, he could always make a living.
EDDIE	It's wonderful. He sings, he cooks, he could make dresses ...
CATHERINE	They get some high pay, them guys. The head chefs in all the big hotels are men. You read about them.
EDDIE	That's what I'm sayin'.
	[*Catherine and Rodolpho continue dancing.*]
CATHERINE	Yeah, well, I mean.
EDDIE	[*to Beatrice*] He's lucky, believe me. [*Slight pause. He looks away, then back to Beatrice.*] That's why the water front is no place for him. [*They stop dancing. Rodolpho turns off the phonograph.*] I mean like me – I can't cook, I can't sing, I can't make dresses, so I'm on the water front. But if I could, if I could sing, if I could make dresses, I wouldn't be on the water front. [*He has been unconsciously twisting the newspaper into a tight roll. They are all regarding him now; he senses he is exposing the issue and he is driven on.*] I would be someplace else. I would be like in a dress store. [*He has bent the rolled paper and it suddenly tears in two. He suddenly gets up and pulls his pants up over his belly and goes to Marco.*] What do you say, Marco, we go to the bouts next Saturday night. You never seen a fight, did you?
MARCO	[*uneasily*] Only in the moving pictures.
EDDIE	[*going to Rodolpho*] I'll treat yiz. What do you say, Danish? You wanna come along? I'll buy the tickets.
RODOLPHO	Sure. I like to go.
CATHERINE	[*goes to Eddie; nervously happy now*] I'll make some coffee, all right?
EDDIE	Go ahead, make some! Make it nice and strong. [*Mystified, she smiles and exits to kitchen. He is weirdly elated, rubbing his fists into his palms. He strides to Marco.*] You wait, Marco, you see some real fights here. You ever do any boxing?
MARCO	No, I never.
EDDIE	[*to Rodolpho*] Betcha you have done some, heh?
RODOLPHO	No.
EDDIE	Well, come on, I'll teach you.
BEATRICE	What's he got to learn that for?
EDDIE	Ya can't tell, one a these days somebody's liable to step on his foot or sump'm. Come on. Rodolpho, I show you a couple of passes. [*He stands below table.*]
BEATRICE	Go ahead, Rodolpho. He's a good boxer, he could teach you.

RODOLPHO   [*embarrassed*] Well, I don't know how to – [*He moves down to Eddie.*]

EDDIE   Just put your hands up. Like this, see? That's right. That's very good, keep your left up, because you lead with the left, see, like this. [*He gently moves his left into Rodolpho's face.*] See? Now what you gotta do is you gotta block me, so when I come in like that you – [*Rodolpho parries his left.*] Hey, that's very good! [*Rodolpho laughs.*] All right, now come into me. Come on.

RODOLPHO   I don't want to hit you, Eddie.

EDDIE   Don't pity me, come on. Throw it, I'll show you how to block it. [*Rodolpho jabs at him, laughing. The others join in.*] 'Ats it. Come on again. For the jaw right here. [*Rodolpho jabs with more assurance.*] Very good!

BEATRICE   [*to Marco*] He's very good!

[*Eddie crosses directly upstage of Rodolpho.*]

EDDIE   Sure, he's great! Come on, kid, put sump'm behind it, you can't hurt me. [*Rodolpho, more seriously, jabs at Eddie's jaw and grazes it.*] Attaboy. [*Catherine comes from the kitchen, watches.*] Now I'm gonna hit you, so block me, see?

CATHERINE   [*with beginning alarm*] What are they doin'?

[*They are lightly boxing now.*]

BEATRICE   [*she senses only the comradeship in it now*] He's teachin'; he's very good!

EDDIE   Sure, he's terrific! Look at him go! [*Rodolpho lands a blow*] 'At's it! Now, watch out, here I come, Danish! [*He feints with his left hand and lands with his right. It mildly staggers Rodolpho. Marco rises.*]

CATHERINE   [*rushing to Rodolpho*] Eddie!

EDDIE   Why? I din't hurt him. Did I hurt you, kid? [*He rubs the back of his hand across his mouth.*]

RODOLPHO   No, no, he didn't hurt me. [*to Eddie with a certain gleam and a smile*] I was only surprised.

BEATRICE   [*pulling Eddie down into the rocker*] That's enough, Eddie; he did pretty good though.

EDDIE   Yeah. [*rubbing his fists together*] He could be very good, Marco. I'll teach him again. [*Marco nods at him dubiously.*]

▷ **Question 2**   Read the following passage and answer the questions beneath it.

LADY MACBETH   How now, my lord? Why do you keep alone,
Of sorriest fancies your companions making,
Using those thoughts which should indeed have died
With them they think on? Things without all remedy
Should be without regard: what's done is done.

MACBETH   We have scotched the snake, not killed it:
She'll close, and be herself, whilst our poor malice
Remains in danger of her former tooth.
But let the frame of things disjoint, both the worlds suffer,
Ere we will eat our meal in fear, and sleep
In the affliction of these terrible dreams
That shake us nightly. Better be with the dead,
Whom we to gain our peace, have sent to peace,
Than on the torture of the mind to lie
In restless ecstasy. Duncan is in his grave;
After life's fitful fever he sleeps well;
Treason has done his worst: nor steel, nor poison,
Malice domestic, foreign levy, nothing,
Can touch him further.

LADY MACBETH   Come on;
Gentle my lord, sleek oe'r your rugged looks;
Be bright and jovial among your guests tonight.

MACBETH   So shall I, love, and so, I pray, be you.
Let your remembrance apply to Banquo;
Present him eminence, both with eye and tongue:
Unsafe the while, that we
Must lave our honours in these flattering streams,
And make our faces vizards to our hearts,
Disguising what they are.

LADY MACBETH	You must leave this
MACBETH	O full of scorpions is my mind, dear wife,
	Thou know'st that Banquo, and his Fleance, lives.
LADY MACBETH	But in them nature's copy's not eterne.
MACBETH	There's comfort yet, they are assailable;
	Then be thou jocund. Ere the bat hath flown
	His cloistered flight, ere to black Hecate's summons
	The shard-borne beetle with his drowsy hums
	Hath rung night's warning peal, there shall be done
	A deed of dreadful note.
LADY MACBETH	What's to be done?
MACBETH	Be innocent of the knowledge, dearest chuck,
	Till thou applaud the deed.

What do you learn of Macbeth from this passage? What sort of relationship is shown between Macbeth and Lady Macbeth in this passage?

▷ **Question 3** In *Arms and the Man* Bernard Shaw uses his characters to discuss ideas on love and war. Show what the characters learn about these things during the course of the play.

 EXAMINATION ANSWERS

▷ **Question 1** *Notes and tutor's answers*

Notes

1 When you watch a play you rely on the actors to show you the feelings of the characters through their actions and their voices. When you re-write a scene as if it is an extract from a novel you must try to provide these feelings yourself through description. You have the advantage that you can tell us directly what the character is thinking which, most of the time, the dramatist cannot do.

2 Follow the stage directions carefully. They give you the basis of the action.

3 Show your knowledge of the rest of the play by including details where appropriate. You do not have to tell the whole story.

4 The following answer is written in the present tense, that is as if it were happening now. You do not have to do this. You can write in the past tense, which is actually easier because we are more used to stories being told in the past tense.

5 The answer is not written in the voice of one of the characters. The question says you can write as one of the characters if you wish but you do not have to do so.

Suggested answer

They are sitting all together in the apartment again. The little family who have been so close for so many years and the two intruders. It was an act of charity to shelter the two illegals, and no more than one would be expected to do for a member of the family, however distant, but already Eddie is regretting that they ever came.

It is evening and dinner is over. Catherine and Rodolpho are not going to the movies tonight. Eddie is grateful for that, but the sight of the boy, slender, with his bright blonde hair and his strange, easy, outgoing manner, is difficult to bear. The tension in the room is heavy. Catherine, rebellious against the disapproval of her uncle, puts 'Paper Doll' on the gramophone so that they can dance. Rodolpho is reluctant to excite any more animosity in Eddie but Catherine is inviting him with love in her eyes and he cannot refuse her. Even the record seems to annoy Eddie: what is the boy doing buying records? They are here to earn money to send back to their families, aren't they? Does he think he'll be here forever? The boy dances stiffly, feeling Eddie's resentment, but Catherine is defiant. However much she loves her uncle she must be allowed to live her own life. She sways in time to the music, young, attractive, a woman now. Eddie, unable to watch, turns his head away and Marco, his eyes always on Eddie, waits, aware of the tension in the man's body and the struggle in his mind. Only Beatrice seems at ease, chattering about the unfamiliar life in Italy, the boats they worked on, when there was work. When Rodolpho was on the boat he did the cooking, for there were no women, the work was too hard. Eddie cannot believe it: what kind of a man is this? He sings, high as a woman sometimes. He made a dress for Katie, as well as a woman could. And now it seems he cooks like a woman. What kind of a man is this? Some kind of punk who has come to take his little girl away when he has slaved and gone without for her sake for nearly twenty years. And now she has become so beautiful she is to be taken away from him by this boy who is no kind of man at all. He can hear what the women say, talents like Rodolpho's are useful, he can earn his living with them. But not in the proper way, not like he does on the waterfront. Something is boiling up inside him that is bound to come out. As he mangles the newspaper in his hands he feels his fingers itch to slap the boy's face, to beat him cleanly with his fists and show him who is the better man. Now the idea is in his mind and he is excited with it. They can go to the bouts next Saturday. He will treat them. He will teach Rodolpho to box now.

They begin slowly. Catherine is happy now. Eddie is making friends and everything will be all right perhaps. She goes to make coffee. Eddie is a good boxer, he is showing Rodolpho what to do, where to put his hands. Beatrice is encouraging, enjoying the men's companionship. Only Marco is wary. What is this for and where will it end? Rodolpho learns quickly and is beginning to enjoy himself as the rhythm of their sparring increases and they start to really box. Catherine, returning from the kitchen, is alarmed, sensing a change. Something is happening. Eddie waits his moment. Now, as he lands the blow with his right, relief and satisfaction flood through him. He hides his smile with the back of his hand. Marco is on his feet. He knows this is no accident despite Eddie's pretence. It is an insult, but what can he do? Rodolpho smiles and in his eyes is the gleam of recognition: Eddie is his enemy. He has shown his hand.

▷ **Question 2** *Notes*

1 Read through the passage carefully.
2 Look at Macbeth's speeches and make notes on the thoughts and feelings he expresses. These notes only need to be a few words.
3 Make a second list noting Lady Macbeth's and Macbeth's reactions to each other.

Suggested answer

'Many students lose marks by re-writing the passage in their own words. Have you really answered the question that was set?'

Macbeth is oppressed by a sense of danger; his mind is full of 'horrible imaginings'. He returns obsessively to thoughts of Duncan's death. Realizing how flimsy his hold on power is, he already feels that it is better to be with the dead, like Duncan, than to live under constant threat. He almost envies Duncan the peace of death for it seems infinitely preferable to the perpetual dread in which he lives. Neither by day nor by night can he rest easy: by day he fears the assassin even as he eats; by night he is plagued by 'terrible dreams'. Yet he will not surrender. He combats the fear with thoughts of more violence: Banquo and Fleance are particularly on his mind. He comforts himself with thoughts of their vulnerability. Night has become his element and he welcomes it with a grim satisfaction at the prospect of more dreadful deeds. These have become the dam that shores up his terrors.

There is still a clear bond of affection between Macbeth and his wife, but Lady Macbeth feels her husband slipping beyond her reach. She knows what afflicts his mind but seems powerless to draw him from the pit of his solitary brooding. Vainly she urges him to forget the past, but can only listen helplessly while Macbeth unburdens his guilt to her. She has no remedy for his state of mind and can only offer rather ineffectual comfort. Macbeth does respond to her appeal to keep up appearances among the guests, understanding the necessity for deceit even though he is disgusted with it. His fear of Banquo and Fleance strikes no chord with Lady Macbeth, consequently she no longer leads him. In the planning of this murder he is acting alone and without her knowledge. The force that she exerted over him has gone.

▷ **Question 3** *Student's answer – examiner's comment*

'An efficient, if obvious introduction.'

Arms and the Man *is a play illustrating how different characters think, react and respond to numerous aspects on love and war, what they learn from each other throughout the play, and how their opinions and decisions would have, and eventually do, affect their lives.*

(continued)

(continued)

At the beginning of the play, Raina lives in a dreamer's world – especially about love. She is so in love with being in love that she fails to look straight at the man she is engaged to. The only things Raina sees are his good breeding, civilized charm, physical hardihood and heroically, young, handsome appearance. The fact that her mother so adores Sergius probably encourages her manufactured adoration towards him. When Raina says to her mother, 'Oh, I know Sergius is your pet . . . you would pet him, and spoil him, and mother him to perfection,' she outwardly confronts this. Like a veil, they just seem to block out anything less than perfect thoughts of him. Sergius' coming back from the war a hero makes Raina's fantasies even more explicit and real. When she hears from her mother of what a success he was, she exclaims, 'what will he care for my poor little worship after the acclamations of a whole army of heroes? But no matter: I am so happy! So proud! It proves that all our ideals were real after all.' Then later, when she is alone, she says out loud, 'oh, I shall never be unworthy of you any more, my soul's hero: never, never, never.' Then 'my hero! my hero!' These two quotations show of Raina's worship and blind devotion to Sergius.

As one gets deeper into the play, one notices that Raina is starting to fall in love with Bluntchli. The emotions that Raina feels, however, are more natural and less forced than the artificial love Raina has for Sergius in the first half of the play. When Bluntchli falls asleep on Raina's bed at the beginning, she subconsciously says what a 'poor darling' he is. She also repeatedly calls him her, 'chocolate cream soldier,' probably not realizing just how affectionate this term really is. The fact that Bluntchli seems to be poor makes him more real and romantic for Raina in the way that he is so unlike Sergius and the 'well-to-do' men that Raina is used to meeting. At the end of the play, Bluntchli explains of his riches to Raina and her family in asking for Raina's hand in marriage; before, she would have been delighted to hear that he was wealthy, but now thinks that their love would be based on materialistic ideals, instead of compatible love. Raina seems to see all the faults in her past 'relationship' with Sergius, and by no means wants a repetition of any of them. She promptly makes it known that she is not there to be married off to the wealthiest man that is available when her parents respond to this piece of delightful news by immediately granting him his wish to marry their daughter. Then she says to Bluntchli that when she gave him her hospitality, shelter and a bed to sleep in in his time of need, that she gave them to a poor, helpless man. Not the Emperor of Switzerland!

It becomes plain to the observer when Raina's and Sergius' 'love' starts to deteriorate as Raina seems to want Sergius to find out about 'her chocolate cream soldier'. An example of these feelings that Raina has at this particular moment in time is when she says to her mother, 'I don't care whether he finds out about the chocolate cream soldier or not. I half hope he may.' When Raina slips a photo of herself to 'her chocolate cream soldier' the apparent significance of this symbolic gesture is simply that Raina has admitted to herself, and to Bluntchli, that she is attracted to him.

By the end of the play, Raina's views on love are no longer those of an irrational young girl, but of a more down to earth, sensible and rational young woman. Apart from this, however, Raina still has one romantic notion. She wants to marry a poor man – not a wealthy one. The same is true with Sergius as it is with Raina. He also believes that he is in love with Raina when, in actual fact, he is not. He worships her because she is young, beautiful, of good social status, and of course, the fact that she seems to do no wrong. Sergius believes he and Raina have found the 'higher love', but in actual fact, he barely knows what this is. This is proven when he asks Louka if she knew what the higher love is. When she replies that she did not know, he commented that it was very tiresome to

(continued)

'Good, apt quotations. Exactly illustrates the points about the characters.'

(continued)

keep up for any length of time. This indicates that it is all an act on Sergius' part and that he has to pretend to himself and to Raina, that he really is as infatuated with her as he would like himself to believe.

So accustomed is Sergius to having any girl he desires, when Louka rejects him, he is flabbergasted, and therefore determined to win her over. At first, Sergius thinks of conquering Louka as a challenge, one that he is sure he can come out on top. But as he starts to see how reluctant she really is, refusing to be toyed with, he begins to realize that love is not a silly game, and therefore starts to take Louka more seriously as a woman. Especially when she says, 'she [Raina] will never marry you now. The man I told you of has come back. She will marry the Swiss.' It is retorts like these that lead up to the irrational and hasty decision Sergius makes at the end of the play, partly to keep his self-dignity, and partly because Sergius is more so naturally attracted to Louka than he is to Raina, that he decides to marry her.

Louka is probably the most cunning character in the whole play. Her social position in the community is very important to her. As a maid, she is not lazy, but overly ambitious, and therefore quite prepared to use love as an excuse to better the quality of her life. At the beginning of the play, it looks as though she might marry the other servant in the household, but it later becomes clear that this will not be the case. She realizes that if she can get engaged to Sergius instead, the standard of her life will be of a much higher ranking. At the end of the play, when Louka is caught eavesdropping outside the door on Sergius', Raina's and Bluntchli's conversation, Louka's determination of marrying Sergius is shown quite clearly. When she is asked why she was listening, she quite matter-of-factly says, 'My love was at stake,' meaning that had she not been there, Sergius mightn't have decided to marry her . . .

. . . At first, Sergius is envious over the fact that Bluntchli has such great capability over both the physical and mental aspects of war, but at the end, this childlike jealously turns into respect when he says, 'what a man! Is he a man!' after Bluntchli bows and walks out the room.

It is safe to say that Sergius, by the end of the play, learns a certain amount about war. He is still overly proud, but nonetheless, if Sergius has to go to war again, he will probably fight in a much saner state of mind! Bluntchli and Louka together, seemed to have neutralized his macho self-esteem by her cutting remarks, 'you don't know what courage is.' And by Sergius observing Bluntchli's true skill and bravery alone.

Like love, at the start of the play, Raina's views on war are purely those of an ignorant, pampered and romantic child. The pain and the agony, the hardship and the suffering, the point (if there is one) – she is oblivious to them all. Handsome young men (in Austrian uniform), fighting proudly for the honour and devotion to their country (against barren like, uncivilized men – take the Serbs for example), is the image that appeals to Raina. She has no idea that one of the main parts of war is staying alive, and believes that avoiding danger (as in Bluntchli's case), is a sign of pure cowardliness. When she says to Bluntchli after being informed that he is hiding in her room to avoid capture from the Austrians, 'Some soldiers I know, are afraid to die' she is implying that because he is not 'volunteering,' to die for the duty of his country, he is unmanly and cowardly.

Raina first sees war as a fairy tale, and when she is first introduced to the reality of it by Bluntchli as he talks of the man being burnt alive, she is shocked and hurt that her wonderful, perfect, shiny bubble has been popped so crudely.

By the end of the play, Raina no longer looks upon war as where men prove their manhood, but comes to understand that it is quite meaningless, ferocious and dirty, to her

(continued)

'Very well structured. Moves clearly from one character to another discussing all aspects of the title.'

'The answer continues . . .'

'This sentence has got rather out of hand!'

(continued)

tastes. She realizes that it is not so grand and exciting as her mother and Sergius made it out to be, and therefore becomes much less patriotic and biased towards her country, but wiser at the same time, on her views to do with war.

As an individual, Louka seems to know as much about war as she feels she needs to, but does not tend to contemplate it a great deal. Her only concerns in life are that she has a good position in the community, and if she has to marry a general to do so, then so be it. However, this is where her interests draw the line. As long as she is not affected by the dramas of war, then Louka probably does not really care which side wins a war. She is not in the least bit patriotic and hardly expresses her views on the matter throughout the play.

'Good concluding discussion of the dramatist's ideas.'

Through his characters, the overall picture that Bernard Shaw is trying to create is that irrational thinking and superficial love simply do not work. Sergius acts irrationally when, at the spur of the moment, he asks Louka to marry him, and also when he makes the cavalry charge. Raina acts irrationally at the beginning, when she is blindly in love with Sergius for all the wrong reasons. However, she makes the only truly brave and thought-out action in the whole play when she saves Bluntchli from almost certain death. Louka acts rationally when she realizes she can marry Sergius to better her life, and Bluntchli too when he climbs up Raina's balcony to save himself.

Another hint that indicates that Bernard Shaw believes unrealistic ideals ruin a person's life is when Bluntchli tells the family that he spoiled all his chances in life by 'an incurably romantic disposition'. When asked what he meant by this remark from Sergius, he goes on to explain, 'I ran away from home twice when I was a boy. I went into the army instead of my father's business.' Therefore regretting taking up the profession as a commercial soldier, and saying that his life would have been less pointless and regretful if he had followed his brain instead of a silly romantic dream.

Bernard Shaw, through his characters, is also trying to tell the viewer that marrying someone for materialistic ideals and social standing will not work as eventually love will conquer all. Raina, for example, although she is betrothed to Sergius, falls in love with Bluntchli because it is natural and not an artificial chemistry, with nothing to do with financial, and false ideals, in contrast to Sergius.

'This short paragraph shows a thoughtful personal reaction in a succinct way.'

At first glance, I did not really think of Arms and the Man as very meaningful – in fact more of a shallow, fictional and uninteresting play. However, after contemplating it afterwards, I realize now that the things Bernard Shaw is trying to point out occur in everyday life – however much exaggerated. On the whole, the play is quite entertaining and not without purpose. It would be interesting to see it performed by a professional cast.

'An excellent discussion of the ideas of this play. The student displays a thorough grasp of the material.'

Question	Assessment Objective(s)	Pre-20th century	20th century
Coursework task – *The Importance of Being Earnest*	1, 2, 4	✓	
1 *A View from the Bridge*	1, 2, 4		✓
2 *Macbeth*	1, 2	✓	
3 *Arms and the Man*	1, 4	✓	

SUMMARY

▷ We learn about characters from:
  – what they do;
  – the way they speak;
  – what they say about themselves;
  – what others say about them.

▷ Well-drawn characters are consistent: their behaviour can be understood and explained.

▷ Some characters are not drawn in depth. They are there to do a specific job in the plot.

▷ Some characters are symbolic, either wholly or in part, and represent ideas.

▷ Dramatists use contrasting characters to portray themes and ideas.

The language of drama

 GETTING STARTED

A number of exam questions may ask you to comment on the language of the play. Often this is in a question based on an extract. We have already seen how the dialogue has a lot of information to convey about character, relationship and feelings. The dialogue can also create atmosphere, generate or intensify emotions and indicate tone. If you are studying a play in verse, like those of Shakespeare, you should pay particular attention to the language. In any play, though, you should always think carefully about the kind of language used. Your knowledge of it will give depth to your comments on other aspects of the play.

The topics covered in this chapter are applicable to all exam boards.

MEG	NEAB	NICCEA	SEG	LONDON	WJEC	IGCSE	**TOPIC**	STUDY	REVISION 1	REVISION 2
✓	✓	✓	✓	✓	✓	✓	Verse and prose			
✓	✓	✓	✓	✓	✓	✓	Atmosphere			
✓	✓	✓	✓	✓	✓	✓	Pause			
✓	✓	✓	✓	✓	✓	✓	Mood			
✓	✓	✓	✓	✓	✓	✓	Tone			
✓	✓	✓	✓	✓	✓	✓	Formality			
✓	✓	✓	✓	✓	✓	✓	Irony			
✓	✓	✓	✓	✓	✓	✓	Colloquial language			
✓	✓	✓	✓	✓	✓	✓	Humour			

WHAT YOU NEED TO KNOW

▷ **Verse and prose**   Some plays, like Shakespeare's, are written in verse or, more usually, a mixture of verse and prose. **Verse** is generally reserved for the more serious and noble characters:

THESEUS   What say you Hermia? Be advised fair maid.
To you your father should be as a God,

Prose is used for comic, unimportant or low characters:

BOTTOM   First, Peter Quince, say what the play treats on; then read the names of the actors and so grow to a point.

By making these distinctions Shakespeare tells us important things about the nature of his characters.

In *A Midsummer Night's Dream* all the lovers, Duke Theseus and his bride, and the fairy king and queen, Oberon and Titania, are all given dialogue in verse. Bottom and his friends, the mechanicals, who provide the broad humour, speak in prose. When these comic characters present their play at court it has to be in verse. However it is not the serious blank verse of the higher characters but a jingling rhymed doggerel. Sometimes a character will have some dialogue in prose and some in verse to distinguish his moods and the seriousness of what he is saying. In *Henry IV Part I* when Prince Hal is cavorting in the tavern with Falstaff he speaks in prose. When he shows his serious side, for instance with his father, the king, he speaks in verse. Falstaff, a comic character, speaks in prose whereas the king always uses verse. This technique of dividing dialogue between verse and prose is an easy way of distinguishing the status of the speaker or the importance and tone of the speech.

▷ **Atmosphere**   When a dramatist uses verse dialogue he can use all the qualities of poetry (see Chapter 3). **Atmosphere** is easily created through verse. In *Julius Caesar* the atmosphere of the wild and dreadful night before Caesar's murder, when the skies seemed to drop fire on the earth and nature itself went mad, is vividly evoked. Throughout *Macbeth* the use of imagery connected with darkness and night helps to create the atmosphere of encompassing evil.

– Come seeling night,
Scarf up the tender eye of pitiful day,
And with thy bloody and invisible hand
Cancel and tear to pieces that great bond
Which keeps me pale. Light thickens, and the crow
Makes wing to the rooky wood.
Good things of day begin to droop and drowse,
While night's black agents to their preys do rouse.

Lines such as these, as much as the appearance of the witches and the foul deeds committed, give the play its increasing sense of a world overwhelmed by dreadful wrong, a man lost in a miasma of evil doing. If you are studying *Macbeth* look through the play and notice how many of these references there are to blackness and night, and things associated with them. Make a note of them and memorize some of the lines.

In plays written in verse the language is vital in conveying mood, theme and action. You should look at some passages from the play (for instance Macbeth's soliloquies) in the same detail and in the same way as you would look at a poem.

Some prose dialogue also creates a very strong atmosphere. This can be so even when the language used is quite simple.

PROCTOR   A fire, a fire is burning! I hear the boot of Lucifer, I see his filthy face! And it is my face, and yours, Danforth! For them that quail to bring men out of ignorance, as I have quailed, and as you quail now when you know in all your black hearts that this be fraud – God damns our kind especially, and we will burn, we will burn together.

(Arthur Miller, *The Crucible*)

The tension, guilt and hysteria of this language generates the atmosphere of a society that believes strongly in hell fire and damnation, for whom God and the Devil are real and present forces. This is created through the use of repeated phrases, through the images of Lucifer which Proctor conjures up and through the rhythm of the language.

▷ **Pause** The use of **pause** often creates a distinctive atmosphere. Harold Pinter frequently uses repetition, pause and silences in his dialogue. This brings a heavy feeling of tension and unease and makes his style very recognizable:

ASTON   You make too much noise.
DAVIES   But ... but ... look ... listen ... listen here ... I mean ...

[*Aston turns back to the window.*]

What am I going to do? [*pause*] What shall I do? [*pause*] Where am I going to go? [*pause*] If you want me to go ... I'll go. You just say the word. [*pause*] I'll tell you what though ... them shoes ... them shoes you give me ... they're working out all right ... they're all right. Maybe I could ... get down. [*Aston remains still, his back to him, at the window.*]
Listen ... if I ... got down ... if I was to ... get my papers ... would you ... would you let ... would you ... if I got down ... and got my ...

Long silence.

You have to hear this speech to appreciate the effect of all those hesitations. Read it aloud to yourself and notice the feeling of helplessness and threat. In any play, remember to look at the pauses. It is easy when you are reading to ignore them, but they are an important part of dramatic language because it is written to be spoken. Much can be conveyed in a pause or a silence. You will rarely come across pause used as much as in this example but it is only taking to great lengths an aspect of language that all dramatists use.

▷ **Mood** Atmosphere affects all the characters onstage. Dialogue also has to express the passing **mood** of the characters. The atmosphere of *The Long and the Short and the Tall* by Willis Hall is tense and threatening, reflecting the harsh situation the soldiers find themselves in. The youngest, Whitaker, starts talking of his girl at home:

WHITAKER   So we'd just walk along be the side of the river, like. Up as far as the bridge. Happen sit down and watch them playing bowls. Sit for ten minutes or so, get up and walk back. Just a steady stroll, you know. I never had much money – only my bus fare there and back sometimes – but it was ... Oh boy! Oh you know – we had some smashing times together me and her.

The mood is soft and nostalgic. The images of the river, the men playing bowls, the familiar quiet sights of a peaceful England, contrast with the strangeness and the danger of the Malayan jungle that now surrounds them. Whitaker's boyish embarrassment about his feelings makes him speak haltingly, and he is unable to express emotion except through exclamations such as 'Oh boy' and 'you know'. The tenderness of this passage makes his death all the more poignant.

We have already seen the power of verse to create an atmosphere of evil throughout *Macbeth*. The atmosphere of *Romeo and Juliet* is much more varied. Here, for instance, is Juliet waiting for Romeo, after they have been married:

Come night, come Romeo; come thou day in night,
For thou wilt lie upon the wings of night
Whiter than new snow on a raven's back.
Come gentle night, come loving, black-browed night,
Give me my Romeo, and when he shall die
Take him and cut him out in little stars,
And he will make the face of heaven so fine
That all the world will be in love with night
And pay no worship to the garish sun.

Juliet's mood is passionate, ecstatic. Shakespeare creates it through the many repetitions, so that her speech becomes almost a chant, an incantation. The usual associations of darkness are contradicted by the use of words like 'loving' and 'gentle', and by comparing Romeo to the day and to snow. Like those he is bright because, although he dare only come to Juliet's bedroom under cover of darkness, he brings joy. The final image of Romeo translated into a brightness which transforms the heavens is the most intense expression of Juliet's sense of her lover's beauty.

Moments before Romeo has killed Tybalt. Juliet knows nothing of this and her mood is in sharp contrast to what has gone before.

▷ Tone

Closely allied to a character's mood is the **tone** of the dialogue. It is often quite difficult to decide on the tone of a speech. Try to imagine the words being spoken and then ask yourself what tone of voice the character is using. The tone shows the attitude of the character who is speaking. Tone can be serious, lighthearted, grave, teasing, formal, informal – there are many possibilities.

Formality

One of the difficulties you may have arises from the way in which our way of speaking to others has changed. These changes in the **mode of address,** as it is called, affect tone.

In modern plays if we hear characters addressing each other as Mr Brown and Miss Gardiner the formality of their tone indicates that they do not know each other well, or they are being very cold towards each other. Formality of address did not always indicate coldness or unfamiliarity. In *The Importance of Being Earnest* Jack and Gwendolen are calling each other Mr Worthing and Miss Fairfax even while Jack is proposing marriage. In the same situation in *She Stoops to Conquer*, written in the eighteenth century, Marlow and Kate call each other 'Sir' and 'Madam'. And in *The Way of the World*, written in the seventeenth century, the lovers, Mirabell and Millamant, never call each other by anything but their surnames. All these reflect the usual forms of address of the time.

In previous centuries it was common to call members of your family and intimate friends 'thee' and other people you were not familiar with 'you'. Shakespeare sometimes makes this distinction, but you have to be careful. He also uses 'thee' and 'you' quite indiscriminately. There is no rule – you have to listen to the tone and decide for yourself.

When thinking about tone it is important to take into account when the play was written and the social customs of the time.

Irony

The most difficult tone to catch is the ironic one, because the character is saying one thing and meaning another. You are being asked to understand the meaning behind the words. We all use irony. For instance we say 'Oh! Great!' when it starts to rain just as we're setting out for a walk. In *The Taming of the Shrew* Petruchio calls Kate:

> pleasant, gamesome, passing courteous,
> But slow in speech, yet sweet as springtime flowers.

Since she has just been shouting, screaming and fighting with him he cannot mean it. He is being ironic. There is another excellent example at the end of the passage from *Romeo and Juliet* used in the exam question at the end of this chapter.

Sometimes a character's words have a different meaning for the audience because the audience knows more about the situation than the character. This is **dramatic irony**. In *An Inspector Calls* Mrs Birling speaks very forcefully against the young man who has got Daisy Renton pregnant. She says he must be made to face his responsibilities, whoever he is. She does not know that the young man in question is her son. But the audience has already guessed this, so they find her words ironic.

There can also be irony in the way events turn out. The witches' predictions to Macbeth all prove true – but not in the way he expected. He believes he cannot be killed until 'Birnam wood be come to Dunsinane' but his enemies order their soldiers to camouflage themselves with leafy branches as they move on his castle and it appears as if the wood is moving. The prophecy, which he thought guaranteed his survival, has come true and he dies.

▷ Colloquial language

Most of us speak **colloquially**. It is the language we use when we are feeling easy, with friends, an off-duty language. Dramatists use it when they want to show a character as belonging to a certain class or part of the country, or to make the dialogue seem natural. Arnold Wesker's Ronnie does not speak in a cockney accent like his brother-in-law, Dave. He is more educated and it shows in his speech. Even so he speaks colloquially:

DAVE	Jesus Christ it's heavy, it's heavy. Drop it a minute.
RONNIE	Lower it gently – mind the edges, it's a work of art.
DAVE	I'll work of art you. And turn that radio off – I can cope with Beethoven but not both of you.
RONNIE	What are you grumbling for? I've been shlapping things to and fro up till now, haven't I?

(I'm Talking About Jerusalem)

Colloquial speech used to be used only for comedy. Nowadays so much of our speech is informal that modern plays conduct serious discussions in this kind of informal language.

▷ **Humour**   We have already seen how **humour** can arise from situation, but much humour also arises out of the language used.

Some plays depend almost completely on the witty dialogue. For an example look back at the extract from *The Importance of Being Earnest* (see Chapter 11). But humour in language does not have to depend on wit like Wilde's, or even jokes. In *Billy Liar* a lot of the humour is created by speech mannerisms, like Billy's father's who punctuates all his utterances with 'bloody':

GEOFFREY	More like one o'clock with your bloody half past eleven! Well you can bloody well start coming in of a night-time. I'm not having you gallivanting round at all hours, not at your bloody age.

Billy's girl-friend, Rita, uses 'rotten' in a similar manner:

RITA	Well, I'm going to see your rotten mother – I'll tell you that. My name's not 'Silly' you know. Either you get me that rotten ring back or I'm going to see your rotten mother.

Shakespeare was very fond of puns. A **pun** is a play on words that has two or more meanings. Here are two of the menservants at the beginning of *Romeo and Juliet*:

SAMSON	. . . I will show myself a tyrant. When I have fought with the men and I will be civil with the maids – I will cut off their heads.
GREGORY	The heads of the maids?
SAMSON	The heads of the maids, or their maidenheads, take it in what sense thou wilt.

This is rather laboured patter, suitable for servants. It is a sixteenth-century equivalent of the stand-up comic and the straight man. The Elizabethans loved puns. They found them humorous and clever. Yet they could also be serious. Shakespeare would use puns in the most serious of situations. 'Ask for me tomorrow and you will find me a grave man', says Mercutio as he is dying.

If you are asked why you find a scene amusing, decide whether the comedy comes from the situation or the language, or both. Look at the language for any exaggerated speech mannerisms, puns or witty dialogue.

▷ **Additional examples**   Use these passages to test your understanding of what you have read in this chapter. Write down your own ideas before you read the key below.

1   What does the language of the following passage tell you about the characters? Look at the manner of the speech rather than the meaning.

SIR TIMOTHY	But thank God, I'm not like thee, Nat Jeffcote. I sometimes think thou'st got a stone where thy heart should be by rights.
JEFFCOTE	Happen I've got a pair of scales.
SIR TIMOTHY	That's nowt to boast on. I'd as soon have the stone.
MRS JEFFCOTE	Beatrice wants to speak to you, Alan.
SIR TIMOTHY	Now my lass –
BEATRICE	Father, I want to speak to Alan.
SIR TIMOTHY	I'd like to have a word with thee first, Bee.
BEATRICE	Afterwards, father.
SIR TIMOTHY	Ay! But it'll be too late afterwards, happen.
JEFFCOTE	Come, Tim, thou can't meddle with this job.
SIR TIMOTHY	I call it a bit thick.

BEATRICE   Please, father.

MRS JEFFCOTE Come into the drawing-room, Sir Timothy. You can smoke there, you know.

(Stanley Houghton, *Hindle Wakes*)

2   What is the mood created by this speech from the end of Tennessee Williams' *The Glass Menagerie*? What features of the writing create the mood?

TOM   Perhaps I am walking along the street at night, in some strange city, before I have found companions. I pass the lighted window of a shop where perfume is sold. The window is filled with pieces of coloured glass, tiny transparent bottles in delicate colours, like bits of a shattered rainbow. Then all at once my sister touches my shoulder. I turn around and look into her eyes ... Oh, Laura, Laura, I tried to leave you behind me, but I am more faithful than I intended to be! I reach for a cigarette, I cross the street, I run into the movies or a bar, I buy a drink, I speak to the nearest stranger – anything that can blow your candles out! – for nowadays the world is lit by lightning! Blow out your candles, Laura – and so good-bye.

Key to the examples

1   The first thing that the language tells you is that the play is set in the North of England, because of the use of words and phrases like 'nowt' and 'my lass' and the use of 'happen' for 'perhaps'. Secondly the way the characters 'thee' and 'thou' each other shows us that the time is probably the past but not too distant past. Sir Timothy and Jeffcote have the strongest dialect. Their down-to-earth speech contrasts with the women, especially Beatrice, who speaks very properly, even in this family situation. They appear to be self-made men who have risen from the working class to positions of wealth and eminence. That Bee has had a very different childhood from her father's is shown in the way she talks.

These are things which the language tells you without considering the content of what is said.

2   The mood of this speech is one of sadness, of regret for the past, though not a wishing to return. It is a lonely, troubled speech, of a man who cannot escape the poignant memories of his sister.

The mood is created partly through imagery. There are the delicate images which remind Tom of Laura: the perfume and the glass, the rainbow – not a beautiful, coloured arch but one shattered. Laura herself appears to him almost as a wistful ghost or vision, without substance but always present. Tom's loneliness comes through his solitariness in a strange city at night. He always appears to be moving on, always in search of new companions. The urgency of that search, in a bar, or the movies, shows Tom's need to run away from the memories of his delicate and tender sister. He speaks of his reaction to his memories in a series of short phrases, 'I reach for a cigarette, I cross the street, I run into the movies'. This manner of speech recreates his mood of restlessness.

'Students often forget to consider imagery in prose.'

SUGGESTIONS FOR COURSEWORK

1   Write a section of dialogue in the style of the playwright you are studying.
2   Re-write a scene of Shakespearean verse in prose.
3   Compare the language of different dramatic genres. For example, compare the language of revenge tragedy and kitchen-sink drama; or compare the language of a scene where Juliet speaks to her parents and Jo speaks to Helen in *A Taste of Honey*.
4   Write a study of the effect of the use of regional or social dialect and accent or non-standard English, for example the rude mechanicals in *A Midsummer Night's Dream*, the characters of *Hindle Wakes*, or Willie Mossop and Maggie in *Hobson's Choice*.

Coursework task   A study of the use of language and dialect in the characterization of Willie Mossop and Maggie in *Hobson's Choice*.

Suggested answer   In *Hobson's Choice* Harold Brighouse uses the manner in which people speak, and in particular dialect, to show character development, to create humour and to place the action in Lancashire.

Maggie's character is established immediately through the way in which she talks. Her first words, 'It isn't', in response to Alice's 'Oh it's you, I thought it was father going out', show her to be direct, to the point, a woman who stands no nonsense. When Maggie intercepts Albert Prosser on the way out her manner is very correct, she is a professional saleswoman, 'What can I do for you Mr Prosser?', but there is a threat behind the formal words. Her determination not to let him leave the shop without making a substantial purchase makes her go on to speak to him in a much more direct and familiar manner. Having pushed him into a chair she examines his boots, declaring, 'It's time you had a new pair. These uppers are disgraceful for a professional man to wear'. While Albert might expect his boss, or even an elder female relative to talk to him in this tone, he hardly expects it from a saleswoman. Harold Brighouse uses the unexpectedness to make his audience laugh. It also makes Albert Prosser buy a pair of boots against his will. As Maggie says after he has left, 'It'll teach him to keep out of here for a bit', though she is well aware that he comes to see her sister Alice. When Alice complains that the shop is the only place where she and Albert can do their 'courting' Maggie retorts that if Albert wants to marry her 'why doesn't he do it?' without more ado. She says:

> See that slipper with a fancy buckle on it to make it pretty? Courting's like that, my lass. All glitter and no use to nobody.

Already by the end of this short scene we can understand a great deal about Maggie Hobson. Her straightforward manner of addressing everyone shows her to be unafraid, clear in her own values and with a sense of her own worth. While her speech is correct certain words and phrases like 'courting', 'my lass', 'no use to nobody', show that she is a Northener and that the play is set at the beginning of this century or earlier. This kind of plain-speaking, down-to-earth, rather overbearing kind of woman later became something of a dramatic stereotype.

Will Mossop is a less educated character than Maggie, a simple boot-hand who has difficulty reading Mrs Hepworth's visiting card because it is printed in italics, thus the dialect features of his speech are more exaggerated. 'I'm not much good at owt but leather' he says of himself and is relieved when Maggie mentions 'partnership' because he 'thought you were axing me to wed you'. When he finds out that this is indeed what Maggie is proposing his first reaction is 'Well, by gum.' This phrase, which later became the typical remark of the archetypal Northern working-class male character, never fails to draw a laugh from the audience. Will has to confess that, unfortunately, he is already 'tokened', a word for which even Maggie needs an explanation. Ada Figgins, the girl to whom Will is tokened, is also given a broad Lancashire accent and dialect. She drops the 'H' of Hobson and uses the old-fashioned 'thine' for 'yours' when defending herself against Maggie:

> You mind your own business, Miss 'Obson. Will Mossop's no concern of thine.

The speech of both these characters is used not just to give a sense of their personality and background, both social and regional, but also to create humour. Tubby Wadlow, the foreman, is given slightly more educated speech to indicate his slightly higher position, but still uses dialect words:

> I'm not going to be responsible to the master with his temper so nowty and all since Miss Maggie went.

Maggie has seen a potential in Will that neither her sisters nor her father recognized, so having married him she sets out on a programme of improvement. The first signs of this come only a month later at the wedding celebration. As the bridegroom Will must make a speech. He has clearly learnt it from Maggie as she has to prompt him in the middle:

WILL   It's an honour you do us and I assure you, speaking for my – my wife as well as for myself, that the – the –

MAGGIE   Generous.

WILL   Oh aye. That's it. That the generous warmth of the sentiments so cordially expressed by Mr Beenstock and so enthusiastically seconded by – no I've gotten that wrong road round – expressed by Mr Prosser and seconded by Mr Beenstock . . .

The words are not Will's own and his lapses of memory are still comic. When he forgets his 'script' he drops quickly into dialect, saying 'aye' for 'yes' and 'road' for 'way'. Nevertheless Alice is impressed. She prevents Albert from speaking again, saying:

You'll not speak as well as he did so we can leave it with a good wind up.

The progress that Will is making with Maggie's tuition shows in the level of language he uses. Later he is able to employ language like this independently of Maggie:

I'll transfer to this address and what I'll do that's generous is this: I'll take you into partnership and give you your half share on the condition that you're sleeping partner and you don't try interference on with me.

This is Will talking to Hobson only a year later and his fluency astonishes even himself:

Words came from my mouth that made me jump at my own boldness.

He has become a different person, a man that Maggie has made and of whom she can be proud. The difference is shown in the way that Will now speaks. Yet, true to Maggie's idea that they should not forget their origins, Will's last words take us back to the person he once was:

Well, by gum!

▷ EXAMINATION QUESTIONS

An exam question may ask you to comment directly on the language of a play, often based on an extract, particularly if it is in verse. Two questions of this type are answered below. Other questions will expect you to use your observations about language in talking about a character, or you might be asked to pretend to be a character and write a diary or a letter, as in the first question below.

▷ **Question 1**   Imagine that you are Marlow in *She Stoops to Conquer*. Write a letter to an imaginary friend telling him about your experiences and the people you have met. You may write your letter about a part of the play or about the whole of the play.

▷ **Question 2**   In Shakespeare's *Romeo and Juliet* Juliet is let down by all those closest to her. Look carefully
'MEG.'   at how each of them speaks to her here, and say what you think of each. How is your opinion influenced by their language as well as their attitude? Comment on the effect of all this on Juliet.

CAPULET   Thursday is near; lay hand on heart, advise:
           An you be mine, I'll give you to my friend;
           An you be not, hang, beg, starve, die in the streets,
           For, by my soul I'll ne'er acknowledge thee,
           Nor what is mine shall never do thee good:
           Trust to't, bethink you; I'll not be forsworn.

           [*He storms out.*]

JULIET   Is there no pity sitting in the clouds,
           That sees into the bottom of my grief?
           O, sweet my mother, cast me not away!
           Delay this marriage for a month, a week;
           Or, if you do not, make the bridal bed
           In that dim monument where Tybalt lies.

LADY CAPULET   Talk not to me, for I'll not speak a word:
                Do as thou wilt, for I have done with thee. [*She leaves.*]

JULIET   O God – O nurse, how shall this be prevented?
           My husband is on earth, my faith in heaven;
           How shall that faith return again to earth,
           Unless that husband send it me from heaven
           By leaving earth? Comfort me, counsel me.
           Alack, alack, that heaven should practise stratagems
           Upon so soft a subject as myself!
           What say'st thou? Hast thou not a word of joy?
           Some comfort, nurse.

NURSE   Faith, here it is.
     Romeo is banished; and all the world to nothing,
     That he dares ne'er come back to challenge you;
     Or if he do, it needs must be by stealth.
     Then since the case so stands as now it doth,
     I think it best you married with the County.
     O, he's a lovely gentleman!
     Romeo's a dishclout to him: an eagle, madam,
     Hath not so green, so quick, so fair an eye
     As Paris hath. Beshrew my very heart,
     I think you are happy in this second match,
     For it excels your first: or if it did not,
     Your first is dead; or 'twere as good he were,
     As living here and you no use of him.
JULIET   Speak'st thou from thy heart?
NURSE   And from my soul too:
     Or else beshrew them both.
JULIET   Amen!
NURSE   What?
JULIET   Well, thou hast comforted me marvellous much.
     Go in; and tell my lady I am gone,
     Having displeas'd my father, to Laurence' cell,
     To make confession and to be absolv'd.
NURSE   Marry, I will; and this is wisely done.

▷ **Question 3**   Choose two scenes from *Macbeth* that take place in darkness. What makes them effective? Look particularly at the language used.

 EXAMINATION ANSWERS

▷ **Question 1**   *Notes and tutor's answer*

Notes
In a question like this you should:

1   Try to imitate the language and tone of the character writing the letter. If this is an open-book exam look carefully at the play for unusual words or phrases which you can use to give the right tone.
2   Show your knowledge of the plot by including appropriate details.
3   Show your understanding of the character by talking about other characters in an appropriate way.

Suggested answer
My dear Lewes,
As I told you, I have been obliged to come into the country to visit Mr Hardcastle, the old friend of my father, and to make my addresses to his daughter. To humour my father I am bound to do it but I assure you I take no pleasure in the task and so far we have had a confoundedly uncomfortable time of it. Hastings has accompanied me, in order to make an assignation with Miss Neville who by chance lives in the same household. A tedious journey of above three-score miles led us to an ale-house which promised but a poor reception, and we were like to have had yet more adventures wandering the countryside had it not been for the help of a young fellow we chanced to meet there. He, though something of a clod-pole, rough and rude in speech in the country manner, though not without some signs of breeding, directed us to an inn. We are to pass the night here, at the Buck's Head, a very well-appointed inn, antique but creditable, and one of the best in the county. However, the comfort and the cleanliness of our lodging are purchased somewhat dear, for the landlord is an impudent, intrusive fellow, a veritable character. He forgets he is an innkeeper and speaks to us for all the world like a country squire of the old school. His talk is all of Prince Eugene and the Duke of

Marlborough. He would, if we had a mind to listen, continue all evening with his accounts of fighting the Turks and the Battle of Belgrade. His uncle, he claims, was a colonel and I don't doubt that I shall shortly make the acquaintance of an aunt who serves as Justice of the Peace! I have already suffered a conversation with his old-fashioned wife, a woman whose mouth is full of the fripperies of London fashion though she cannot tell St James's from Tower Wharf.

Yet the worst of all this is: by some infernal mischance Miss Hardcastle, happening to dine in the neighbourhood, called here to take fresh horses, and I was obliged to meet her, despite the disorder of my dress after our long journey. You well know my difficulties in the company of women of reputation. Often I resolve to break the ice and rattle away but as soon as I see a modest woman, dressed out in all her finery, I freeze. They petrify me. While I was able to converse with a modicum of sense when Hastings was with us, as soon as he left us to our tête-à-tête I could hardly stammer out a rational response. Though Miss Hardcastle claimed to understand me perfectly it was more than I did myself. However it is no matter because she is a maypole and I think she squints.

At the last one encounter compensated for all these difficulties. There is in the house the prettiest child who serves in the office of a bar-maid. With her, as with all women of that class, my tongue was loosened. If I could say half the things to ladies of Miss Hardcastle's class that I lavished upon this handsome little keeper of the keys I would not lack a charming companion. As it is I can only enjoy the company of this little maid and return to London tomorrow having had some pleasure from this unprofitable journey.

Yours,
Marlow.

▷ Question 2 *Notes and tutor's answer*

Notes

1 Read the passage carefully.
2 Look at Capulet's speech. Note down anything that strikes you about the form of the verse and the kind of language he uses. What is his tone? What impression do you get of him?
3 Do the same for Lady Capulet and the Nurse.
4 Note Juliet's reaction to each speaker.
5 Write four paragraphs – on Capulet, Lady Capulet, the Nurse and Juliet.

Suggested answer

Capulet rages at Juliet. He is furious that she should not meekly accept the husband he has arranged for her. His daughter is his property to be given away to whomsoever he pleases. Although this seems an extraordinary attitude now it would be less so at the time when Shakespeare was writing. Even now brides are 'given away' in church by their fathers. Even when allowance is made for this historical difference, Shakespeare makes Capulet appear callous in the harsh way he speaks, never pausing for a moment to hear Juliet's fears or objections. He threatens and thunders, never seeking to persuade. His threats are real: Juliet knows he has the power to turn her friendless on to the streets if she does not obey him and marry Paris on Thursday. His temper is so great that he almost chokes on his words. The verse becomes very disjointed as a sign of his anger. Each line is broken up by pauses and the normal Iambic rhythm disappears completely. In the line:

'Note how the answer looks at the words as verse and at the way they sound when spoken. Have you done this?'

An you be not, hang, beg, starve, die in the streets

his voice seems to be rising in a crescendo of anger as he roars each awful word at his daughter. The manner of Capulet's speech, as much as what he is saying, robs him of all our understanding for his position: we feel only pity for Juliet suffering the onslaught of this tirade. He appears so unreasonable and tyrannical, a man so used to having his way that his temper immediately flares when he is crossed.

Lady Capulet can only follow her husband. The coolness of her manner is shown by her short, clipped phrases, which make her appear too fearful to contradict her husband. She cannot afford to have an independent opinion.

Left alone with Juliet, even the Nurse is cowed, though her natural talkativeness does not desert her completely. In her peasant's manner she can think of no other way than taking the easiest course in the present circumstances. Her tone is comforting, gentle and practical, but she has no idea of Juliet's feelings. Since Romeo is miles away and can do her no harm, she thinks that Juliet had better make the best of a bad job. Morality does not enter her calculations. Clumsily she tries to manipulate Juliet's feelings, denigrating Romeo by calling him a 'dishclout' and praising Paris by comparing him to an eagle, just as earlier she had praised Romeo. For all her affectionate good intentions the Nurse appears despicable here, a base character, unable to rise to Juliet's needs.

Juliet's first reaction, if she cannot prevent or delay this marriage, is to see death as the only way out. Her passionate words are a counter-threat, but once her mother leaves her she feels unable to cope with the situation she is entangled in. She is well aware that she is in danger of committing a mortal sin. In wild despair she turns to the Nurse as her only comfort and as she listens to the Nurse's words she becomes quiet. By the time she answers her whole manner has changed, as if, in this short space, she has ceased to be a child and become independent. Her words:

> Well, thou hast comforted me marvellous much

are ironic. The Nurse has not comforted her at all. She hides her feelings and her intentions from the Nurse and determines to seek help from the only other person she can trust: Friar Laurence.

▷ **Question 3**   *Student's answer – examiner's comment*

'Good. Points to Macbeth's fear as making the scenes effective.'

The scene between Macbeth and Lady Macbeth before the banquet is one of the scenes that takes place at night and Macbeth refers to the night and darkness all through the scene. Lady Macbeth is trying to comfort him and turn his mind away from what they have done but Macbeth can only think about his terrible nightmares which come to him every night so that he can't get any sleep or rest from his guilty thoughts. One of the things that makes this scene effective is Macbeth's fear of night which brings the dreams that shake him. He uses the metaphor of being on a rack to describe his state.

'Good. Explains the metaphor and chooses an appropriate quotation to the point.'

>   Than on the torture of the mind to lie
>   In restless ecstasy

Later on he compares his thoughts to scorpions to show what mental agony he is in.

>   O full of scorpions is my mind dear wife

'Good. Identifies the language used to create atmosphere. Notices the personification.'

Although he is frightened of the night he wants it to come quickly so that Banquo can be killed. Shakespeare uses words like 'bat' and 'black Hecate' to create an evil atmosphere. Night is personified and Macbeth calls on it to come quickly. He speaks as though Night is going to do a murder.

>   Come seeling Night
>   Scarf up the tender eye of pitiful day
>   And with thy bloody and invisible hand
>   Cancel and tear to pieces that great bond

He describes the dark coming as 'light thickens' and as the good things of the day fade and go to sleep the evil things of Night wake up to stalk their prey.

By mentioning these things Shakespeare builds a picture of evil which makes the scene very effective.

'This scene comes first in the play, so it should come first in the essay.'

Another scene which takes place at night is the one where Macbeth is getting ready to murder Duncan. This scene begins peacefully with Banquo and Fleance going to bed and commenting on how dark the night is. When Macbeth appears they speak about the

(continued)

'Good. Points out the imagery to do with night and tries to explain its effect.'

(continued)

Weird Sisters, which together with the darkness gives a sinister feeling. When Banquo has gone Macbeth sees the vision of the dagger in the darkness. It seems he would not have seen it if it had been light because the night affected his imagination. In his speech Macbeth speaks of all the frightening things connected with night, like witchcraft, murder and death. Even before he has done the murder he is talking about bad dreams. He personifies a wolf howling and then walking stealthily towards its prey like a ghost. Shakespeare uses these images to make the atmosphere effective.

'The student's observation is good. However the discussion of language needs to be much more detailed and the imagery needs to be analysed more carefully.'

Question	Assessment Objective(s)	Pre-20th century	20th century
Coursework task – *Hobson's Choice*	1, 2, 4		✓
1 *Romeo and Juliet*	1, 2, 4	✓	
2 *She Stoops to Conquer*	1, 2, 4	✓	
3 *Macbeth*	1, 2, 4	✓	

SUMMARY

▷ Shakespeare, and other verse dramatists, use **verse** for serious characters and **prose** for low characters.

▷ **Imagery** creates atmosphere and mood. This applies particularly, but not solely, to verse plays.

▷ The use of **pause** and **silence** is important in dramatic language.

▷ **Formality** in language may be a question of period. This is important in deciding tone.

▷ **Colloquial** language may be used to make the play authentic or to show class or region.

▷ **Humour** is a product of language as much as situation.

Reading to understand narrative

▷ **GETTING STARTED**

We have all been familiar with reading stories from a young age. This probably makes the novel or short story section of the course the easiest to cope with. On the other hand, familiarity may also cause us to overlook difficulties. We have to remember that studying a novel or short story means looking at the question of *how the story is told* as well as what it is about. This chapter will help you to ask this question and show you how to answer it.

The topics in this chapter are applicable to all exam boards.

MEG	NEAB	NICCEA	SEG	LONDON	WJEC	IGCSE	TOPIC	STUDY	REVISION I	REVISION 2
✓	✓	✓	✓	✓	✓	✓	Who is telling the story?			
✓	✓	✓	✓	✓	✓	✓	To whom is the story told?			
✓	✓	✓	✓	✓	✓	✓	How many stories are there?			

WHAT YOU NEED TO KNOW

▷ **Who is telling the story?**

A story can be told in the **first person**. This is a grammatical term used to describe the use of 'I'.

> When I was nine years old I found myself completely alone in the world. The way that came about is very painful for me to recount.

Alternatively it can be told in the **third person**. This term means referring to people as 'he' and 'she'.

> Anne bent down and peered into the dark hole of the tunnel. She did not want to enter it. The enveloping blackness was the suffocation of her dream that could not be pushed away. She turned her head. It was day. She turned back and quickly went into the tunnel.

A story written in the third person has a different effect from one written in the first person. If someone says something happened to them, personally, it may make the incident seem more real, and the listener may become more involved. Even so, more novels are written in the third person.

The word we use for story-telling is **narration**. A story-teller is a **narrator**. Here are some questions to ask about narration:

i) Is the story all told by one person?
ii) Does the narrator have any part in the events of the story?
iii) Is the narrator telling his or her own story?
iv) How does the narrator know about the events?
v) If the narrator is looking back on himself at a younger age, has his viewpoint changed?

All these things will alter the way in which the story comes across to the reader. The story of *Wuthering Heights* is told at first by Mr Lockwood, then it is taken up by his housekeeper Nellie Dean. One of the effects of having a second narrator take over from the first is to make the previous events seem distant. The events are moved back in time and yet another person is placed between the reader and the characters of the story. This allows the reader to accept the sometimes strange events and violent passions of the novel. Nellie Dean is a different kind of character from Mr Lockwood and so tells the story in a different way. Her viewpoint is that of a servant in the household of the major characters. It is because Nellie Dean plays a small part in the story she is telling that she knows what happened. Sometimes it seems that she should not be present at a private scene but we tend not to notice such intrusions when we are reading.

When the narrator is telling his own story, like Pip in *Great Expectations* or Scout in *To Kill a Mocking Bird*, this difficulty does not arise. Both these narrators are looking back on their younger selves. This gives them the opportunity to comment on their own behaviour. In Pip's case he continually criticizes himself, regretting his earlier ingratitude to the good-natured Joe.

One of the restrictions of a first-person narrative is that it can only be told from one person's point of view. Therefore, in most novels the story is told from the outside. The narration does not come through a person's voice at all. The author simply tells the story as though she knows everything that happened, even down to what all the characters are thinking. This method of story-telling is most popular probably because the author then does not have to worry about how the narrator knows anything. Readers are accustomed to accepting a God-like knowledge in the author.

▷ **To whom is the story told?**

The story is, in the end, told to us, the readers. But some stories are told to a particular listener or a reader named or suggested by the narrator. Here are two examples of stories with special readers in mind:

i) **A Diary.** Is this a private diary, supposedly written only for the person writing it? If so how does this affect the way it is written and our views of what we read?
ii) **Letters.** Stories written in the form of a correspondence between two people used to be popular. A letter assumes that one particular person is reading it and so is written to appeal to him or her.

In both these cases readers may feel in the privileged position of someone eavesdropping on intimacies.

When you are reading a novel it helps you to sort out who is telling the story and to whom if you ask the following questions:

▶ Is there a character in the book who is listening to the story? The character of the listener will affect the way the story is told.

▶ If there is no stated listener or reader, to what sort of person does the author *seem* to be addressing the book?

If you can answer the question 'Who is the story told to?' as well as the question 'Who is telling it?' it may help you to understand the way in which it is written.

▷ How many stories are there?

Just as many plays have sub-plots, novels often have several narrative lines. The separate strands of the story usually come together at some point. Often there is a linking idea or theme between the stories. For instance, in *Great Expectations* there are several strands which may appear at first to be unrelated: the stories of Pip, Miss Haversham and Magwich. All these are connected, as we discover later on in the novel, by criminal activity. One of the ways of discovering the themes of a book is to look for links between the different threads of the story.

▷ Additional examples

Use the following passage as an exercise to test your understanding of what you have read. Work out your own ideas before reading the key below.

'Don't confuse the "I" of the story with the author.'

1 What can you say about the narrator and narration of the following passage? (Look back at all the possible questions and decide which are appropriate to ask and answer here.)

> When I came back from the East last autumn I felt that I wanted the world to be in uniform and at a moral attention forever; I wanted no more excursions with privileged glimpses into the human heart. Only Gatsby, the man who gives his name to this book, was exempt from my reaction – Gatsby, who represented everything for which I have an unaffected scorn. If personality is an unbroken series of successful gestures, then there was something gorgeous about him, some heightened sensitivity to the promises of life, as if he were related to one of those intricate machines that register earthquakes ten thousand miles away. This responsiveness had nothing to do with that flabby impressionability which is dignified under the name of the 'creative temperament' – it was an extraordinary gift for hope, a romantic readiness such as I have never found in any other person and which it is not likely that I shall ever find again. No – Gatsby turned out all right at the end; it is what preyed on Gatsby, what foul dust floated in the wake of his dreams that temporarily closed out my interest in the abortive sorrows and short-winded elations of men.
>
> *The Great Gatsby*, (F. Scott Fitzgerald)

2 Read the following five extracts from *Ethan Frome* by Edith Wharton. How many people are there telling the story? What is the difference in the narrative between number 4 and number 5?

> 1 I had the story bit by bit, from various people, and, as generally happens in such cases, each time it was a different story.
>
>   If you know Starkfield, Massachusetts, you know the post-office. If you know the post-office you must have seen Ethan Frome drive up to it, drop the reins on his hollow-backed bay and drag himself across the brick pavement to the white colonnade: and you must have asked who he was.
>
>   It was there several years ago, I saw him for the first time; and the sight pulled me up sharp. Even then he was the most striking figure in Starkfield, though he was but a ruin of a man. It was not so much his great height that marked him, for the 'natives' were easily singled out by their lank longitude from the stockier foreign breed: it was the careless powerful look he had, in spite of a lameness checking every step like the jerk of a chain. There was something bleak and unapproachable in his face, and he was so stiff and grizzled that I took him for an old man and was surprised to hear that he was not more than fifty-two. I had this from Harmon Gow, who had driven the stage from Bettsbridge to Starkfield in pre-trolley days and knew the chronicle of all the families on his line.
>
>   'He's looked that way ever since he had his smash up; and that's twenty-four years ago come next February,' Harmon threw out between reminiscent pauses.
>
> 2 Though Harmon Gow developed the tale as far as his mental reach permitted there were perceptible gaps between his facts, and I had the sense that the deeper meaning of the story was in the gaps.

3   In the 'best parlour', with its black horse-hair and mahogany weakly illuminated by a gurgling Carcel lamp, I listened every evening to another and more delicately shaded version of the Starkfield chronicle.

4   Frome stamped on the worn oil-cloth to shake the snow from his boots, and set down the lantern on a kitchen chair which was the only piece of furniture in the hall. Then he opened the door.

'Come in,' he said; and as he spoke the droning voice grew still . . .

It was that night that I found the clue to Ethan Frome, and began to put together this vision of his story . . .

5   The night was perfectly still, and the air so dry and pure that it gave little sensation of cold. The effect produced on Frome was rather of a complete absence of atmosphere, as though nothing less tenuous than ether intervened between the white earth under his feet and the metallic dome over head. 'It's like being in an exhausted receiver,' he thought.

Key to the examples

1   This is a narrative in the first person by someone who clearly has his own part in the story, but not the main part. He says the book is chiefly about Gatsby. The narrator's part seems to be mainly that of an observer who has watched some strongly emotional events, for he speaks of 'abortive sorrows and short-winded elations'. Some of what he has witnessed has disgusted him and left him disillusioned with human nature: 'it is what preyed on Gatsby, what foul dust floated in the wake of his dreams'. These remarks, together with his earlier ones about wanting 'the world to be in uniform and at a moral attention' shows the narrator to be a principled person with scruples and concerned about decent behaviour. He also seems to have admired and appreciated Gatsby despite initially feeling scorn for him. This confession and the sense that he has principles makes us willing to accept the narrator's judgement. His authority for telling the story, the reason he knows what he does, is that he had 'privileged glimpses into the human heart', meaning that he was a confidante of Gatsby and possibly others too.

The narrator has no particular listener or reader in mind, but seems to assume that he is telling his story to someone fairly like himself: educated, decent and down to earth, with similar values to his own because he does not strive to justify what he says. He expects it to be accepted.

2   There are three people telling the story. The first narrator is the 'I' of extracts 1–4. The second person is Harmon Gow; the third is the person in extract 3, whose name is Mrs Ned Hale. Between extracts 4 and 5 we move from first-person narrative to third-person narrative. The 'I' narrator has put together all his facts and starts to tell the story like an omniscient (i.e. all-knowing) author. This is what Edith Wharton herself wrote about the construction and narration of her story:

I had to find a means to bring my tragedy, in a way at once natural and picture-making, to the knowledge of its narrator. I might have sat him down before a village gossip who would have poured out the whole affair in a breath, but in doing this I should have been false to two essential elements of my picture: first the deep-rooted reticence and inarticulateness of the people I was trying to draw, and secondly the effect of roundness (in the plastic sense) produced by letting their case be seen through eyes as different as those of Harmon Gow and Mrs Ned Hale. Each of my chroniclers contributes to the narrative *just so much as he or she is capable of understanding* [EW's italics] of what, to them, is a complicated and mysterious case; and only the narrator of the tale has scope enough to see it all . . .

As you read Edith Wharton's story you can judge how far she has been successful in these aims.

SUGGESTIONS FOR COURSEWORK

1   Re-write a chapter of a novel in the form of letters written by the characters to each other or to another character in the novel.

2   Make a comparison of two different kinds of narrative, for example a story told in the first person and a story told in the third person. You might compare *Roll of Thunder,*

Hear My Cry, with *Of Mice and Men*; or compare *The Loneliness of the Long Distance Runner* with *A Kestrel for a Knave*.

3   Imagine you are a character in a novel at a key moment in your life. Write a letter to a friend, explaining how you feel and what your hopes are for the future.

4   Choose a novel written in the third person. Select a chapter. Re-tell the story from the viewpoint of one of the characters.

▷ **Coursework task**   Rewrite an episode from *Silas Marner* from the point of view of one of the characters. You may write as that character if you wish.

▷ **Notes**   1   *Silas Marner* is told in the third person. The author, George Eliot, tells us what many of the characters are thinking and feeling. That is to say we get many points of view. The question asks you to write from a single point of view.

2   The following answer is written in the first person in the character of Mrs Nancy Cass. This means we get only her point of view of this incident.

▷ **Suggested answer**   'Mrs Nancy Cass Visits Silas and Eppie With Her Husband'

As soon as everything was quiet again at the Stone Pits Godfrey and I walked to Silas Marner's cottage. All I felt was a deep regret that we had not made this journey earlier, for I would not have opposed Godfrey's idea of adopting Eppie if I had known then that she was his child. When we reached the cottage it was Eppie who opened the door and I realized what a pretty, delicate girl she is, with eyes exactly like Godfrey's and the same golden hair. I had seen Eppie many times but had no cause to notice her particularly and so the likeness had not struck me before. The cottage was very clean and neat, a credit to Eppie's housewifery and the good instruction she has received from Dolly Winthrop. The gold which had been recovered from the Stone Pit lay ranged on the table and indeed it was a goodly sum for working people, enough to keep Marner comfortable in his old age, although it could not approach the comfort and privileges that should have been Eppie's from the beginning and which Godfrey was now going to offer her.

Godfey had great difficulty in broaching the subject, which was only to be expected after the wrong he had done in not claiming the child from the beginning. Now that he had opened himself to me I could see that he was determined to do right and make amends for the past insofar as he could. We had agreed that it would be better to leave aside the subject of father-hood and break it slowly to Eppie. To my mind it would be difficult for the girl to forgive Godfrey for the way he treated her mother. Consequently Godfrey spoke only of the wrong which his bother Dunsey had done to Marner in robbing him all those years ago. Marner is a good, simple, hard-working man. He and Eppie seemed content with their lot and were grateful for what my husband had already done for them, which indeed had been as much as he could without raising suspicions. All that Eppie seemed to desire was a garden and I sympa-thized with that for I spend a good deal of time in the garden myself.

Well, it was finally said: that we had the intention of taking Eppie into our own home and treating her as our own daughter. Marner seemed not at first to understand and Godfrey had to explain that Eppie would be allowed to come to see him often and everything would be done to make him comfortable, in recognition of the care that he had given to Eppie for sixteen years. I thought that Marner was going to object for it was clear that he was struggling with himself, as well he might for he would lose the child he had cared for. But he could see that the offer was for her good and he said what was right and that he would not stand in Eppie's way. Then to my astonishment Eppie herself said no. She was very polite and near to tears and so was I. I could see that her feeling for Marner was too strong to break. My heart grieved for Godfrey, for now he must surely tell her that he was her natural father and her duty was to him. I could hear the agitation in his voice as he revealed the truth to her, a truth that could only appear brutal when presented in this way and Eppie was visibly shaken by the news. Now it was Marner who opposed Godfrey. When he said that God had given Eppie to him because Godfrey had turned his back on her I could not help feeling the truth of his words. I thought too that Godfrey had made a noble resolution to do his duty, whatever the cost to our reputation, and I was prepared to support him however hard it was, for it would be hard to tell the world of the great wrong he had done, especially hard to tell father and

Priscilla. I told Eppie that I would care for her as a daughter and she would be a great treasure to me. With her as a daughter I would wish for nothing more, for she would fill the only vacancy in our lives.

I was unprepared and shocked when once again Eppie refused to leave Marner. The great tenderness between the old man and the child was a blessing and a joy to see but there was also the question of her duty to her lawful father and, as I felt bound to tell her, perhaps there was something to be given up on more sides than one. However she was adamant in her determination and shed passionate tears, saying she was already promised in marriage to a working man and wanted nothing more. My poor Godfrey could hardly hold back his own tears. There was no more to say and indeed he could not speak so I said our farewells and withdrew.

It is a bitter thing for Godfrey but he has resigned himself to it and I think after all he is a better man now than he was and I cannot find it in my heart to blame him for the past.

 ## EXAMINATION QUESTIONS

You may be asked if you think it is a good or a bad idea to let a character tell his or her own story. Other questions may ask you what view you have formed of the character or point of view of the narrator, for instance Laurie Lee in *Cider with Rosie*. Sometimes you will be asked to change the way the story is narrated by imagining you are a certain character and explaining how you feel and why you react in the way you do. (Look at the previous coursework answer for one example of this kind of question, and the student's answer at the end of the chapter for another.)

▷ **Question 1**
'Higher Tier.'

In *To Kill a Mockingbird*, Harper Lee lets Scout tell her own story. Do you think this is a good idea? Use as evidence to support your opinion Scout's accounts of two or more of the following: her family, Boo Radley, Mrs Dubose, Calpurnia's church, the night outside the jail, the trial.

1   List any general advantages and disadvantages you can think of to first-person narrative.
2   Decide on the two or more events you wish to write about and jot down notes on Scout's part in each scene and any thoughts you have on the way it is told. Is it convincing? What difference does it make having it told by a child?
3   Use your general points for your opening paragraph.
4   Use the events of the book to bring out the points you have made in your opening paragraph.

▷ **Question 2**

Writing a letter from a character is another way of changing the narrative point of view. The following question is based on *Her First Ball* by Katherine Mansfield.

Imagine you are Leila. Write a letter to your mother explaining what happened at the ball and how you felt.

 ## EXAMINATION ANSWERS

▷ **Question 1**   *Tutor's answer*

The advantage of allowing Scout to tell her own story is that it has the immediacy of any first-hand account. It is convincing because she herself has taken part in the events she is narrating. Readers feel involved because there is as little distance as possible between themselves and the narrator: they feel they know the person to whom all these things have appeared. Scout is only a small child when the events of the story take place and this gives a second advantage. Because it is told through a child's eyes the story has the freshness of a child's point of view. However there is a disadvantage: Scout can only tell of things she has seen, or been told about, and this is occasionally awkward. She has to be present at events a child would not perhaps witness, or have conversations a child would not have.

We might feel that it is a disadvantage to have Scout as a narrator when Jem is ordered to

'Have you used the story to make points which answer the question? Many candidates lose marks because they just re-tell the story.'

read to Mrs Dubose as a punishment for destroying her camellias. It is not necessary for Scout to go with him. Atticus says, 'You don't have to go with Jem you know.' The author overcomes this by making Scout so devoted to Jem that it seems natural for her to accompany him, even though she finds it unpleasant.

Mrs Dubose is sick, old and a morphine addict. Jem is ordered to read *Ivanhoe* to her for two hours every afternoon for a month. Sitting beside Jem as he reads, Scout can obviously observe more than he. Without Scout's presence this part of the story would have to be told first by Jem to Scout. The detail and freshness of firsthand impressions would be lost. As Jem reads Mrs Dubose interrupts and corrects him but then Scout notices she has drifted off into a fit, which is horrible to watch. With a child's limited experience Scout is not aware of the cause; she simply recounts the events. Finally the alarm clock rings and they are sent away by Jessie the maid. Every day is the same. Eventually Scout realizes that the time before the fit starts and the alarm rings has gradually lengthened. Finally Mrs Dubose is conscious and cantankerous right up until they leave. The advantage of a child as narrator is that Mrs Dubose's behaviour is never questioned, a purpose beyond that of the whim of a nasty old woman is never sought. Her morphine addiction is only revealed to us when she dies a month later. Then we understand her behaviour and our sympathy with the character is the greater for being delayed: we always feel sorry when we say 'if only I'd known at the time'.

The author's purpose in including this episode is to contrast what is normally thought of as brave with the kind of courage Mrs Dubose showed in breaking her morphine addiction before she died. This is done through Atticus' admiration of her. He calls her a 'great lady'. He uses Mrs Dubose to teach Jem that courage is fighting even when you know from the start you're licked, which is exactly what he himself is doing in the case of Tom Robinson. By having a child as narrator the author is able to use the parent–child relationship to point a simple moral to the reader.

The difficulty of needing Scout to be present in situations where she might not be expected to be is cleverly overcome, indeed exploited, in the scene outside the jail the night before Tom Robinson's trial. Atticus knows there might be trouble. The previous night Scout and Jem overheard the Sheriff and other men predicting that some out-of-town folks might take the law into their own hands. Scout tells this part of the story as if she is somewhat baffled by the behaviour of Jem, who is four years her senior. When Atticus takes an extension cord and light bulb and goes out instead of going to bed Jem gets jumpy and prepares to follow him. Scout insists on going too, although she appears not to understand why. This lack of understanding means that the story can be told very simply. It also means that we, the readers, have to work out the significance of the events for ourselves, which helps to hold our interest and attention.

Jem, Scout and Dill find Atticus quietly reading outside the jail and are about to sneak quietly home when several car-loads of men arrive and confront him. In reply to their threats Scout hears Atticus say, 'Do you really think so', which she knows is his deadly question. This, Scout says, was too good to miss. She runs to Atticus. This action is the weakest point of the narrative. Even though Scout is presented as an impetuous, even wilful child, it does not seem a sufficiently strong reason for her to run out and risk punishment for not being at home in bed. On this occasion the author has not completely overcome the difficulty of getting the narrator on to the scene.

After that, however, the author uses Scout's age to enormous advantage. First she defends Jem by kicking one of the men. It is only because she is a small girl that this does not spark off violence in retaliation. She has no idea of what is happening so she is not frightened. She launches into a conversation with Mr Cunningham about his son and a lawsuit she has heard Atticus talking about. Finally her chatter defuses an ugly situation because it makes Cunningham and his gang look at Atticus as a person again and not an enemy or merely something in their way. The author uses the innocence of the child to comment on the morality and behaviour of the men.

Most of the time during this episode we feel we know more about the situation than Scout does. The author appears to describe the scene exactly as an eight year old would see it. We are left to draw the implications lost on a child. The language, though, is not that of a child, except when Scout speaks. We are told at the beginning that Scout is looking back on these incidents so the language used is that of an adult. Moreover Scout is presented to us as a bright little tomboy, a precocious child who could read and write before she went to school. This allows the author to put her into situations and give her thoughts which might otherwise have been unconvincing.

▷ **Question 2**   *Student's answer – examiner's comments*

Dearest Mother,

I am writing just a quick letter to tell you about the ball. So if you are standing, sit down and turn the wireless off. My feelings about the ball are so mixed I don't know where to begin.

The feeling of excitement that I experienced in the cab really came alive as I entered the ladies' room, simply because my first ball was really going to happen. It was very crowded but it did not matter. Soon a basket of programmes was passed around. I felt a little nervous as I took one and wondered what I was supposed to do with it.

As we entered the drill hall my nervous feelings vanished and I felt so happy. Everything in the room looked lovely. I was introduced to some other girls but I am sure that they didn't even look at me as they were too interested in the men on the other side of the room. It was curious how they all lined up on that side and didn't come across. Then suddenly they all came at once and before I knew it a young man who had signed Meg's programme took mine and scribbled his name down. This was very exciting but then a bald, fat old man came across to me and compared our programmes. I felt ashamed as it seemed so much trouble for him to go to, but as soon as the music started he disappeared.

I could hardly wait for my partner to arrive and when he came he smiled and bowed so politely. I was so happy when we glided on to the floor. I couldn't understand his astonishment as I commented that it was nice and slippery. When he asked me if I'd been at the ball last week I explained that this was my first and that it was very exciting for me. Soon the music stopped and we sat down. Although he had nothing to say it really didn't matter. It was blissful just watching everybody else. When the music started again my second partner arrived. It was very strange because he said exactly the same things as the first one. I felt a bit disappointed that nobody was interested that this was my very first ball. This time when the music ended we went out through the double doors to find an ice. They looked so pretty on their little glass plates with little frosted spoons and it was so refreshing. As we returned to the hall the fat man was waiting for me. It was a shock to see how old he was. As we 'walked' around the floor he astonished me by telling me he had been doing this for thirty years. I felt quite sorry for him with his baldness and his fatness and his age. He said I would soon be sitting on the stage like the fat mothers watching my own daughter dancing and that made me feel quite depressed. I laughed and tried not to show how much he had upset me but he had depressed me so much that I did not want to dance any more. When he left at the end of the dance I just wanted to be home with you.

Out of politeness I carried on dancing with my next partner and within moments the music and twirling round the floor, the lights and colours and the smells of the flowers all carried me off. Until I started writing about it just now I forgot all about the old man with his depressing view of the future and I enjoyed the present. I had a wonderful evening and I hope you will allow me to go to another ball very soon.

Your loving daughter,
Leila.

'This story is all about feelings so this is a good letter because it accurately describes Leila's feelings and shows the way they change.

The tone of the letter is also good: it sounds as though it were written by a girl to her mother earlier this century. The word 'wireless' for 'radio' is a good attempt to create the period, unfortunately there was no wireless at the time when the story is set.

'Ashamed' picks out a good word concerning Leila's feelings for the fat man but does not really convey her reaction to this important incident. 'Enjoy the present' sums up Leila's feeling at the end.

This is a good account but there are two reasons why this piece of work falls short of the top grade. First there is a vagueness in the descriptions: the story has good specific details and one or two of these could have been picked out to supply colour. Secondly elements of the feeling of the story have not been conveyed completely. In the original there is a sense that Leila's excitement will soon fade and that the person she calls "the fat man" has a much more realistic view of life than she has.'

Question	Assessment Objective(s)	Pre-20th century	20th century
Coursework task – *Silas Marner*	1, 2, 4	✓	
1 *To Kill a Mocking Bird*	1, 2, 4		✓
2 *Her First Ball*	1, 2, 4		✓

SUMMARY

▷ The type of narrator alters the way the story is told.

▷ First-person narratives give an impression of intimacy to the reader, but they can only be told from one person's point of view.

▷ Third-person narratives allow the author to know everything about all the characters. They can present several points of view.

▷ Where there is an imaginary person to whom the story is told this also affects the way it is told.

▷ Stories often have several strands linked by a common theme.

Plots in novels

 GETTING STARTED

When we read a novel or short story it is frequently the desire to know what happens next that keeps us reading. Just like a dramatist a novelist uses suspense, tension, conflict and surprise to keep us interested. If you have not read the chapter on plots in drama (Chapter 10) you should do so to see how these elements work. In the exam you will be asked to recall what happened in the story and why it was important. But you should always try to do more than simply re-tell the story. That will earn you some marks, but not very many. So from the beginning you must learn to ask what is significant about the events. In other words you must ask not 'what' but 'how' and 'why'. Try to decide how the author has aroused and held your interest in each chapter. The sections that follow give you specific questions and ideas, first on the opening chapter and then on the rest of the novel.

The topics covered in this chapter are applicable to all exam boards.

MEG	NEAB	NICCEA	SEG	LONDON	WJEC	IGCSE	**TOPIC**	STUDY	REVISION I	REVISION 2
✓	✓	✓	✓	✓	✓	✓	Arousing interest			
✓	✓	✓	✓	✓	✓	✓	Development of the plot			
✓	✓	✓	✓	✓	✓	✓	The order of the story			
✓	✓	✓	✓	✓	✓	✓	Endings			

WHAT YOU NEED TO KNOW

▷ **Arousing interest**
Authors must arouse the interest of their readers and make them want to go on reading. How do they do it?

Character

They can immediately introduce a character that we are fascinated by or sympathize with, like the Emperor Claudius in the first sentence of *I Claudius*:

> I, TIBERIUS CLAUDIUS DRUSUS NERO GERMANICUS
> This-that-and-the-other (for I shall not trouble you yet with all my titles) who was once, and not so long ago either, known to my friends and relatives and associates as 'Claudius the Idiot' or 'That Claudius' or 'Claudius the Stammerer', or 'Clau-Clau-Claudius' or at best as 'Poor Uncle Claudius' am now about to write this strange history of my life;

We do not have to like the character. Any strong reaction will do.

Situation

Another way is to plunge us into a situation that we then want to follow. This does not necessarily mean finding ourselves in the middle of a tense conflict on the first page. Consider the opening paragraphs of *To Kill a Mockingbird*:

> When he was nearly thirteen, my brother Jem got his arm badly broken at the elbow. When it healed, and Jem's fears of never being able to play football again were assuaged, he was seldom self-conscious about his injury. His left arm was somewhat shorter than his right; when he stood or walked, the back of his hand was at right angles to his body, his thumb parallel to his thigh. He couldn't have cared less, so long as he could pass and punt.
>   When enough years had gone by to enable us to look back on them, we sometimes discussed the events leading to his accident. I maintain that the Ewells started it all, but Jem, who was four years my senior, said it started long before that. He said it began the summer Dill came to us, when Dill first gave us the idea of making Boo Radley come out.

Already we are asking ourselves questions. Why was Jem's arm broken so badly? Who were the Ewells and what had they done to start it? Who was the peculiarly named person, Boo Radley, and what did he or she have to come out from? Because we are curious to know the answer to all these questions we go on reading.

Setting or atmosphere

A third way is to create a strong atmosphere or sense of place. This does not have to be an exotic place. Thomas Hardy begins *The Return of the Native* with a chapter describing a stretch of moorland in Dorset. It is not particularly beautiful. Nothing happens, no characters appear, but by the end of the chapter we are so immersed in the scene that it seems charged with significance. Dickens opens *Bleak House* with a similarly significant description. The first paragraph concentrates on mud, the second on fog:

> Fog everywhere. Fog up the river, where it flows among green aits and meadows; fog down the river where it rolls defiled among the tiers of shipping, and the waterside pollutions of a great (and dirty) city. Fog on the Essex marshes, fog in the Kentish heights. Fog creeping into the cabooses of the collier-brigs; fog lying out on the yards, and hovering off the rigging of the great ships; fog drooping on the gunwales of barges and small boats. Fog in the eyes and throats of ancient Greenwich pensioners, wheezing by the firesides of their wards; fog in the stem and bowl of the afternoon pipe of the wrathful skipper, down in his close cabin; fog cruelly pinching the toes and fingers of his shivering little 'prentice boy on deck.

And so it goes on. Dickens seems to draw us into the novel by creating the most unpleasant conditions that he can devise. He arouses our interest through distaste and imagined discomfort as much as through sympathy for the poor wretches who have to endure such weather. We also begin to suspect that this description has to do with more than simply weather. We read on to find out its significance.

Comedy

Yet another way to keep the readers is to make them laugh, or at least smile:

> I suppose that the high water mark of my youth in Columbus, Ohio, was the night the bed fell on my father.

That is the promising opening sentence of James Thurber's *My Life and Hard Times*. Promising because it suggests irreverent descriptions of hilarious situations. We read on.

How does the novelist arouse interest in the opening chapter of the novels you are studying?

▷ Development of the plot

Having aroused our interest the author must then keep it. The characters or the situation must develop just as in drama (again see Chapter 10). One of our most basic interests is in other people, so the portrayal and development of characters is one of the novelist's strongest weapons. Another is the unfolding of a situation in a way that we recognize as a representation of life. Some of the ways that novelists have of keeping our interest are as follows:

i) The development of **relationships** between characters. All novels involving courtship and 'romance' do this but there are many other kinds of developing relationships. For example there are family relationships and social relationships. Many novels include all these types. Think about whether – and how – relationships change from chapter to chapter in the novels you are reading.

ii) The solving of a **problem** or a mystery. The detective novel is a popular form which uses this method. Other novels may incorporate less obvious mysteries as one part of the plot. For instance, who is Pip's benefactor in *Great Expectations*?

iii) The development and resolution of a **conflict** between characters or groups. This may range from war between countries, through gang war, down to rivalry between individuals. The conflict does not have to be physical. The popularity of fights and trial scenes in literature (and on television) shows how potent the idea of conflict is.

iv) The overcoming of some **difficulty** or disaster, as in many adventure novels.

v) A **search** or discovery, whether it is a search for lost empires, the discovery of penicillin or some kind of more personal inner quest.

These are just some suggestions. Most novels include many of these features at different points of the story. *Pride and Prejudice* includes a number of unfolding relationships, conflict (though never violent) between various characters, self-discovery by both Elizabeth and Darcy, and the overcoming of numerous difficulties on the way to fortunate marriage by Jane and Elizabeth.

How does the novelist maintain interest in the novels you are reading?

▷ The order of the story

Remember that stories are constructed. An author decides not just what shall be told but the order of telling it. In life we learn things about people and events in a great jumble. We know that the lady next door is a nurse and we see her going to work regularly at the hospital. This gives us a particular view of her. Then suddenly we find out that she used to be a trapeze artiste in a circus and our view of her changes with a jolt. Just the same happens in novels; the author quite deliberately gives us information in a certain order. Our view of the characters may unfold smoothly, or we may be brought up short by an unexpected revelation, just as the novelist pleases. Ask yourself these questions:

i) Is the story presented chronologically? That is, in the order in which the events happen?

ii) If the story does not begin at the beginning, where does it begin? Why has the author chosen to begin at that point?

iii) Does the plot move us back in time to some earlier point in the story? If so, how often and for what reasons?

iv) Are we ever taken into the future and if so how is it done?

v) Are we ever told things twice?

vi) Are there any gaps or jumps in the story?

▷ **Endings**   The end of a story should show events brought to a conclusion which we feel is right and in keeping with what has gone before. Even when the end is a sad one we should feel that such an ending is justified. A sense of rightness has a lot to do with the themes and ideas of the book being worked out satisfactorily. Chapter 17 deals with this.

▷ **Additional examples**   Use these examples as exercises to test your understanding of this chapter. Write down your own ideas before looking at the key. The first two passages are openings, of a novel and a short story. Try to say what in them arouses our interest. What does the novelist do in the third passage to maintain interest?

1   Mr Tench went out to look for his ether cylinder, into the blazing Mexican sun and the bleaching dust. A few vultures looked down from the roof with shabby indifference: he wasn't carrion yet. A faint feeling of rebellion stirred in Mr Tench's heart, and he wrenched up a piece of the road with splintering fingernails and tossed it feebly towards them. One rose and flapped across the town: over the tiny plaza, over the bust of an ex-president, ex-general, ex-human being, over the two stalls which sold mineral water, towards the river and the sea. It wouldn't find anything there. The sharks looked after the carrion on that side. Mr Tench went on across the plaza.

(Graham Greene, *The Power and the Glory*)

2   There was a man who loved islands. He was born on one but it didn't suit him, as there were too many other people on it, besides himself. He wanted an island all of his own: not necessarily to be alone on it, but to make it a world of his own.

(D. H. Lawrence, *The Man Who Loved Islands*)

3   'Hymn number one-seven-five, "New every morning is the love".' The navy blue covers of the hymn books, inconspicuous against the dark shades of the boys' clothing, bloomed white across the hall as they were opened and the pages flicked through. The scuff and tick of the turning pages was slowly drowned under a rising chorus of coughing and hawking; until Mr Gryce, furious behind the lectern, scooped up his stick and began to smack it vertically down the face.
      'STOP THAT INFERNAL COUGHING.'
      The sight and swishsmack of the stick stopped the throat noises and the boys and the teachers, posted at regular intervals at the ends of the rows, all looked up to the platform. Gryce was straining over the top of the lectern like a bulldog up on its hind legs.
      'It's every morning alike! As soon as the hymn is announced you're off revving up! Hm-hmm! Hm-hmm! It's more like a race track in here than an assembly hall!' – Hall – ringing across the hall, striking the windows and lingering there like the vibrations of a tuning fork.
      No one muffed. Not a foot scraped. Not a page stirred. The teachers looked seriously into the ranks of the boys. The boys stood looking up at Gryce, each one convinced that Gryce was looking at him.
      The silence thickened. The boys began to swallow their adam's apples, their eyes skittering about in still heads. The teachers began to glance at each other and glance sideways up at the platform.
      Then a boy coughed.
      'Who did that?'
      Everybody looking round.
      'I said WHO DID THAT?'
      The teachers moved in closer, alert like a riot squad.
      'Mr Crossley! Somewhere near you! Didn't you see the boy?'
      Crossley flushed, and rushed amongst them, thrusting them aside in panic.
      'There Crossley! That's where it came from! Around there!' Crossley grabbed a boy by the arm and began to drag him into the open.
      'It wasn't me, Sir!'
      'Of course it was you.'
      'It wasn't, Sir, honest!'
      'Don't argue lad, I saw you.' Gryce thrust his jaw over the front of the lectern, the air whistling down his nostrils.
      'MACDOWALL! I might have known it! Get to my room, lad!'

(Barry Hines, *Kestrel for a Knave*)

Key to the examples

1 This is an interesting opening because it immediately provokes us to ask questions about the character and the situation he is in. Why is he looking for an ether cylinder? Why does he feel rebellious? A strong, exotic atmosphere is established by the blazing Mexican sun, vultures on the roof, the sharks. Mr Tench does not seem to fit in here but his gesture of rebellion is an ineffectual one: the piece of tarmac he feebly throws displaces only one of the vultures. Why isn't he able to do something positive? The vultures and the sharks, with their associations of death, produce a tension and a strong sense of foreboding. The only other sign of humanity is an ex-human being.

2 The question raised here is will the man get what he wants: an island all of his own? It seems to be the opening of a search or a struggle to achieve that ambition.

3 The interest in this passage depends on the portrayal of Mr Gryce, the headmaster, his relation-ships with the other staff and the boys, and the tension produced by his anger. The beginning is also quite grimly comic with the description of the boys' chorus of throat noises which sound like racing cars. By comparing Mr Gryce to a 'bulldog up on its hind legs' and by showing him smacking his stick down on the lectern while roaring furiously at the assembled school, Barry Hines creates a figure which is both funny and frightening. He conveys to us the trepidation of the boys as they stand silently, hardly daring to breathe. Even the teachers are affected by the tension. Mr Crossley appears almost as much in awe as the boys and panics when action is demanded of him. Then the blow falls on MacDowall. The tension is broken when he is carted off to await punishment.

Notice how many of the sentences are very short. This is one of the ways tension is created. Another is by putting some of Gryce's words in capital letters to suggest his roaring. This device also adds humour. The fact that MacDowall is shown as being picked from the crowd indiscrimi-nately – and probably unjustly – because Mr Crossley cannot confess that he does not know who did it, adds to our interest. It raises questions about the fairness of the behaviour of Gryce and Crossley. We sympathize with MacDowall. Perhaps we even sympathize with Mr Crossley. When we read the book these questions of fairness recur.

'Did you note the character of Mr Gryce, relationships and comedy? These are points that will gain marks.'

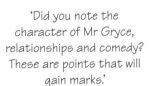 **SUGGESTIONS FOR COURSEWORK**

1 Write a new opening or final chapter to a novel you are studying.
2 Find a chapter in a novel where you feel the plot takes an unfortunate turn – you would like a different twist to the plot. Write a new chapter which would satisfy your needs at this stage in the novel.
3 Write about the part which weather plays in a novel of your choice.
4 Write a comparison of two opening chapters which you find effective in different ways.
5 Write a review of a novel which uses 'flashbacks', for example *Ethan Frome* or *Wuthering Heights,* and suggest what these techniques add to the story.
6 Choose a novel which you think might have started at a different part of the story. Write the new opening chapter.
7 Write about the end of a novel. How satisfactory do you find it?

▷ **Coursework task**   Write about the ending of *Of Mice and Men*. Do you think that Steinbeck's ending is a satisfy-ing one?

▷ **Outline answer**
1 **Introduction.** The ending of Steinbeck's short novel *Of Mice and Men* is extremely sad but completely in keeping with the rest of the story.
2 **Describe** Lennie's character and physical characteristics. Include his childlike behaviour, such as his complete dependence on George, his desire to have rabbits to look after and the way he likes to pet things. Describe his physical size and strength, giving examples such as the way he always unintentionally kills his pets and the crushing of Curley's hand.
3 **Describe the relationship** George has with Lennie, including how he tries to instruct Lennie to keep out of trouble, how he grumbles that life could be so much easier without Lennie but continues to look after him. Note that other men on the ranch find it odd that

George and Lennie travel together (look for a quotation) and that one of the problems of ranch life is loneliness.

4 **Relate the end of the story** telling how Lennie came to kill Curley's wife and, as previously instructed by George, goes to wait for George in the brush. Describe how George shoots Lennie while telling him once again the story of the land they are going to buy.

5 **Consider alternative endings** to the story:
   i)   George and Lennie hide and escape as they did after the incident in Weed when Lennie was accused of rape. (How would they live?)
   ii) The other men find Lennie first and, Curley especially, subject him to brutal treatment before finally killing him. (How would George react?)
   iii) Lennie is handed over to the law. (Look at what Slim says about this alternative.)

6 **Conclusion.** George has to steel himself to shoot Lennie. His hand shakes violently until he sets his face and makes a great effort of will. He makes sure that Lennie is happy and absorbed in the thought of what life will be like when they have bought their little bit of land. George shoots Lennie directly in the back of the neck and then throws away the gun, staring at his hand as though it doesn't belong to him. Earlier in the story Candy's old dog has to be shot to put it out of its misery. Candy allows Carlson to take the dog away and shoot it but later regrets his own cowardice. He should have done it himself. It is clear that Lennie has to die, because he has long been a danger to others and now he has murdered a woman. George kills his friend himself in the kindest way possible because otherwise he would not be able to face himself.

EXAMINATION QUESTIONS

In the exam you may be asked your opinion about the opening or the ending of a novel. Or you may be asked to choose an exciting episode and explain why you find it exciting, or how the author holds your attention. You could be asked to show the part played by a particular aspect of the plot, such as conflict or violence. You may be given a passage and asked how the writer creates suspense.

▷ **Question 1**   How successful do you find Chapter 1 of *Great Expectations*? In what ways does it prepare you for what is going to happen in the rest of the novel?

▷ **Question 2**   What is the role of the conch in *Lord of the Flies*?
'Higher Tier.'

EXAMINATION ANSWERS

▷ **Question 1**   *Notes and tutor's answer*

Notes

1 This question is set for an open-book exam so your first task is to look at the chapter to remind yourself of the work you have done on it.

NOTE: You will only have time to refresh your memory. Do not expect to be able to go into the exam room and write on a question like this without having prepared yourself.

2 Note that the question asks you to relate the chapter to the rest of the book. You should not, therefore, write just about the opening chapter.

3 Jot down notes on the general areas you want to cover before beginning to write. (Look back at the section on arousing interest.) Use the following headings, expanding each one with detailed points and supporting evidence from the text:
   – Character and situation of Pip;
   – Character and significance of convict;
   – Atmosphere of marshes;
   – Tension of situation;
   – Later significance of this meeting.

Suggested answer

The opening chapter of *Great Expectations* introduces us to Pip, the central character and narrator of the story, and to the convict who so influences the course of his life. This meeting leads to Pip's 'great expectations' and many changes in his life.

The opening paragraphs arouse our interest in Pip by showing him to have survived while his mother and father and five of his brothers have died. As he is an orphan we feel sympathy for him. Almost immediately he is plunged into a terrifying situation which grips our attention.

The man who confronts him is a fearsome sight: wet, dirty with mud, shivering with cold and with a great iron on his leg. He strikes terror into Pip's heart not only by his appearance but also by turning him upside down and balancing him dangerously on top of a high tombstone while he threatens him. All this, and the strangeness of the man, his looks and behaviour, further excites our interest and raises questions that we expect the novelist to answer. Why is he lurking in the churchyard? What has he done? Will he escape? His physical condition – filthy, cold, hungry and hunted – also elicits our sympathy, but his treatment of Pip, his dire threats of having Pip's heart and liver torn out and roasted whole, sets up an unequal conflict in which we hope Pip will not be harmed.

The place in which Dickens chooses to set the scene gives it a strong and eerily melancholy atmosphere. It is a raw afternoon on the 'dark, flat wilderness' of the marshes. The wind rushes in from the sea and the only living creatures to be seen are the scattered cattle. Pip is alone among the gravestones when suddenly the figure arises from among them. The convict's first words voice the threat to cut Pip's throat. It is a memorably dramatic scene. When Pip runs home across the marshes the lone figure outlined against the darkening sky is limping towards the gibbet – a further suggestion of crime and suffering, to be developed later in the novel. Everything in this scene is calculated to increase the atmosphere of grim mystery.

At the end of the chapter we are left wondering whether Pip will keep his meeting secret and if he will manage to return with the file and the food the convict has demanded. Our curiosity about the fate of both Pip and the convict has been awakened. We expect the meeting to have an uncommon effect on Pip's life, although we have to wait a long time before we see what it is.

The presence of a convict in the first chapter alerts us to one of the themes in the novel. A good deal of the book is concerned with crime and criminals and many of the characters are affected as well as Pip. Miss Havisham's plight is the result of a criminal deception; the same man affects Estella, the convict's child; Pip's sister, Mrs Joe Gargery, is maimed by Orlick, who also attacks Pip and represents unredeemable criminal brutishness; we see the effect of work among the criminal classes on Jagger and on Wemmick who has to become a different person to do his work; we are taken into the prison at Newgate.

A second theme is developed through the relationship of Pip and the convict. Pip's kindness as a child is rewarded with his 'great expectations', but these, perversely, lead him to behave badly, squander his money and neglect the good and faithful Joe. When Magwich re-enters the story Pip cannot, for shame, be unkind to the man who has done and promised so much. Pip loses the money which was intended to buy him the status of 'gentleman'. Nevertheless he learns how to be the true gentleman that Magwich wanted him to be.

'Have you answered the question fully? You will lose marks if you do not refer to the rest of the book, as the question asked.'

▷ **Question 2** *Student's answer – examiner's comment*

'Good. Correctly states the central importance of the conch.'

At the beginning of the book the conch is found by Ralph. It stays with Ralph and symbolizes his power and authority. As people begin to listen less to Ralph and more to fact they seem to disregard the conch.

But there was a stillness about Ralph as he sat that marked him out: there was his size, and attractive appearance; and most obscurely, yet most powerfully, there was the conch.

At the beginning of the book the conch was used as a call for all the boys to come to the

(continued)

'"At the beginning" is used twice. The first paragraph should make a general statement, leaving illustration or quotation to later paragraphs.'

'Good specific detail from the story, linking the conch with an idea.'

'Good. Identifies how attitudes towards the conch change as the story progresses.'

'There is not enough plot detail of how the conch came to represent order and civilization. This continues throughout; few points are backed up by enough reference to events.'

(continued)

beach in order to discuss their position. It represented a meeting of civilized schoolboys waiting to organize things, vote on matters etc. All things that happen in the ordinary civilized world. Thus the conch gets associated with civilization.

'This toy of voting was almost as pleasing as the conch.' Here, William Golding is linking the conch with voting, one of the most civilized things that happens in the world. It's fair, democratic and far from barbaric.

Whenever anyone holds the conch they have power over everyone else. They have the right to express their wishes and rules are put forward. Thus through the conch rules are put forward and they make grand plans. Rules run parallel with civilization. You need both and so the conch becomes the symbol of both.

As the story goes on the boys begin to forget the real world and they turn to hunting. Their grand plans dissolve and they begin to forget the rules. The conch begins to lose its power. First they tell Piggy to 'shut up' when he has the conch and then Jack starts to speak and call out when he hasn't got the conch.

'Jack! Jack! You haven't got the conch! Let him speak.' Once the conch is disregarded so are the rules and civilization loses its foothold over the boys.

'The rules!' shouted Ralph, 'you're breaking the rules.' From then on things go from bad to worse. The rules slip and the conch loses its meaning; when Ralph and Jack split up Jack says:

You haven't got it with you. You left it behind. See, clever? And the conch doesn't count at this end of the island.

In the book the colour of the conch fades to white like the fading of civilization. In the end the conch is pure white. Ralph begins to lose faith in the conch. Only Piggy clings to the conch. He is the only one who is unaffected by barbarism and so he is linked with the conch. They both stand for the civilization that was.

In the end the conch is shattered into a thousand pieces and Piggy dies with it. Roger the hunter shattered both.

Question	Assessment Objective(s)	Pre-20th century	20th century
Coursework task – *Of Mice and Men*	1, 2		✓
1 *Great Expectations*	1, 2, 4	✓	
2 *Lord of the Flies*	1, 2		✓

SUMMARY

▷ The first task of the novelist is to **arouse our interest**. This may be done through character, situation, setting or atmosphere and sometimes humour.

▷ The **development of the plot** maintains that interest through portraying characters and their relationships.

▷ Conflict, problems which have to be solved, struggle and discovery all help to maintain interest.

▷ The **order** in which the story is told is important for creating suspense, showing different points of view and developing our views about characters and events.

Character in novels

GETTING STARTED

Just as with drama, a great many of the questions on novels are about character. Much of what was said in Chapter 11 about characters in plays also applies to novels. If you have not already done so you should study that chapter. The difference with the novel is that the character is in the hands of the author and reader alone. The novelist has complete control over what the character does, says, thinks and all the external circumstances of the character's life. The reader's contribution is understanding and interpreting the text.

This chapter helps you to understand how novelists create characters. As you read a novel, make notes about each important character under headings like those in the section below. If you do this for every chapter you will have a record of the characters' development and changing feelings throughout the novel.

The topics covered in this chapter are applicable to all boards.

MEG	NEAB	NICCEA	SEG	LONDON	WJEC	IGCSE	TOPIC	STUDY	REVISION 1	REVISION 2
✓	✓	✓	✓	✓	✓	✓	Appearance			
✓	✓	✓	✓	✓	✓	✓	Speech and actions			
✓	✓	✓	✓	✓	✓	✓	Surroundings			
✓	✓	✓	✓	✓	✓	✓	Thoughts			
✓	✓	✓	✓	✓	✓	✓	Introducing a character			
✓	✓	✓	✓	✓	✓	✓	Development			
✓	✓	✓	✓	✓	✓	✓	Character types			
✓	✓	✓	✓	✓	✓	✓	Names			
✓	✓	✓	✓	✓	✓	✓	Relationships			
✓	✓	✓	✓	✓	✓	✓	Author's attitude			

WHAT YOU NEED TO KNOW

▷ **Appearance**   Some novelists give us detailed descriptions of the **appearance** of their characters, or at least of the main ones. Appearance is not character; but it is an indication, in some novels a strong indication, of character.

Showing personality

Physical appearance can be used directly to show **personality**.

> Such a voice could only come from a broad chest, and the broad chest belonged to a large-boned muscular man nearly six feet high, with a back so flat and a head so well poised that when he drew himself up to take a more distant survey of his work, he had the air of a soldier standing at his ease. The sleeve rolled up above the elbow showed an arm that was likely to win the prize for feats of strength; yet the long supple hand, with its broad finger-tips looked ready for works of skill.

This is George Eliot's description of her hero at the opening of *Adam Bede* and she goes on to compare Adam with his brother Seth in a way that makes it clear that Adam's physical strength also denotes moral strength. His upright stance indicates a spiritual uprightness. The face and the eyes are frequently used to indicate personality: here George Eliot has used the whole body.

Contrast

Occasionally there is a **contrast** between the appearance and personality of a character.

> Mr Denny addressed them directly, and entreated permission to introduce his friend, Mr Wickham, who had returned with him the day before from town, and he was happy to say he had accepted a commission in their corps. This was exactly as it should be; for the young man wanted only regimentals to make him completely charming. His appearance was greatly in his favour; he had all the best part of beauty, a fine countenance, a good figure, and very pleasing address. The introduction was followed up on his side by a happy readiness of conversation . . .

This is our first introduction to Mr Wickham in *Pride and Prejudice* and if we are attracted by his appearance it is not surprising. One of the meanings of 'prejudice' is 'to form a judgement too hastily'. Jane Austen deliberately blinds us to Wickham's real character. It is part of her purpose to prejudice us in his favour so that we understand how her heroine is prejudiced. Later we, like her, discover that he is not what he appears to be and that is part of the meaning of the novel.

Dress

The way characters **dress** may also be used to suggest character. At the beginning of *Tess of the d'Urbervilles* Tess is dressed in white as befits her innocent maidenhood. 'She was so modest, so expressive, she had looked so soft in her thin white gown', thinks the man who will become her husband. In *Oliver Twist* Dickens dresses the Artful Dodger in the clothes of a man. They are too big for him: he has to roll up the sleeves of his jacket. He is only a boy but his situation forces him to be 'street-wise' and act like a man. His clothes show how he has had to become prematurely adult. George Eliot contrasts the plain sensible dress of Dinah Morris with Hetty Sorrel's rust-coloured ribbons, which show her frivolousness (*Adam Bede*). Likewise in *Jane Eyre* Charlotte Bronte contrasts Jane's plain dark dresses with Blanche's fashionable silks.

Think carefully and decide what the description of the characters' appearance is telling you about them.

▷ **Speech and**   Everything that was said about the speech and actions of characters in Chapter 11 also
actions   applies here. The novelist, however, depends only upon the reader's imagination, not on the actor's interpretation of the character's words. A novelist can tell us that a character has a soft and gentle voice, or a firm, decisive walk. These details of the way in which characters **speak** and **act** add to the picture of them along with what they do and say.

You should note your reactions as you read and ask yourself what it is in the author's words that creates your reaction. You can see from the following extract from *Lord of the Flies* how much can be conveyed in a very short space:

> Piggy took off his shoes ands socks, ranged them carefully on the ledge, and tested the water with one toe.
>   'It's hot!'
>   'What did you expect?'
>   'I didn't expect nothing. My auntie –'
>   'Sucks to your auntie!' Ralph did a surface dive and swam under water with his eyes open; the sandy edge of the pool loomed up like a hillside. He turned over, holding his nose, and a golden light danced and shattered just over his face. Piggy was looking determined and began to take off his shorts. Presently he was palely and flatly naked. He tip-toed down the sandy side of the pool, and sat there up to his neck in water smiling proudly at Ralph.
>   'Aren't you going to swim?' Piggy shook his head. 'I can't swim. I wasn't allowed. My asthma –'
>   'Sucks to your ass-mar!'

The novelist, William Golding, has made all Piggy's actions careful, cautious and deliberate. Notice the way he arranges his shoes and socks. He enters the water somewhat nervously. He cannot swim. Taking off his shorts takes some determination. Entering the water makes him feel proud. His auntie obviously put a firm brake on all such activities and as a result he is physically timid. Notice too how his appearance – pale and fat – adds to this impression. Ralph, on the other hand, is presented as very competent in the water. He dives in, swims under water with his eyes open and knows he must hold his nose when he turns over. His manner of speech is decisive, if boyish: 'Sucks to your auntie'. Twice he interrupts Piggy. Ralph's speech is also more educated than Piggy's: he speaks in complete, grammatical sentences, while Piggy's contains errors, such as the double negative in 'I didn't expect nothing' and the incomplete sentence 'I wasn't allowed'.

Even from these few sentences we have a clear initial impression of the character of the two boys from their speech and actions.

Take a short passage near the beginning of a novel, or where a new character is introduced, and look at it in detail. What you observe will probably be confirmed in later passages.

▷ Surroundings

Many of our impressions of characters may be created by the **surroundings** in which the novelist places them. Our view of someone who is always seen in dark, dirty or unpleasant places, or always in the company of unpleasant people, like Fagin in *Oliver Twist*, is going to be affected by the nature of those surroundings. Adam Bede and Dinah Morris are always seen in clean and orderly surroundings so we associate them with those qualities. Remember, though, that a character's reactions to his or her surroundings is also important. Dickens refuses to let Oliver be contaminated by Fagin's world and so eventually he escapes. Nancy, although retaining some sense of what is good and right, is shown as having been immersed in that world for so long that she cannot accept the offer of escape when it comes.

These ideas are explored further in Chapter 16 on setting.

▷ Thoughts

Novelists have the great advantage of being able to get inside a character's mind and describe their **thoughts** and feelings:

> Poor Fanny! She sang little, and looked beautiful through that inappropriate hymn ... Brilliant she looked, and brilliant she felt, for she was hot and angrily miserable and inflamed with a sort of fatal despair. Because there was about him a physical attraction that she hated, but which she could not escape from. He was the first man who had ever kissed her. And his kisses, even while she rebelled from them, had lived in her blood and sent roots down into her soul. After all this time she had come back to them. And her soul groaned, for she felt dragged down, dragged down to earth, as a bird which some dog has got down in the dust.
>
> (D. H. Lawrence, *Fanny and Annie*)

Notice how Lawrence moves from describing things that can be observed from the outside, 'looked beautiful', through things that can be guessed from her appearance, 'she was hot and angrily miserable', to things which only Fanny herself can know – 'And his kisses, even while she rebelled from them, had lived in her blood and sent roots down into her soul . . . And her soul groaned, for she felt dragged down'.

Sometimes writers clearly signal that they are moving inside a character's head by writing 'she thought' or 'he felt'. More often, like Lawrence, they gradually move from describing appearance or actions into describing thoughts and feelings. You should look out for these indications of a character's inner life for it is these that make the reader feel they really 'know' a character.

▷ Introducing a character

We may be **introduced** to a character directly, through a description of appearance, actions and speech. Alternatively we may be introduced indirectly, through other characters' words, opinions and reactions to them. This happens most obviously when a narrator is used. (Look back at the passage quoted from *The Great Gatsby* in Chapter 13.) But it can also accumulate through information given by other characters and their attitude:

> 'Why my dear you must know, Mrs Long says that Netherfield is taken by a young man of large fortune from the north of England; that he came down on Monday in a chaise and four to see the place, and was so much delighted with it that he agreed with Mr Morris immediately; that he is to take possession before Michaelmas, and some of his servants are to be in the house by the end of the next week.'
>
> 'What is his name?'
>
> 'Bingley.'
>
> 'Is he married or single?'
>
> 'Oh! Single, my dear, to be sure! A single man of large fortune; four or five thousand a year. What a fine thing for our girls!'

Mrs Bennet, speaking here at the beginning of *Pride and Prejudice*, has not even met Bingley yet she manages to convey a great deal of information about him, such as his status, his willingness to be pleased and take immediate action, and, most importantly, his significance for the other characters.

In the same novel Mr Collins is introduced through a letter he sends to Mr Bennet. When he arrives in the flesh he confirms the fatuous impression given by his letter.

How are the characters introduced in the novels you are reading?

▷ Development

Novelists show their characters in as many situations, and over whatever length of time, they choose. This allows them to **develop** characters, show them changing through their lives, or perhaps remaining constant as things change around them. We may find some of their behaviour unexpected. Before we dismiss it as unconvincing we must ask *why* the novelist portrays the character like this. Does it fit in the the larger purpose of the book? Look at all the different facets of a character which the novelist has chosen to display. Ask yourself why the novelist shows one character as always the same, while another changes.

Pip's character in *Great Expectations* goes through several stages, both in his own behaviour and his relationship with others. Joe, his kind and generous uncle, remains constant. Wemmick, the lawyer's clark, has two distinct modes of behaviour, one for his work and one for home, which are never allowed to overlap. Each of these kinds of characterization tells us something. Pip develops because he has to learn what is true gentlemanly behaviour; Joe remains the same because he is the standard of goodness against which other characters are measured; Wemmick's dual personality represents the contrast between the debased values of the city and the better values of his domestic life. Dickens shapes each character differently because they fulfil different functions.

Your notes on each chapter should record the *changes* in each developing character and the reason why those who do *not* change remain the same.

▷ Character types

Despite the three different ways Dickens presents the characters of Pip, Joe and Wemmick, they are all fully developed, realistic characters. Some characters in novels are neither of these things. The animals in George Orwell's *Animal Farm* are obviously not realistic. They stand for certain characteristics. For instance, Boxer, the cart-horse, stands for the honest, unquestioning, hard-working peasant.

Characters who have only one or very few characteristics are said to be 'flat' or 'unrounded'. Most novelists employ such characters as part of their background.

Some characters have one characteristic exaggerated to such an extent that they become caricatures. George Eliot's Silas Marner is a caricature of a miser, poring over his gold and counting it every night, until he is suddenly given a child to care for.

All these **character types** can have a place in the author's scheme. The questions to ask are: Why have they been put there? What purpose do they serve?

▷ Names

In novels, as in plays, **names** can sometimes reveal a character's personality. We would expect a man called Gabriel Oak to be a sturdy, reliable person, with a good heart and true. He is probably a countryman. These characteristics, suggested by the oak tree, are all found in Gabriel Oak (in *Far from the Madding Crowd* by Thomas Hardy). Mr Gradgrind is a hard, uncompromising person, totally lacking in sentiment, who believes only in facts and figures. His name has the right associations and the right sound for such a person.

Not all novelists use this technique. Think about the names of characters in the novels you are studying to see if they express anything of their nature.

▷ Relationships

Just as important as each of the characters in themselves are the **relationships** between them. These can be traced in the same way as individual characters. Look at the things they say and think about each other; how they act and react to each other; whether their thoughts about, reactions about and reactions towards each other change. Sometimes the whole point of a book is shown through these changing relationships. The courtship of a couple is often used to show the novelist's ideas of goodness, propriety and virtue. When Rochester proposes to Jane, in *Jane Eyre*, neither she nor anyone else can believe that she, a mere governess, is the proper wife for him, a gentleman. When it is revealed that he is already married their relationship seems over, for Jane will not yield to his pleas to stay with him as his mistress. She abandons him but remains true to her love for him despite another offer of marriage. Rochester loses his sight while trying, but failing, to rescue his mad first wife from a fire. When he has suffered and expiated his sins he and Jane are reunited and the novelist finally allows them to marry. Jane's virtue and love earn her the reward of marriage. Marriage is often used as a reward for virtue triumphant or difficulties overcome.

Remember to record in your notes the character's thoughts and feelings about each other, showing how they develop and how they express the novel's themes.

▷ Author's attitude

An **author's attitude** to the characters is not always clear. Harper Lee obviously approves of Atticus in *To Kill a Mockingbird*: everything he does is presented to us in a good light and we are shown nothing bad about him at all; the whole town looks up to him. William Golding equally obviously disapproves of Roger in *Lord of the Flies* because he never does or says anything good and is shown as the initiator of evil. The other boys fear him but do not like or admire him.

Few judgements are as clear-cut as this. What, for instance, is Emily Bronte's attitude towards Heathcliff? He is adjudged at best uncouth and ill-tempered, and at worst wicked, by every other character in the novel, including Cathy who says she loves him as she loves her own soul. His actions reinforce these judgements. So why do I not despise him? Because Emily Bronte depicts him, with all his faults, with sympathy, understanding and even admiration. His enormous love for Cathy and overwhelming pain at her loss is allowed to outweigh everything else. Through her attitude to this character the novelist displays her judgement, in this case of the importance of passion.

Always ask yourself: what is the author's attitude to the characters? What does it show about the author's judgement and values?

▷ Additional examples

Use these passages as exercises to test your understanding of this chapter. Write down your own thoughts before reading the key below.

1   What do we find out about each character in this passage? What is the author's attitude
and what is your own response to the characters?

George turned the bean cans so that another side faced the fire. He pretended to be
unaware of Lennie so close beside him.

'George,' very softly. No answer. 'George!'

'Whatta you want?'

'I was only foolin', George. I don't want no ketchup. I wouldn't eat no ketchup if it was
right here beside me.'

'If it was here you could have some.'

'But I wouldn't eat none, George. I'd leave it all for you. You could cover your beans with
it and I wouldn't touch none of it.'

George still stared morosely at the fire.

'When I think of the swell time I could have without you, I go nuts. I never get no
peace.'

Lennie still knelt. He looked off into the darkness across the river. 'George, you want I
should go away and leave you alone?'

'Where the hell could you go?'

'Well, I could. I could go off in the hills there. Some place I'd find a cave.'

'Yeah? How'd you eat? You ain't got sense enough to find nothing to eat.'

'I'd find things George. I don't need no nice food with ketchup. I'd lay out in the sun and
nobody'd hurt me. An' if I foun' a mouse, I could keep it. Nobody'd take it away from me.'

George looked quickly and searchingly at him. 'I been mean, ain't I?'

'If you don' want me I can go off in the hills an' find a cave. I can go any time.'

'No – Look! I was jus' foolin' Lennie. 'Cause I want you to stay with me. Trouble with
mice is you always kill 'em.' He paused. 'Tell you what I'll do, Lennie. First chance I get I'll
give you a pup. Maybe you wouldn't kill it. That'd be better than mice. And you could pet it
harder.'

Lennie avoided the bait. He had sensed his advantage. 'If you don't want me, you only
jus' got to say so, and I'll go off in those hills right there – right up in those hills and live by
myself. An' I won't get no mice stole from me.'

George said, 'I want you to stay with me Lennie. Jesus Christ, somebody'd shoot you for
a coyote if you was by yourself. No, you stay with me. Your Aunt Clara wouldn't like your
running off by yourself, even if she is dead.'

Lennie spoke craftily, 'Tell me – like you done before.'

'Tell you what?'

'About the rabbits.'

George snapped, 'You ain't gonna put nothing over on me.'

Lennie pleaded, 'Come on, George. Tell me. Please, George. Like you done before.'

'You get a kick outa that, don't you? Awright, I'll tell you, then we'll eat our supper . . .'
George's voice became deeper. He repeated his words rhythmically as though he had said
them many times before. 'Guys like us, that work on ranches, are the loneliest guys in the
world. They got no family.'

(John Steinbeck, *Of Mice and Men*)

2   What do you find interesting about these two characters?

Cabbage-Stump Charlie was our local bruiser – a violent, gaitered, gaunt-faced pigman,
who lived only for his sows and for fighting. He was a nourisher of quarrels, as some men
are of plants, growing them from nothing by the heat of belligerence and watering them
daily with blood. He would set out each evening, armed with his cabbage-stalk, ready to
strike down the first man he saw. 'What's up then Charlie? Got no quarrel with thee.'
'Wham!' said Charlie, and hit him. Men fell from their bicycles or back-pedalled violently
when they saw Charlie coming. With his hawk-brown nose and whiskered arms he looked
like a land-locked Viking; and he would take up his stand outside the pub, swing his great
stump round his head, and say 'Wham! Bash!' like a boy in a comic, and challenge all-
comers to battle. Often bloodied himself, he left many a man bleeding before crawling
back home to his pigs. Cabbage-Stump Charlie, like Jones' goat, set the village to bolting its
doors.

Percy-from-Painswick, on the other hand, was a clown and a ragged dandy, who used to
come over the hill dressed in a frock-coat and leggings, looking for local girls. Harmless,
half-witted, he wooed only with his tongue: but his words were sufficient to befuddle the

girls and set them shrieking with pleasure and shock. He had a sharp pink face and a dancer's light body and the girls used to follow him everywhere, teasing him on into cheekier fancies and pinning ribbons to his swallowtail coat. Then he'd spin on his toes, and say something quick and elaborate, uttered smoothly from smiling teeth – and the girls would run screaming down over the bank, red-faced, excited, incredulous, hiding in bushes to exclaim to each other was it possible what Percy just said? He was a gentle, sharp, sweet-moving man, but he died of his brain soon after.

(Laurie Lee, *Cider With Rosie*)

Key to the examples

1   There are very few actions in this extract, so we learn about the characters almost entirely through their speech. George's words show him to be a rough, plain man but one who has sympathetic and tender feelings. That George cares for Lennie, even though he is a nuisance, is clear from the way he drops into telling the old story that Lennie wants to hear. He has been angry with Lennie but despite all the trouble Lennie causes, George is sorry to have hurt him. He knows the story will calm and comfort Lennie. George is also a practical man, realizing that a pup would satisfy Lennie's need for something to pet while being big enough to withstand Lennie's over-enthusiastic caresses. George changes from being glum about his own situation and resentful of Lennie's presence to feeling sorry and wishing to make amends.

Lennie's words show us that he is affectionate to George but simple-minded and childlike in the way he tries to earn forgiveness. George can have all the ketchup, when there is any. His idea of going off to live in the hills is like a child's reaction to wrongdoing, with no realization of the difficulties he would encounter. He has a simple need to love things, but does not realize his own strength, unintentionally killing the mice he pets. Like a child he reacts instinctively to George's almost parental concern, sensing when he can get his own way. And like a child he loves stories and listens contentedly to George.

There is nothing in this passage to tell us directly the author's attitude to his characters so we have to deduce it from the way they are presented to us. The author's own language, in the few words and phrases of narration, is educated and much more sophisticated than anything George and Lennie would say: 'morosely' and 'looked quickly and searchingly' are too clever for them. Yet the educated author does not look down on his uneducated characters. He presents them seriously, not mocking their failings or showing them in a comic way. We therefore feel he is sympathetic towards them and understands their situation.

Because of this my own response to the characters is to feel sympathy. George's shouldering of responsibility for Lennie, despite the difficulties and the restrictions Lennie imposes on his own behaviour and pleasures, seems admirable. Steinbeck excites my sympathy for Lennie through his childlike qualities and his vulnerability.

2   Both these characters are made interesting by making them unusual people with extraordinary mannerisms and appearance. Both provoke a strong reaction in other people.

Cabbage-Stump Charlie's unusual features are his devotion to his pigs and aggression to all men. His appearance – he is compared to a Viking – is a warning of his attitude to fights, which he seems to enjoy and practise as entertainment. His chosen weapon, the cabbage-stalk, is comic and so too is the language he uses – '"Wham! Bash!" like a boy in a comic'. Laurie Lee describes the villagers scampering out of his way or cowering behind locked doors to avoid the bloody results of Charlie's nightly excursions in search of victims or sparring partners.

Percy-from-Painswick is depicted as harmless but capable of creating as much of a stir as Charlie. Laurie Lee concentrates on his quaint dress, idiosyncratic speech and movements and his effect on the village girls. In his swallow-tailed coat trimmed with ribbons, his strange, balletic movements and rapid, shocking speech, he seems like a visiting entertainer rather than a half-wit from over the hill. But the final sentence of the extract quells the comedy and evokes pity for Percy.

▷ **SUGGESTIONS FOR COURSEWORK**

1   Re-write an episode from the point of view of one of the less important characters. (See student's answer below.)

2   Imagine you are a character in a novel. Select a chapter or a brief section from the novel. Re-write the events and happenings in the form of a diary. Describe what has happened to you and give your thoughts on the events.

3   Write a letter from a character in one novel to a character in another novel. In it describe the predicament you are in and ask for advice. You could also write the reply.

4   Write a study of character types in a novel genre. You might choose from one of the following: gothic horror, comic novel, historical romance, detective fiction.

5   A character from a family in one novel goes to stay with a family in a different one. Describe what happens.

6   Compare two characters from different novels by the same author.

7   Invent a completely new episode in a novel involving the characters of a novel. You could if you wish introduce a new character and show how the existing characters react.

8   Choose an episode from a novel which illustrates a character well. Re-write it as a scene from a play.

▷ **Coursework task**   Re-write the episode in the furmity tent from the first chapter of *The Mayor of Casterbridge* as a scene from a play, in order to bring out the character of Michael Henchard.

▷ **Notes**   1   Write stage directions to set the scene as vividly as possible.
2   Use the author's dialogue, adapting and adding to it in an appropriate way.
3   Include further stage directions to show the reactions of characters, tone of voice and movements.

▷ **Suggested answer**   *(The scene is a large tent with long narrow tables arranged down each side. At one end is an old-fashioned stove. A woman in a large white apron is stirring a large, round, metal pot which hangs over the fire. She looks rather the worse for wear and not very respectable. A nearby table, covered with a white cloth, carries bowls of corn, flour, milk, raisins and currants. From time to time the furmity woman adds handfuls of these to the pot she is stirring. Sitting at the tables, eating and chatting, is an assortment of country people, some of them none too sober. A young couple appear in the doorway of the tent, their shoes and clothes covered with the dust of a long journey on foot. He is carrying a bag of tools, she a young child.)*

SUSAN	We'll go in here, not the other one. I've always liked furmity and it's nourishing after a long day.
MICHAEL	[*without enthusiasm*] I've never tasted it. [*He follows Susan to a table near the furmity woman. To her*] We'll have a bowl each, good and hot.
SUSAN	[*taking her bowl and offering a spoonful to the child*] Come on Elizabeth-Jane, you like furmity.

[*Other customers come in in a regular stream. Michael observes them closely.*]

MICHAEL	Oh, I see what the game is. [*He passes his bowl back to the furmity woman, giving her a broad wink. She surreptitiously laces it with rum and then slips the bottle back under the table*]
FURMITY WOMAN	Most things are better for a bit o' seasonin'.
MICHAEL	Aye, it has a taste to it now. [*to Susan*] Have a drop. It'll do you good.
SUSAN	I'm not sure. Now I hope you won't take too much Mike.
MICHAEL	Oh cease your whittlin' woman.
SUSAN	Very well, just a drop. [*She passes up her bowl.*]
MICHAEL	And another one for me. The stronger the better. [*He quickly downs his second bowl and passes it up again to be refilled. This happens again and again during the rest of the conversation.*]
SHEPHERD	You've been walking a long ways by the look of 'ee. You'll be looking for trade I should think.
MICHAEL	Aye, anything in the hay-trussing line.
TURNIP-HOER	Why have you come to Weydon for a job o' that sort at this time o' year?
MICHAEL	Well, that's my trade, though I can turn my hand to others if need be.
COACHMAN	Aye, if you've wife and child to support you've need to look about. I thank my stars I never shackled myself with a woman.

SUSAN	[*cradling the child, who is beginning to whimper*] Mike, it's getting late. We should go now. How about our lodging, we may have trouble …
MICHAEL	[*ignoring Susan and beginning to talk too loudly*] You're a wise man. I did for myself that way, fool that I was, and this is the consequence. [*He gestures contemptuously at Susan and the child.*]
SUSAN	[*turning away*] Come now Elizabeth-Jane. There's a good girl.
MICHAEL	[*resentfully*] If I were a free man again I'd be worth a thousand pound before I was finished. But a fellow never knows these things till the chance is past.
COACHMAN	That's about the way of it, young fella.
AUCTIONEER	[*his voice coming in from outside the tent*] Now this is the last lot. Who'll take the lot for a song. Forty shillings.
MICHAEL	[*gloomily to himself, the idea is not new*] For my part I don't see why men that have wives and don't want them shouldn't sell them at auction like an old horse. I'd sell mine this minute if anyone would have her.
TURNIP-HOER	There's some would do it.
COACHMAN	[*looking appreciatively at Susan*] She's got true cultivation, though it wants a bit o' bringing out. I've worked in some good families and I know breeding.
MICHAEL	[*gazing drunkenly at Susan*] Well, now's your chance. I'm open to an offer for this gem o' creation.
SUSAN	[*quietly and bitterly*] Michael you've talked this nonsense before in public places. A joke is a joke but you'll make it once too often.
MICHAEL	I know I said it before and I meant it too. [*lurching up and addressing the whole tent*] All I want is a buyer. This woman is no good to me. Who'll have her?
SUSAN	[*whispering, pulling at his coat*] Come, it's getting dark, this nonsense won't do. If you won't come along I'll go without you.
MICHAEL	[*swaying down the aisle between the tables*] Nobody's answered my question. Will any of ye buy my goods?
SUSAN	[*grimly*] Mike, this is getting serious.
MICHAEL	Will anybody buy her?
SUSAN	[*firmly*] I wish somebody would; her present owner is not to her liking.
MICHAEL	No, nor you to mine. So we're agreed to part. [*striding up and down between the tables and rubbing his hands*] Gentlemen, do you hear it's an agreement to part? She shall take the girl and go her ways. Stand up, Susan.
WOMAN	Don't do it child. Your good man don't know what he's saying.

[*She holds on to Susan to try to prevent her and throughout the following scene she shakes her head, moaning 'Oh dearie me' behind her hand. Susan, careful not to disturb Elizabeth-Jane, stands up quietly and remains still, looking at the floor.*]

| MICHAEL | Right, now who'll be auctioneer? |

[*A short man, rather drunk, jumps up and runs round behind the furmity woman's table. He calls out loudly, imitating an auctioneer's manner.*]

AUCTIONEER	Who'll make an offer for this lady?
TURNIP-HOER	Five shillings. [*Everybody laughs.*]
MICHAEL	[*not laughing*] That's insulting; who'll say a guinea?
WOMAN	Behave yourself moral good man, for heaven's sake. Ah what a cruelty is the poor soul married to. It's not worth bed and board to be treated like that.
MICHAEL	Set it higher.
AUCTIONEER	Two guineas. [*More laughter, particularly from the men, many of whom are less than sober. Calls of 'Half a crown', 'Two shillings, take it or leave it'.*]
MICHAEL	If they don't take it at that in ten seconds they'll have to give more. Very well, add another guinea.
AUCTIONEER	Three guineas.
MICHAEL	[*excitedly*] Good lord! Why, she's cost me fifty times that. Go on.
AUCTIONEER	Four guineas. [*Cries of 'For a woman?' and 'I could buy two good horses for that'. Much ribald laughter.*]
MICHAEL	I tell you what. I won't sell her for less than five. [*banging the table hard*] I'll sell her for five guineas to any man that will treat her well. Now then, five guineas and she's yours. Susan, you agree? [*Susan remains silent, her head bowed.*]
AUCTIONEER	Five guineas or she'll be withdrawn. For the last time. Do anybody give it, yes or no?

SAILOR	[*from the doorway of the tent, not shouting, but loud enough to be heard over the continuing laughter and snide remarks*] Yes.

[*Immediately there is silence. Everyone turns towards the door.*]

MICHAEL	[*slowly, collecting his thoughts*] You say you do.
SAILOR	[*crossing the tent, deliberately*] Yes I say so.
MICHAEL	[*gazing at the Sailor disbelievingly*] Saying is one thing, paying is another.
SAILOR	[*hesitating, looking at Susan, then carefully laying down each banknote and coin as he speaks*] One, two, three, four, five and five shillings.
SUSAN	[*looking at the money, then, searchingly, at the Sailor; in a low voice*] Michael, if you touch that money I and my little girl go with this man. It's a joke no longer.
MICHAEL	[*shouting, quite drunk*] Of course it's not a joke. I take the money, the sailor takes you. It's been done elsewhere, why not here?
SAILOR	[*turning to Susan and speaking very gently*] 'Tis quite on the understanding that she's willing. I wouldn't hurt her feelings for the world.
MICHAEL	She's willing as long as she can have the child. We talked about it only the other day.
SAILOR	[*to Susan*] Is that true?
SUSAN	Yes, it's true.
MICHAEL	Very well, she shall have the child and the bargain's complete. [*He sweeps up the money and puts it into his inside pocket then sits down with an air of finality and unconcern.*]
SAILOR	[*smiling*] Come along, the little one too, the more the merrier.
SUSAN	[*once again looking closely at the Sailor's face, then lifting up Elizabeth-Jane and following him to the door; she turns*] Mike, I've lived with thee two years and had nothing but temper. Now I'm nothing to you. I'll try my luck elsewhere. It'll be better for me and better for Elizabeth-Jane. So goodbye. [*Pulling off her wedding ring she throws it at Michael before she disappears.*]

▶ **EXAMINATION QUESTIONS**

A great many exam questions are asked about character, either in response to a passage printed on the exam paper, or in the book as a whole. A question might ask about:

▶ a character's thoughts and feelings;
▶ character development;
▶ relationships between characters;
▶ a character's part in the plot;
▶ characters in relation to the ideas, themes or background;
▶ the author's attitude towards the characters;
▶ your own response to the characters.

I have tried to touch on all these things in this chapter, but since questions of character are so much linked to *other aspects* of the novel you need to study these aspects, dealt with in other chapters. You cannot look at characters in isolation.

▷ **Question I**
'Foundation Tier.'

The following questions, set by SEG on a passage from Thomas Hardy's *Far from the Madding Crowd* are typical questions on character in a given passage.

'Miss Everdene!' said the farmer.

She trembled, turned, and said 'Good morning.' His tone was so utterly removed from all she had expected as a beginning. It was lowness and quiet accentuated: an emphasis of deep meanings, their form, at the same time, being scarcely expressed. Silence has sometimes a remarkable power of showing itself as the disembodied soul of feeling wandering without its carcase, and it is then more impressive than speech. In the same way, to say little is often to tell more than to say a great deal. Boldwood told everything in that word.

As the consciousness expands on learning that what was fancied to be the rumble of wheels is the reverberation of thunder, so did Bathsheba's at her intuitive conviction.

'I feel – almost too much – to think,' he said, with a solemn simplicity. 'I have come to speak to you without preface. My life is not my own since I have beheld you clearly, Miss Everdene – I come to make you an offer of marriage.'

Bathsheba tried to preserve an absolutely natural countenance, and all the motion she made was one of closing her lips which had previously been a little parted.

'I am now forty-one years old,' he went on. 'I may have been called a confirmed bachelor, and I was a confirmed bachelor. I had never any views of myself as a husband in my earlier days, nor have I made any calculation on the subject since I have been older. But we all change, and my change, in this matter, came with seeing you. I have felt lately, more and more, that my present way of living is bad in every respect. Beyond all things, I want you as my wife.'

'I feel, Mr Boldwood, that though I respect you much, I do not feel – what would justify me to – in accepting your offer,' she stammered.

This giving back of dignity for dignity seemed to open the sluices of feeling that Boldwood had as yet kept closed.

'My life is a burden without you,' he exclaimed in a low voice. 'I want you – I want you to let me say I love you again and again!'

Bathsheba answered nothing, and the mare upon her arm seemed so impressed that instead of cropping the herbage she looked up.

'I think and hope you care enough for me to listen to what I have to tell!'

Bathsheba's momentary impulse was to ask why he thought that, till she remembered that, far from being a conceited assumption on Boldwood's part, it was but the natural conclusion of serious reflection based on deceptive premises of her own offering.

'I wish I could say courteous flatteries to you,' the farmer continued in an easier tone, 'and put my rugged feelings into graceful shape: but I have neither power nor patience to learn such things. I want you for my wife – so wildly that no other feeling can abide in me; but I should not have spoken out had I not been led to hope.'

'The valentine again! O that valentine!' she said to herself, but not a word to him.

'If you can love me say so, Miss Everdene. If not – don't say no.'

What do you learn about Boldwood in this passage? What do you learn about Bathsheba's feelings from her reaction to Boldwood?

 Question 2   *To Kill a Mocking Bird* is told in the first person by Scout. Write about the trial of Tom Robinson from the point of view of one of the other characters. You may write as one of the characters if you wish.

EXAMINATION ANSWERS

▷ Question 1   *Notes and tutor's answer*

Notes

1 Read through the passage carefully.
2 Go through the passage underlining everything relating to Boldwood and his character, feelings and behaviour.
3 Write a substantial paragraph in answer to the first part of the question.
4 Go back and underline points about Bathsheba's feelings and reactions, then write a second paragraph in answer to the second part.

Suggested answer

Boldwood is overwhelmingly in love with Bathsheba. His voice betrays the depth of his feelings as soon as he speaks her name. He says he is forty-one and has been a confirmed bachelor, never thinking of marriage, until he saw Bathsheba. She has changed his life. He speaks of his love with great directness, his passion being so great that he cannot hide it. He is, in any case, unused to flattering people; he does not know, and does not want to know, how to proceed with a courtship in a gallant manner, although he speaks with dignity. All he wants, with great impatience, is for Bathsheba to be his wife. Until she is, he feels that his life is worthless. All other concerns have been driven out of his head and he can think of nothing else. He is determined that she shall not turn him down and is confident, given the evidence of the valentine which Bathsheba sent him, that he can win her. It is only her action which has led him to speak to her in this manner.

The intensity of Boldwood's voice makes Bathsheba tremble from the first words he speaks. She guesses what he has come to say, and is fearful, not knowing how to respond. She tries to give none of her feelings away in her face and stammers a non-committal reply. She feels very guilty about sending the valentine and wishes that she had not done so because it has stirred up Boldwood's feelings to a pitch she is incapable of dealing with. Realizing that this situation is all her own fault, she is paralysed and unable to reject him.

▷ **Question 2** *Student's answer – examiner's comments*

It's been many years now since my Tom left this earth, yet whenever I come out here and set on the front porch I still gets to thinkin' 'bout that ev'nin' when Mr Finch come an tell me that he dead. I didn't need no words to tell me. I could tell from Mr Finch's face, all sombre and unsmilin', which ain't usual for Mr Finch. All I could manage was to offer him a seat afore my grief took over an' I collapsed on the floor. My Tom was such a good man, a lovin' man, an' he knew how to care for his chillun. Him dyin' all but broke my heart. Ever since, I bin a strong woman 'cos I got my chillun to care for, but I bin mighty lonesome.

I guess that all this started the day Tom came runnin' home from the fields. He was shakin' an' he looked terrified out of his mind. Miss Mayella had called him into her place as he was passin' by and asked him to bust up a chiffarobe. But there weren't no chiffarobe, only a door which she said needed mendin' but which Tom said looked good and safe to him. Then she asked him to get somethin' down off the top of another chiffarobe an' as he was doin' it she sort of grabbed him an' started a-kissin' him. I knew my Tom wasn't tellin' no lies as he was a good honest man, but when Tom told me that Mr Ewell had seen what Mayella done I was frightened 'cos I knew he'd come after Tom when he'd finished with beatin' Mayella. Well they shut him up an' Mr Finch had to stand guard to stop the out of town folks from lynchin' him.

When the day of the court case came I felt I owed it to Tom to go an' watch, but I knew it would be awful upsettin'. So as not to let my tears show if he were convicted I sat right at the back of the balcony an' wrapped up well in a scarf so not too many folks would get to recognizin' me. I guess I knew Tom wouldn't stand no chance agin them white folks but I knew he was innocent so I just kept hopin'. The first witness was Mr Tate. Now our sheriff was a good man but he was white an' no amount of goodness could take away his feelin' about us black folk. He jis couldn't help it. He told the jury that Mr Ewell called him to come an' see that his girl had been raped, an' sure enough when he got there he found Miss Mayella lyin' on the floor all beat up an' accusin' Tom of havin' taken advantage of her. Then Mr Finch found out Mr Tate didn't call no doctor 'cos it was obvious she bin beat up. I wanted to stan' up an' shout that didn't mean she bin raped but o' course I kept quiet so's I could stay in court where I could keep seein' Tom. Mr Finch got Mr Tate to tell us all about Mayella's injuries an' after a bit I realized what Mr Finch was drivin' at. He knew that Tom's left arm was damaged an' he couldn't have beat Miss Mayella on her right side, or held her throat.

When Mr Gilmer called up Mr Ewell he said he was goin' to tell the truth but I thought otherwise. Mr Ewell is a black mark on the white folk which you can tell from his language. He said he saw my Tom havin' his way with Mayella, an' how he brought himself to speak such a lie when he'd sworn to tell the truth on the Holy Bible I didn't know. I said then he'd be struck down sooner or later an' I was right. I knew he'd go to hell for such lies. Then it was Mr Finch's turn with Mr Ewell, an' bein' cleverer than any man I know he asked him to write his name, which he went right on an' did with his left

(continued)

(continued)

hand. I was so happy I could have gev Mr Finch a huge hug right then 'cept it wouldn't have bin proper.

When Miss Mayella went up on the stand, in the middle of tellin' it she all of a sudden burst into tears. Now I'm not a cold-hearted woman but I had no pity for the snivellin' girl. She was doin' her best play actin'. She told the judge it was Mr Finch she was frightened of, with his questions, and how that could be is beyond me, he bein' as kind an' understandin' a man as he is. Judge Taylor told her not to be afraid of nothin' so she carried on tellin' us how she called Tom into the yard to bust up a chiffarobe an' when she went into the house to get him a nickel he took advantage. She said she screamed real loud, but if she had someone would 've heard her. Then her father came an' she fainted, so she said.

Mr Finch was as polite as polite could be in his questionin' but Miss Mayella jis thought he was mockin' her an' got upset. She said she could write real good even though she only got to go to school for three years an' she had seb'n brothers an' sisters but she didn't have no friends. An' you could tell from her answerin' that she wasn't of a good homely upbringin' and was kinda lonely. When she said her father was tollable an' didn't beat her none I knew she was lyin'. You could tell from her stumblin' an' bein' so defiant. She couldn't remember 'bout invitin' Tom into the house afore, then she went 'bout changin' her mind. She was mighty confused. Mr Finch got Tom to stand up so that everyone could see his poor withered arm an' Miss Mayella got more an' more confused but kept right on sayin' Tom beat her when he couldn't ha' done. She got so upset she was screamin' at everyone that Tom was guilty. I was so mad 'cos she was jis lyin' an' there wasn't nothin' I could do to stop her. Then she started cryin' an' I hated her even more.

Finally Tom was called to the stand an' I could see his sad face that I loved so much. I wanted to reach out an' tell him to be strong. Tom told the folk jis what he told me when he run home. He told Mr Finch that Miss Mayella said she'd saved a whole year to get enough nickels to send the chillun off to get ice creams an' let her alone. He said when Mr Ewell came back an' saw what Miss Mayella was doin' he shouted that he'd kill her. Mr Gilmer's questions were mighty sly. He made out that Tom was strong enough to beat anybody. An' then came the worst thing Tom could ha' done. He said he felt sorry for the white girl an' that's why he helped her out. That made the white folks real mad, that a nigger felt sorry for a white girl. 'T ain't our fault God gave us feelin's too.

The end of the case came pretty soon after an' we all had a break. They sure took their time comin' to a verdict an' I began to hope maybe Mr Finch had worked a miracle. But in the end the white folks pronounced him guilty even though everyone in that court room could see he was dead plain innocent. I was just pushed outside by the crowd, knowin' it would be a long time before I saw my Tom agin. I realized jis how long that time would be when Mr Finch came to tell me how he died. I'll allus love my Tom an' I know in my heart that it were the Ewells who was guilty, not him. God bless his soul.

'This excellent piece of work captures the voice of Tom's wife, Helen, and puts her point of view with sympathy and conviction.

Notice how the student cleverly uses certain words to create the sense of Helen's dialect. These have been chosen from the speech of other black characters in the book, and from listening to the accents of the actors in the film of the book.

The description of the court proceedings with Helen's reaction to each witness shows excellent knowledge and understanding of the text.

This is an outstanding piece of work showing great sensitivity and skill in writing.'

Question	Assessment Objective(s)	Pre-20th century	20th century
Coursework task – *The Mayor of Casterbridge*	1, 2, 4	✓	
1. *Far from the Madding Crowd*	1	✓	
2. *To Kill a Mocking Bird*	1, 2, 4		✓

SUMMARY

▷ We learn about characters directly from their **speech** and **actions**, indirectly from their **appearance, dress, surroundings** and the **opinions of others**.

▷ The novelist's exploration of **thoughts** and **feelings** reveal the characters' inner life.

▷ Characters may be **flat** or **rounded**..

▷ Characters may **develop** or **remain unchanged**, according to their function in the plot.

▷ **Relationships** are developed in the same way as characters and may express the theme of the novel.

▷ The way the characters are **presented** and the **language** used to describe them shows the author's attitude to them.

GETTING STARTED

A novelist has to create in words all the sights and sounds of the characters' world. The setting of a novel can do more than produce atmosphere. It can be used to tell us about the feelings of characters and their relation to the world around them. Because the author creates the world in which the characters live, as well as the characters themselves, it is equally important in the ideas and structure of the novel.

The questions you have to ask are: What is my response to this world? Why has the author created it in this way? Different aspects of background and setting may be important at different points in the novel and, of course, all novels are different. This chapter shows you some ways of thinking about the background and setting of novels.

The topics covered in this chapter are applicable to all exam boards.

MEG	NEAB	NICCEA	SEG	LONDON	WJEC	IGCSE	**TOPIC**	STUDY	REVISION I	REVISION 2
✓	✓	✓	✓	✓	✓	✓	Atmosphere			
✓	✓	✓	✓	✓	✓	✓	Mood			
✓	✓	✓	✓	✓	✓	✓	Landscape and weather			
✓	✓	✓	✓	✓	✓	✓	Setting and characters			
✓	✓	✓	✓	✓	✓	✓	Social context			

WHAT YOU NEED TO KNOW

▷ **Atmosphere**

The mood of a whole book is often produced by the author's use of the background against which the story is set. There may be many different settings during the course of a novel. They all add up to give the general **atmosphere** of the book. An author who dwells on the dirt and misery of a setting, whether it be a rural hovel or urban slum, will produce an atmosphere of hopelessness and oppression. Graham Greene has become so well known for seedy, dirty, run-down settings in his novels that his typical setting has been given a name: Greeneland.

An author can move between widely different settings in a novel and yet produce a strong sense of place and a dominant atmosphere. In *The Mayor of Casterbridge* Thomas Hardy moves from the elegant Lucetta's drawing-room at one end of the scale to the crowded slum of Mixen Lane, haunt of the undesirables of the town. He produces the feeling of life in the provincial town of Casterbridge with its encircling countryside.

'The examiners are looking for a personal response. What is your response to the author's setting?'

The many descriptions of the town make us feel we know it in the same way we know a town that we have visited. The nature of the town is conveyed through references to its long history and remarks like this:

> 'What an old-fashioned town it seems to be!' said Elizabeth-Jane . . . 'It is huddled all together and it is shut in by a square wall of trees, like a plot of garden ground by a box edging.'

Here the visual description of the town, especially the comparison to an enclosed garden, is also an indication of its nature: inward looking and backward, a comfortable, close-knit community shut off from the world. This sense of the place is important for the relationships between the characters and for the way in which we will view the downfall and exclusion from Casterbridge of Michael Henchard.

Other descriptions of settings in the same novel give a solemn atmosphere to the book which intensifies into tragedy: the strange, lonely, Roman amphitheatre; the stone bridge over the river to which the unhappy resort.

Notice the settings of the novels you read. Do they produce a particular atmosphere? Of what sort is it? How is it related to the characters and themes of the novel?

▷ **Mood**

Just as the setting can create a general atmosphere, so a particular environment can be used to convey the **mood** of a character. The red room in which Jane Eyre is shut up as a punishment is so oppressive that she falls ill. The room, with its dark furnishings and red hangings, feels like a jail to Jane. Locked in this solemn, silent and chill room, the scene of Mr Reed's death, she waits as darkness falls:

> Daylight began to forsake the red room; it was past four o'clock, and the beclouded afternoon was tending towards drear twilight. I heard the rain still beating continuously on the staircase window, and the wind howling in the grove behind the hall; I grew by degrees cold as a stone, and then my courage sank. My habitual mood of humiliation, self-doubt, forlorn depression, fell damp on the embers of my decaying ire. All said I was wicked, and perhaps I might be so.

The mood created by the dreariness of the winter twilight in the cold, dark room and the sound of the rain and the wind matches Jane's 'habitual' mood. The setting is an influence on Jane's mood and it is also a symbol of what she feels. The description of the scene attempts to produce in us the feeling that Jane has most of the time.

▷ **Landscape and weather**

Descriptions of the **landscape** and the **weather** are very effective in producing atmosphere and mood. Many people respond emotionally to the weather. In novels rain often figures in dismal scenes, as it did in the one above from *Jane Eyre*, sunshine figures in happy ones. Leafy lanes and green valleys are pleasant and comfortable; barren hills are grim. George Eliot uses a contrast of this kind in two settings, Loamshire and Stoneyshire, in *Adam Bede*. The most difficult and depressing events happen in Stoneyshire: the death of Hetty Sorrel's baby and her imprisonment. The setting is used to emphasize the meaning or moral that Hetty must suffer for the wrongs she has done.

We have already seen how Dickens uses fog in *Bleak House* (see Chapter 14). The fog which literally envelops the city evokes a powerful mood at the beginning of the book. It also stands as a symbol for the processes of the law which enmesh the characters throughout the story.

In *The Go-Between* by L.P. Hartley the mounting heat is used to denote mounting tension. Leo, the boy who narrates the story, frequently checks the rising temperature through the long, hot summer. The heat becomes oppressive. As it does so, the situation between the adult characters gathers to a storm. Leo is only imperfectly aware of what is going on; he is excited by the heat but when the storm breaks he is devastated. The weather is being used as a metaphor.

Can you find examples of landscape or weather being used to create a mood or being used as a symbol or metaphor?

▷ Setting and characters

There can be a distinct relationship between **characters and the background** against which they are set. Heathcliff belongs on the bleak, wild moors around Wuthering Heights: their character reflects his character. The Lintons live in the softer, more comfortable environment of Thrushcross Grange and are correspondingly gentler characters. The conflict in Emily Bronte's novel begins when Cathy deserts the first for the second. Why does she do it, because it seems from her character that she too belongs at Wuthering Heights?

A second point to note is the one already mentioned in Chapter 15: setting can evoke in the reader a particular response towards a character. Henchard dying in a hovel evokes more pity than if he died in a good clean bed, particularly because we see him reduced to this from a position of wealth and strength. Read this passage and see what kind of response the setting creates. In *Tess of the d'Urbervilles*, Tess, abandoned by her husband, penniless, is grubbing up swedes for a living through the winter.

> ...the whole field was in colour a desolate drab; it was a complexion without features, as if a face from chin to brow should be only an expanse of skin. The sky wore, in another colour, the same likeness; a white vacuity of countenance ...They worked on hour after hour, unconscious of the forlorn aspect they bore in the landscape ... In the afternoon the rain came on again and Marian said that they need not work any more. But if they did not work they would not be paid; so they worked on. It was so high a situation, this field, that the rain had no occasion to fall, but raced along horizontally upon the yelling wind, sticking into them like glass splinters till they were wet through. Tess had not known till now what was really meant by that.

Many readers find the situation of the two girls very distressing. The awful conditions through which they work makes us respond with an increased sympathy.

When reading a novel you should note any connections between setting and personality. Then decide whether your response to a character is affected by the settings that the author puts him or her in.

▷ Social context

The **society** that the characters live in is just as important, and in some novels far more important, than the landscape or other surroundings. *To Kill a Mockingbird*, for example, contains people from all levels of society, from the shiftless and anti-social Ewells, through the poor but hard-working Cunninghams, to Aunt Alexandra with her land and her long family tradition. Alongside, yet interrelated, is the distinct society of the blacks. We get to know the town of Maycomb very well through its people. We know Thomas Hardys' Casterbridge not only through the many descriptions of the town, but also the variety of the townspeople and their relationships.

Some novelists are very interested in society and use their novels to criticize its faults. Dickens often displays the city as a place where villainy and hypocrisy thrive. For example, he does this in both *Oliver Twist* and *Great Expectations*. Jane Austen is interested in social relationships but only depicts the small section of society, the upper middle class, which she feels qualified to write about. Some writers invent whole societies of their own, often setting them in the future, in order to express their ideas. In *1984*, written in 1948, George Orwell invents a state which has complete control over its citizens, with Thought Police to control their thoughts. The television set becomes a two-way instrument, a camera as well as a receiver, acting as a spy in the corner of the room, transmitting details of everyone's every action. Orwell was trying to show the dangers of allowing the state to take over too much of people's lives. Aldous Huxley had similar intentions when he invented the very different society in *Brave New World*.

When reading a novel, think about how important the social setting is. What aspects of society has the novelist chosen to write about? Is the society shown in a bad or a good light?

▷ **Additional examples**
Use these examples as exercises to test your understanding of this chapter. Write down your own ideas before looking at the key below.

1 What kind of society is the novelist describing here?

> 'Well, well, do as you like, Bessy,' said Mr Tulliver, taking up his hat and walking out to the mill. Few wives were more submissive than Mrs Tulliver on all points unconnected with her family relations; but she had been a Miss Dodson, and the Dodsons were a very respectable family indeed – as much looked up to as any in their own parish, or the next to it. The Miss Dodsons had always been thought to hold up their heads very high, and no one was surprised the two eldest had married well – not at an early age, for that was not the practice of the Dodson family. There were particular ways of doing everything in that family: particular ways of bleaching the linen, of making the cowslip wine, curing the hams, and keeping the bottled gooseberries; so that no daughter of the house could be indifferent to the privilege of having been born a Dodson.

> (George Eliot, *The Mill on the Floss*)

2 On a beautiful summer evening, under a chestnut tree, with the nightingales singing, Mr Rochester proposes to Jane Eyre. Then comes the following passage. If you have not read the book, what does this passage suggest to you about Jane and Rochester's relationship? If you have read the book, your knowledge of the story will help you explain the meaning of this passage.

> But what had befallen the night? The moon was not yet set and we were all in shadow: I could scarcely see my master's face, near as I was. And what ailed the chestnut tree? It writhed and groaned; while wind roared in the laurel walk and came sweeping over us. 'We must go in,' said Mr Rochester; 'the weather changes. I could have sat with thee till morning, Jane.' 'And so,' thought I, 'could I with you.' I should perhaps have said so, but a livid, vivid spark leapt out of a cloud at which I was looking, and there was a crack, a crash, a close rattling peal; and I thought only of hiding my dazzled eyes against Mr Rochester's shoulder. The rain rushed down. He hurried me up the walk, through the grounds and into the house; but we were quite wet before we could cross the threshold ... Before I left my bed in the morning, little Adele came running in to tell me that the great horse-chestnut at the bottom of the orchard had been struck by lightning, and half of it split away.

> (Charlotte Bronte, *Jane Eyre*)

'Look for symbols and metaphors in the action of the novels you are studying.'

Key to the examples

1 The kind of society described in this passage is a small, settled village community. We know that the world is a narrow one because we are told it is a source of pride if one is looked up to by everyone in the parish and the next one to it. The wider world beyond that does not concern them. It is very conservative, always doing things in a particular way. Rural skills are still important: all the activities described – bottling, curing hams, winemaking – are those of the well-regulated country household in the last century. The family is comfortably off, though not wealthy. It is large, with a strong sense of family pride.

2 From the way the weather changes we might expect that there is something wrong in the relationship between Jane and Rochester and their future will not go smoothly. The beautiful evening is destroyed by a terrible storm, rending apart the tree under which they have been sitting. This is a bad omen. It is as though the heavens are protesting at the event, the proposal, which has just taken place on this spot, and nature is signalling its disapproval of some wrong which has been done. Later we discover that Rochester is already married and he cannot marry Jane without committing the crime of bigamy.

Charlotte Bronte is using the storm as an indication of the moral judgement on Rochester. (The thunderbolt is traditionally a sign of God's displeasure.) The description is of a real storm but it is equally a symbolic one.

▷ **SUGGESTIONS FOR COURSEWORK**

1 Write a comparison of the setting used in two novels. Show the similarities and the differences between the different settings.

2 Show how actual historical events have played an important part in fictional works, for example in *A Tale of Two Cities*.

3 Write a study on the way a novelist uses the society in which a novel is set. Suitable examples might be the novels of Jane Austen, Elizabeth Gaskell, Edith Wharton, Charles Dickens, Joan Lingard, Barry Hines. Show how important the social setting is to the novel.

4 Take a scene from a novel out of its social context and time. For example, imagine a Jane Austen novel set on a twentieth-century housing estate, or a Thomas Hardy novel set in the Caribbean. Re-write two pages of the novel making the necessary changes.

5 Write a study of a novel set in a particular culture: for example, Asia, the Caribbean, industrial areas, rural settings.

6 Choose a passage from a novel you are studying which uses setting to convey any of the following: atmosphere, a symbolic expression of a character's mood, an expression of a theme, a striking scene in its own right. Write about the use the author makes of the setting of the scene. (See the student's answers below for examples of this kind of question.)

▷ **Coursework task** Choose a novel in which the weather plays a significant part. Write about the contribution which it makes to the novel.

▷ **Suggested answer** *Ethan Frome* is a winter story. Almost every one of its scenes is set amid the snows of the New England winter. The visit of the narrator to the Frome household, which enables him to construct his 'vision' of Ethan's story, takes place in the worst storm of the winter when the bitter cold and the heaviness of the snowfall compel him to pass the night there. The story ends in the snow of the night before the thaw when Ethan and Mattie coast down the frozen sled track to their deliberate accident. From beginning to end, the cold is pervasive: the houses huddle 'against the white immensities of land and sky'; Ethan's farmhouse looks 'as mute and cold as a gravestone'; indoors the kitchen has 'the deathly chill of a vault', so 'powerful cold' that Ethan cannot stay up to do his accounts. This frozen landscape and bitter weather reflects the harsh, restricted lives of the characters. When the narrator exclaims that Ethan, at the age of fifty-two, 'looks as if he were dead and in hell', Harmon Gow simply replies 'Guess he's been in Starkfield too many winters'.

Life in Starkfield is hard. Even the name indicates the bleakness of the place. Ethan Frome is hard put to it to wring a living from his mill and his farm and all his life he has had 'troubles' with sickness. His studies in Worcester, interrupted when his father fell sick and died, were never resumed. Having cared for his father Ethan then had to nurse his mother until she died and then look after his perpetually sick wife. Illness is a continual drain on his meagre income. No one in the community is rich. Mr Hale, to whom Ethan sells his timber, never pays before the end of three months and then sometimes with difficulty. Only Michael Eady, 'the ambitious Irish grocer, whose suppleness and effrontery had given Starkfield its first notion of "smart" business methods' is conspicuously successful. There is little entertainment once the snows come and communication between Starkfield and the bigger towns becomes difficult. The village is 'beleaguered'; life is 'negated'.

Under these conditions emotions cannot thrive. The narrator is struck by 'the contrast between the vitality of the climate and the deadness of the community'. However, once he has experienced the storms of February and the winds of March he begins to understand the sense of being under siege. This stark landscape and harsh climate produces characters who speak little. Their feelings are dammed up behind walls of reticence and inarticulateness. When the new railroad left the farmhouse 'side-tracked' Ethan's mother fell into a silence that was only broken for her by the voices in her head. After an initial volubility Ethan's wife also becomes increasingly silent so that he fears she too may be going crazy. Ethan himself cannot express his delight in the beauty of the landscape, admiring Mattie's ability to find the words, 'It looks just as if it were painted' which seem to him to say precisely what he is feeling. Later, searching for the 'all-expressive word' to tell her of his pleasure in her presence he 'found only a deep "Come along"'.

This natural reticence is re-enforced by the strict rectitude of the society. Ruth Varnum may kiss Ned Hale because the whole village knows they are engaged, but the discussion of it still causes Mattie to blush. Thus Ethan, overwhelmed as he is with love for Mattie cannot, during the whole of the evening they are alone together, bring himself so much as to touch her hand but kisses instead the piece of stuff she is sewing. Even when Mattie is forced to leave by Ethan's wife, Mattie and Ethan can only communicate by looks and their feelings might have remained unsaid had Mattie not found a letter which Ethan meant to destroy. Yet however strongly he may wish it Ethan cannot carry through into action the desires voiced in the letter. Even if he could borrow the money necessary to take Mattie away to 'the West', which he cannot because the farm is already mortgaged up to the hilt, the strict moral code by which he has always lived prevents him. This is a society in which to survive neighbour must help neighbour and everyone bears a responsibility to his kin: the harsh conditions of life as well as the teachings of Christianity enforce these values. Between poverty and his own strict values Ethan is caught as in a vice.

The perpetual snow and cold are literal representations of the difficulties under which the characters labour. At the same time the winter is a metaphorical expression of the emotional bleakness of their lives in which happiness cannot be grasped, suffering cannot be evaded and the only course is to patiently endure.

▷ **Notes** 1 You could answer the same question choosing *The Go-Between*, which is another novel which uses weather in a similar way, in this case summer heat.

2 You could write a comparison between *Ethan Frome* and *The Go-Between*.

3 *Ethan Frome*, *The Crucible* and the poems of Robert Frost all have a New England setting. You could write a comparison between any two of these.

EXAMINATION QUESTIONS

Exam questions on setting may ask you to examine why setting is important in the novel you have been studying. You could be asked to discuss:

▶ the impact of the setting and of any changes of setting;
▶ the effect this has on the characters and their relationships;
▶ ways in which the setting is presented by the writer;
▶ ways in which the setting reflects important themes in the text.

The following question is from an open-book exam: the relevant passage is printed below. If you have not read the book, you can use the passage as practice for a prose unseen, answering the first two parts of the question but ignoring the part about the wedding.

▷ **Question 1** Read again the beginning of Part Four, Chapter 1 of *Brighton Rock* by Graham Greene. What impression do you get from this passage of a Bank Holiday in Brighton in the 1930s? What do you find particularly vivid in Greene's description and how does this scene, in your opinion, relate to the wedding which is about to take place?

It was a fine day for the races. People poured into Brighton by the first train. It was like Bank Holiday all over again, except that these people didn't spend money; they harboured it. They stood packed deep on the tops of trams rocking down to the Aquarium, they surged like some natural and irrational migration of insects up and down the front. By eleven o'clock it was impossible to get a seat on the buses going out to the course. A negro, wearing a bright striped tie, sat on a bench in the Pavilion garden and smoked a cigar. Some children played touch wood from seat to seat, and he called out to them hilariously, holding his cigar at arm's length with an air of pride and caution, his great teeth gleaming like an advertisement. They stopped playing and stared at him, backing slowly. He called out to them again in their own tongue, the words hollow and unformed and childish like theirs, and they eyed him uneasily and backed farther away. He put his cigar patiently back between his cushiony lips and went on smoking. A band came up the pavement through Old Steyne, a blind band playing drums and trumpets, walking in the gutter, feeling the kerb with the edge of their shoes, in Indian file. You heard the music a long way off, persisting through the rumble of the crowd, the shots of exhaust pipes and the grinding of the buses starting uphill for the racecourse. It rang out with spirit, marched like a regiment, and you raised your eyes in expectation of the tiger skin and the twirling drumsticks and saw the pale blind eyes, like those of pit ponies going by along the gutter.

In the public school grounds above the sea the girls trooped solemnly out to hockey: stout goal-keepers padded like armadillos; captains discussing tactics with their lieutenants; junior girls running amok in the bright day. Beyond the aristocratic turf, through the wrought-iron main gates they could see the plebeian procession, those whom the buses wouldn't hold, plodding up the down, kicking the dust, eating buns out of paper bags. The buses took the long way round through Kemp Town, but up the steep hill came the crammed taxicabs – a seat for anyone at ninepence a time – a Packard for the members' enclosure, old Morrises, strange high cars with family parties, keeping the road after twenty years. It was as if the whole road moved upwards like an Underground staircase in the dusty sunlight, a creaking, shouting, jostling crowd of cars moving with it. The junior girls took to their heels like ponies racing on the turf, feeling the excitement going on outside, as if this were a day on which life for many people reached a kind of climax. The odds on Black Boy had shortened, nothing could ever make life quite the same after that rash bet of a fiver on Merry Monarch. A scarlet racing model, a tiny rakish car which carried about it the atmosphere of innumerable road-houses, of tootsies gathered round swimming pools, of furtive encounters in by-lanes off the Great North Road, wormed through the traffic with incredible dexterity. The sun caught it: it winked as far as the dining-hall windows of the girls' school. It was crammed tight: a woman sat on a man's knee, and another man clung on the running board as it swayed and hooted and cut in and out uphill towards the downs. The woman was singing, her voice faint and disjointed through the horns, something traditional about brides and bouquets, something which went with Guinness and oysters and the old Leicester Lounge, something out of place in the bright little racing car. Upon the top of the down the words blew back along the dusty road to meet an ancient Morris rocking and receding in their wake at forty miles an hour, with flapping hood, bent fender and discoloured windscreen.

▷ **Question 2**   This question involves the 'setting' of *Far from the Madding Crowd*. How does Hardy create an appropriate atmosphere and background to the events of the story?

▷ **Question 3**   Write about your response to these two passages. You could write about the similarities and differences in the setting, the situations described, the presentation of the characters, how you feel about the descriptions.

Passage 1 James Joyce, **A Portrait of the Artist as a Young Man**

Fleming knelt down squeezing his hands under his armpits, his face contorted with pain, but Stephen knew how hard his hands were because Fleming was always rubbing rosin into them. But perhaps he was in great pain for the noise of the pandies was terrible. Stephen's heart was beating and fluttering.

– At your work all of you! shouted the prefect of studies. We want no lazy idle little loafers here, lazy idle little schemers. At your work, I tell you. Father Dolan will be in to see you every day. Father Dolan will be in tomorrow.

He poked one of the boys with the pandybat, saying:

– You, boy! When will Father Dolan be in again?

– Tomorrow, sir, said Tom Furlong's voice.

– Tomorrow and tomorrow and tomorrow, said the prefect of studies. Make up your minds for that. Every day Father Dolan. Write away. You, boy, who are you?

Stephen's heart jumped suddenly.

– Dedalus, sir.

– Why are you not writing like the others?

– I . . . my . . .

He could not speak with fright.

– Why is he not writing, Father Arnall?

– He broke his glasses, said Father Arnall, and I exempted him from work.

– Broke? What is this I hear? What is this your name is? said the prefect of studies.

– Dedalus, sir.

– Out here, Dedalus. Lazy little schemer. I see schemer in your face. Where did you break your glasses?

Stephen stumbled into the middle of the class, blinded by fear and haste.

–Where did you break your glasses?' repeated the prefect of studies.
– The cinderpath sir.
– Hoho! The cinderpath! cried the prefect of studies. I know that trick.

Stephen lifted his eyes in wonder and saw for a moment Father Dolan's whitegrey not young face, his baldy whitegrey head with fluff at the sides of it, the steel rims of his spectacles and his nocoloured eyes looking through the glasses. Why did he say he knew that trick?

– Lazy idle little loafer! cried the prefect of studies. Broke my glasses! An old schoolboy trick! Out with your hand this moment!

Stephen closed his eyes and held out in the air his trembling hand with the palm upwards. He felt the prefect of studies touch it for a moment at the fingers to straighten it and then the swish of the sleeve of the soutane as the pandybat was lifted to strike. A hot burning stinging tingling blow like the loud crack of a broken stick made his trembling hand crumple together like a leaf in the fire: and at the sound and the pain scalding tears were driven into his eyes. His whole body was shaking with fright, his arm was shaking and his crumpled burning livid hand shook like a loose leaf in the air. A cry sprang to his lips, a prayer to be let off. But though the tears scalded his eyes and his limbs quivered with pain and fright he held back the hot tears and the cry scalded his throat.

– Other hand! shouted the prefect of studies.

Stephen drew back his maimed hand and his quivering right arm and held out his left hand. The soutane sleeve swished again as the pandybat was lifted and a loud crashing sound and a fierce, maddening tingling burning pain made his hand shrink together with the palms and fingers in a livid quivering mass. The scalding water burst forth from his eyes and, burning with shame and agony and fear, he drew back his shaking arm in terror and burst out into a whine of pain. His body shook with a palsy of fright and in shame and rage he felt the scalding cry come from his throat and the scalding tears falling out of his eyes and down his flaming cheeks.

– Kneel down, cried the prefect of studies.

Stephen knelt down quickly pressing his beaten hands to his side. To think of them beaten and swollen with pain all in a moment made him feel so sorry for them as if they were not his own but someone else's that he felt sorry for. And as he knelt, calming the last sobs in his throat and feeling the burning tingling pain pressed in to his sides, he thought of the hands which he had held out in the air with the palms up and the firm touch of the prefect of studies when he steadied the shaking fingers and of the beaten swollen reddened mass of the palm and fingers that shook helplessly in the air.

– Get at your work, all of you, cried the prefect of studies from the door. Father Dolan will be in every day to see if any boy, any lazy idle little loafer wants flogging. Every day. Every day.

The door closed behind him.

The hushed class continued to copy out the themes. Father Arnall rose from his seat and went among them helping the boys with gentle words and telling them the mistakes they had made. His voice was very gentle and soft. Then he returned to his place and said to Fleming and Stephen:

–You may return to your places, you two.

Fleming and Stephen rose and, walking to their seats, sat down. Stephen, scarlet with shame, opened a book quickly with one weak hand and bent down upon it, his face close to the page.

Passage 2 D. H. Lawrence, The Rainbow

'Go in front, Wright,' she said.

She was trembling in every fibre. A big sullen boy, not bad but difficult, slouched out to the front. She went on with the lesson, aware that Williams was making faces at Wright, and that Wright was grinning behind her. She was afraid. She turned to the map again. And she was afraid.

'Please Miss, Williams –' came a sharp cry, and a boy on the back row was standing up, with drawn, pained brows, half a mocking grin on his face, half real resentment against Williams.

'Please Miss, he's nipped me,' and he rubbed his leg ruefully.

'Come in front, Williams,' she said.

The rat-like boy sat with his pale smile and did not move.

'Come in front,' she repeated, definite now.

'I shan't,' he cried, snarling, rat-like, grinning. Something went click in Ursula's soul. Her face and eyes set, she went through the class straight. The boy cowered before her glowering, fixed eyes. But she advanced on him, seized him by the arm, and dragged him from his seat. He clung to the form. It was a battle between him and her. Her instinct had suddenly become calm and quick. She jerked him from his grip, and dragged him, kicking and struggling to the front. He kicked her several times and clung to the forms as he passed, but she went on. The class was on its feet in excitement. She saw it but made no move.

She knew that if she let go the boy he would dash to the door. Already he had run home once out of her class. So she snatched her cane from the desk and brought it down on him. He was writhing and kicking. She saw his face beneath her, white, with eyes like the eyes of a fish, stony, yet full of hate and horrible fear. And she loathed him, the hideous writhing thing that was nearly too much for her. In horror lest he should overcome her, and yet at the heart quite calm, she brought down the cane again and again, whilst he struggled making inarticulate noises, and lunging vicious kicks against her. With one hand she managed to hold him, and now and then the cane came down on him. He writhed like a mad thing. But the pain of the strokes cut through his writhing vicious coward's courage, bit deeper, till at last, with a long whimper that became a yell, he went limp. She let him go, and he rushed at her, his teeth and eyes glinting. There was a second of agonized terror in her heart: he was a beast thing. Then she caught him, and the cane came down on him. A few times, madly, in a frenzy, he lunged and writhed, to kick her. But again the cane broke him, he sank with a howling yell to the floor, and like a beaten beast he lay there yelling.

Mr Harby had rushed up towards the end of this performance.

'What's the matter?' he roared.

Ursula felt as if something was going to break in her.

'I've thrashed him,' she said, her breast heaving, forcing out the words on the last breath. The headmaster stood choking with rage, helpless. She looked at the writhing, howling figure on the floor.

'Get up,' she said. The thing writhed away from her. She took a step forward. She had realized the presence of the headmaster for one second and then she was oblivious of it again.

'Get up,' she said. And with a little dart the boy was on his feet. His yelling dropped to a mad blubber. He had been in a frenzy.

'Go and stand by the radiator,' she said.

As if mechanically, blubbering, he went.

The headmaster stood robbed of movement and speech. His face was yellow, his hands twitched convulsively. But Ursula stood stiff not far from him. Nothing could touch her now: she was beyond Mr Harby. She was violated as if to death.

The headmaster muttered something, turned and went down the room, whence, from the far end, he was heard roaring in a mad rage at his own class.

The boy blubbered wildly by the radiator. Ursula looked at the class. There were fifty pale, still faces watching her, a hundred round eyes fixed on her in an attentive, expressionless stare.

'Give out the history readers,' she said to the monitors.

There was dead silence. As she stood there, she could hear again the ticking of the clock, and the chock of piles of books taken out of the low cupboard. Then came the faint flap of books on the desks. The children passed in silence, their hands working in unison. They were no longer a pack, but each one separated into a silent, closed thing.

 EXAMINATION ANSWERS

 Question I *Notes and tutor's answer*

Notes

1   Read through the passage carefully.
2   Make a list of as many *different* aspects of the scene as you can find.
3   Decide what the general atmosphere is and try to put a word to it – or several words if you think there is more than one element to it.
4   Make a second list of comparisons, images, particular expressions and anything else you find striking about the writing.
5   Look at the reference to brides and bouquets and think of what Pinkie's reaction to this might be.
6   Write three paragraphs:
      – one on different aspects of the scene using your first list;
      – one on what you find vivid in the description using your second list;
      – one relating the passage to the wedding.

Suggested answer

Brighton is full of people: they cram the trams, the buses, the taxis, and jostle in a seething mass along the seafront. There is an air of excitement from the multitude of people, all intent on enjoying themselves and winning money. Even the girls shut away from the crowds in the school grounds are infected by it. There is an enormous amount of noise, from the people themselves and from the traffic – car exhausts and overloaded buses straining their engines to climb the hill. A band plays with gusto and the sound gives a festive air. Even the private cars are crammed with people. Every conceivable vehicle, from ancient, unfashionable family cars to a zippy modern sports car, has taken to the road. All kinds of people, rich and poor, have taken the day off, for this is not actually a Bank Holiday, to attend the races. There is an air of teeming, tatty confusion, as people trail through the dust eating out of paper bags, and a sense that the normal rules of life have been relaxed and anything can happen.

The writing is made vivid by the numerous details, and through particular, unexpected features. The solitary negro, brightly dressed and smoking a cigar, is a sufficiently unusual sight for the children to back away in alarm when he speaks. The band is not, as you might expect, a regimental marching band, but a group of blind beggars. Greene notices how they guide themselves along the street by keeping one foot against the kerb. Many of the people in this extract are compared to animals. The band is like a group of blind pit ponies, the girls keeping goal are armadillos, the younger girls, ponies on the turf. The whole crowd is like a mass of insects moving mindlessly as if compelled by some force of nature rather than reason. These comparisons, particularly the last, are dehumanizing and vividly create the feeling of the crowd, where individuals are submerged and the mass takes on a life of its own. Further comparisons add to this effect. The noise of the crowd is like that of a machine: it 'rumbles'. The movement of the crowd is mechanical too, as if on a creaking escalator. Yet the sports car is alive: it 'worms' its way through the traffic. The sun, reflecting off it, seems to be giving a great wink, as though it is in the know about some of its rakish activities.

The woman in the car sings incongruously about brides and bouquets. The connection between this scene and the wedding is made through the song from the car. The words float down to Pinkie following in his battered old Morris and remind him of his marriage. He resents being in a situation where he has to marry Rose, but he must do it so that she cannot give evidence against him. The whole idea of marriage disgusts him. What is more, Rose is poor, unglamorous and innocent. She comes from the very background from which he is trying to escape. The sports car is a symbol of what Pinkie wants. He is envious of people who own scarlet racing cars and of their life-style. It is ironic that the romantic and traditional song should come from the car, with its associations of smutty sexual encounters 'in by-lanes off the Great North Road'. The song is out of place in such a car. Pinkie wants nothing to do with brides and bouquets but he does want the car.

There is another, more general, connection between this scene and Pinkie's wedding. A wedding is usually a celebratory, festive occasion, as this scene is. Pinkie's wedding is grimly functional, performed in a bare, official room with only the two necessary witnesses present and without even a wedding ring. The only similarity with this scene is in the general seediness of the surroundings.

'Have you given examples of vivid writing? Have you answered both parts of the question?'

▷ **Question 2**   *Student's answer – examiner's comment*

'Much better to refer to an event rather than a chapter number.'

'Good. Identifies the atmosphere.'

Hardy has many ways of capturing our attention and creating our emotions in chapters twenty-eight and forty-four.

At the beginning of chapter twenty-eight Hardy describes the landscapes: the words he uses are plump, radiant, clear and untainted. We can see that this is not unlike Bathsheba at this time – her body or her mind. We obtain a feeling of warmness and self-indulgence, 'bristling balls of gold' and 'luxuriant rays'. The branches caress Bathsheba, perhaps showing promises of what is to come. Hardy describes throughout the chapter Bathsheba's feelings: she ran 'literally trembling and panting' because of the danger she is in. Bathsheba is excited and therefore we feel much of this excitement ourselves. She is

(continued)

(continued)

afraid of the sword and overwhelmed at the end which creates these emotions in the reader. Hardy is very keen to divulge Bathsheba's emotions so that we can understand and sympathize with her but it is noticeable that not once in the chapter does Hardy pinpoint Troy's feelings, so we imagine Troy as merely a figure and an object, not a person, who sets off the fire in Bathsheba. Troy is ready and waiting, and when he produces the sword, it is introduced as a living thing which first may give us the idea that it is an extension of his manhood. He then performs the 'cuts and thrusts' which are noticeably 'entering' movements. The exercises overall are a symbol of foreplaying – a taste of what is to come for Bathsheba. During the chapter, many phrases are used to describe the movement of the sword and its effect on Bathsheba. 'A rainbow' is a very good one because it symbolizes a mirage – something that is enchanting but soon disappears which is Troy's love and their marriage. It 'resembles a sky full of meteors close at hand', which shows that this was new to her, something alien and exciting. And finally 'like a twanged harpstring' which describes Troy's sword arm. This is a strange simile for Troy, but perhaps Bathsheba thought she was in heaven!

Troy deceives her when he tells her the sword is blunt, which is a symbol of their whole relationship.

The sword, as it moved past her, Hardy says, has left the shape of her which shows that at that time Troy had summed up her character totally and knew just what she wanted. It is because of this that Troy can go on to cut off the lock of her hair and remove the caterpillar from her bosom.

'The essay has moved away from the title. It is now concerned with the character's feelings rather than with atmosphere. Although this student continues to write well about the language, it is not until much later that he/she gets back to answering the question actually set! You cannot afford to ramble.'

'Good. Points out the symbolic nature of the action.'

'Good. Getting back to the atmosphere and background to the story.'

▷ **Question 3** *Student's answer – examiner's comments*

The two passages are both set in the classroom: they are also not modern schools. We can tell this because of the beatings and because of the number of pupils in the class. The two passages both involve boys being beaten, one with a 'pandybat' and one with a cane.

The school Joyce has created is extremely strict: Stephen is beaten because he has broken his glasses, yet we learn at the end of the passage what we suspected all along, that he has been telling the truth because he has great difficulty in reading his book. This is unjust and unfair. The prefect of study ferociously punishes the boy for no proper reason. He almost seems to enjoy it.

In Lawrence's school the teacher is a young and inexperienced girl and the class is rude and uncooperative. She has developed a strong dislike for Williams, who is a rat-like, snarling, nasty boy. Her feelings towards him seem to be justified and yet she has no desire to hurt him. When he answers back he is caned, but with great difficulty on Ursula's part. He fights viciously to avoid the pain of the punishment. In Joyce's school the young boys are more disciplined and they obediently respond when they are called to the front of the class for a painful beating.

Stephen, in Joyce's passage, is very sensitive and responsive to feelings. He pities his beaten hands as if they were independent of himself and had human feelings. He is very polite and truthful, obedient and well behaved. He is also terrified of the pandybat and Father Dolan. He becomes so tense he can barely think properly and almost loses his senses. Williams, in Lawrence's passage, is quite the opposite. He is insensitive, rude, inconsiderate, spiteful and vicious and wild as a beast. He is very disobedient and undisciplined.

(continued)

'A very effective and well-written answer. Points out the similarities of the situation in the two passages and then goes on to point out the differences. Good observations covering many aspects of the texts: setting, characters, relationships and language. Evidence from the passages is carefully used to back up all the points made. Gives a strong and well-reasoned personal response.

One criticism would be of the organization: the answer begins by talking about setting and then comes back to it in the fifth paragraph. It would be better to group all these remarks together. The last paragraph would have been better placed before the strong statement about emotions and sympathies, which would make a good conclusion.'

(continued)

The setting in each passage is fairly similar, in the sense they are both in a classroom, but I feel the schools differ a great deal. Joyce's boys seem to be of a higher class than Lawrence's. The school also seems better for they have individual classrooms whereas in Lawrence's school it seems that the whole school is in one large hall. Ursula appears to be teaching fifty pupils at one end and Mr Harby another fifty at the other end. This seems to show that Lawrence's school is in a poor village or town. Another aspect which shows the difference between the schools is the language of the pupils. In Joyce's school their language is more correct and structured. Moreover the boys know better than to call out across the room. In Lawrence's school the language is not only not so well structured but also the children speak in dialect.

Even though the passages are similar in setting they create opposing emotions. After reading Joyce's passage I felt desperately sorry for Stephen and the other children because they were so unjustly treated: Father Dolan was so unfair and far too strict. In the second passage my response changed from sympathy for the children to sympathy for the teacher. Immediately I was on Ursula's side. I felt she had tried to be fair and just and the children were difficult and full of resentment towards her. I loathed the thought of ever being in Ursula's situation. I felt so sorry for Ursula having to deal with a child like Williams and had no pity for him when she beat him: he deserved it.

The relationships between the pupil and the teacher are very different in the two schools. Although Father Dolan is resented by all the children in Joyce's passage Father Arnall is appreciated because he is kind and helpful. Ursula also seems to have tried being kind before but the children are too ignorant to appreciate her and she has to act as she does to prevent them overcoming her. She has no help from her superior who ought to help her to keep order.

Question	Assessment Objective(s)	Pre-20th century	20th century
Coursework task – *Ethan Frome*	1, 2, 4		✓
1 *Brighton Rock*	1, 2, 4		✓
2 *Far from the Madding Crowd*	1, 2	✓	
3 *A Portrait of the Artist as a Young Man, The Rainbow*	1, 2, 3, 4		✓

SUMMARY

▷ The **setting** of the novel is a whole, distinctive world, created by the novelist.

▷ Settings can produce the general **atmosphere** of the novel but also reflect a character's particular **mood**.

▷ **Landscape** and **weather** are effective in creating atmosphere and reflecting character.

▷ Landscape, weather and other aspects of setting may be used symbolically as well as literally, to help convey a theme or idea.

▷ Settings may show character and may affect our response to a character.

▷ The **social context** is often important in conveying the author's views and criticisms of society.

Themes and ideas

GETTING STARTED

Some exam questions will test whether you understand what the book is about. That is not what the story is about, but the ideas it expresses. Every author has an outlook on life which the story expresses. Some stories set out very clearly to put forward the author's point of view, even to teach or preach. Ideas may be aired through a character's thoughts or conversation. More often, the author's ideas will be buried in the story. The themes will emerge only gradually as these ideas become clear. You will only be able to say what the book is 'about' when you have finished reading, and the pattern is complete. This is why re-reading is essential. The second time through you can pick up hints and indications you overlooked before because you did not realize their importance. That is not to say you should not be looking for themes from the beginning. As you read, ask yourself, 'What seems to be important to the novelist?'

The topics covered in this chapter are applicable to all exam boards.

MEG	NEAB	NICCEA	SEG	LONDON	WJEC	IGCSE	**TOPIC**	STUDY	REVISION 1	REVISION 2
✓	✓	✓	✓	✓	✓	✓	Titles			
✓	✓	✓	✓	✓	✓	✓	Characters and ideas			
✓	✓	✓	✓	✓	✓	✓	Plots and ideas			
✓	✓	✓	✓	✓	✓	✓	Endings			
✓	✓	✓	✓	✓	✓	✓	Significant events			
✓	✓	✓	✓	✓	✓	✓	Contrasting pairs			
✓	✓	✓	✓	✓	✓	✓	Setting			

WHAT YOU NEED TO KNOW

Every part of a novel can express its theme.

▷ **Titles**　The **title** often gives a good idea of the themes of a novel. This is not surprising because in it the author may try to sum up in a few words what is important and significant in a book. Jane Austen is very good on titles: *Pride and Prejudice* and *Sense and Sensibility* tell us what her books are about before we begin to read. We expect to find in these novels characters who have the qualities mentioned in the titles and we do. We also find out what Jane Austen's verdict on these qualities is through her handling of the characters.

Do not, however, always expect the title to give you a clue to the theme. *Oliver Twist* tells us who, not what, the book is about.

An interesting exercise is to compose alternative titles which express the novel's theme.

▷ **Characters and ideas**　Novelists show their views in the kind of **characters** they create and what befalls them. Which of the characters are condemned and shown in a bad light, which are approved of? The answers to these questions may show you the novelist's values. Among other things in *Pride and Prejudice*, Jane Austen disapproves of Mr Collins' pomposity, Mrs Bennet's silliness, Lady Catherine's snobbishness, Mary's self-absorption and above all Wickham's selfish opportunism and deceit. All these characters are commented on adversely, sometimes openly, sometimes by implication. Elizabeth and Darcy are admired for their ability to learn. They are rewarded with wealth and happiness.

Another way novelists show disapproval is to bring characters to a bad end. Fagin, who throughout *Oliver Twist* has no pity for anyone, is mercilessly shown suffering in the condemned cell before he is hanged.

Some characters embody an idea so completely that they become types, or caricatures. Mr Bounderby, as his name implies, is a walking example of a 'bounder', a Victorian word for a person without principles. Big Brother, in Orwell's *1984*, is totalitarianism personified. (Look back at Chapter 11 on character types and names in drama for more examples of characters who embody ideas.)

▷ **Plots and ideas**　Plots, unlike life, can be organized however the novelist wishes. Therefore they can be specially tailored to show what the novelist thinks ought to happen. A novelist who wants to discuss the class system, for example, will construct a story that includes class conflicts. One who thinks that marriage is a good and necessary thing for women, like most nineteenth-century novelists, will show events leading to happy and successful marriages. One who thinks, as the present-day writer Fay Weldon does, that marriage is a poor deal for most women, will construct stories that show marriage in a poor light. George Orwell constructed a story, *1984*, which he hoped showed the evil of totalitarian rule. The ideas came first; the working out of the plot, in which the individual is crushed by the state machine, is designed to demonstrate those ideas.

Ask yourself these questions about the novels you are studying: What is the purpose of the story? What works out successfully for the characters? What fails? What is shown to be good and what bad? Who wins the conflicts? Are we made to feel that the right side won?

▷ **Endings**　Not all bad characters die or are punished in the **end** and not all good characters receive rewards. And by no means can all characters be divided neatly into good and bad – most are a mixture. In working out the plot the novelist may deliberately offend the reader's idea of what is fair in order to make a point. At the end of *Of Mice and Men*, for example, Steinbeck has George shoot his friend Lennie. George does it quickly and cleanly, while Lennie is happily dreaming of the future, in order to save him from far worse. We see that it is not fair that Lennie should die; we also see that it is inevitable. Lennie is a simpleton in a hard world where there is no place for him. The author produces complex responses in his readers. Our recognition of the appropriateness of the end of the novel shows that we have understood Steinbeck's ideas, as expressed through the novel's plot and structure. Happy endings, or fairly happy endings, should strike us in the same way, as justified and inevitable. It is right that Adam Bede and Dinah Morris should marry. But first Adam has to learn that his first choice, Hetty, is the wrong woman for him, although Hetty is more beautiful. It is a painful lesson, but necessary, so that the book may reach the conclusion which we recognize as proper.

We may not always feel the ending is satisfying. At the end of *The Mayor of Casterbridge* Henchard dies just before Elizabeth-Jane finds him. Is this inevitable? Some people would say not. They grumble that it is artificial that Elizabeth-Jane should arrive just too late so that Henchard dies miserable and lonely. In fact, they grumble that Thomas Hardy does this kind of thing far too often. This criticism is really saying that Hardy does not express his ideas through his plots in a satisfactory way. The idea that Hardy is expressing by having Henchard die is the folly of his strongly impetuous nature. He destroys what he loves right from the beginning when he sells his wife. All events point to the fact that Henchard cannot win, but the manner of his death also points to Hardy's deeply fatalistic view of life. Hardy is artistically right even if not completely realistic. His novel ends in a way that is appropriate to the scheme and ideas of the book even if this is not a way which is likely to happen in real life.

▷ Significant events

While endings are very important because they complete the pattern of the story, many other events in the story can be **significant** in stating the theme. These can often be seemingly quite small. In *A Passage to India*, when Mrs Callendar takes an Indian doctor's carriage without permission, it is significant because it shows the relationship between the races. In the same novel Mrs Moore finds a wasp on the coat-peg – not a very earth-shattering event:

> Going to hang up her cloak she found that the tip of the peg was occupied by a small wasp. She had known this wasp or his relatives by day; they were not as English wasps, but had long yellow legs which hung down behind when they flew. Perhaps he mistook the peg for a branch – no Indian animal has any sense of an interior . . . There he clung, asleep while jackals in the plain bayed their desires and mingled with the percussion of drums. 'Pretty dear,' said Mrs Moore to the wasp.

This tiny event is made significant because it is used to show the difference between India and England. The distinctions which the English are used to do not seem to apply: the animals cannot be shut outside – indoors and outdoors do not seem to count; a peg and a branch are the same to a wasp. This implies that animals and people cannot be divided into separate categories. Mrs Moore can see this. She calls the wasp a pretty dear, though most people – English people – would shoo it away or kill it. Later in the novel there is another reference to a wasp when a character tries to explain why, in the Hindu religion, even the life of an insect is valuable. The little incident in this passage shows that Mrs Moore understands this instinctively.

Look out for such events as these. When apparently small things are mentioned several times they are usually significant in the novel's theme.

▷ Contrasting pairs

Many plots are built around contrasts and these are often instructive in revealing the author's ideas and the theme of the novel. **Contrasting pairs** occur frequently throughout literature and several have already been mentioned in the course of this book. In settings we have had the contrast of Wuthering Heights and Thrushcross Grange and of Loamshire and Stoneyshire (see Chapter 16). In character we have had Kate and Bianca, and Maggie Hobson and her sisters (see Chapter 11). In *The Mayor of Casterbridge* the impetuous Henchard is contrasted with the calm and methodical Farfrae: as Henchard falls so Farfrae rises, taking over Henchard's business and his house. Henchard's failure is the result of his character, which contains what is often called a 'fatal flaw'. Hardy uses the opposing character of Farfrae to expose Henchard's faults and to show how he could have behaved differently.

▷ Setting

Chapter 16 showed how the **setting** of a novel can create a particular atmosphere or a distinct world. The nature of this world, or the atmosphere it generates, also show the author's views. Dickens' city is cruel; Orwell's state is oppressive and all-pervasive; Graham Greene's world is degraded. There is a very general idea, found frequently in English literature, that the town or city tends to be bad and harbour vice, while the countryside is wholesome and good. This idea goes back to classical literature and the biblical paradise in the Garden of Eden and can be traced from Shakespeare down through Dickens and the nineteenth century and on to *Lark Rise to Candleford* and *Cider with Rosie*.

Apart from such general ideas, setting can give more specific indications of the ideas or themes of a novel. The opening of *A Passage to India* is a description of the city of Chandrapore where the novel is set. In the description the author, E. M. Forster, mentions much that is important for the rest of the novel. He begins:

> Except for the Marabar Caves – and they are twenty miles off – the city of Chandrapore presents nothing extraordinary.

He then seems to forget the caves and goes on to the city, where everything seems to be made of mud. This is where the Indians live. On a hill above the city the British, the rulers, live. The positions are significant – in fact everything is significant. The caves, which seem only to have been mentioned in passing, become the scene of the most important event in the novel. The mud becomes a symbol of life. The whole novel deals with the difficult relationships between British and Indian and the prejudices of oppressor and oppressed, westerner and oriental.

We cannot see the significance of everything immediately. We have to store the details in our minds and wait for the significance to be revealed. That is what we have to do all the time when we are reading.

▷ **Additional examples**

Use these examples as exercises to test your understanding of what you have read in this chapter. Write down your own ideas before reading the key below.

1   This passage, from the end of *A Passage to India*, restates the themes of the novel quite clearly. What are the ideas expressed in this passage?

> 'Down with the English anyhow. That's certain. Clear out, you fellows, double quick, I say. We may hate one another, but we hate you most. If I don't make you go, Ahmed will, Karim will, if it's fifty-five hundred years we shall get rid of you, yes, we shall drive every blasted Englishman into the sea, and then,' – he rode against him furiously – 'and then,' he concluded, half-kissing him, 'you and I can be friends.'
>
> 'Why can't we be friends now?' said the other, holding him affectionately. 'It's what I want. It's what you want.' But the horses didn't want it – they swerved apart; the earth didn't want it, sending up rocks through which riders must pass in single file; the temples, the tank, the jail, the palace, the birds, the carrion, the Guest House, that came into view as they issued from the gap and saw Mau beneath them: they didn't want it, they said in their hundred voices, 'No, not yet,' and the sky said 'No, not there.'

2   What ideas are being expressed in the following extract from *Animal Farm*? Why does George Orwell choose to present them through the characters of animals?

> Major continued: 'I have little more to say. I merely repeat, remember always your duty of enmity towards Man and all his ways. Whatever goes on two legs, is an enemy. Whatever goes on four legs, or has wings, is a friend. And remember also that in fighting against Man, we must not come to resemble him. Even when you have conquered him, do not adopt his vices. No animal must ever live in a house, or sleep in a bed, or wear clothes, or drink alcohol, or smoke tobacco, or touch money, or engage in trade. All the habits of Man are evil. And, above all, no animal must ever tyrannize over his own kind. Weak or strong, clever or simple, we are all brothers. No animal must ever kill any other animal. All animals are equal.
>
> 'And now, comrades, I will tell you about my dream of last night. I cannot describe that dream to you. It was a dream of the earth as it will be when Man has vanished. But it reminded me of something I had long forgotten. Many years ago, when I was a little pig, my mother and the other sows used to sing an old song of which they knew only the tune and the first three words. I had known that tune in my infancy, but it had long since passed out of my mind. Last night, however, it came back to me in my dream. And what is more, the words of the song also came back – words, I am certain, which were sung by the animals of long ago and have been lost to memory for generations. I will sing you that song now, comrades. I am old and my voice is hoarse, but when I have taught you the tune, you can sing it better for yourselves. It is called "Beasts of England".'
>
> Old Major cleared his throat and began to sing. As he had said, his voice was hoarse, but he sang well enough, and it was a stirring tune, something between 'Clementine' and 'La Cucuracha'. The words ran:

Beasts of England, beasts of Ireland,
Beasts of every land and clime,
Hearken to my joyful tidings
Of the golden future time.

Soon or late the day is coming,
Tyrant Man shall be o'erthrown,
And the fruitful fields of England
Shall be trod by beasts alone.

Rings shall vanish from our noses,
And the harness from our back,
Bit and spur shall rust forever,
Cruel whips no more shall crack.

Riches more than mind can picture,
Wheat and barley, oats and hay,
Clover, beans and mangel-wurzels
Shall be ours upon that day.

Key to the examples

1 The Indian and the Englishman who are talking in this passage want to be friends. They each feel affection for the other but they cannot be friends because the Indians want the British out of the country so that they can rule it themselves. Only then will individuals be able to come together. As it is everything around them in society, the whole way that life is organized in India, is a barrier to their friendship and understanding. Perhaps the Indians and the English can never come together because even the landscape, the rocks, seem to be against it, and the sky says 'No, not there.'

2 George Orwell is using an old tradition when he chooses animals as his characters. Just as in Aesop's Fables they are used to stand for human characters. We understand that he is really writing about human society. By writing about animals he is able to simplify the characters, the events and the ideas, so that he can put them across more directly and with greater force. He also avoids stirring up our prejudices. We feel that animals are removed from us so we can view their activities dispassionately.

Major is addressing all the animals 'of every land and clime'. His speech is a rallying cry to unify them against their common enemy, Man. He has a vision of a better life for all, when the tyrant will no longer rule over them with cruelty. They will be their own masters and everyone will share in the good things of life. This is an ancient and long-felt desire of the animals, for it has come to Major in a dream of something he heard in infancy. Once Man has been conquered and over-thrown, all the evils of his rule will be abolished and never allowed to return.

Major represents the visionary seer calling on his fellows to revolt. He could be any leader with a dream of the future, and the animals any group which feels itself oppressed. The promises of the golden age to come are the promises that every leader makes: the wheat and barley that the animals will receive represent any unfulfilled desires. Because the animals' hatred for the present system is so great, Major says everything must be swept away. Revolutionaries generally want to break completely with the past. They cannot admit that anything is good, so everything must go.

Like other revolutionary thinkers, Major is sincere. He wants to better the lot of everyone and to make them all equal. He warns against backsliding in the future. The animals must not over-throw Man just to become like him. He sees that there is always the danger of the strong taking advantage of the weak. Orwell is saying that despite the sincerest intentions there is the danger that self-interest will prevail.

By the end of the book Major's revolution has suffered the fate that he foresaw. The pigs have taken the place of Man.

▷ SUGGESTIONS FOR COURSEWORK

1   Write an alternative last chapter of a novel. Change the events in any way you like, but make the new ending:

(a) convincing in terms of character – would the characters have behaved the way you make them?

(b) appropriate to the themes of the novel. How are the characters treated in the new conclusion in comparison to the original ending?

2 Write a piece of dialogue between two characters from different novels. Possible suggestions, Jane Eyre and Billy Liar; Miss Havisham and Elizabeth Bennet.

3 Take a dramatic event from a novel you are studying. Imagine that you are to conduct a television interview with one of the characters involved in that incident. Write the interview.

4 Take a leading character in a novel of your choice. Imagine that your chosen character has gone to live in a different place altogether, for example, Fagin has retired to the country; Billy Casper has gone to live in New York. As your chosen character write a diary about a week's events in your new home.

▷ **Coursework task**   Take a dramatic event from a novel you are studying. Imagine that you are to conduct a television interview with one of the characters involved in that incident. Write that interview.

▷ **Suggested**   The interview is with Cassie Logan, the heroine of *Roll of Thunder, Hear My Cry* by Mildred
  answer   D. Taylor. The interview is based on the events of Chapter 11.
            'I' is the interviewer and 'C' stands for Cassie.

I   I know it must have been a very distressing time for you, but could you tell the viewers what happened that night?

C   Yes, it was. It was sheer terror.

I   How did it start?

C   Well, I couldn't sleep – it was a hot, muggy night. I was trying to get to sleep by trying to count the states. It's odd really – I was trying to do it geographically – when T. J. burst in.

I   T. J.? Who's that?

C   T. J. is bad news. He hangs about with white boys. Sucks up to them, you know. The Simmses – they're a bad lot – but T. J. – T. J. Avery, that is, is too easily led.

I   Led? In what way?

C   Well, this time, he had his heart set on this pearl-handled pistol and they found one in a shop in Strawberry.

I   Strawberry? Where's that?

C   Strawberry is the town where we take things to sell in a market there. We've not got much of a pitch, right at the back, out of the way, but we got loyal customers.

I   And what did T. J. want?

C   Want? He was running scared. Wanted to hide, I suppose. You see, the owner of the store, Mr Barnett, caught T. J. and the Simmses' kids breaking in, and R. W. had hit Mr Barnett on the head with an axe.

I   That was a terrible thing to do.

C   Not if you knew Mr Barnett. He always served white people first. Even white kids. One day he ignored me and T. J. to serve a white girl.

I   Do you think the owner would be able to recognize T. J. again?

C   Oh yes. You see, he wasn't wearing a mask, not like the Simmses' kids were. Barnett thought all of them were black. There was a struggle and Mrs Barnett was thrown down and knocked out.

I   So they all decided to run?

C   They would have, but T. J. threatened to tell everybody that it was the Simmses who had killed the Barnetts. So they beat T. J. up and left him in the back of a truck. Funnily enough, this time I had to believe him. Normally T. J. is a great big liar but this time I knew he was speaking the truth.

I   What did you do about T. J.?

C   Me? Nothing. Stacey – my brother – tried to persuade him to stay. He should have stayed. Blood was spurting out of his mouth. But he said he should get home and tell his mom and pa that some white boys had beat him up.

I   So what did you decide to do?

C   Stacey – he's always had a soft spot for T. J. – feels he's his responsibility or something – said he was going to see T. J. home. I said I'd help.

ı   That was taking a big risk, wasn't it?

c   Sure thing! First we had to sneak past Mr Morrison who slept on the porch.

ı   Mr Morrison?

c   Yes, he's a giant of a man, but soft as cotton. Pa brought him home from work one day and he's been with us ever since. Works for nothing, the big soft baby. We got past him all right. The weather was awful – thunder and lightning. We just wanted to get T. J. home and dump him there.

ı   Did you manage to do that?

c   We thought we had. We saw him climb through an open window, but then the next problem was we had to get home.

ı   Problem? What kind of a problem?

c   Well, just as we got close to the forest, the sky was all lit up. There were lights everywhere. We hid in the bush and saw pickups and cars full of men shouting. One of the men was that Kaleb Wallace.

ı   What was he doing?

c   He and his brother Thurston were beating on the Averys' front door. Thurston was really mad, 'cos our gentle giant – you know, Mr Morrison – had broken his arm earlier. It was awful. The Averys were dragged out of their home. T. J. had his jaw broken. The Simmses were kicking him in the stomach.

ı   Did anybody try to help?

c   Poor Mrs Avery was screaming and tried to save her son, but she was pushed against the side of the house and knocked out.

ı   Couldn't you find anybody to help?

c   No way. Mr Jamieson came by and tried to persuade Kaleb Wallace to have T. J. tried in a proper court, but Kaleb was having none of it.

ı   But what about the local sheriff? Couldn't he do anything?

c   Well, the sheriff arrived, and told everybody that there would be no hanging on Granger's land.

ı   So that was the end of the affair?

c   You don't know Kaleb. He said he'd got three ropes and it would be a shame not to use them.

ı   And did he?

c   All we could think of was getting Pa. We had to get Papa. Stacey said he'd stay on in case the men moved T. J. to a different place – he'd be able to follow him. I wasn't happy about this but I had to get home to tell Papa what had happened.

ı   So what did you decide to do?

c   I took my two brothers by the hand – they had come along with us – and ran back. It was awful. I daren't turn on the flashlight in case the men saw us. The storm was worse than before. So we ran on in the dark. We had to get Papa. He was T. J.'s only hope.

ı   I know how distressing it has been to relive the events of that night, but thank you for telling the viewers your terrible story.
Don't forget to look in tomorrow night to find out if Cassie did manage to rescue T. J.

EXAMINATION QUESTIONS

▷ **Question 1**
'MEG Foundation Tier.'

R.L. Stevenson's *Dr Jekyll and Mr Hyde* contains a number of incidents that create a feeling of horror in a reader. Which particular incident do you think is most horrifying? Remember to give reasons for your choice.

    In order to answer this question first select the particular incident and then find reasons for its being the most horrifying. To do this you also need to look at other incidents and compare them.

▷ **Question 2**
'SEG Foundation Tier.'

The Mayor of Casterbridge – Thomas Hardy. Give your opinion on Michael Henchard's troubles in the novel.

    You may wish to consider some of the following: Henchard's words and actions in different parts of the novel, his behaviour regarding other characters, the change in his fortunes, the role of fate in his downfall.

▷ **Question 3**
'London Foundation Tier.'

Great Expectations – Charles Dickens. How has wealth affected Pip's attitude to Joe Gargery? Are these effects unavoidable?

    In your answer you ought to consider the pressures Pip has been subjected to and the constant nature of Joe throughout the course of the novel. Reference ought to be made to the contrast which Pip would feel between his early behaviour when he became rich and the present when he has lost all his money.

▷ **Question 4**
'WJEC Higher Tier.'

Paddy Clarke Ha Ha Ha – Roddy Doyle. At the end of the story the narrator says: 'I didn't listen to them. They were only kids.' What do you think has contributed to his growing up throughout the book?

▷ **Question 5**
'Foundation Tier.'

Pride and Prejudice – Jane Austen. Explain the importance for the novel as a whole of Mr Bennet's remark: 'One cannot know what a man is by the end of a fortnight.'

▷ **Question 6**
'Higher Tier.'

What is the primary meaning of *Lord of the Flies*?

EXAMINATION ANSWERS

▷ **Question 5**   *Notes and tutor's answer*

Notes

1 As preparation make a list of all the occasions in the novel when longer acquaintance causes one character to change his or her opinion of another.

2 Make a plan along these lines:
    i)   remark applies generally – note title;
    ii)   Elizabeth's misconceptions – Wickham, Darcy;
    iii) Darcy's misconceptions – Elizabeth, Jane;
    iv) other characters.

Suggested answer

'Do all your references to the book illustrate the central idea of the question, that it takes time to know someone?

Although it is their new acquaintance with Mr Bingley which causes Mr Bennet to make this remark, the assertion applies less to Bingley than it does to other characters. As the title suggests, the idea of 'prejudice' is central to the novel. Several characters make a judgement after an initial impression, which proves to be unsound or inaccurate.

    The theme is worked out most importantly through Elizabeth Bennet. Elizabeth is a lively and witty girl. She trusts to her intelligence to provide her with sound opinions of people and her judgement is often shown to be correct. She immediately dislikes and distrusts Miss Bingley and Mrs Hurst. Elizabeth's good-natured sister, Jane, accepts their friendliness at face value and points to their kindnesses to her, but Elizabeth is shown to be right. Elizabeth's opinion of Mr Collins is formed immediately on reading the letter which announces his visit. He appears to her to be pompous, complacent and foolish to a laughable degree. Again, she is proved right. It is all the more disconcerting, therefore, when in two important cases her prejudice leads her into errors of judgement.

    On her first encounter with Mr Darcy she finds him proud and disdainful. She is piqued by his cool remarks about her appearance and his refusal to dance with her. This initial impression of Darcy is reinforced when she meets Wickham and hears the story of how Darcy deprived him of the living promised to him by Darcy's father. Because Wickham is pleasant and attentive, and moreover, good looking, Elizabeth believes his stories and sympathizes with him. Therefore, when Darcy unexpectedly proposes to her Elizabeth declares that she cannot marry a man who, as well as being insufferably haughty and ruining Jane's relationship with Bingley, has treated Wickham very badly. Elizabeth can hardly accept Darcy's version of the events. She is mortified when events prove her to be mistaken in her assessment both of Wickham and Darcy. Wickham's unprincipled behaviour towards her sister, Lydia, could have ruined her life. It is Darcy who arranges a financial settlement which persuades Wickham to marry Lydia. In making Wickham Lydia's seducer and Darcy the saviour of the family honour, Jane Austen shows how mistaken Elizabeth's first views are. And since even her intelligent heroine succumbs to such an error, we see how difficult it is to withhold judgement and form a true and fair view.

Darcy also makes mistakes. Blinded by his pride and reserve he fails to assess Elizabeth correctly at first. He judges her on her family status until her liveliness and wit compel him to look at her as an individual. He falls in love with her almost against his will. He also fails to understand the reticence of Jane's character and so advises his friend Bingley against marrying her, on the ground that she lacks real ardour and is merely fortune hunting. In both cases Darcy's error is based on giving undue weight to the value of position and fortune. However, unlike other members of his class – Lady Catherine de Bourgh, for example – he is willing to learn. Darcy, as well as Elizabeth, is shown as having to reserve his judgement on people.

The force of Mr Bennet's remark is lost on Mrs Bennet and her younger daughters. She and they persist in their silly and superficial opinions of people and never attempt to reach a right view. Jane is shown as always kind and good, but she errs in her reluctance ever to believe ill of anyone. Jane Austen makes her heroine fall into the same error as her mother and younger sisters but then gives her the wit and wisdom to overcome her prejudices and understand that you cannot know a man in a fortnight. The whole story is constructed around the misapprehensions which keep the hero and heroine apart. Only when they overcome them are they allowed to come together.

▷ **Question 6**   *Student's answer – examiner's comment*

'Tell enough of the story to show that you know it in detail, but not so much that you wander off the point. Keep the question in mind.'

'Good. Clearly states the argument of the essay in the opening sentence.'

'Good. Uses a direct quotation which exactly illustrates the point about Jack's feelings.'

'A good choice of incidents to illustrate the idea stated at the start of the essay. This is so throughout the essay.'

'The unfolding of the argument is not signposted in paragraphs which clearly indicate the progression of ideas. The paragraphs become shorter and shorter.'

The primary meaning of Lord of the Flies *is that which illustrates the fact that in any society, however big, once we are left up to our own means, without rules and regulations the standard begins to drop. So, the primitive spirit, which is present in each one of us, begins to get the better of us. The book illustrates this, throughout the steady decline of civilization amongst the marooned boys, progressing throughout the novel. The decline begins with the very first chapter, where Ralph tears off his clothes, and comparatively tears off a part of civilization.*

'He kicked his shoes off fiercely and ripped off each stocking with its elastic garter.' It progressed then to apathy about necessities required, in order to be rescued or survive, on Jack's part. He became obsessed with the hunt, and killing. The passage reads:

He tried to convey the compulsion to track down and kill that was swallowing him up.

It began to decline steadily when the hunters, led by Jack, painted their faces, and then later when the fire – a sign of civilization – was neglected in order to hunt and kill. This was an important point because it distinctly showed the two paths: one being the path leading to disorder, through the hunt and kill; and the other being the path leading to civilization, through the fire and rescue. He also indicated that, at this point, only a handful of boys were following the latter path. Another important incident which showed the definite decline, was when Piggy's glasses were half-broken, and so a part of civilization was broken. Simon said: 'One side's broken.'

The path towards disorder was followed further as the boys began to succumb to the pleasures of the hunt. The passage reads:

Ralph too was fighting to get near . . . The desire to squeeze and hurt was over-mastering.
The pig-run . . . , Ralph was content to follow Jack along it.

This latter quote was symbolic, in that it indicated that Ralph was content to follow Jack along the pig-run – the path to disorder; although he never continued any further. Then the group separates, which is an important part in the book because Golding thus shows that when a society crumbles, the different parts cannot exist humanely. Jack said, 'I'm going off by myself.'

(continued)

'Much more detail is needed to explain events like Simon's murder and, a little later, the breaking of Piggy's glasses and the destruction of both Piggy and the conch.'

(continued)

Gradually things become worse, as Simon is murdered, by the evil he knew was the source of the fear, and so religion and reason are wiped off the island of the other boys.

Then in chapter ten it is evident that the evil rules, when the hunters steal Piggy's glasses – a symbol of civilization – and so civilization diminishes. The quote, talking of Jack, reads:

He was chief now in truth . . . from his left hand dangled Piggy's broken glasses.

Piggy, a sign of common sense and intellect, Ralph a sign of authority, and the conch, a symbol of order and rule, still remained and so a thread of civilization still existed at this point.

Question	Assessment Objective(s)	Pre-20th century	20th century
Coursework task – Mildred D. Taylor	1, 2, 4		✓
1 *Dr Jekyll and Mr Hyde*	1, 2	✓	
2 *The Mayor of Casterbridge*	1, 2		✓
3 *Great Expectations*	1, 2	✓	
4 *Paddy Clarke Ha Ha Ha*	1, 2		✓
5 *Pride and Prejudice*	1, 2	✓	
6 *Lord of the Flies*	1, 2		✓

SUMMARY

▷ **Titles** can sum up what a story is about.

▷ The author's ideas can be shown through the treatment of the characters, particularly **contrasting characters**, and through comment on their behaviour.

▷ The events of the story, particularly the **ending**, show the author's concerns and judgements.

▷ The setting of the story can show the author's **general outlook** or point to the **theme** of the story.

The language of prose

▷ **GETTING STARTED**

Some questions will ask you how an author achieves a particular effect in a passage of prose. Some of the terms and techniques used in writing about the language of poetry are useful. Although we cannot look at a whole novel or even a short story with the close attention we would give to a poem, it is worth looking at some passages closely to see how the language works. The chapter on Language in Drama (Chapter 12) also contains sections that can be applied to prose.

The topics in this chapter are applicable to all exam boards.

MEG	NEAB	NICCEA	SEG	LONDON	WJEC	IGCSE	**TOPIC**	STUDY	REVISION 1	REVISION 2
✓	✓	✓	✓	✓	✓	✓	Comparisons			
✓	✓	✓	✓	✓	✓	✓	Contrasts			
✓	✓	✓	✓	✓	✓	✓	Association words			
✓	✓	✓	✓	✓	✓	✓	Repetition			
✓	✓	✓	✓	✓	✓	✓	Sentences			
✓	✓	✓	✓	✓	✓	✓	Dialogue			

WHAT YOU NEED TO KNOW

▷ **Comparisons**   As in poetry, **comparisons** help to make prose writing vivid and interesting. Prose writers do use metaphors, but they are far more likely to use similes. (If you have forgotten the meaning of these terms, look back at Chapter 4. If you have not read that chapter you should do so.)

Charlotte Bronte shows the cold, hard and inhuman characteristics of Mr Brocklehurst in *Jane Eyre* by comparing him to an inanimate thing:

> presently beside Miss Temple, who herself had risen, stood the same black column which had frowned on me so ominously from the hearthrug at Gateshead.

At other times he is compared to 'black marble' and a 'black pillar' with a face like a 'carved mask placed above the shaft by way of capital'. These comparisons help to create the physical appearance of Mr Brocklehurst and a sense of his towering, forbidding presence. They also tell us a lot about his nature, which is solemn and unfeeling. Notice how all the comparisons are similar. Novelists often cluster images in this way. D. H. Lawrence, writing of the boy in *The Rocking Horse Winner*, uses two contrasting similes about his eyes. When he is winning and things are going well his eyes are like blue fire; when he is sick and exhausted from seeking the name of the Derby winner on his rocking-horse his eyes are like blue stones. The whole condition of the boy is summed up in the difference of his eyes, fire for life and stones for death. Lawrence is a writer who uses many comparisons, quite a lot of them metaphors. These are often quite brief. 'A bomb of rage exploded in her breast' is his telling description of a woman's anger. Later he speaks of 'the risen viper of the little elderly woman' (*The Blue Moccasins*).

When you are reading ask yourself whether the author is making comparisons. Work out what the character or thing is being compared with. Then think about what effect this comparison creates for the reader.

▷ **Contrasts**   Few writers use **contrast** as deliberately as Dickens does at the opening of *A Tale of Two Cities*:

> It was the best of times, it was the worst of times, it was the age of wisdom, it was the age of foolishness, it was the epoch of belief, it was the epoch of incredulity, it was the season of Light, it was the season of Darkness, it was the spring of hope, it was the winter of despair ...

The mention of two contrasting qualities together helps to emphasize them both. Black stands out against white, light against dark.

When you read, notice the way that writers use contrast. Ask yourself what effect it creates.

▷ **Association words**   Prose works very strongly through the kinds of **associations** which the words arouse in the reader. We have already looked at the kind of feelings we get from associations to do with the weather (see Chapter 16). We have also seen how names like Gabriel Oak have certain associations which novelists sometimes use to help characterization (Chapter 15). Many words carry these kinds of associations. Some words work on us very strongly: 'gloom' carries unpleasant associations, 'rainbow' pleasant ones. Poets use such associations very freely and deliberately – again you should look back at the chapter on figurative language (Chapter 4). Prose writers use them more sparingly.

When you are asked to say how a writer creates atmosphere or makes the writing vivid, look at the pleasant and unpleasant associations of the words used.

There is a tendency to think that it is adjectives and adverbs that make description lively:

'Use your dictionary whenever you are in any doubt about the meaning of a word.'

> He looked scornfully (adverb) down his aquiline (adjective) nose. Languidly (adverb) she raised a slender (adjective) arm to the bell-pull and he glanced suspiciously (adverb) round the room.

We can get tired of this sort of writing very quickly. Of course good writers do use adverbs and adjectives in a striking and original way, but not usually in quantity. It is often the single well-placed word that strikes us:

> A bell began to toll with a *peremptory* clang. (Thomas Hardy)
> Suddenly Piggy was a-bubble with *decorous* excitement. (William Golding)

We must expect writers to use unusual words that we have to look up in the dictionary. Liveliness in the writing can just as frequently be a product of verbs:

> I *hurled* myself across the room, *seized* him round the chest, *squeezed* as hard as I could to prevent his escape, and then *flung* him with a dextrous twist of my wrist towards the nearest chair. (*My Family and Other Animals* by Gerald Durrell)

The vigour of this sentence comes from a succession of verbs which re-create the actions for us rather than simply describe them.

Look at all the kinds of words the writer uses and be especially attentive to unusual words or words used in an unusual way.

▷ Repetition

This is one of the prose writer's most useful techniques for heightening atmosphere, creating tension or simply giving an increased importance to what is being said. We have already had an excellent example of the **repetition** of a single word many times in Dickens' passage on fog (see Chapter 14).

We do not expect a high degree of patterning in prose, so patterns rapidly become obvious and we can quickly feel that they are overdone. Nevertheless, arrangements in threes is a favourite device:

> 'You must be admired, you must be courted, you must be flattered – you must have music, dancing and society – or you languish and die away.'

says Eliza of her sister Georgiana in *Jane Eyre*. The weight of her scorn is increased by the thrice-stated phrase and the three frivolities that Georgiana relishes. A little later Mrs Reed recalls Jane's childhood behaviour and her distaste is expressed through a similar method of listing three items of Jane's conduct:

> I could not forget your conduct to me, Jane – the fury with which you once turned on me; the tone in which you declared you abhorred me the worst of anybody in the world; the unchildlike look and voice with which you affirmed that the very thought of me made you sick ...

Repetition is not always in threes of course, nor is it always used for unpleasant statements or adverse criticisms like these.

Look out for repetitions, not just of the same word, but of the same kind of phrase as in the example above. Ask yourself why the writer uses them, and whether they are successful.

▷ Sentences

'Notice how writers use sentences and then follow their example in your own writing.'

Different kinds of **sentences** give different effects. A succession of short sentences might give speed, urgency, or might show simplicity and directness. Long sentences bring intricacy and complexity in thought, feeling or situation. When a short sentence comes after a long one it is usually emphatic or dramatic:

> 'Never listen when they tell you that Man and the animals have a common interest, that the prosperity of the one is the prosperity of the others. It is all lies.'

says Major in *Animal Farm*, and we can imagine the dramatic pause before he snaps 'It is all lies.'

Notice the kinds of sentences which writers use in describing different situations and how they vary them. Think carefully about what this variation adds to the effect of the writing.

▷ Dialogue

If a writer uses a great deal of **dialogue** it makes for a quite different style from that of one who uses more passages of action, explanation and description. In the extract from *Of Mice and Men* in Chapter 15 the author gives little information in his own voice because he uses so much dialogue. This gives more prominence to the voice of the characters and we feel we come to know them more directly.

Notice how much dialogue a writer uses and how the voices of the characters vary, as in dramatic dialogue.

▷ **Additional example**

Use the following passage to test your understanding of what you have read in this chapter. Try to say what makes it a vivid piece of writing. Write down your own ideas before reading the key below.

> The creepers and the bushes were so close that he left his sweat on them and they pulled together behind him. When he was secure in the middle he was in a little cabin screened off from the open space by a few leaves. He squatted down, parted the leaves and looked out into the clearing. Nothing moved but a pair of gaudy butterflies that danced round each other in the hot air. Holding his breath he cocked a critical ear at the sounds of the island. Evening was advancing towards the island; the sounds of the bright fantastic birds, the bee-sounds, even the crying of the gulls that were returning to their roosts among the square rocks were fainter. The deep sea breaking miles away on the reef made an undertone less perceptible than the susurration of the blood.
>
> Simon dropped the screen of leaves back into place. The slope of the bars of honey-coloured sunlight decreased; they slid up the bushes, passed over the green candlelike buds, moved up towards the canopy, and darkness thickened under the trees. With the fading of the light the riotous colours died and the heat and urgency cooled away. The candle-buds stirred. Their green sepals drew back a little and the white tips of the flowers rose delicately to meet the open air.
>
> Now the sunlight had lifted clear of the open space and withdrawn from the sky. Darkness poured out, submerging the ways between the trees till they were dim and strange as the bottom of the sea. The candle-buds opened their wide white flowers glimmering under the light that pricked down from the first stars. Their scent spilled out in to the air and took possession of the island.

(William Golding, *Lord of the Flies*)

Key to the example

One of the things that we can notice about this passage is the appeal that it makes to the senses. First there is the heat, so intense that Simon leaves sweat on the creepers as he brushes past them. Colours are emphasized: the green candle-buds contrast with the white flowers; the tropical brightness of birds is depicted in words that describe not their hue but their dazzling effect on the eye – 'gaudy', 'fantastic', 'riotous'. The brightness of the day contrasts with the dimness of the night lit only by the pin-pricks of the stars.

Sounds are mentioned, but not distinguished from each other. They are simply 'bee-sounds' and 'bird' sounds, as though they all merge into one, except for the cry of the gulls. Even this grows fainter as the evening comes. Underneath them all is the murmuring of the sea. In an exceptional simile Golding compares this to blood in the veins, which is more of a sensation than a sound. The image works, however, because the sound of the word 'susurration' is onomatopoeic. The sound echoes the sense (it means whispering or murmuring), and conveys the distance and lowness of the sound of the sea. Finally there is the overwhelming scent of the flowers.

The coming of the evening is described with verbs that seem to make the landscape and vegetation active and give it will and purpose. The evening 'advanced', the colours 'died'. The sunlight is purposeful: it 'slides' up the bushes and 'withdraws' from the sky. The darkness is active: it pours from the sky. Most of all, the candle-buds seem to possess a will and a strength of their own. The sepals 'drew back' and the flowers 'rose to meet the air'. When they open, their scent takes possession of the island. By using verbs in this way Golding gives a strange vibrancy and life to the island which seems appropriate to the tropical setting.

▷ **SUGGESTIONS FOR COURSEWORK**

1 Write the opening chapter of a novel in the style of an author you admire or detest.
2 Write a conversation you might have had with an author, in which you ask questions about his or her favourite book.

3   From a novel you are studying, choose a page or chapter which you find dull and uninteresting. Re-write it to give it more life and excitement.

4   From a novel you are studying, pick out some of the author's favourite words and phrases. Write about how these words and phrases make the writing effective. You may also wish to criticize some of the author's choice.

▷ **Coursework task**   Write a conversation you might have had with an author, in which you ask questions about his or her favourite book.

▷ **Suggested answer**   A conversation I would like to have would be with Mildred D. Taylor.

ME   You have written several books, but which one has given you the most pleasure?

MDT   The choice is a difficult one, but my favourite has to be *Roll of Thunder, Hear My Cry*.

ME   Why is that?

MDT   Well, I suppose one reason is that other writers thought it was a good novel. It was awarded the Newbery Medal in 1977.

ME   What else makes it your favourite?

MDT   Writing this novel was a chance to write about my own experiences. My family grew up in Mississippi during the depression, where life really was hard. In the book I was able to tell readers what life was really like.

ME   What were the things which you remember in particular?

MDT   Usually the bad things. The worst thing, apart from the fact we were always poor, was the way in which the blacks were treated by white folks. In the book I could show others the terror my family felt by describing the night-riders burning down our houses.

ME   In the novel you describe the night when T.J. came to the house. That must have been awful.

MDT   It sure was! Cassie never thought they would ever make it home to warn Papa.

ME   Did you enjoy writing the character of T.J.?

MDT   Yes, because I didn't want to show all black people as good and all white people as bad. T.J. was a person with faults, and weak characters make for interesting reading.

ME   You mean, the way he was easily led and the fact that he was a liar.

MDT   Yes, but in spite of all those things, Cassie believed in him that night and took pity on him.

ME   Was that Cassie really you?

MDT   Well, you could say that there's a bit of me in her. She went through things that I had to suffer.

ME   Do you see Jeremy Simms as a sort of white T.J.?

MDT   In a way. He doesn't feature a lot in the novel. That might have been a mistake.

ME   Who is your favourite character in the novel?

MDT   Apart from Cassie, I suppose Mr Morrison.

ME   Why is that?

MDT   Because he is so big and yet so gentle. He is what I would like men to be, not like Kaleb Wallace. If there were more Morrisons this world would be a better place.

ME   Most of the characters speak in a funny kind of English.

MDT   Well, I tried to get the characters to speak in the way we did in Mississippi.

ME   You mean with 'gonna', 'yes, 'm' and 'y'all'?

MDT   That's right. If the book were to sound real, then the characters would have to speak as we did.

ME   Do you think that might put some people off reading your book?

MDT   Yes, I was aware of that problem. I couldn't let my characters speak exactly as we spoke or nobody would have understood us! I had to tone it down a bit.

ME   Did you have any other problems in writing this book?

MDT   I must admit I could easily have become very bitter about the way blacks were treated. You remember in the novel the trick played on the white children's school bus? That was one way of getting back at those white children. I put it in as a joke. When we were young we were angry about the way we were treated. But I hope that when the reader laughs he or she will feel some of my anger coming through.

ME   Why did you spend so much time describing mud on the walks to school?

MDT   Because it sort of showed where the children were – down in the mud. They couldn't escape. Wherever they turned they were bogged down in the stuff.

ME   But Uncle Hammer managed to escape. He came to see Cassie in a shiny automobile and gave Stacey a new coat.

MDT   That's true. As a black you could make it if you went to work in the Northern states where the wages were higher. But, as you remember, he had to sell the car in order to help out the Logans.

ME   So really there was no hope for you, as there wasn't for Cassie?

MDT   Well, I tried to show in the final chapter there was some hope. I know in the final sentence I wrote that Cassie would weep for the land. But I also wrote that she would still be free to run and wander. And her Mama and Papa did soften the hurt.

ME   Well, you certainly made it, because you have become a world-famous novelist. Thank you for taking the time to talk with me.

MDT   Thank you.

EXAMINATION QUESTIONS

▷ **Question 1**
'WJEC Higher Tier.'

What impressions of country life are given in *Silas Marner* and how are they conveyed?

▷ **Question 2**
'MEG Foundation Tier.'

Huckleberry Finn – Mark Twain. Life at this time in America seems to have been very violent. Explore any one episode that seems to you particularly violent, bringing out how Mark Twain presents it to the reader.

▷ **Question 3**
'SEG Foundation Tier.'

What qualities make *Great Expectations* such a good novel?
   You may wish to consider some of the following: the style of writing including story-telling and descriptions of characters, the use of Pip as narrator, Pip's story, the importance of other characters, the structure of the novel, the variety of setting and atmosphere.

▷ **Question 4**

Short Stories of Our Time – edited by Douglas Barnes. 'Ernest Brown is misunderstood.' How far do you agree with this comment on the story, 'Uncle Ernest'?
   You may wish to consider some of the following: the events of the story, Sillitoe's description of Ernest and the two girls, Ernest's past, his loneliness, his relationship with the two girls, the ending of the story, any different opinions on Ernest's relationship with the girls.

▷ **Question 5**
'MEG Foundation Tier.'

A good horror story is meant to shock you. What are your feelings as you read through this extract from *Dr Jekyll and Mr Hyde* by R. L. Stevenson? How has the way it is written helped to create these feelings?

'And now,' said he, 'to settle what remains. Will you be wise? will you be guided? will you suffer me to take this glass in my hand, and to go forth from your house without further parley? or has the greed of curiosity too much command of you? Think before you answer, for it shall be done as you decide. As you decide, you shall be left as you were before, and neither richer nor wiser, unless the sense of service rendered to a man in mortal distress may be counted as a kind of riches of the soul. Or, if you shall so prefer to choose, a new province of knowledge and new avenues to fame and power shall be laid open to you, here, in this room, upon the instant; and your sight shall be blasted by a prodigy to stagger the unbelief of Satan.'

'Sir,' said I, affecting a coolness that I was far from truly possessing, 'you speak enigmas, and you will perhaps not wonder that I hear you with no very strong impression of belief. But I have gone too far in the way of inexplicable services to pause before I see the end.'

'It is well,' replied my visitor. 'Lanyon, you remember your vows: what follows is under the seal of our profession. And now you who have so long been bound to the most narrow and material views, you who have denied the virtue of transcendental medicine, you who have derided your superiors – behold!'

He put the glass to his lips, and drank at one gulp. A cry followed: he reeled, staggered, clutched at the table and held on, staring with injected eyes, gasping with open mouth; and as I looked there came, I thought a change – he seemed to swell – his face became suddenly black, and the features seemed to melt and alter – and the next moment I had sprung to my feet and leaped back against the wall, my arm raised to shield me from that prodigy, my mind submerged in terror.

'O God!' I screamed, and 'O God!' again and again; for there before my eyes – pale and shaken, and half-fainting, and groping before him with his hands, like a man restored from death – there stood Henry Jekyl'.

What he told me in the next hour I cannot bring my mind to set on paper. I saw what I saw, I heard what I heard, and my soul sickened at it; and yet, now that sight has faded from my eyes, I ask myself if I believe it, and I cannot answer. My life is shaken to its roots; sleep has left me; the deadliest terror sits by me at all hours of the day and night; I feel that my days are numbered, and that I must die; and yet I shall die incredulous. As for the moral turpitude that man unveiled to me, even with tears of penitence, I cannot, even in memory, dwell on it without a start of horror. I will say one thing, Utterson, and that (if you can bring your mind to credit it) will be more than enough. The creature who crept into my house that night was, on Jekyll's own confession, known by the name of Hyde and hunted in every corner of the land as the murderer of Carew.

▷ **Question 6**

'WJEC Foundation Tier.'

Read the following extract from Hard Times by Charles Dickens. What impression of Mr Gradgrind does Dickens give here? Look at how he is described as well as what he says and does.

'Now what I want is, Facts. Teach these boys and girls nothing but Facts. Facts alone are wanted in life. Plant nothing else, and root out everything else. You can only form the minds of reasoning animals upon Facts; nothing else will ever be of any service to them. This is the principle on which I bring up my own children, and this is the principle on which I bring up these children. Stick to Facts, sir!'

The scene was a plain, bare, monotonous vault of a schoolroom, and the speaker's square forefinger emphasized his observations by underscoring every sentence with a line on the schoolmaster's sleeve. The emphasis was helped by the speaker's square wall of a forehead, which had his eyebrows for its base, while his eyes found commodious cellarage in two dark caves, overshadowed by the wall. The emphasis was helped by the speaker's mouth, which was wide, thin, and hard-set. The emphasis was helped by the speaker's voice, which was inflexible, dry, and dictatorial. The emphasis was helped by the speaker's hair, which bristled on the skirts of his bald head, a plantation of firs to keep the wind from its shining surface, all covered with knobs, like the crust of a plum pie, as if the head had scarcely warehouse-room for the hard facts stored inside. The speaker's obstinate carriage, square coat, square legs, square shoulders – nay, his very neckcloth, trained to take him by the throat with an unaccommodating grasp, like a stubborn fact, as it was – all helped the emphasis.

'In this life, we want nothing but Facts, sir; nothing but Facts!'

The speaker and the schoolmaster, and the third grown person present, all backed a little, and swept with their eyes the inclined plane of little vessels then and there arranged in order, ready to have imperial gallons of facts poured into them until they were full to the brim.

EXAMINATION ANSWERS

▷ **Question 5** *Notes and tutor's answer*

Notes

1 Read through the passage carefully.
2 Make a note of your feelings.
3 Jot down those parts of the extract which are typical of a horror story.
4 Underline/jot down those words and phrases which convey a sense of shock.
5 Think carefully about how they are effective.

Suggested answer

I enjoyed this horror story because the author was able to involve me in the story. He drew me in by using the device of one character re-telling an incident to another. In this way the reader becomes like the listener Utterson as Lanyon unfolds his horrific story.

'Establishes narrative technique.'

I sympathized with Lanyon, becoming impatient to learn what had happened. Jekyll, or the author, very skilfully keeps the reader in suspense by asking if Lanyon will allow him to tell what happened to him. This feeling of delay makes the reader impatient for Jekyll to finish his

'How the author prepares
for the horror.'

questioning ('will you be guided? will you suffer me to take this glass into my hand?'). The reader wants to know what is in the glass, and as Jekyll delays even more by reminding Lanyon to remember his vows, the reader wants him to get on to an account of the actual horror.

When Jekyll reaches the point when he puts the glass to his lips there follows a series of dramatic actions: 'reeled, staggered, clutched at the table'. The author here gets the reader to visualize what is happening. He directs us to look at Jekyll's face. The detail here is really horrific, with the eyes 'injected' – you can almost feel the needle going in. The face becomes non-human. It seems to melt. The reader is reacting with Lanyon: 'O God!' Lanyon thinks he is drowning in fear: 'my mind submerged in terror'. Jekyll seems like a living corpse: 'like a man restored from death'.

'Analyses the horrific
details.'

In the final paragraph the author continues the sense of horror by describing Lanyon's reaction to what he has just witnessed. There is a sense of physical revulsion ('my soul sickened at it'). He had been totally amazed by what he had just seen: 'My life is shaken to its roots'. He imagines a physical presence which will not go away. He even feels that Jekyll has not really gone away ('the deadliest terror sits by me at all hours of the day').

'Aftermath of horror.'

'An effective answer because it structures the horror by placing it in context of the author's technique. It is not simply a list of shocking details.'

▷ **Question 6** *Student's answer – examiner's comments*

'The student makes a
factual error. Gradgrind is
not the teacher.'

'Makes the point but
rather loosely.'

'This is better. Clear
discussion of technique.'

'Good. Beginning to
develop some useful
associations.'

'Still on target.'

'Good, clinching argument.'

'Effective over-view of
technique.'

Mr Gradgrind is a teacher with a simple attitude towards teaching. All he wants to teach is about facts. Nothing else seems to interest him. He is not like a teacher today who likes to interest the kids in his or her subject, or wants to take the children on school trips or get them to read interesting books.

The classroom seems to fit in with Gradgrind's style of teaching. It is 'bare, monotonous'. The room is large ('a vault') and probably the children feel lost in it. Gradgrind's forefinger is described as 'square' which emphasizes the 'facts'. They do not have any interesting shapes. The man looks unimaginative: 'square wall of a forehead'. He looks empty of feeling with his eyes like 'two dark caves'. He even looks mean with his 'wide, thin' mouth. He speaks in a dull way too with his 'dry' voice.

The author pokes fun at Gradgrind's method of teaching. The man looks ridiculous, with his hair being compared to clumps of fir trees and the top of his head looking like the crust on a plum pie. His head is large and hollow-sounding, like a huge warehouse. It sounds an uninteresting place, like a storehouse. You can imagine the dust on the things stored there.

The man is obstinate like his teaching methods. Everything about him is 'square', his coat, legs and shoulders. There are no interesting curves. Everything seems hard and forbidding. Even the neckcloth seems to be strangling the man 'like a stubborn fact'.

The pupils are not looked upon as human beings. They are simply storage jars for the facts. The author describes them sitting there as if waiting for liquid to be poured into them. When they are full up with facts, they will, presumably, be full of education. The comic picture of the children sitting there like empty milk bottles waiting to be filled shows how ridiculous Gradgrind's teaching methods are.

Throughout the extract the writer uses repetition effectively. By constantly hammering home the word 'facts' he reveals a boring education system. There is no variety – just boring repetition.

Question	Assessment Objective(s)	Pre-20th century	20th century
Coursework task – Mildred D. Taylor	1, 2, 4		✓
1 Silas Marner	1, 2	✓	
2 Huckleberry Finn	1, 2	✓	
3 Great Expectations	1, 2	✓	
4 Short Stories of our Time	1, 2		✓
5 Dr Jekyll and Mr Hyde	1, 2	✓	
6 Hard Times	1, 2	✓	

SUMMARY

▷ Prose writers use **comparisons** and **associations** in the same ways but usually not to the same extent as poets.

▷ **Contrast** and **repetition** are used to emphasize effects.

▷ Differences in style depend on:

    the kind of **words** used;
    the kind of **sentences**;
    the amount and kind of **dialogue**.

All these need to be looked at carefully.

Index

Longman - for all your study guide needs

Addison Wesley Longman publishes a wide range of curriculum-related books to help you with your studies. If you have enjoyed using this book and have found it useful, you can now order others directly from us - simply follow the ordering instructions below.

Don't forget to tell your fellow students about *Longman Study Guides* - they might find them useful too!

HOW TO ORDER

A full list of titles is given overleaf. Decide which title(s) you require and then order in one of the following ways:

by post
Fill in the quantity alongside the title(s) you require, select your method of payment, complete your name and address details and return your completed order form and payment to:
Addison Wesley Longman Ltd
PO BOX 88
Harlow
Essex CM19 5SR

by phone
Call our Customer Information Centre on 01279 623923 to place your order, quoting mail number: HESG1

by fax
complete the order form overleaf and fill in your name and address details and method of payment, and fax it to us on 01279 414130.

by e-mail
E-mail your order to us on awlhe.orders@awl.co.uk listing title(s) and quantity required and providing full name and address details as requested here. Please quote mail number: HESG1. Please do not send credit card details by e-mail.

Mail no: HESG1

Your Name _____

Your Address _____

_____

Postcode _____ Telephone _____

Method of payment

☐ I enclose a cheque or a P/O for £ _____ made payable to Addison Wesley Longman Ltd
☐ Please charge my Visa/Access/AMEX/Diners Club card

Number _____ Expiry Date _____

Signature _____ Date _____

(please ensure that the address given above is the same as for your credit card)

Prices and other details are correct at time of going to press but may change without notice. All orders are subject to status.

☐ *Please tick this box if you would like a complete listing of York Notes Literature Guides (suitable for GCSE and A-level English students)*

LONGMAN

Addison
Wesley
Longman

LONGMAN HOMEWORK HANDBOOKS (KEY STAGE 3)

£7.99 each unless otherwise stated

QTY *(0582)*

1	_____ 29330 8	English (KS3)
2	_____ 29331 6	French (KS3)
3	_____ 30423 7	French pack*(KS3) (£12.99)
4	_____ 30425 3	French cassette (KS3) (£6.00)
5	_____ 29329 4	German (KS3)
6	_____ 30427 X	German pack*(KS3) (£12.99)
7	_____ 30428 8	German cassette (KS3) (£6.00)
8	_____ 29328 6	Mathematics (KS3)
9	_____ 29327 8	Science (KS3)

LONGMAN GCSE STUDY GUIDES

£9.99 each unless otherwise stated

10	_____ 30481 4	Biology
11	_____ 31538 7	Business Studies
12	_____ 30482 2	Chemistry
13	_____ 31539 5	Economics
14	_____ 30484 9	English
15	_____ 30483 0	English Literature
16	_____ 30485 7	French
17	_____ 03839 1	French pack* (£14.99)
18	_____ 03836 7	French cassette (£6.00)
19	_____ 30486 5	Geography
20	_____ 30487 3	German
21	_____ 03837 5	German pack* (£14.99)
22	_____ 03838 3	German cassette (£6.00)
23	_____ 30495 4	Higher Level Mathematics
24	_____ 30494 6	Information Technology (£10.99)
25	_____ 30496 2	Mathematics
26	_____ 30497 0	Music
27	_____ 31540 9	Physics
28	_____ 28700 6	Psychology
29	_____ 31542 5	Religious Studies
30	_____ 30498 9	Science (£10.99)
31	_____ 22651 1	Sociology
32	_____ 22652 X	Spanish
33	_____ 24509 5	Spanish pack* (£14.99)
34	_____ 24511 7	Spanish cassette (£6.00)
35	_____ 23771 8	Technology
36	_____ 30545 4	World History

LONGMAN GCSE EXAM PRACTICE KITS

37	_____ 30381 8	Biology £4.99)
38	_____ 30383 4	Business Studies (£4.99)
39	_____ 31191 8	English (£4.99)
40	_____ 30384 2	Geography (£4.99)
41	_____ 30385 0	Mathematics (£4.99)
42	_____ 30379 6	Physics (£4.99)
43	_____ 30380 X	Science (£5.99)

LONGMAN GCSE REFERENCE GUIDES *£6.99 each*

44	_____ 05788 4	Biology
45	_____ 05790 6	Chemistry
46	_____ 05072 3	English
47	_____ 05077 4	French
48	_____ 05074 X	Mathematics
49	_____ 05794 9	Physics
50	_____ 05076 6	Science

GCSE SURVIVAL GUIDE *£2.95*

51	_____ 05078 2

_____ **YORK NOTES LITERATURE GUIDES** *(see overleaf)*

LONGMAN A-LEVEL STUDY GUIDES

£9.99 each unless otherwise stated

52	_____ 22569 8	Accounting (£10.99)
53	_____ 31545 X	Biology
54	_____ 31652 9	Business Studies
55	_____ 31546 8	Chemistry
56	_____ 05782 5	Computer Science
57	_____ 27688 8	Economics (£10.99)
58	_____ 31656 1	English
59	_____ 05784 1	French
60	_____ 24495 1	French pack* (£14.99)
61	_____ 24497 8	French cassette (£6.00)
62	_____ 05173 8	Geography
63	_____ 31654 5	German
64	_____ 24498 6	German pack* (£14.99)
65	_____ 24508 7	German cassette (£6.00)
66	_____ 28702 2	Government and Politics (£10.99)
67	_____ 31549 2	Law (£10.99)
68	_____ 31550 6	Mathematics (£10.99)
69	_____ 31551 4	Modern History
70	_____ 27690 X	Physics
71	_____ 31655 3	Psychology
72	_____ 27691 8	Sociology

LONGMAN A-LEVEL EXAM PRACTICE KITS *£6.99 each*

73	_____ 30386 9	Biology
74	_____ 30387 7	Business Studies
75	_____ 30388 5	Chemistry
76	_____ 30389 3	Mathematics
77	_____ 30390 7	Psychology
78	_____ 30382 6	Sociology

LONGMAN A-LEVEL REFERENCE GUIDES *£6.99 each*

79	_____ 06394 9	Biology
80	_____ 06390 6	Chemistry
81	_____ 06396 5	English
82	_____ 06398 1	Mathematics
83	_____ 06392 2	Physics (£7.99)

LONGMAN HANDBOOKS *£7.99 each*

84	_____ 09965 X	Botany
85	_____ 08810 0	Chemistry

LONGMAN PARENT'S AND STUDENTS' GUIDES

£2.99 each

86	_____ 29971 3	Longman Parent's Guide to Pre-school Choices and Nursery Education
87	_____ 29975 6	Longman Parent's Guide to Key Stage 1 of the National Curriculum
88	_____ 29974 8	Longman Parent's Guide to Key Stage 2 of the National Curriculum
89	_____ 29973 X	Longman Parent's Guide to Key Stage 3 of the National Curriculum
90	_____ 29972 1	Longman Parent's Guide to GCSE and Key Stage 4 of the National Curriculum
91	_____ 29978 0	Longman A-level Survival Guide
92	_____ 29969 1	Longman Students' Guide to Vocational Education
93 to	_____ 29970 5	Longman Students' Guide to Returning Learning
94	_____ 29976 4	Longman Students' Guide to Higher Education

* pack = book and cassette